Taste of Home

QUICK COOKING

ANNUAL RECIPES

Taste of Home

RDA ENTHUSIAST BRANDS, LLC • MILWAUKEE, WI

QUICK COOKING

ANNUAL RECIPES 2018

RASPBERRY CHOCOLATE PUFFS
(p. 289)

Cover Photography:
Taste of Home Photo Studio

Pictured on front cover: Broccoli-Cheddar Beef Rolls, p. 67; Pretzel Jell-O Dessert, p. 259; Bacon-Wrapped Pesto Pork Tenderloin, p. 116; Pina Colada Fruit Salad, p. 248; Asian Long Noodle Soup, p. 65; Taco Noodle Dish, p. 119

Pictured on back cover: Sweet & Salty Peanut Butter Bites, p. 150; Grilled Bean Burgers, p. 209; Cucumber Shell Salad, p. 310; Slow Cooker Carnitas, p. 307; Barbecued Chicken Pizzas, p. 212

Pictured on page 1: Grandma's Spinach Salad, p. 32; Skillet Ham & Rice, p. 79; Caramel Apple Cupcakes, p. 295; Butternut Thyme Tartlets, p. 8

© 2018 RDA Enthusiast Brands, LLC
1610 N. 2nd St., Suite 102, Milwaukee WI
53212-3906

International Standard Book Number:
978-1-61765-752-8
International Standard Serial Number: 1552-6603

Component Number: 117800063H

Printed in USA
1 3 5 7 9 10 8 6 4 2

CHICKEN & GOAT CHEESE SKILLET (p. 76)

DUTCH WAFFLE COOKIES (p. 151)

BISTRO BEEF BARBECUE SANDWICHES (p. 182)

STRAWBERRY KALE SALAD (p. 38)

MEAT LOAF MUFFINS (p. 149)

Because great food shouldn't be complicated!

SOUTHWESTERN FISH TACOS (p. 94)

SWEET POTATO & CRAB SOUP (p. 58)

CHOCOLATE CHIP
CREAM CHEESE BARS (p. 294)

BAKED MAC & CHEESE (p. 117)

There's always time to put scrumptious home-cooked meals on the table with *Quick Cooking Annual Recipes*.

TASTY YET SIMPLE DISHES are go-to favorites for family cooks. After all, these recipes offer delicious results without much work or long ingredient lists...and they always fit busy schedules,

This edition of *Quick Cooking Annual Recipes* is brimming with 553 new sensations. In fact, you'll find a full year of recipes from *Simple & Delicious* magazine, plus more than 100 bonus dishes specially chosen to free up time for today's multitasking cooks.

Each dish is easy to prepare and uses kitchen staples you likely have on hand. Step-by-step instructions, color photos and handy tips make *Quick Cooking Annual Recipes* one book you simply can't do without.

ICONS IN THIS BOOK

FAST FIX
Recipes that are table-ready in 30 minutes or less.

(5) INGREDIENTS
Recipes that use five or fewer ingredients (they may also call for water, salt, pepper, and canola or olive oil).

EAT SMART
Dietitian-approved recipes that are lower in calories, fat and sodium.

FREEZE IT
Freezer-friendly recipes that include directions for freezing and reheating.

SLOW COOKER
Recipes that use a slow cooker.

STRAWBERRY WATERMELON SLUSH (p. 259)

BROILED LOBSTER TAIL (p. 228)

Discover surprisingly easy favorites with these
650+ RECIPES & TIPS.

IN THIS EDITION
Slow-Cooked Selections
You'll find more than 60 recipes for this best-loved appliance, from braised meats and yummy soups to "Aha!" dishes such as homemade Irish soda bread (p. 257) and luscious pudding cake (p. 196).

Fuss-Free Techniques
Step-by-step photos and helpful hints throughout will help you master broiled lobster tail for the holidays (pictured above), make homemade ice cream with no special equipment (p. 292), and layer up the ultimate in lasagna (p. 112).

Spirited Holidays
We've included a round-up of the best Christmas treats, simple bites and sips for a holiday open house, and a traditional St. Patrick's Day. Find frosty sweets to celebrate the red, white and blue. Plus, thrill all of your boys and ghouls with adorable Halloween foods such as hot ham and cheese sammies that look like spiders (p. 265) .

Potlucks & Parties
This new chapter brings you make-and-take salads, big-batch sandwiches, irresistible snacks, and popular picnic foods such as baked beans, corn on the cob and candy-loaded crispy bars.

Weeknight Dinners
Fresh, easy suppers for your busiest days are the hallmark of *Quick Cooking Annual Recipes*. Inside, you'll discover more than 130 simple mains that are table-ready in 30 minutes or less.

Nutrition Insights
Our registered dietitian nutritionist shares her best secrets to help you make healthy eating choices. Look for the **HEALTH TIP** icon throughout.

PLUS...
Treat your family to comforting soups, homemade breakfasts, showstopping desserts, barbecue dishes and more!

Appetizers & Beverages

Party time, snack time, relaxation time—they're all good! Whether you're hosting a big bash or simply need movie-night munchies, this chapter is for you. It's time to celebrate with 20 no-fuss finger foods and beverages.

BUTTERNUT
THYME TARTLETS

SESAME PORK APPETIZERS

The honey marinade give this hearty pork appetizer added flavor. You might find other uses for the yummy dipping sauce.
—Joyce Moynihan, Lakeville, MN

Prep: 15 min. + marinating • **Bake:** 40 min.
Make: 2 dozen (½ cup sauce)

- ½ cup sherry or chicken broth
- 1 tablespoon reduced-sodium soy sauce
- 2 pork tenderloins (¾ pound each)
- ½ cup honey
- ½ cup sesame seeds

DIPPING SAUCE

- ⅓ cup reduced-sodium soy sauce
- 1 green onion, finely chopped
- 1 tablespoon sherry or chicken broth
- 1 tablespoon sesame oil
- 1 garlic clove, minced
- ½ teaspoon minced fresh gingerroot

1. In a large resealable plastic bag, combine sherry and soy sauce; add pork. Seal bag and turn to coat; refrigerate for 8 hours or overnight.
2. Drain and discard marinade; pat pork dry. Place honey and sesame seeds in separate shallow bowls. Roll the pork in honey, then sesame seeds. Place on a rack in a shallow roasting pan. Bake at 350° for

40-45 minutes or until a thermometer reads 160°. Let pork stand for 5 minutes before slicing.
3. Meanwhile, in a small bowl, combine sauce ingredients. Serve with pork.
**Per 1 ounce cooked pork with
1 teaspoon sauce:** 70 cal., 3g fat (0 sat. fat), 16mg chol., 155mg sodium, 5g carb. (4g sugars, 0 fiber), 6g pro.
Diabetic Exchanges: 1 lean meat.

BUTTERNUT THYME TARTLETS

A great teaser for what's to come, this light and crunchy appetizer is filled with my favorite flavors for late fall. Make the creamy filling a few days early, then fill phyllo cups right before guests arrive.
—Arlene Erlbach, Morton Grove, IL

Prep: 25 min. • **Bake:** 10 min. + cooling
Makes: 2½ dozen

- 2 packages (1.9 ounces each) frozen miniature phyllo tart shells
- 1 package (8 ounces) reduced-fat cream cheese
- 1½ cups frozen cubed butternut squash (about 8 ounces), thawed and patted dry
- ½ cup crumbled goat cheese

- 1 shallot, finely chopped
- 1 tablespoon minced fresh thyme
- 1½ teaspoons grated lemon peel
- ½ teaspoon rubbed sage
- ⅛ teaspoon salt
- ⅛ teaspoon ground nutmeg
- ⅛ teaspoon pepper
  Fresh thyme leaves

1. Preheat oven to 350°. Place shells in a 15x10x1-in. pan. Bake until golden brown, 8-10 minutes. Cool completely.
2. For filling, beat cream cheese on medium speed until fluffy, about 2 minutes. Coarsely chop squash; add to cream cheese. Add goat cheese, shallot, minced thyme, lemon peel and the seasonings; beat until blended.
3. To serve, spoon about 1 tablespoon filling into each shell. Top with thyme. Refrigerate leftovers.
Per tartlet: 49 cal., 3g fat (1g sat. fat), 8mg chol., 60mg sodium, 4g carb. (1g sugars, 0 fiber), 2g pro.

❋
TEST KITCHEN TIP
 Try this filling as a topper for crostini or alongside veggies as a tasty dip. You can even make the filling ahead and store it in the refrigerator until it's party time.

SALMON PARTY SPREAD

Living in Alaska, we love serving our delicious salmon to guests. Set out some crackers, and this slightly smoky spread will be gone in no time!
—Kathy Crow, Cordova, AK

Prep: 10 min. + chilling
Makes: 2 cups

- 1 package (8 ounces) cream cheese, softened
- 1 can (7½ ounces) pink salmon, drained, flaked and cartilage removed
- 3 tablespoons chopped fresh parsley
- 2 tablespoons finely chopped green pepper
- 2 tablespoons finely chopped sweet red pepper
- 2 teaspoon lemon juice
- 1 teaspoon prepared horseradish
- ½ teaspoon liquid smoke, optional
  Finely chopped pecans or additional parsley
  Crackers

In a small bowl, combine the first eight ingredients; stir until well blended. Cover and chill 2-24 hours. Transfer to a serving bowl; sprinkle with pecans or parsley. Serve with crackers.

Per 2 tablespoons: 71 cal., 6g fat (3g sat. fat), 21mg chol., 115mg sodium, 1g carb. (0 sugars, 0 fiber), 4g pro.

SALMON PARTY SPREAD

(5) INGREDIENTS

SAVORY POTATO SKINS

For a hot snack that really hits the spot on cool evenings, put together a plate of these crisp potato skins.
—Andrea Holcomb, Torrington, CT

Prep: 1¼ hours • **Broil:** 5 min.
Makes: 32 appetizers

- 4 large baking potatoes (about 12 ounces each)
- 3 tablespoons butter, melted
- 1 teaspoon salt
- 1 teaspoon garlic powder
- 1 teaspoon paprika
  Sour cream and chives, optional

1. Preheat oven to 375°. Scrub potatoes; pierce several times with a fork. Place on a greased baking sheet; bake until tender, 1 to 1¼ hours. Cool slightly.
2. Cut each potato lengthwise in half. Scoop out pulp, leaving ¼-in. thick shells (save pulp for another use).
3. Cut each half shell lengthwise into quarters; return to baking sheet. Brush insides with butter. Mix seasonings; sprinkle over butter.
4. Broil 4-5 in. from heat until golden brown, 5-8 minutes. If desired, mix sour cream and chives and serve with the potato skins.

Per piece: 56 cal., 2g fat (1g sat. fat), 6mg chol., 168mg sodium, 8g carb. (0 sugars, 1g fiber), 1g pro.

TACO MEATBALL RING

PICTURED ON P. 7

While it looks complicated, this attractive meaty ring is really very easy to assemble. My family loves tacos, and we find that the crescent roll dough is a nice change from the usual tortilla shells or chips.
—Brenda Johnson, Davison, MI

Prep: 30 min. • **Bake:** 15 min.
Makes: 16 servings

- 2 cups shredded cheddar cheese, divided
- 2 tablespoons water
- 2 to 4 tablespoons taco seasoning
- ½ pound ground beef
- 2 tubes (8 ounces each) refrigerated crescent rolls
- ½ medium head iceberg lettuce, shredded
- 1 medium tomato, chopped
- 4 green onions, sliced
- ½ cup sliced ripe olives
- 2 jalapeno peppers, sliced
  Sour cream and salsa, optional

1. In a large bowl, combine 1 cup cheese, water and taco seasoning. Crumble the beef over mixture and mix well. Shape into 16 balls.
2. Place meatballs on a greased rack in a shallow baking pan. Bake, uncovered, at 400° for 12 minutes or until meat is no longer pink. Drain the meatballs on paper towels. Reduce heat to 375°.
3. Arrange crescent rolls on a greased 15-in. pizza pan, forming a ring with the pointed ends facing outer edge of the pan and wide ends overlapping.
4. Place a meatball on each roll; fold point over meatball and tuck under wide end of roll (meatball will be visible). Repeat. Bake for 15-20 minutes or until the rolls are golden brown.
5. Carefully transfer to a serving platter. Fill the center of the ring with lettuce, tomato, onions, olives, jalapenos, remaining cheese, and sour cream and salsa if desired.
Note: Wear disposable gloves when cutting hot peppers; the oils can burn skin. Avoid touching your face.
Per serving: 203 cal., 12g fat (5g sat. fat), 24mg chol., 457mg sodium, 14g carb. (3g sugars, 1g fiber), 8g pro.

APRICOT WRAPS

(5) INGREDIENTS
APRICOT WRAPS

I accumulated a large recipe collection from around the world while my husband served in the Air Force for 25 years. This mouthwatering appetizer is one of our all-time favorites.
—Jane Ashworth Beavercreek, OH

Prep: 20 min. • **Bake:** 20 min.
Makes: about 4½ dozen

- 1 pound bacon strips
- 3 cups dried apricots (about 14 ounces)
- ½ cup whole almonds

SAUCE
- ¼ cup plum preserves or apple jelly
- 2 tablespoons soy sauce

1. Preheat oven to 375°. Cut each bacon strip into thirds. Fold each apricot piece around an almond; wrap with a piece of bacon. Secure with toothpicks.
2. Place on two ungreased 15x10x1-in. pans. Bake until bacon is crisp, 20-25 minutes, turning the wraps halfway.
3. Place sauce ingredients in a small saucepan; cook and stir until heated through. Drain wraps on paper towels. Serve with sauce.
Per appetizer: 46 cal., 2g fat (1g sat. fat), 2mg chol., 79mg sodium, 6g carb. (4g sugars, 1g fiber), 1g pro.

Note: If desired, replace toothpicks with decorative picks after baking.

EAT SMART | FAST FIX ▸
LAYERED HUMMUS DIP

PICTURED ON P. 7

My love for Greece inspired this fast-to-fix Mediterranean dip. It's great for parties, and it's a delicious way to add a few garden-fresh veggies to your menu.
—Cheryl Snavely, Hagerstown, MD

Prep/Total Time: 15 min.
Makes: 12 servings

- 1 carton (10 ounces) hummus
- ¼ cup finely chopped red onion
- ½ cup Greek olives, chopped
- 2 medium tomatoes, seeded and chopped
- 1 large English cucumber, chopped
- 1 cup crumbled feta cheese
  Baked pita chips

Spread the hummus into a shallow 10-in. round dish. Layer with the onion, olives, tomatoes, cucumber and cheese. Refrigerate dip until serving. Serve with chips.
Per serving without chips: 88 cal., 5g fat (2g sat. fat), 5mg chol., 275mg sodium, 6g carb. (1g sugars, 2g fiber), 4g pro.
Diabetic Exchanges: 1 fat, ½ starch.

APPLE PEAR SALSA WITH CINNAMON CHIPS

For a treat that's always a hit at get-togethers, try this easy appetizer. The salsa is packed with crunchy apples, grapes and pears, which perfectly complement the homemade chips.
—Courtney Fons, Brighton, MI

Prep: 25 min. • **Bake:** 10 min.
Makes: 12 servings

- 3 tablespoons sugar
- 1 teaspoon ground cinnamon
- 6 flour tortillas (8 inches)
  Cooking spray

SALSA
- 4 cups finely chopped tart apples (about 2 large)
- 1 medium ripe pear, finely chopped
- ½ cup quartered seedless red grapes
- ½ cup chopped celery
- ¼ cup chopped walnuts
- 2 teaspoons grated orange peel
- 3 tablespoons orange juice
- 1 tablespoon brown sugar

1. Preheat oven to 350°. Mix sugar and cinnamon. Spritz both sides of tortillas with cooking spray; sprinkle with sugar mixture. Cut each tortilla into eight wedges. Spread in a single layer on baking sheets. Bake until lightly browned, for 10-12 minutes, rotating pans as needed.
2. Place salsa ingredients in a large bowl; toss to combine. Serve with chips.
Per serving: 154 cal., 4g fat (1g sat. fat), 0 chol., 123mg sodium, 28g carb. (12g sugars, 3g fiber), 3g pro.
Diabetic Exchanges: 1 starch, 1 fruit, ½ fat.

RISOTTO BALLS (ARANCINI)

My Italian Grandma made these for me. I still ask for them when I visit her, and so do my children. They freeze well, so I make them ahead of time.
—Gretchen Whelan, San Francisco, CA

Prep: 35 min. • **Bake:** 25 min.
Makes: about 3 dozen

- 1½ cups water
- 1 cup uncooked arborio rice
- 1 teaspoon salt
- 2 large eggs, lightly beaten
- ⅔ cup sun-dried tomato pesto
- 2 cups panko (Japanese) bread crumbs, divided
  Marinara sauce, warmed

1. Preheat oven to 375°. In a large saucepan, combine water, rice and salt; bring to a boil. Reduce heat; simmer, covered, 18-20 minutes or until liquid is absorbed and rice is tender. Let stand, covered, 10 minutes. Transfer to a large bowl; cool slightly. Add eggs and pesto; stir in 1 cup bread crumbs.
2. Place remaining bread crumbs in a shallow bowl. Shape rice mixture into 1¼-in. balls. Roll in bread crumbs, patting to help coating adhere. Place on greased 15x10x1-in. baking pans. Bake 25-30 minutes or until golden brown. Serve with marinara sauce.
Per appetizer without marinara sauce: 42 cal., 1g fat (0 sat. fat), 10mg chol., 125mg sodium, 7g carb. (1g sugars, 0 fiber), 1g pro.
Diabetic Exchanges: ½ starch.

APPLE PEAR SALSA WITH CINNAMON CHIPS

ALMOND-BACON CHEESE CROSTINI

Try these baked bites for a change from the usual tomato-based crostini. Loaded with cheese, bacon and nuts, they offer comforting goodness in every bite.
—Leondre Hermann, Stuart, FL

Prep: 30 min. • **Bake:** 15 min.
Makes: 3 dozen

- 1 French bread baguette (1 pound), cut into 36 slices
- 2 cups shredded Monterey Jack cheese
- ⅔ cup mayonnaise
- ½ cup sliced almonds, toasted
- 6 bacon strips, cooked and crumbled
- 1 green onion, chopped
  Dash salt
  Additional toasted almonds, optional

1. Place bread slices on an ungreased baking sheet. Bake at 400° for 8-9 minutes or until lightly browned.
2. Meanwhile, in a large bowl, combine the cheese, mayonnaise, almonds, bacon, onion and salt. Spread over bread. Bake for 7-8 minutes or until cheese is melted. Sprinkle with additional almonds if desired. Serve warm.

Per crostini: 120 cal., 8g fat (2g sat. fat), 8mg chol., 160mg sodium, 10g carb. (0 sugars, 1g fiber), 3g pro.

HONEY BUFFALO MEATBALL SLIDERS

FREEZE IT SLOW COOKER

HONEY BUFFALO MEATBALL SLIDERS

These little sliders deliver big Buffalo chicken flavor without the messiness of wings. The spicy-sweet meatballs are a hit on game day with kids and adults alike.
—Julie Peterson, Crofton, MD

Prep: 10 min. • **Cook:** 2 hours
Makes: 6 servings

- ¼ cup packed brown sugar
- ¼ cup Louisiana-style hot sauce
- ¼ cup honey
- ¼ cup apricot preserves
- 2 tablespoons cornstarch
- 2 tablespoons reduced-sodium soy sauce
- 1 package (24 ounces) frozen fully cooked Italian turkey meatballs, thawed
  Additional hot sauce, optional
  Bibb lettuce leaves
- 12 mini buns
  Crumbled blue cheese
  Ranch salad dressing, optional

1. In a 3- or 4-qt. slow cooker, mix first six ingredients until smooth. Stir in meatballs until coated. Cook, covered, on low until meatballs are heated through, 2-3 hours.
2. If desired, stir in additional hot sauce. Serve meatballs on lettuce-lined buns; top with cheese and, if desired, dressing.

Per 2 sliders: 524 cal., 21g fat (6g sat. fat), 110mg chol., 1364mg sodium, 61g carb. (29g sugars, 1g fiber), 28g pro.

STRAWBERRY FRUIT DIP

If you're thinking about taking a fruit tray to a brunch or morning social, consider whipping up this creamy treat. Not only does the pretty dip come together easily in a blender, but it also calls for only five ingredients.

—Lydia Graf, Norton, OH

Prep: 15 min. + chilling
Makes: 1½ cups

- 1 cup sliced fresh strawberries
- ¼ cup sour cream
- 1 tablespoon sugar
- ¼ teaspoon vanilla extract
- ½ cup heavy whipping cream
  Assorted fresh fruit

1. In a blender, combine the strawberries, sour cream, sugar and vanilla. Cover and process until smooth.
2. In a small bowl, beat cream until stiff peaks form. Fold into strawberry mixture. Cover and refrigerate for at least 1 hour. Serve with fruit.

Per 2 tablespoons dip: 53 cal., 5g fat (3g sat. fat), 17mg chol., 6mg sodium, 2g carb. (2g sugars, 0 fiber), 0 pro.

SPICY EDAMAME

Edamame are young soybeans in their pods, and they're quickly becoming a busy cook's best friend. In our Test Kitchen, we boiled and seasoned them with salt, ginger, garlic powder and red pepper flakes. Yum!

—*Taste of Home* Test Kitchen

Start to Finish: 20 min.
Makes: 6 servings

- 1 package (16 ounces) frozen edamame pods
- 2 teaspoons kosher salt
- ¾ teaspoon ground ginger
- ½ teaspoon garlic powder
- ¼ teaspoon crushed red pepper flakes

Place edamame in a large saucepan and cover with water. Bring to a boil. Cover and cook for 4-5 minutes or until tender; drain. Transfer to a large bowl. Add the seasonings; toss to coat.

Per serving: 52 cal., 2g fat (0 sat. fat), 0 chol., 642mg sodium, 5g carb. (1g sugars, 2g fiber), 4g pro.

SPARKLING WHITE GRAPE JUICE

I love this versatile non-alcoholic drink. It's fun to serve all year, but it really goes well with cake at weddings or baby showers. It's not too sweet, so there's no sugar overload. Sometimes I come up with excuses to mix up a batch.

—Dana Moore, Alvaton, KY

Start to Finish: 5 min.
Makes: 14 servings (¾ cup each)

- 1 liter ginger ale, chilled
- 4 cups white grape juice, chilled
- 4 cans (6 ounces each) unsweetened pineapple juice, chilled

In a large pitcher, combine ginger ale, grape juice and pineapple juice. Serve punch immediately.

Per ¾ cup: 94 cal., 0 fat (0 sat. fat), 0 chol., 12mg sodium, 24g carb. (21g sugars, 0 fiber), 0 pro.

Pizza by the Bite

Slice up that zucchini, then top it like a pizza for a speedy, garden-fresh take on everybody's favorite dish!

On a greased pan, broil zucchini 3–4 in. from heat, 2 minutes per side. Top with pizza sauce, cheese and pepperoni; broil 1 minute. Add basil.

REUBEN ROUNDS

3. Bake 6 minutes. Sprinkle with the remaining cheese blend; bake 2-3 minutes longer or until cheese is melted.

Freeze option: Freeze cooled taco cups in a freezer container, separating layers with waxed paper. To use, reheat on a baking sheet in a preheated 350° oven until crisp and heated through.

Per each: 63 cal., 3g fat (1g sat. fat), 11mg chol., 156mg sodium, 4g carb. (0 sugars, 0 fiber), 4g pro.

(5) INGREDIENTS

MINT JULEP

Show off your bartending know-how with a drink that's sure to wow guests—this Kentucky Derby Day staple. You make the syrup up ahead of time so the drinks are ready to stir up when friends arrive.
—*Taste of Home* Test Kitchen

Prep: 30 min. + chilling
Makes: 10 servings (2½ cups syrup)

MINT SYRUP
- 2 **cups sugar**
- 2 **cups water**
- 2 **cups loosely packed chopped fresh mint**

EACH SERVING
- ½ **to ¾ cup crushed ice**
- ½ **to 1 ounce bourbon**
   Mint sprig

1. For syrup, combine the sugar, water and chopped mint in a saucepan. Bring to a boil over medium heat; cook until sugar is dissolved, stirring occasionally. Remove from the heat; cool to room temperature.
2. Line a mesh strainer with a double layer of cheesecloth or a coffee filter. Strain syrup; discard mint. Cover and refrigerate syrup for at least 2 hours or until chilled. For each serving, place ice in a metal julep cup or rocks glass. Pour ¼ cup mint syrup and bourbon into the glass; stir until mixture is well chilled. Garnish with mint sprig.

Per ⅓ cup: 197 cal., 0 fat (0 sat. fat), 0 chol., 6mg sodium, 42g carb. (39g sugars, 1g fiber), 1g pro.

Mock Mint Julep: Prepare mint syrup as directed. After straining, add ½ cup lemon juice. Cover and refrigerate for at least 2 hours or until chilled. For each serving, combine ½ cup club soda and ¼ cup mint syrup in a glass filled with crushed ice. Garnish with mint.

FAST FIX

REUBEN ROUNDS

Fans of the classic Reuben sandwich will go crazy for baked pastry spirals of corned beef, Swiss and sauerkraut. They're a breeze to make, and bottled Thousand Island dressing is the perfect dipping sauce.
—Cheryl Snavely, Hagerstown, MD

Start to Finish: 30 min.
Makes: 16 appetizers

- 1 **sheet frozen puff pastry, thawed**
- 6 **slices Swiss cheese**
- 5 **slices deli corned beef**
- ½ **cup sauerkraut, rinsed and well drained**
- 1 **teaspoon caraway seeds**
- ¼ **cup Thousand Island salad dressing**

1. Preheat oven to 400°. Unfold the puff pastry; layer with cheese, corned beef and sauerkraut to within ½-in. of edges. Roll up jelly-roll style. Trim ends and cut crosswise into 16 slices. Place the slices on greased baking sheets, cut side down. Sprinkle with caraway seeds.
2. Bake 18-20 minutes or until golden brown. Serve with salad dressing.

Per appetizer: 114 cal., 7g fat (2g sat. fat), 8mg chol., 198mg sodium, 10g carb. (1g sugars, 1g fiber), 3g pro.

FREEZE IT (5) INGREDIENTS

MINI PHYLLO TACOS

PICTURED ON P. 7

Crispy phyllo cups are the secret to creating an appetizer that has all the flavor and appeal of a taco but is much easier to eat! The two-bite treats of spicy ground beef and zesty shredded cheese will be a surefire hit with any hungry crowd.
—Roseann Weston, Philipsburg, PA

Prep: 30 min. • **Bake:** 10 min.
Makes: 2½ dozen

- 1 **pound lean ground beef (90% lean)**
- ½ **cup finely chopped onion**
- 1 **envelope taco seasoning**
- ¾ **cup water**
- 1¼ **cups shredded Mexican cheese blend, divided**
- 2 **packages (1.9 ounces each) frozen miniature phyllo tart shells**

1. Preheat oven to 350°. In a small skillet, cook beef and onion over medium heat until meat is no longer pink; drain. Stir in taco seasoning and water. Bring to a boil. Reduce heat; simmer, uncovered, for 5 minutes. Remove from heat; stir in ½ cup cheese blend.
2. Place tart shells in an ungreased 15x10x1-in. baking pan. Fill with the taco mixture.

MINT JULEP

Oh, You Little Devils

Have 20 minutes to spare? Turn a dozen eggs into an irresistible snack when you crack the how-to mystery of perfect deviled eggs.

HOW-TO
Prep Perfect Deviled Eggs

1. Hard cook the eggs
In a pan, arrange eggs in a single layer; add water to cover by 1 inch. Cover and bring water to a rolling boil. Remove from the heat. Let pan stand, covered, for 15 minutes. Drain; cover eggs with cold water. Crack shells and return to cold water for 1 hour. Peel off shells.

2. Trim the bottoms
Trim a small part off the egg white from both long sides.

3. Make the filling
Halve the eggs lengthwise and squeeze the whites to remove the yolk. Mash yolks with until crumbly. Stir in mayonnaise and seasonings. Spoon filling into a plastic bag. Snip off one corner.

4. Finish the eggs
Pipe filling into the whites. Garnish with paprika or your favorite herbs or spices.

GARLIC-DILL DEVILED EGGS

I like to experiment with recipes and was pleasantly pleased with how the fresh dill really perked up the flavor of these irresistible appetizers.
—Kaml Horch, Franktort, Maine

Prep: 20 min. + chilling
Makes: 2 dozen

- 12 hard-boiled large eggs
- ⅔ cup mayonnaise
- 4 teaspoons dill pickle relish
- 2 teaspoons snipped fresh dill
- 2 teaspoons Dijon mustard
- 1 teaspoon coarsely ground pepper
- ¼ teaspoon garlic powder
- ⅛ teaspoon paprika or cayenne pepper

Per deviled egg: 81 cal., 7g fat (1g sat. fat), 94mg chol., 81mg sodium, 1g carb. (0 sugars, 0 fiber), 3g pro.

HOT APPLE PUNCH

With its soothing cinnamon seasoning, this fresh and flavorful apple punch is a must for fall and winter get-togethers.
—Dawn Supina, Edmonton, AB

Prep: 5 min. • **Cook:** 35 min.
Makes: 2 quarts

- 2 cinnamon sticks (about 3 inches each), broken
- 10 whole cloves
- 6 whole allspice or 2 whole nutmeg
- 2 quarts apple juice
  Additional cinnamon sticks, optional

Place the cinnamon sticks, cloves and allspice on a double thickness of cheesecloth; bring up the corners and tie with string to form a bag. Place in a large saucepan with apple juice (or place loose spices in pan and strain before serving). Bring to a boil. Reduce heat; cover and simmer for 30 minutes. Remove spice bag. Serve punch hot in mugs. Garnish with cinnamon sticks if desired.

Per cup: 119 cal., 0 fat (0 sat. fat), 0 chol., 7mg sodium, 29g carb. (28g sugars, 0 fiber), 0 pro.

ASIAGO-BASIL STUFFED MUSHROOMS

Even if you don't like mushrooms, you'll have to try them again with this pretty appetizer, which tastes divine. If you want to make them a main dish, double the filling and use large portobellos.
—Lorraine Caland, Shuniah, ON

Prep: 25 min. • **Bake:** 10 min.
Makes: 2 dozen

- 24 baby portobello mushrooms (about 1 pound), stems removed
- ½ cup reduced-fat mayonnaise
- ¾ cup shredded Asiago cheese
- ½ cup loosely packed basil leaves, stems removed
- ¼ teaspoon white pepper
- 12 cherry tomatoes, halved
  Sliced Parmesan cheese, optional

1. Preheat oven to 375°. Place the mushroom caps in a greased 15x10x1-in. baking pan. Bake 10 minutes. Meanwhile, place mayonnaise, Asiago cheese, basil and pepper in a food processor; process until blended.

2. Drain juices from mushrooms. Fill each with 1 rounded teaspoon mayonnaise mixture; top each with a tomato half.
3. Bake 8-10 minutes or until lightly browned. If desired, top the mushroom caps with Parmesan cheese.

Per appetizer: 35 cal., 3g fat (1g sat. fat), 5mg chol., 50mg sodium, 2g carb. (1g sugars, 0 fiber), 2g pro.

Italian Sausage Mushrooms: Bake mushrooms as directed. In a large skillet, cook 1 pound bulk Italian sausage over medium heat until no longer pink; drain. In a bowl, mix 6 ounces softened cream cheese, 3 tablespoons minced fresh parsley and sausage; spoon into mushroom caps. Bake as directed. Sprinkle with an additional 1 tablespoon minced fresh parsley.

★ ★ ★ ★ ★ **READER REVIEW**

"Very easy to make and quite tasty. My husband had been wanting me to make a portobello dish, and I thought this one sounded yummy. It was."

NINAVERBEENA TASTEOFHOME.COM

HOT APPLE PUNCH

Side Dishes & Salads

The crisp slaws, cool fruit salads and hot veggie sides in this chapter round out any main dish with ease. Here you will also find savory grain favorites, heartwarming wintertime casseroles and satisfying entree salads for warmer months.

Swiss Corn Casserole (p. 25) **Oven-Roasted Asparagus** (p. 25) **Berry Nectarine Salad** (p. 23)
Garlic Shrimp & Rice Salad (p. 20) **Zucchini Pancakes** (p. 37)

BACON AVOCADO SALAD

EAT SMART **FAST FIX**

GARLIC SHRIMP & RICE SALAD

PICTURED ON P. 19

For this easy main dish, you can prepare the rice mixture and chop the vegetables ahead of time. Cook the shrimp at the last minute, then assemble it all together for a light yet satisfying meal.

—Diane Nemitz, Ludington, MI

Start to Finish: 30 min.
Makes: 4 servings

- 1 pound uncooked shrimp (31-40 per pound), peeled and deveined
- 2 tablespoons olive oil
- 2 garlic cloves, minced
- 1 teaspoon dried oregano
- 1 package (8.8 ounces) ready-to-serve brown rice
- ¼ cup mayonnaise
- ¼ cup sour cream
- 2 tablespoons minced fresh basil or 1 teaspoon dried basil
- 2 tablespoons lemon juice
- 1 celery rib, chopped
- ¼ cup minced fresh parsley
- 2 tablespoons chopped green pepper
- 4 cups fresh baby arugula or baby spinach

1. Toss shrimp with the oil, garlic and oregano; let stand 15 minutes. Meanwhile, cook rice according to package directions. Transfer rice to a large bowl; cool slightly. For dressing, mix mayonnaise, sour cream, basil and lemon juice.

2. In a large skillet, saute shrimp mixture over medium-high heat until shrimp turns pink, 2-3 minutes. Add to the rice; stir in celery, parsley and pepper. Add arugula and toss lightly; serve with dressing.

Per serving: 397 cal., 23g fat (5g sat. fat), 142mg chol., 232mg sodium, 21g carb. (1g sugars, 2g fiber), 22g pro.

FAST FIX

BACON AVOCADO SALAD

Everyone in my family loves this summery salad—even the younger kids! I serve it at pretty much every get-together I host and, at this point, the recipe's been shared too many times to count.

—Noreen McCormick Danek, Cromwell, CT

Start to Finish: 25 min.
Makes: 10 servings

- ¾ cup extra virgin olive oil
- ¼ cup red wine vinegar
- 4 teaspoons sugar
- 2 garlic cloves, minced
- 1 teaspoon salt
- 1 teaspoon Dijon mustard

SALAD
- 1 bunch romaine, chopped (about 12 cups)
- ¾ pound bacon strips, cooked and crumbled
- 3 medium tomatoes, chopped
- 1 medium red onion, halved and thinly sliced
- 3 medium ripe avocados, peeled and cubed
- 2 tablespoons lemon juice
- 1 cup (4 ounces) crumbled Gorgonzola or feta cheese

1. Place first six ingredients in a jar with a tight-fitting lid; shake well until blended. Refrigerate until serving.

2. In a large bowl, combine romaine, bacon, tomatoes and onion. Toss the avocados with lemon juice and add to salad. Sprinkle with cheese. Serve with dressing, shaking to blend again if needed.

Per 1⅓ cups: 339 cal., 31g fat (7g sat. fat), 22mg chol., 626mg sodium, 10g carb. (4g sugars, 5g fiber), 9g pro.

CARROT & KALE VEGETABLE SAUTE

Thanks to fresh veggie dishes like this one, I almost forget I'm wheat- and gluten-free. Bacon adds yet another layer of flavor and depth to this gorgeous side dish.
—Darla Andrews, Schertz, TX

Prep: 15 min.
Cook: 20 min.
Makes: 8 servings

- 8 bacon strips, coarsely chopped
- 4 large carrots, sliced
- 2 cups peeled cubed butternut squash (½-inch pieces)
- 1 poblano pepper, seeded and chopped
- ½ cup finely chopped red onion
- 1 teaspoon smoked paprika
- ¼ teaspoon salt
- ¼ teaspoon pepper
- 2 plum tomatoes, chopped
- 2 cups chopped fresh kale

1. In a large skillet, cook bacon over medium heat until crisp, stirring occasionally. Using a slotted spoon, remove bacon to paper towels. Pour off all but 1 tablespoon drippings.
2. Add carrots and squash to drippings; cook, covered over medium heat for 5 minutes. Add poblano pepper and onion; cook until vegetables are tender, about 5 minutes, stirring occasionally. Stir in seasonings. Add tomatoes and kale; cook, covered, until kale is wilted, 2-3 minutes. Top with bacon.
Per ¾ cup: 101 cal., 5g fat (2g sat. fat), 10mg chol., 251mg sodium, 11g carb. (4g sugars, 3g fiber), 4g pro.
Diabetic Exchanges: 1 vegetable, 1 fat, ½ starch.

DID YOU KNOW?

The sweet, rich flavor of smoked paprika is made by slowly drying peppers over a fire for several weeks.

Poblano peppers are dark green and mild in flavor. When dried, they turn reddish black and are known as anchos.

CARROT & KALE VEGETABLE SAUTE

SALMON & FETA WILTED SPINACH SALAD

My friend mentioned a Turkish salmon and grain dish that sounded fantastic, so I started experimenting. I prefer this salad warm, but it's also tasty served cold.
—Jeni Pittard, Statham, GA

Start to Finish: 30 min.
Makes: 2 servings

- 1 salmon fillet (8 ounces)
- 2 teaspoons lemon juice
- ½ teaspoon Greek seasoning
- ½ cup quinoa, rinsed
- 1 cup reduced-sodium chicken broth
- 1 teaspoon olive oil
- 4 cups coarsely chopped fresh spinach
- 1 cup grape tomatoes, halved
- ¼ cup crumbled feta cheese
- 2 tablespoons chopped fresh parsley
- 1 tablespoon minced fresh oregano
- ⅛ teaspoon pepper
  Lemon wedges

1. Preheat oven to 375°. Place salmon on a foil-lined baking sheet, skin side down. Sprinkle with lemon juice and Greek seasoning. Bake until fish just begins to flake easily with a fork, 15-18 minutes.
2. Meanwhile, in a small saucepan, combine quinoa, broth and oil; bring to a boil. Reduce heat; simmer, covered, until liquid is absorbed and quinoa is tender, 12-15 minutes.
3. To serve, break salmon into 1-in. pieces using a fork. Place spinach, tomatoes, quinoa and salmon in a large bowl. Add cheese, herbs and pepper; toss gently to combine. Serve with lemon wedges.
Per 2 cups: 427 cal., 18g fat (4g sat. fat), 64mg chol., 773mg sodium, 34g carb. (3g sugars, 6g fiber), 32g pro.
Diabetic Exchanges: 3 lean meat, 2 vegetable, 1½ starch, 1 fat.

EAT SMART

SESAME-GINGER CUCUMBER SALAD

I love the marinated sides and salads that come with meals at Japanese restaurants and wanted to try some at home. After some research, I came up with this cool and crisp salad with a little Asian zing. We love it with meat hot off the grill!
—Kimberly Ludvick, Newburgh, NY

Prep: 15 min.
Makes: 6 servings

- 2 tablespoons rice vinegar
- 4 teaspoons soy sauce
- 1 tablespoon olive oil
- 2 teaspoons minced fresh gingerroot
- 2 teaspoons sesame oil
- 1 teaspoon honey
- ¼ teaspoon Sriracha Asian hot chili sauce
- 2 English cucumbers
- 1 teaspoon sesame seeds, toasted
  Thinly sliced green onions

1. For dressing, mix the first seven ingredients. Trim ends and cut cucumbers crosswise into 3-in. sections. Cut sections into julienne strips.
2. To serve, toss cucumbers with sesame seeds and dressing. Sprinkle salad with green onions.
Per ¾ cup: 64 cal., 4g fat (1g sat. fat), 0 chol., 293mg sodium, 7g carb. (4g sugars, 1g fiber), 1g pro.
Diabetic Exchanges: 1 vegetable, 1 fat.

STRAWBERRY SALAD WITH POPPY SEED DRESSING

FAST FIX

STRAWBERRY SALAD WITH POPPY SEED DRESSING

My family is always happy to see this fruit and veggie salad on the table. If fresh strawberries aren't available, substitute mandarin oranges and dried cranberries.
—Irene Keller, Kalamazoo, MI

Start to Finish: 30 min.
Makes: 10 servings

- ¼ cup sugar
- ⅓ cup slivered almonds
- 1 bunch romaine, torn (about 8 cups)
- 1 small onion, halved and thinly sliced
- 2 cups halved fresh strawberries

DRESSING
- ¼ cup mayonnaise
- 2 tablespoons sugar
- 1 tablespoon sour cream
- 1 tablespoon 2% milk
- 2¼ teaspoons cider vinegar
- 1½ teaspoons poppy seeds

1. Place sugar in a small heavy skillet; cook and stir over medium-low heat until melted and caramel colored, about 10 minutes. Stir in almonds until coated. Spread on foil to cool.
2. Place romaine, onion and strawberries in a large bowl. Whisk together dressing ingredients; toss with salad. Break candied almonds into pieces; sprinkle over salad. Serve immediately.
Per ¾ cup: 110 cal., 6g fat (1g sat. fat), 1mg chol., 33mg sodium, 13g carb. (10g sugars, 2g fiber), 2g pro.
Diabetic Exchanges: ½ starch, 1 vegetable, 1 fat.

BERRY NECTARINE SALAD
PICTURED ON P. 19

I've been making this recipe for years. Whenever my family has a summer get-together, everyone requests it. The nectarines and berries look beautiful together, and the creamy topping is a perfect accent.
—Mindee Myers, Lincoln, NE

Prep: 15 min. + chilling
Makes: 8 servings

 4 medium nectarines, sliced
 ¼ cup sugar
 1 teaspoon lemon juice
 ½ teaspoon ground ginger
 3 ounces reduced-fat cream cheese
 2 cups fresh raspberries
 1 cup fresh blueberries

1. In a large bowl, toss nectarines with sugar, lemon juice and ginger. Refrigerate, covered, 1 hour, stirring once.
2. Drain the nectarines, reserving juices. Gradually beat reserved juices into cream cheese. Gently combine nectarines and berries; serve with cream cheese mixture.
Per serving: 109 cal., 3g fat (2g sat. fat), 8mg chol., 46mg sodium, 21g carb. (15g sugars, 4g fiber), 2g pro.
Diabetic Exchanges: 1 fruit, ½ starch, ½ fat.

CHERRY WALDORF SALAD
Classic Waldorf salad gets a fun fall spin when tart cherries and dried cranberries are added to the crunchy mix.
—Marie Hattrup, Sonoma, CA

Prep: 15 min. + chilling
Makes: 8 servings

 ¼ cup mayonnaise
 ¼ cup sour cream
 2 tablespoons honey
 ⅛ teaspoon salt
 2 large apples (about 1 pound), cubed
 1 tablespoon lemon juice
 2 celery ribs, chopped
 ½ cup dried cranberries
 ½ cup slivered almonds, toasted
 1 cup fresh or frozen pitted tart cherries, thawed

1. For dressing, whisk together first four ingredients. In a large bowl, toss apples with lemon juice. Add celery, cranberries and almonds; toss with dressing. Gently stir in cherries.
2. Refrigerate salad, covered, 1 hour before serving.
Note: To toast nuts, bake in a shallow pan in a 350° oven for 5-10 minutes or cook in a skillet over low heat until lightly browned, stirring occasionally.
Per ¾ cup: 181 cal., 10g fat (2g sat. fat), 2mg chol., 84mg sodium, 23g carb. (19g sugars, 3g fiber), 2g pro.

BROCCOLI WITH SAUTEED RED PEPPER
Slivered almonds and sweet red peppers add crunch to fresh broccoli.
—*Taste of Home* Test Kitchen

Start to Finish: 20 min.
Makes: 4 servings

 1 cup chicken broth
 1 pound fresh broccoli spears
 1 cup julienned sweet red pepper
 2 tablespoons chopped shallot
 2 tablespoons olive oil
 ⅓ cup slivered almonds
 ½ teaspoon lemon-pepper seasoning
 ¼ teaspoon salt

1. In a large saucepan, bring broth to a boil. Cut broccoli spears in half lengthwise; add to broth. Reduce the heat; cover and simmer for 5-8 minutes or until broccoli is crisp-tender.
2. Meanwhile, in a large skillet, saute red pepper and shallot in oil for 5 minutes or until crisp-tender. Drain broccoli; add broccoli, almonds, lemon-pepper and salt to skillet. Cook and stir for 2 minutes or until broccoli is tender.
Per ¾ cup: 157 cal., 12g fat (1g sat. fat), 0 chol., 468mg sodium, 10g carb. (4g sugars, 5g fiber), 6g pro.

CHERRY WALDORF SALAD

CHICKEN QUINOA SALAD

EAT SMART **FAST FIX ▶**

CHICKEN QUINOA SALAD

We pile our favorite gyro fixin's (plus quinoa) into bowls. Our local gyro guy has a spicy yogurt sauce that really transforms his sandwiches. It's a must here, too.
—Leah Lyon, Ada, OK

Start to Finish: 25 min.
Makes: 4 servings

    1½ cups plus 2 tablespoons water,
         divided
     ¾ cup quinoa, rinsed
      2 tablespoons reduced-fat plain yogurt
      1 tablespoon reduced-fat mayonnaise
      1 teaspoon Sriracha Asian hot chili
         sauce
     ¼ cup crumbled reduced-fat feta
         cheese
      1 medium cucumber, seeded and diced
     ¾ cup finely chopped fresh parsley
      2 green onions, chopped
     ¼ cup extra virgin olive oil
      3 tablespoons lemon juice
     ¾ teaspoon Greek seasoning
      1 package (6 ounces) ready-to-use
         grilled chicken breast strips
      1 medium tomato, finely chopped

1. In a small saucepan, bring 1½ cups water to a boil. Add quinoa. Reduce heat; simmer, covered, until liquid is absorbed, 12-15 minutes.
2. For dressing, place remaining water, yogurt, mayonnaise, chili sauce and cheese in a small food processor or blender. Cover; process until blended.
3. In a fine-mesh strainer, rinse cooked quinoa with cold water; drain well. In a bowl, toss quinoa with cucumber, parsley, green onions, oil, lemon juice and Greek seasoning. Top mixture with chicken, tomato and dressing.

Per serving: 341 cal., 19g fat (3g sat. fat), 30mg chol., 590mg sodium, 27g carb. (3g sugars, 4g fiber), 19g pro.
Diabetic Exchanges: 3 fat, 2 starch, 2 lean meat.

---

⑤ INGREDIENTS

CUCUMBERS WITH DRESSING

It wouldn't be summer if Mom didn't make lots of these creamy cucumbers. Just a few simple ingredients— mayonnaise, sugar, vinegar and salt— dress up the cool slices of this crisp garden vegetable.
—Michelle Beran, Claflin, KS

Prep: 10 min. + chilling
Makes: 6 servings

      1 cup mayonnaise
     ¼ cup sugar
     ¼ cup white vinegar
     ¼ teaspoon salt
      4 cups thinly sliced cucumbers

In a large bowl, mix first four ingredients; toss with the cucumbers. Refrigerate, covered, 2 hours.
Per ¾ cup: 283 cal., 27g fat (4g sat. fat), 3mg chol., 286mg sodium, 11g carb. (10g sugars, 0 fiber), 0 pro.

ZUCCHINI MUSHROOM BAKE

This simple recipe dresses up my garden-fresh zucchini with mushrooms, onion, cheddar and a sprinkle of basil.
—Jacquelyn Smith, Carmel, ME

Prep: 10 min. • **Bake:** 30 min.
Makes: 4 servings

- 3 cups sliced zucchini
- 2 cups sliced fresh mushrooms
- ⅓ cup sliced onion
- ½ teaspoon dried basil
- ¼ teaspoon salt
- ½ cup shredded cheddar cheese

1. Preheat oven to 350°. Toss together first five ingredients; place in a greased 2-qt. shallow baking dish.
2. Bake, covered, 30 minutes. Sprinkle with cheese; bake, uncovered, until vegetables are tender, about 10 minutes.
Per ⅔ cup: 83 cal., 5g fat (3g sat. fat), 14mg chol., 249mg sodium, 5g carb. (3g sugars, 1g fiber), 5g pro.
Diabetic Exchanges: 1 medium-fat meat, 1 vegetable.

OVEN-ROASTED ASPARAGUS

PICTURED ON P. 19

Asparagus spears have never tasted so good! Simply seasoned with butter and green onions, they have fresh flavor and keep their bright green color, too. They're so good, you might want to make extra.
—Jody Fisher, Stewartstown, PA

Start to Finish: 20 min.
Makes: 6 servings

- 2 pounds fresh asparagus, trimmed
- ¼ cup butter, melted
- 2 to 4 green onions, chopped
- ½ teaspoon salt

1. Preheat oven to 425°. Place asparagus in a 15x10x1-in. pan. Toss with melted butter and green onions; spread evenly. Sprinkle with salt.
2. Roast until crisp-tender, 10-15 minutes.
Per serving: 87 cal., 8g fat (5g sat. fat), 20mg chol., 266mg sodium, 4g carb. (1g sugars, 1g fiber), 2g pro.

SWISS CORN CASSEROLE

PICTURED ON P. 19

My mom shared this recipe with me back in the '80s and now it's a Turkey Day mainstay. We freeze locally grown corn during peak season, and I love to use it in this special side.
—Wendy Young, Cordova, MD

Prep: 20 min. • **Bake:** 35 min. + standing
Makes: 8 servings

- 4 large eggs
- 1 can (12 ounces) evaporated milk
- ½ teaspoon salt
- ¼ teaspoon pepper
- 4 cups frozen corn (about 20 ounces), thawed
- 3 cups shredded Swiss cheese, divided
- ¼ cup chopped onion
- 3 cups soft bread crumbs
- ¼ cup butter, melted

1. Preheat oven to 350°. In a large bowl, whisk together first four ingredients; stir in corn, 1½ cups cheese and onion. Transfer to a greased 11x7-in. baking dish.
2. Toss bread crumbs with melted butter; distribute over casserole. Sprinkle with remaining cheese.
3. Bake, uncovered, until golden brown and heated through, 35-45 minutes. Let stand 10 minutes before serving.
Note: To make soft bread crumbs, tear bread into pieces and place in a food processor or blender. Cover and pulse until crumbs form. One slice of bread yields ½ to ¾ cup crumbs.
Per ⅔ cup: 412 cal., 25g fat (14g sat. fat), 161mg chol., 434mg sodium, 28g carb. (7g sugars, 2g fiber), 21g pro.

✱

TEST KITCHEN TIPS

Any leftover bread can be used to make the bread crumbs. Egg bread gives a golden hue, whole grain bread makes for heartier texture, and sourdough offers a hint of tang.

Try using finely chopped red onion or shallots to add a touch of color to the casserole. For a sharper cheese flavor, use an aged Swiss.

ZUCCHINI MUSHROOM BAKE

SPINACH BLUEBERRY SALAD

EAT SMART ⑤ INGREDIENTS
ROASTED BALSAMIC RED POTATOES

I was intrigued when I found a potato recipe that called for vinegar. I didn't have the seasonings on hand, so I had to improvise. I gave the recipe a whirl using Italian seasoning and balsamic vinegar, and it turned out great!
—Lisa Varner, El Paso, TX

Prep: 10 min. • **Bake:** 30 min.
Makes: 6 servings

- 2 pounds small red potatoes, cut into wedges
- 2 tablespoons olive oil
- ¾ teaspoon garlic pepper blend
- ½ teaspoon Italian seasoning
- ¼ teaspoon salt
- ¼ cup balsamic vinegar

1. Preheat oven to 425°. Toss potatoes with oil and seasonings; spread in a 15x10x1-in. pan.
2. Roast 25 minutes, stirring halfway. Drizzle with vinegar; roast until potatoes are tender, 5-10 minutes.
Per ¾ cup: 159 cal., 5g fat (1g sat. fat), 0 chol., 143mg sodium, 27g carb. (4g sugars, 3g fiber), 3g pro.
Diabetic Exchanges: 2 starch, 1 fat.

⑤ INGREDIENTS FAST FIX
SPICY GRILLED EGGPLANT

This side goes well with pasta or meats also made on the grill. Thanks to the Cajun seasoning, it gets more attention than most ordinary veggies.
—Greg Fontenot, The Woodlands, TX

Start to Finish: 20 min.
Makes: 8 servings

- 2 small eggplants, cut into ½-inch slices
- ¼ cup olive oil
- 2 tablespoons lime juice
- 3 teaspoons Cajun seasoning

1. Brush eggplant slices with oil. Drizzle with lime juice; sprinkle with Cajun seasoning. Let stand 5 minutes.
2. Grill eggplant, covered, over medium heat or broil 4 in. from heat until tender, 4-5 minutes per side.
Per serving: 88 cal., 7g fat (1g sat. fat), 0 chol., 152mg sodium, 7g carb. (3g sugars, 4g fiber), 1g pro.
Diabetic Exchanges: 1½ fat, 1 vegetable.

FAST FIX
SPINACH BLUEBERRY SALAD

Blueberries are a fun surprise in this salad. I received the recipe from a co-worker's wife, and it's become one of my favorites.
—Heidi Gilleland, Lee's Summit, MO

Start to Finish: 15 min.
Makes: 8 servings

- ¼ cup raspberry vinegar
- 2 teaspoons Dijon mustard
- 1 teaspoon sugar
- ½ teaspoon salt
- ½ cup canola oil

SALAD
- 12 cups fresh baby spinach (about 10 ounces)
- 1 cup fresh blueberries
- 1 cup (4 ounces) crumbled blue cheese
- ½ cup chopped pecans, toasted

Mix first four ingredients; gradually whisk in oil until blended. In a large bowl, combine salad ingredients; toss with the dressing.
Per serving: 254 cal., 24g fat (5g sat. fat), 13mg chol., 407mg sodium, 6g carb. (3g sugars, 2g fiber), 6g pro.

EAT SMART FAST FIX
CILANTRO SALAD DRESSING

Use this zippy dressing over greens or hot or cold boiled potatoes. You'll love it.
—Sara Laber, Shelburne, VT

Start to Finish: 10 min.
Makes: about ½ cup

- ¼ cup buttermilk
- ¼ cup fat-free mayonnaise
- 3 to 6 drops hot pepper sauce
- ¼ teaspoon salt
- ¼ teaspoon garlic powder
- ⅛ teaspoon sugar
- ½ cup fresh cilantro leaves

Place all ingredients in a blender; cover and process until blended. Refrigerate, covered, until serving.
Per 2 tablespoons: 18 cal., 0 fat (0 sat. fat), 1mg chol., 298mg sodium, 4g carb. (2g sugars, 0 fiber), 1g pro.

**PESTO CORN SALAD
WITH SHRIMP**

PESTO CORN SALAD
WITH SHRIMP

*This recipe showcases the beautiful
bounty of summer with its fresh corn,
tomatoes and delicious basil. Prevent
browning by placing plastic wrap directly
on the salad or spritzing with lemon juice.*
—Deena Bowen, Chico, CA

Start to Finish: 30 min.
Makes: 4 servings

- 4 medium ears sweet corn
- ½ cup packed fresh basil leaves
- ¼ cup olive oil
- ½ teaspoon salt, divided
- 1½ cups cherry tomatoes, halved
- ⅛ teaspoon pepper
- 1 medium ripe avocado, peeled and chopped
- 1 pound uncooked shrimp (31-40 per pound), peeled and deveined

1. In a pot of boiling water, cook corn
until tender, about 5 minutes. Drain; cool
slightly. Meanwhile, in a food processor,
pulse the basil, oil and ¼ teaspoon salt
until blended.
2. Cut corn from cob and place in a bowl.
Stir in tomatoes, pepper and remaining
salt. Add avocado and 2 tablespoons basil
mixture; toss gently to combine.
3. Thread shrimp onto metal or soaked
wooden skewers; brush with remaining
basil mixture. Grill, covered, over medium
heat until shrimp turn pink, 2-4 minutes
per side. Remove shrimp from skewers;
serve with corn mixture.
Per serving: 371 cal., 22g fat (3g sat.
fat), 138mg chol., 450mg sodium, 25g
carb. (8g sugars, 5g fiber), 23g pro.

GREEN BEAN SALAD
WITH CREAMY DRESSING

*My grandmother passed this refreshing
side dish recipe on to me. It's always
devoured at my house.*
—Jodi Galanis, Murray, UT

Prep: 15 min. + chilling
Makes: 2 servings

- 1 cup cut fresh green beans (2 inch)
- ½ medium cucumber, halved lengthwise and sliced
- ⅓ cup julienned sweet red pepper
- ¼ cup thinly sliced onion

DRESSING

- 2 tablespoons cream cheese, softened
- 1 tablespoon 2% milk
- 1 tablespoon tarragon vinegar
- 2 teaspoons sugar
- ¼ teaspoon salt
- ¼ teaspoon pepper

1. In a saucepan of boiling water, cook
green beans, uncovered, until crisp-
tender, 3-5 minutes. Remove beans with a
slotted spoon; drop immediately into ice
water. Drain and pat dry.
2. Place cucumber, red pepper, onion and
beans in a large bowl. Whisk together
dressing ingredients; toss with vegetables.
Refrigerate, covered, until cold.
Per cup: 107 cal., 5g fat (3g sat. fat),
15mg chol., 349mg sodium, 13g carb.
(9g sugars, 3g fiber), 3g pro.
Diabetic Exchanges: 1 vegetable, 1 fat.

NECTARINE & BEET SALAD

Beets and nectarines sprinkled with feta cheese make a scrumptious new blend for a mixed green salad. The combination of ingredients may seem unlikely, but I think it will become a favorite.
—Nicole Werner, Ann Arbor, MI

Start to Finish: 10 min.
Makes: 8 servings

- 2 packages (5 ounces each) spring mix salad greens
- 2 medium nectarines, sliced
- ½ cup balsamic vinaigrette
- 1 can (14½ ounces) sliced beets, drained
- ½ cup crumbled feta cheese

On a serving dish, toss greens and nectarines with vinaigrette. Top with beets and cheese; serve immediately.
Per cup: 84 cal., 4g fat (1g sat. fat), 4mg chol., 371mg sodium, 10g carb. (6g sugars, 3g fiber), 3g pro.
Diabetic Exchanges: 2 vegetable, ½ fat.

SAUTEED GREEN BEANS

These beans are seasoned with some of my favorite herbs. I've found that basil, oregano and parsley are great flavor accents for canned, frozen or fresh beans. It's easy to throw together this delicious side for last-minute potlucks.
—Heidi Wilcox, Lapeer, MI

Start to Finish: 15 min.
Makes: 4 servings

- 1 package (9 ounces) frozen cut green beans, thawed
- 2 tablespoons butter
- 1 teaspoon dried minced onion
- ¼ teaspoon salt
- ¼ teaspoon each dried basil, oregano and parsley flakes

In a large skillet, saute beans in butter for 4-5 minutes. Add onion and seasonings. Reduce heat; cook and stir for 5 minutes or until heated through.
Per ½ cup: 71 cal., 6g fat (4g sat. fat), 15mg chol., 279mg sodium, 4g carb. (2g sugars, 2g fiber), 1g pro.

SPINACH SALAD WITH WARM BACON DRESSING

My spinach salad with bacon dressing is a recipe I turn to again and again in winter. It's quick, elegant and so delicious.
Count on compliments when you serve this tasty side.
—Sandy Davis, Prescott, AZ

Start to Finish: 30 min.
Makes: 4 servings

- 3 bacon strips, chopped
- 2 tablespoons red wine vinegar
- 1 small garlic clove, minced
- ½ teaspoon packed brown sugar
- ½ teaspoon Dijon mustard
- ¼ teaspoon salt
- ⅛ teaspoon coarsely ground pepper
  Dash ground nutmeg
  Dash crushed red pepper flakes
- ¼ cup olive oil
- 6 ounces fresh baby spinach (about 8 cups)
- ⅓ cup thinly sliced red onion
- 4 hard-boiled large eggs, chopped

1. In a skillet, cook bacon over medium heat until crisp, stirring occasionally. Using a slotted spoon, remove bacon to paper towels. Discard all but 1 tablespoon of drippings.
2. Add vinegar, garlic, brown sugar, mustard and seasonings to drippings; heat through, stirring to blend. Transfer to a small bowl; gradually whisk in oil. Stir in half of the bacon.
3. Place spinach, onion and eggs in a large bowl; toss with warm dressing. Sprinkle with remaining bacon; serve immediately.
Per 1¾ cups: 280 cal., 25g fat (6g sat. fat), 196mg chol., 373mg sodium, 5g carb. (2g sugars, 1g fiber), 10g pro.

DID YOU KNOW?

Using baby spinach saves prep time because you don't have to remove the tough stems of mature spinach. Some people also prefer the tender texture of baby spinach in salads.

NECTARINE & BEET SALAD

FAST FIX

CREAMY LEMON RICE

This bright rice dish has a creamy texture that's reminiscent of a lemon risotto, but without all the work. Keep this one in your back pocket for hosting dinner guests— or for a great side any old day!
—Lyndsay Wells, Ladysmith, BC

Start to Finish: 30 min.
Makes: 4 servings

    2½ cups chicken broth
     2 ounces cream cheese, cubed
     ½ teaspoon grated lemon peel
     1 tablespoon lemon juice
     ¼ teaspoon salt
     ¼ teaspoon coarsely ground pepper
     1 cup uncooked long grain rice
     ¼ cup minced fresh basil

1. In a saucepan, combine first six ingredients; bring to a boil. Stir with a whisk to blend.
2. Stir in rice; return to a boil. Reduce heat; simmer, covered, until liquid is absorbed and rice is tender, about 15 minutes. Stir in basil.
Per ¾ cup: 246 cal., 6g fat (3g sat. fat), 17mg chol., 806mg sodium, 42g carb. (1g sugars, 1g fiber), 5g pro.

YUMMY CORN CHIP SALAD

FAST FIX

YUMMY CORN CHIP SALAD

Corn chips give a special crunch and unexpected flavor to this potluck-favorite salad. Bacon adds a hint of smokiness while the cranberries bring a touch of sweetness. We've found it to be the perfect picnic companion!
—Nora Friesen, Aberdeen, MS

Start to Finish: 25 min.
Makes: 12 servings

    ¾ cup canola oil
    ¼ cup cider vinegar
    ¼ cup mayonnaise
    2 tablespoons yellow mustard
    ½ teaspoon salt
    ¾ cup sugar
    ½ small onion
    ¾ teaspoon poppy seeds

SALAD
    2 bunches leaf lettuce, chopped (about 20 cups)
    1 package (9¼ ounces) corn chips
    8 bacon strips, cooked and crumbled
    1 cup shredded part-skim mozzarella cheese
    1 cup dried cranberries

1. For dressing, place first seven ingredients in a blender. Cover; process until smooth. Stir in poppy seeds.
2. Place salad ingredients in a large bowl; toss with dressing. Serve immediately.
Per 1⅓ cups: 436 cal., 30g fat (4g sat. fat), 12mg chol., 456mg sodium, 38g carb. (24g sugars, 2g fiber), 7g pro.

ROSEMARY RED POTATOES

Great with steak or any meat, this is one of our best-loved potato sidekicks. Sometimes, after the potatoes have baked about 15 minutes, I add sliced fresh mushrooms and sliced fresh zucchini tossed with a little olive oil.

—Kelly Ward-Hartman, Cape Coral, FL

Start to Finish: 30 min.
Makes: 4 servings

- 1¾ pounds small red potatoes, quartered
- 1 small onion, quartered
- ¼ cup olive oil
- 1½ teaspoons dried rosemary, crushed
- 2 garlic cloves, minced
- ¼ teaspoon garlic salt

In a bowl, combine the potatoes, onion, oil, rosemary, garlic and garlic salt; toss to coat. Transfer to a foil-lined 15x10x1-in. baking pan. Bake, uncovered, at 425° for 25-30 minutes or until the potatoes are tender and browned.

Per cup: 273 cal., 14g fat (2g sat. fat), 0 chol., 126mg sodium, 34g carb. (3g sugars, 4g fiber), 4g pro.

CHEESY CHEDDAR BROCCOLI CASSEROLE

People who don't even like broccoli beg me to make this fabulous recipe. It's similar to a classic green bean casserole, but the melted cheese just puts it over the top.

—Elaine Hubbard, Pocono Lake, PA

Prep: 15 min. • **Bake:** 35 min.
Makes: 8 servings

- 1 can (10¾ ounces) condensed cream of mushroom soup, undiluted
- 1 cup (8 ounces) sour cream
- 1½ cups shredded sharp cheddar cheese, divided
- 1 can (6 ounces) french-fried onions, divided
- 2 packages (16 ounces each) frozen broccoli florets, thawed

1. Preheat oven to 325°. In a large saucepan, combine soup, sour cream, 1 cup cheese and 1¼ cups onions; heat through over medium heat, stirring until blended, 4-5 minutes. Stir in broccoli. Transfer to a greased 2-qt. baking dish.
2. Bake, uncovered, until bubbly, about 25-30 minutes. Sprinkle with remaining cheese and onions. Bake until cheese is melted, 10-15 minutes.

Per ¾ cup: 359 cal., 26g fat (11g sat. fat), 30mg chol., 641mg sodium, 19g carb. (4g sugars, 3g fiber), 8g pro.

CHEESY CHEDDAR BROCCOLI CASSEROLE

SIDE DISHES & SALADS

TURKEY & PASTA RANCH SALAD

This easy pasta salad is loaded with fresh veggies, and the classic ranch dressing makes it appealing to kids.
—Julie Peterson, Crofton, MD

Start to Finish: 25 min.
Makes: 6 servings

- 2 cups uncooked whole wheat spiral pasta (about 5 ounces)
- 2 medium sweet peppers, chopped
- 1 medium zucchini, thinly sliced
- 1 yellow summer squash, thinly sliced
- ½ cup finely chopped red onion
- 2 cups cubed cooked turkey or chicken
- 3 tablespoons chopped fresh parsley
- ½ cup peppercorn ranch salad dressing
- ¼ teaspoon salt
- ¼ cup shredded Parmesan cheese

1. Cook pasta according to package directions. Drain and rinse with cold water; drain well.

2. Place pasta, vegetables, turkey and parsley in a large bowl; toss with dressing and salt. Sprinkle with cheese.

Per 1⅔ cups: 256 cal., 11g fat (2g sat. fat), 50mg chol., 383mg sodium, 20g carb. (4g sugars, 4g fiber), 19g pro.
Diabetic Exchanges: 3 lean meat, 1½ fat, 1 starch, 1 vegetable.

STRAWBERRY KALE SALAD

This fresh, zingy salad is super easy and always a crowd pleaser! The sliced strawberries and fresh mint give it an extra summery feel, and crumbled bacon and toasted almonds add the perfect amount of crunch.
—Luanne Asta, Hampton Bays, NY

Start to Finish: 25 min.
Makes: 10 servings

- ½ cup olive oil
- ⅓ cup cider vinegar
- 1 teaspoon honey
- ¼ teaspoon salt
- ⅛ teaspoon pepper
- 1 bunch kale (about 12 ounces), trimmed and chopped (about 14 cups)
- 2 cups sliced fresh strawberries
- ¾ pound bacon strips, cooked and crumbled
- ¼ cup minced fresh mint
- 1 cup crumbled feta cheese
- ¼ cup slivered almonds, toasted

1. For dressing, whisk together first five ingredients.

2. To serve, place kale, strawberries, bacon and mint in a large bowl; toss with dressing. Sprinkle with the cheese and slivered almonds.

Note: To toast nuts, bake in a shallow pan in a 350° oven for 5-10 minutes or cook in a skillet over low heat until lightly browned, stirring occasionally.

Per 1⅓ cups: 231 cal., 19g fat (4g sat. fat), 18mg chol., 399mg sodium, 8g carb. (2g sugars, 2g fiber), 8g pro.

WAFFLE IRON ACORN SQUASH

I love to get the kids involved in cooking, and this squash is so simple even a small child can cook it with minimal adult supervision. The recipe is fun, fast and no-fuss, and doesn't use valuable oven space before big family meals.
—Donna Kelly, Orem, UT

Prep: 10 min. • **Bake:** 5 min./batch
Makes: 4 servings

- 3 tablespoons maple syrup
- ¾ teaspoon ground chipotle pepper
- ½ teaspoon salt
- 1 small acorn squash

1. Preheat a greased waffle maker. Mix syrup, chipotle pepper and salt.

2. Cut squash crosswise into ½-in.-thick slices. Using round cookie cutters, cut out centers to remove squash strings and seeds. If necessary, halve slices to fit in waffle maker.

3. Bake slices in waffle maker just until tender and lightly browned, 3-4 minutes. Serve with syrup mixture.

Per serving: 98 cal., 0 fat (0 sat. fat), 0 chol., 463mg sodium, 25g carb. (12g sugars, 2g fiber), 1g pro.
Diabetic Exchanges: 1½ starch.

❋

TEST KITCHEN TIPS
Cut slices just ½ inch thick. If slices are thicker, the waffle iron won't close all the way. A panini press also works to make this squash.

The squash will be very tender after cooking this way. To keep the squash intact, drizzle the maple mixture over the squash instead of brushing it on.

MANGO & JICAMA SALAD

This pretty salad has become part of my regular summertime rotation because of its freshness and versatility—it goes great with everything from grilled chicken to seafood! Try it with coconut-flavored vinegar for a fun tropical twist.
—Carla Mendres, Winnipeg, MB

Start to Finish: 25 min.
Makes: 8 servings

- ½ cup white wine vinegar
- ¼ cup canola oil
- ¼ cup honey
- 1 teaspoon minced fresh gingerroot
- ¼ teaspoon salt
- ⅛ teaspoon pepper
- 1 medium jicama (about 1½ pounds), peeled
- 1 medium mango, peeled
- 1 medium sweet red pepper
- 2 tablespoons lime juice
- ½ cup chopped fresh cilantro
- ⅓ cup minced fresh chives

1. For dressing, whisk together the first six ingredients.

2. Cut jicama, mango and red pepper into matchsticks; place in a large bowl. Toss with lime juice. Add herbs and dressing; toss to combine. Refrigerate, covered, until serving.

Per cup: 143 cal., 7g fat (1g sat. fat), 0 chol., 78mg sodium, 20g carb. (16g sugars, 3g fiber), 1g pro.
Diabetic Exchanges: 1½ fat, 1 vegetable, ½ starch.

WAFFLE IRON ACORN SQUASH

LINGUINE WITH FRESH TOMATOES

FAST FIX ▸

SESAME RAMEN SALAD

This spicy Asian sausage and noodle salad is equally good for lunch or a potluck.
—Denese Johnson, Chico, TX

Start to Finish: 30 min.
Makes: 8 servings

- 3 packages (3 ounces each) shrimp ramen noodles
- 6 cups hot water
- 1 pound bulk spicy pork sausage
- ¾ cup Asian toasted sesame salad dressing
- ¾ cup sliced green onions (about 6 medium), divided
- ½ cup chopped fresh cilantro
- ½ teaspoon grated lime peel
- 3 tablespoons lime juice
- 3 cups fresh snow peas, halved diagonally (about 8 ounces)
- 1½ cups julienned carrots
- 4 tablespoons chopped dry roasted peanuts, divided

1. Break the ramen noodles into quarters and place in a large bowl; reserve one seasoning packet. Cover noodles with hot water; let stand until softened, about 5 minutes.
2. Drain noodles; rinse with cold water. Drain well and return to bowl.
3. In a large skillet, cook and crumble sausage over medium heat until no longer pink, 5-7 minutes. Drain on paper towels.
4. Mix salad dressing, ½ cup green onions, cilantro, lime peel, lime juice and contents of reserved seasoning packet; add to noodles. Toss with snow peas, carrots, 3 tablespoons peanuts and sausage. Sprinkle with the remaining green onions and peanuts.
Per cup: 402 cal., 25g fat (8g sat. fat), 31mg chol., 972mg sodium, 33g carb. (8g sugars, 2g fiber), 12g pro.

✳
TEST KITCHEN TIP

Easily upgrade instant ramen noodles by stirring in some peanut butter, chopped green onion or sliced boiled egg. Or stir a raw beaten egg into the ramen during the last 30 seconds of cooking. Cook and stir until egg pieces are firm.

FAST FIX ▸
LINGUINE WITH FRESH TOMATOES

This garlic and basil pasta is a perfect way to use up your late-summer tomato harvest. It makes a great light supper when paired with a salad, or make it heartier with some chopped chicken.
—Susan Jones, Downers Grove, IL

Start to Finish: 20 min.
Makes: 6 servings

- 8 ounces uncooked linguine
- 3 medium tomatoes, chopped
- 6 green onions, sliced
- ½ cup grated Parmesan cheese
- ¼ cup minced fresh basil or 4 teaspoons dried basil
- 2 garlic cloves, minced
- 1 teaspoon salt
- ½ teaspoon pepper
- 3 tablespoons butter

1. Cook linguine according to package directions. Meanwhile, place all remaining ingredients except butter in a large bowl.
2. Drain linguine; toss with butter. Add to tomato mixture and toss to combine.

Per cup: 233 cal., 9g fat (5g sat. fat), 21mg chol., 567mg sodium, 32g carb. (3g sugars, 3g fiber), 8g pro.

EAT SMART **FAST FIX**
ALMOND STRAWBERRY SALAD

Everyone loves this pretty salad that's topped with strawberries and sliced almonds. With just a few ingredients, it's loaded with flavor.
—Renae Rossow, Union, KY

Start to Finish: 10 min.
Makes: 4 servings

- 3 cups fresh baby spinach
- ½ cup sliced fresh strawberries
- ¼ cup honey-roasted sliced almonds
- 1 tablespoon cider vinegar
- 1 tablespoon honey
- 1½ teaspoons sugar

Place spinach, strawberries and almonds in a large bowl. Mix vinegar, honey and sugar until blended; toss with salad.
Per ¾ cup: 75 cal., 4g fat (0 sat. fat), 0 chol., 98mg sodium, 9g carb. (8g sugars, 1g fiber), 2g pro.
Diabetic Exchanges: 1 vegetable, 1 fat.

TARRAGON ASPARAGUS SALAD

I love asparagus, and I love it even more when drizzled with my light, lemony vinaigrette dressing with a touch of tarragon. It's so perfect as a side for fresh spring meals.
—Linda Lacek, Winter Park, FL

Prep: 15 min. + chilling • **Cook:** 5 min.
Makes: 4 servings

- 2 tablespoons lemon juice
- 2 tablespoons olive oil
- 1 teaspoon minced fresh tarragon or ¼ teaspoon dried tarragon
- 1 garlic clove, minced
- ½ teaspoon Dijon mustard
- ¼ teaspoon pepper
  Dash salt
- 1 pound fresh asparagus, cut into 2-inch pieces

1. Place first seven ingredients in a jar with a tight-fitting lid; shake contents well. Refrigerate at least 1 hour.
2. In a large skillet, bring ½ in. of water to a boil. Add asparagus; cook, covered, until crisp-tender, 1-3 minutes. Remove asparagus and immediately drop into ice water. Drain and pat dry. Refrigerate, covered, until serving.
3. To serve, shake dressing again. Spoon over asparagus.
Per serving: 77 cal., 7g fat (1g sat. fat), 0 chol., 387mg sodium, 3g carb. (1g sugars, 1g fiber), 2g pro.
Diabetic Exchanges: 1½ fat, 1 vegetable.

BROCCOLI SLAW

Here's a sweet twist on traditional coleslaw. It's so easy to make and has an irresistible tangy crunch.
—Konny Thomas, Citrus Heights, CA

Prep: 15 min. + chilling
Makes: 6 servings

- 4 cups broccoli florets
- 2 cups shredded red cabbage
- 1 small sweet onion, finely chopped
- 1 medium carrot, shredded
- ½ cup raisins
- 1 cup coleslaw salad dressing

In a large bowl, combine all ingredients and toss. Refrigerate, covered, at least 2 hours. Stir before serving.
Per cup: 225 cal., 12g fat (2g sat. fat), 4mg chol., 325mg sodium, 25g carb. (19g sugars, 3g fiber), 3g pro.

CURRIED QUINOA SALAD

Quinoa is such a fantastic salad base— it's full of protein, adds a nutty flavor, and is the perfect vehicle to soak up any kind of dressing. If you like a little more heat, add more cayenne or curry to the dressing.
—Shannon Dobos, Calgary, AB

Prep: 20 min. + chilling
Cook: 15 min. + standing
Makes: 6 servings

- 1 cup quinoa, rinsed
- 1 teaspoon ground turmeric
- ¼ teaspoon ground cumin
- 1 can (14½ ounces) vegetable or chicken broth
- 1½ cups grape tomatoes, halved
- 1 small cucumber, diced
- ⅓ cup diced red onion

DRESSING
- 2 tablespoons lemon juice
- 2 tablespoons olive oil
- 1 tablespoon honey
- 1 teaspoon yellow mustard
- ½ teaspoon curry powder
- ¼ teaspoon salt
- ⅛ teaspoon cayenne pepper

1. In a small saucepan, bring first four ingredients; bring to a boil. Reduce heat; simmer, covered, until liquid is absorbed, 12-15 minutes. Remove from heat; let stand, covered, 15 minutes. Transfer to a large bowl; cool slightly.
2. Add tomatoes, cucumber and onion to quinoa. In a small bowl, whisk together the dressing ingredients; toss with the salad. Refrigerate, covered, until cold, about 2 hours. Stir before serving.
Per ¾ cup: 176 cal., 6g fat (1g sat. fat), 0 chol., 320mg sodium, 25g carb. (5g sugars, 3g fiber), 5g pro.
Diabetic Exchanges: 1½ starch, 1 fat.

TARRAGON ASPARAGUS SALAD

Soups & Sandwiches

Turn here for the dynamic duo of the fast-to-fix set! A longtime standby for busy cooks, soups and sandwiches come together quickly, and they always satisfy. For soul-soothing comfort on busy days or man-cave cravings during the game, the perfect combo is right here.

CHEDDAR PEAR SOUP

FAST FIX ▶

GARLIC TORTELLINI SOUP

PICTURED ON P. 43

Tender cheese tortellini comes together with spinach, tomatoes and a garlicky broth in this comforting soup. A hunk of crusty bread takes it over the top.
—Donna Morgan, Hendersonville, TN

....

Start to Finish: 25 min.
Makes: 6 servings

- 1 tablespoon butter
- 2 garlic cloves, minced
- 3 cans (14½ ounces each) reduced-sodium chicken broth or vegetable broth
- 1 package (9 ounces) refrigerated cheese tortellini
- 1 can (14½ ounces) diced tomatoes with green chilies, undrained
- 1 package (10 ounces) frozen chopped spinach, thawed and squeezed dry

In a large saucepan, heat butter over medium heat; saute garlic until tender, about 1 minute. Stir in broth; bring to a boil. Add tortellini; cook, uncovered, until tender, 7-9 minutes. Stir in tomatoes and spinach; heat through.

Per cup: 189 cal., 6g fat (3g sat. fat), 23mg chol., 1074mg sodium, 25g carb. (2g sugars, 3g fiber), 11g pro.

HEALTH TIP The broth adds nearly 600mg sodium, despite being reduced-sodium. Instead of broth, add 5½ cups water plus just 3 tsp. reduced-sodium chicken bouillon granules. That brings total sodium to just 636mg.

CHEDDAR PEAR SOUP

Pears and sharp cheddar have always been one of my favorite flavor combos. This recipe brings the two together in a creamy, delicious soup. I like to serve it with a warm baguette and fresh fruit for lunch or a light supper.
—Trisha Kruse, Eagle, ID

....

Prep: 15 min.
Cook: 35 min.
Makes: 8 servings (2 quarts)

- ¼ cup butter, cubed
- 1 large onion, chopped
- 2 garlic cloves, minced
- ⅓ cup all-purpose flour
- 2 teaspoons smoked paprika
- 5 cups chicken broth
- 3 medium ripe pears, peeled and chopped
- ¾ pound sharp cheddar cheese, shredded (about 3 cups)
- ¼ teaspoon freshly ground pepper
  Fresh pear slices, optional

1. In a Dutch oven, heat butter over medium-high heat; saute onion and garlic until tender, 7-9 minutes. Stir in flour and paprika until blended; cook and stir 2 minutes. Gradually stir in broth. Add chopped pears; bring to a boil. Reduce heat; simmer, covered, until pears are tender, about 15 minutes, stirring occasionally.

2. Puree soup using an immersion blender. Or, cool slightly and puree soup in batches in a blender; return to pan. Add cheese and pepper; cook and stir over low heat until cheese is melted, 3-5 minutes. If desired, top with pear slices.

Per cup: 299 cal., 20g fat (12g sat. fat), 60mg chol., 938mg sodium, 18g carb. (8g sugars, 3g fiber), 12g pro.

ITALIAN JOES ON TEXAS TOAST

This is great for a weeknight on the go. If you double the crushed tomatoes, meat and wine, you'll have enough sauce to freeze for busy days.

—Ashley Armstrong, Kingsland, GA

Start to Finish: 30 min.
Makes: 8 servings

- 1 pound ground beef
- 1 small green pepper, finely chopped
- 1 medium onion, finely chopped
- 3 garlic cloves, minced
- ½ cup dry red wine or beef broth
- 1 can (14½ ounces) diced tomatoes, undrained
- ¼ cup tomato paste
- ¼ teaspoon salt
- ⅛ teaspoon pepper
- 1 package (11¼ ounces) frozen garlic Texas toast
- 8 slices part-skim mozzarella cheese

1. Preheat oven to 425°. In a large skillet, cook and crumble beef with green pepper, onion and garlic over medium-high heat until no longer pink, 5-7 minutes; drain. Stir in wine. Bring to a boil; cook until wine is reduced by half, about 2 minutes. Stir in tomatoes, tomato paste, salt and pepper; return to a boil. Reduce heat; simmer, uncovered, until mixture is thickened, 2-3 minutes, stirring occasionally.

2. Meanwhile, place Texas toast on a foil-lined 15x10x1-in. pan; bake until lightly browned, 8-10 minutes.

3. Spoon beef mixture onto toast slices; top with cheese. Bake until cheese is melted, 3-4 minutes. Serve immediately.

Per open-faced sandwich: 353 cal., 19g fat (7g sat. fat), 58mg chol., 626mg sodium, 25g carb. (5g sugars, 2g fiber), 22g pro.

ITALIAN JOES ON TEXAS TOAST

SOUTHWEST TURKEY BURGERS
PICTURED ON P. 43

I made these turkey burgers with corn, green chilies and taco seasoning for my parents. They originally weren't sold on an untraditional burger, but they absolutely loved these! The burgers are gobbled up quickly every time I serve them.

—Katie Ring, Menasha, WI

Start to Finish: 30 min.
Makes: 6 servings

- ½ cup seasoned bread crumbs
- ½ cup frozen corn, thawed
- 1 can (4 ounces) chopped green chilies
- 1 tablespoon reduced-sodium taco seasoning
- 1 pound lean ground turkey
- 6 whole wheat hamburger buns, split
- 6 wedges The Laughing Cow queso fresco chipotle cheese, halved Lettuce leaves, optional

1. Preheat the broiler. Mix the first four ingredients. Add ground turkey; mix lightly but thoroughly. Shape into six ½-in.-thick patties.

2. In a large nonstick skillet coated with cooking spray, cook burgers in batches over medium heat until a thermometer reads 165°, 4-6 minutes per side. Keep burgers warm.

3. Meanwhile, place buns on a baking sheet, cut side up. Broil 3-4 in. from heat until toasted, about 30 seconds. Spread tops with cheese. Serve burgers in buns, with lettuce if desired.

Freeze option: Place uncooked patties on a plastic wrap-lined baking sheet; cover and freeze until firm. Remove from pan and transfer to a large resealable plastic bag; return to freezer. To use, cook frozen patties in a nonstick skillet coated with cooking spray over medium-low heat until a thermometer reads 165°, 6-8 minutes per side.

Per burger: 316 cal., 10g fat (3g sat. fat), 57mg chol., 812mg sodium, 35g carb. (6g sugars, 4g fiber), 22g pro.
Diabetic Exchanges: 3 lean meat, 2 starch, ½ fat.

BISTRO TURKEY SANDWICH

FAST FIX

PORTOBELLO MELTS

We're always looking for satisfying vegetarian meals, and this one tops the list. These melts are especially delicious in the summer when we have so many juicy homegrown tomatoes to use.
—Amy Smalley, Morehead, KY

Start to Finish: 20 min.
Makes: 2 servings

    2 large portobello mushrooms
       (4 ounces each), stems removed
    ¼ cup olive oil
    2 tablespoons balsamic vinegar
    ½ teaspoon salt
    ½ teaspoon dried basil
    4 tomato slices
    2 slices mozzarella cheese
    2 slices Italian bread (1 inch thick)
       Chopped fresh basil

1. Preheat broiler. Place mushrooms in a shallow bowl. Mix oil, vinegar, salt and dried basil; brush onto both sides of mushrooms. Let stand 5 minutes.
2. Place mushrooms on a greased rack of a broiler pan, stem side down; reserve remaining marinade. Broil mushrooms 4 in. from heat until tender, 3-4 minutes per side. Top stem sides with tomato and cheese. Broil until cheese is melted, about 1 minute.
3. Place bread on a baking sheet; brush with reserved marinade. Broil 4 in. from heat until lightly toasted, 45-60 seconds. Top with mushrooms. Sprinkle with chopped basil.

Per open-faced sandwich: 460 cal., 35g fat (7g sat. fat), 22mg chol., 934mg sodium, 26g carb. (8g sugars, 3g fiber), 12g pro.

HEALTH TIP If you skip the bread in these portobello melts to make them low-carb, you can also use half the vinaigrette, saving almost 15g fat and 400mg sodium.

FAST FIX

BISTRO TURKEY SANDWICH

As a turkey lover who can't get enough during fall and winter, I was inspired to come up with a restaurant-worthy sandwich. I love it with Brie.
—Grace Voltolina, Westport, CT

Start to Finish: 30 min.
Makes: 4 servings

    2 tablespoons butter, divided
    1 large Granny Smith or Honeycrisp
       apple, cut into ¼-inch slices
    ½ teaspoon sugar
    ¼ teaspoon ground cinnamon
    ½ medium sweet onion, sliced
    ¼ cup whole-berry or jellied cranberry
       sauce
    4 ciabatta rolls, split
    1 pound cooked turkey, sliced
    8 slices Camembert or Brie cheese
       (about 8 ounces)
    3 cups arugula (about 2 ounces)

1. Preheat broiler. In a large skillet, heat 1 tablespoon butter over medium heat; saute apple with sugar and cinnamon until crisp-tender, 3-4 minutes. Remove from the pan.
2. In same pan, melt remaining butter over medium heat; saute onion until lightly browned, 3-4 minutes. Remove from heat; stir in sauteed apple.
3. Spread cranberry sauce onto bottom of rolls; layer with turkey, apple mixture and cheese. Place on a baking sheet alongside roll tops, cut side up.
4. Broil 3-4 in. from heat until cheese begins to melt and roll tops are golden brown, 45-60 seconds. Add arugula; close sandwiches.

Per sandwich: 797 cal., 28g fat (14g sat. fat), 171mg chol., 1196mg sodium, 87g carb. (16g sugars, 6g fiber), 55g pro.

PORTOBELLO MELTS

FREEZE IT FAST FIX

WHITE BEAN SOUP WITH MEATBALLS

It tastes like it's from scratch, but my Italian-inspired soup uses lots of shortcuts. For a meatball in every bite, chop them up—with an egg slicer!
—Carole Lotito, Hillsdale, NJ

Start to Finish: 30 min.
Makes: 6 servings

- 2 teaspoons olive oil
- 1 medium onion, chopped
- 2 garlic cloves, minced
- ⅛ teaspoon coarsely ground pepper
- 12 ounces frozen fully cooked Italian meatballs (about 3 cups), thawed
- 1 cup julienned carrots
- 1 carton (32 ounces) reduced-sodium chicken broth
- 1 can (15½ ounces) cannellini beans, rinsed and drained
- 8 cups coarsely chopped escarole (1 bunch) or fresh spinach
  Thinly sliced fresh basil, optional

1. In a 6-qt. stockpot, heat oil over medium heat; saute onion until tender, 3-4 minutes. Add garlic and pepper; cook and stir 1 minute.
2. Stir in meatballs, carrots and broth; bring to a boil. Reduce heat; simmer, covered, 5 minutes. Stir in beans and escarole; return to a boil. Reduce heat; simmer, covered, until escarole has wilted, about 10 minutes. If desired, top servings with basil.
Freeze option: Freeze cooled soup in freezer containers. To use, partially thaw in refrigerator overnight. Heat through in a saucepan, stirring occasionally.
Per cup: 301 cal., 15g fat (6g sat. fat), 27mg chol., 1050mg sodium, 26g carb. (3g sugars, 8g fiber), 19g pro.

MOZZARELLA BEEF ROLL-UPS

FREEZE IT FAST FIX

MOZZARELLA BEEF ROLL-UPS

The kids will love these wraps. They're easy to assemble because each tortilla is simply wrapped around a portion of meat filling with a piece of string cheese.
—*Taste of Home* Test Kitchen

Start to Finish: 30 min.
Makes: 6 servings

- 1 pound ground beef
- 1 medium green pepper, chopped
- ⅓ cup chopped onion
- 1 can (8 ounces) pizza sauce
- 2 ounces sliced pepperoni (about ⅔ cup)
- ½ teaspoon dried oregano
- 6 flour tortillas (10 inches), warmed
- 6 pieces string cheese (about 6 ounces)

1. Preheat oven to 350°. In a large skillet, cook and crumble beef with pepper and onion over medium-high heat until no longer pink, 5-7 minutes; drain. Stir in pizza sauce, pepperoni and oregano.
2. Spoon ½ cup mixture across center of each tortilla; top with a piece of string cheese. Fold bottom and sides of tortilla over filling and roll up.
3. Place on an ungreased baking sheet, seam side down. Bake until heated through, about 10 minutes.
Freeze option: Cool beef mixture before assembly. Individually wrap roll-ups in foil and freeze in a resealable plastic freezer bag for up to 2 months. To use, partially thaw overnight in refrigerator. Reheat foil-wrapped roll-ups on a baking sheet in a preheated 350° oven until heated through. To reheat individually, remove foil and rewrap in paper towel; place on a microwave-safe plate. Microwave on high until heated through, turning once. Let stand 15 seconds.
Per roll-up: 513 cal., 25g fat (11g sat. fat), 71mg chol., 1064mg sodium, 41g carb. (5g sugars, 4g fiber), 30g pro.

LOADED AVOCADO BLT

My husband invented this twist on a bacon, lettuce and tomato sandwich. I like to make it with eight slices of bacon, and sometimes add Gorgonzola cheese to the avocado spread.
—Lori Grant, Kingsport, TN

Start to Finish: 15 min.
Makes: 2 servings

- ½ small ripe avocado, peeled
- 2 tablespoons mayonnaise
- ½ teaspoon lemon juice
- 2 tablespoons crumbled Gorgonzola cheese
- 4 slices Italian bread, toasted
- 1½ cups fresh baby spinach
- 4 tomato slices
- 4 thick-sliced applewood smoked bacon strips, cooked

1. Mash avocado with a fork; stir in mayonnaise and lemon juice. Gently stir in the cheese.
2. Spread over toast slices. Top two of the slices with spinach, tomato, bacon and remaining slices of toast.

Per sandwich: 420 cal., 29g fat (7g sat. fat), 27mg chol., 921mg sodium, 27g carb. (3g sugars, 5g fiber), 15g pro.

HAM & CHEESE CHOWDER

Chowder makes chilly days instantly cozier. This easy one, with cheddar, potatoes and smoky ham, warms you up from head to toe.
—Mandy Beerman, Houstonia, MO

Start to Finish: 30 min.
Makes: 6 servings

- 1½ pounds potatoes (about 3 medium), peeled and diced
- ¼ teaspoon baking soda
- 3 tablespoons butter
- 1 small onion, finely chopped
- 3 tablespoons all-purpose flour
- 3½ cups whole milk
- 4 ounces process cheese (Velveeta), cubed (about 1 cup)
- ½ cup shredded sharp cheddar cheese
- 1½ cups cubed fully cooked ham
  Minced chives and coarsely ground pepper, optional

1. Place potatoes and baking soda in a large saucepan. Add water to cover; bring to a boil. Reduce heat; cook, uncovered, until potatoes are tender, 6-8 minutes. Drain, reserving ½ cup potato water.
2. In same pan, heat the butter over medium heat; saute onion until tender, 2-4 minutes. Stir in flour until blended; cook and stir 2 minutes. Gradually stir in milk and reserved potato water. Bring to a simmer, stirring constantly; cook and stir until thickened, 1-2 minutes.
3. Stir in cheeses until melted. Stir in ham and potatoes; heat through. If desired, sprinkle with chives and pepper.

Per cup: 366 cal., 20g fat (11g sat. fat), 78mg chol., 888mg sodium, 28g carb. (10g sugars, 1g fiber), 19g pro.

LOADED AVOCADO BLT

FAST FIX >

TUNA BURGERS

My family was so accustomed to a typical beef burger that they were hesitant to try these when I first made them. Any skepticism disappeared after one bite.
—Kim Stoller, Smithville, OH

Start to Finish: 20 min.
Makes: 4 servings

- 1 large egg, lightly beaten
- ½ cup dry bread crumbs
- ½ cup finely chopped celery
- ⅓ cup mayonnaise
- ¼ cup finely chopped onion
- 2 tablespoons chili sauce
- 1 pouch (6.4 ounces) light tuna in water
- 2 tablespoons butter
- 4 hamburger buns, split and toasted
  Lettuce leaves and sliced tomato, optional

1. Mix first six ingredients; fold in tuna. Shape into four patties.
2. In a large skillet, heat butter over medium heat. Cook patties until lightly browned, 4-5 minutes per side. Serve on buns, with lettuce and tomato if desired.
Per burger: 417 cal., 23g fat (7g sat. fat), 79mg chol., 710mg sodium, 35g carb. (6g sugars, 2g fiber), 17g pro.
HEALTH TIP Lighten up this burger by using reduced-fat mayo and brushing the patties with 1 tablespoon butter. Then use your broiler instead of pan-frying. You'll save 75 calories and 10g fat.

LEMONY TURKEY RICE SOUP

FAST FIX >

LEMONY TURKEY RICE SOUP

While growing up in Texas, I spent a lot of time helping my grandma cook. I took her classic turkey soup recipe and gave it a deliciously different twist with lemon and cilantro. It's ready in no time!
—Margarita Cuellar, East Chicago, IN

Start to Finish: 30 min.
Makes: 8 servings (2 quarts)

- 2 cups diced cooked turkey
- 2 cups cooked long grain rice
- 1 can (10¾ ounces) condensed cream of chicken soup, undiluted
- ¼ teaspoon pepper
- 6 cups chicken broth, divided
- 2 tablespoons cornstarch
- ¼ to ⅓ cup lemon juice
- ¼ to ½ cup minced fresh cilantro

1. In a large saucepan, combine first four ingredients and 5½ cups broth. Bring to a boil; cook 3 minutes.
2. In a small bowl, mix cornstarch and remaining broth until smooth; gradually stir into soup. Bring to a boil; cook and stir until thickened, 1-2 minutes. Remove from the heat; stir in the lemon juice and minced cilantro.
Per cup: 166 cal., 4g fat (1g sat. fat), 42mg chol., 1047mg sodium, 17g carb. (1g sugars, 1g fiber), 13g pro.

FAST FIX >

GRILLED HUMMUS TURKEY SANDWICH

PICTURED ON P. 43

I created this toasted sandwich last summer using homemade hummus and veggies from our garden. We really can't get enough.
—Gunjan Gilbert, Franklin, ME

Start to Finish: 15 min.
Makes: 2 servings

- ½ cup hummus
- 4 slices whole wheat bread
- 4 ounces thinly sliced deli turkey
- 4 slices tomato
- 2 slices pepper jack cheese
- 4 teaspoons butter, softened

1. Spread hummus on two bread slices; top with turkey, tomato, cheese and remaining bread. Spread outsides of sandwiches with butter.
2. In a large skillet, toast sandwiches over medium heat until golden brown and cheese is melted, 2-3 minutes per side.
Per sandwich: 458 cal., 23g fat (10g sat. fat), 63mg chol., 1183mg sodium, 36g carb. (3g sugars, 7g fiber), 28g pro.
HEALTH TIP Cut saturated fat in half by omitting the butter and browning the sandwich in nonstick cooking spray instead.

APPLE CHICKEN QUESADILLAS

My sister came up with this easy recipe that can be served as a main course or an appetizer. People are surprised by the combination of chicken, apples, tomatoes and corn inside the crispy tortillas.
—Stacia Slagle, Maysville, MO

Start to Finish: 25 min.
Makes: 6 servings

- 2 medium tart apples, sliced
- 1 cup diced cooked chicken breast
- ½ cup shredded cheddar cheese
- ½ cup shredded part-skim mozzarella cheese
- ½ cup fresh or frozen corn, thawed
- ½ cup chopped fresh tomatoes
- ½ cup chopped onion
- ¼ teaspoon salt
- 6 flour tortillas (8 inches), warmed
  Optional toppings: shredded lettuce, salsa and sour cream

1. Preheat oven to 400°. Toss together first eight ingredients. Place ¾ cup mixture on one half of each tortilla. Fold tortillas to close; secure with toothpicks.
2. Place on a baking sheet coated with cooking spray. Bake until golden brown, 13-18 minutes, turning halfway through. Discard toothpicks. Serve with toppings as desired.

Per quesadilla: 300 cal., 10g fat (4g sat. fat), 33mg chol., 475mg sodium, 38g carb. (6g sugars, 3g fiber), 16g pro.
Diabetic Exchanges: 2½ starch, 2 medium-fat meat.

FAST FIX ▸
PARMESAN CHICKEN SANDWICHES

Quickly coat tender chicken breasts with seasoned bread crumbs and smother them in marinara sauce. Served on hoagie rolls, they're really winners!
—Sue Bosek, Whittier, CA

Start to Finish: 25 min.
Makes: 2 servings

- ½ cup all-purpose flour
- 1 large egg, lightly beaten
- ¾ cup seasoned bread crumbs
- 3 tablespoons grated Parmesan cheese
- 2 boneless skinless chicken breast halves (5 ounces each)
- ⅛ teaspoon salt
- ⅛ teaspoon pepper
- 2 tablespoons olive oil
- 2 Italian rolls, split
- 2 slices provolone cheese
- ⅓ cup marinara or other meatless pasta sauce, warmed

1. Place flour and egg in separate shallow bowls. In another bowl, toss bread crumbs with Parmesan cheese.
2. Pound chicken with a meat mallet to ½-in. thickness; sprinkle with salt and pepper. Dip chicken in flour to coat both sides; shake off excess. Dip in egg, then in crumb mixture.
3. In a large skillet, heat oil over medium heat. Add chicken; cook until golden brown and chicken is no longer pink, 4-5 minutes per side. Serve in rolls with provolone cheese and sauce.

Per sandwich: 669 cal., 32g fat (10g sat. fat), 198mg chol., 1124mg sodium, 45g carb. (3g sugars, 3g fiber), 48g pro.
Sourdough Chicken Sandwiches: Prepare chicken as directed. If desired, spread four slices sourdough bread with mayonnaise; top two slices with a lettuce leaf, a slice of Swiss cheese, tomato slice, 1 bacon strip cooked and cut in half, and the chicken breast. Top with remaining sourdough bread.

PARMESAN CHICKEN SANDWICHES

FREEZE IT **FAST FIX** ▶

ASIAN TURKEY SLIDERS

We make weeknights fun with these fast and easy grilled sliders. I like to serve them with tangy slaw on the side.

—Trinity Saffer, Golden, CO

Start to Finish: 25 min.
Makes: 4 servings

- 1 large egg, lightly beaten
- ⅓ cup panko (Japanese) bread crumbs
- ¼ cup teriyaki sauce
- 2 garlic cloves, minced
- 2 teaspoons minced fresh gingerroot
- 1 teaspoon sesame oil
- ½ teaspoon onion powder
- ⅛ teaspoon white pepper
- 1 pound lean ground turkey
- 8 Hawaiian sweet rolls, split and warmed
  Optional toppings: sliced cucumber, shredded carrot and fresh cilantro leaves

1. Combine first eight ingredients. Add turkey; mix lightly but thoroughly. Shape into eight ½-in.-thick patties.
2. Place sliders on an oiled grill rack over medium heat; grill, covered, until a thermometer reads 165°, 3-4 minutes per side. Serve in Hawaiian rolls with toppings as desired.

Freeze option: Cover and freeze patties on a plastic wrap-lined baking sheet until firm. Transfer to a large resealable plastic bag; return to freezer. To use, grill the frozen patties as directed, increasing time as necessary for a thermometer to read 165°.

Per 2 sliders: 433 cal., 16g fat (6g sat. fat), 155mg chol., 868mg sodium, 38g carb. (14g sugars, 2g fiber), 34g pro.

DECONSTRUCTED
WONTON SOUP

DECONSTRUCTED WONTON SOUP

Wonton is one of my favorite types of soup. When I wanted to whip up a homemade version, I decided to take a shortcut and combined pork meatballs with wide egg noodles. If I have them on hand, I'll add sliced water chestnuts, barbecued pork or sesame seeds to switch it up.

—Joanne Neidhamer, Tuolumne, CA

Prep: 20 min.
Cook: 20 min.
Makes: 4 servings

- 6 ounces bulk pork sausage
- ⅓ cup panko (Japanese) bread crumbs
- 1 large egg, lightly beaten
- 2 tablespoons plus ⅓ cup thinly sliced green onions, divided
- 1 carton (32 ounces) reduced-sodium chicken broth
- 1 tablespoon reduced-sodium soy sauce
- 1 bunch baby bok choy, coarsely chopped, or 2 cups fresh spinach
- 2 celery ribs, thinly sliced
- 1 cup uncooked extra-wide egg noodles
- ½ cup coarsely chopped fresh basil

1. Combine sausage, bread crumbs, egg and 2 tablespoons green onion; mix lightly but thoroughly. Shape into ¾-in. balls.
2. In a large saucepan, bring the broth and soy sauce to a boil. Carefully drop meatballs into soup. Stir in the bok choy, celery and noodles; return to a boil. Cook, uncovered, until meatballs are cooked through and noodles are tender, 10-12 minutes. Stir in basil and remaining green onions; remove from heat.

Per cup: 234 cal., 13g fat (4g sat. fat), 83mg chol., 1193mg sodium, 15g carb. (2g sugars, 1g fiber), 14g pro.

INDIAN SPICED CHICKPEA WRAPS

Raita, an Indian condiment made with yogurt, elevates this vegetarian dish into a satisfying gourmet wrap. If you're in the mood to experiment, substitute mango or cucumber for the pineapple and add fresh herbs like cilantro or mint.
—Jennifer Beckman, Falls Church, VA

Start to Finish: 30 min.
Makes: 4 servings

- 1 cup (8 ounces) reduced-fat plain yogurt
- ½ cup unsweetened pineapple tidbits
- ¼ teaspoon salt
- ¼ teaspoon ground cumin

WRAPS
- 2 teaspoons canola oil
- 1 small onion, chopped
- 1 tablespoon minced fresh gingerroot
- 2 garlic cloves, minced
- ½ teaspoon curry powder
- ¼ teaspoon salt
- ¼ teaspoon ground coriander
- ¼ teaspoon ground cumin
- ¼ teaspoon cayenne pepper, optional
- 1 can (15 ounces) chickpeas, rinsed and drained
- 1 cup canned crushed tomatoes
- 3 cups fresh baby spinach
- 4 whole wheat tortillas (8 inches), warmed

1. For pineapple raita, mix the first four ingredients.
2. For wraps, in a large nonstick skillet coated with cooking spray, heat oil over medium-high heat; saute onion until tender. Add ginger, garlic and seasonings; cook and stir until fragrant, about 1 minute. Stir in chickpeas and tomatoes; bring to a boil. Reduce heat; simmer, uncovered, until slightly thickened, for 5-8 minutes, stirring occasionally.
3. To serve, place spinach and chickpea mixture on tortillas. Top with the raita and roll up.

Per wrap: 321 cal., 7g fat (1g sat. fat), 3mg chol., 734mg sodium, 55g carb. (15g sugars, 10g fiber), 13g pro.

HEALTH TIP This wrap has it all: fruit, veggies, whole grains, reduced-fat dairy and protein-packed pulses. Oh, and it tastes amazing, too!

INDIAN SPICED CHICKPEA WRAPS

MEXICAN CHORIZO & CORN SOUP

This filling soup is great when you need to warm up on a blustery day! If you want a chowder consistency, use a potato masher to break down some of the spuds.
—Laura Davis, Chincoteague, VA

Prep: 15 min. • **Cook:** 35 min.
Makes: 10 servings (3½ quarts)

- ¾ pound bulk fresh chorizo or spicy pork sausage
- 1 large onion, chopped
- 1 medium sweet red pepper, chopped
- 1 poblano pepper, seeded and chopped
- 3 garlic cloves, minced
- ⅓ cup all-purpose flour
- 1 teaspoon ground cumin
- ½ teaspoon salt
- ½ teaspoon pepper
- 2 cartons (32 ounces each) reduced-sodium chicken broth
- 1½ pounds potatoes (about 4 medium), peeled and cut into ½-inch cubes
- 3 cups frozen corn (about 16 ounces)
- ½ cup sour cream
- 1 cup crumbled queso fresco or shredded Monterey Jack cheese Chopped fresh cilantro

1. In a Dutch oven, cook and crumble chorizo over medium heat until cooked through, 4-6 minutes. Using a slotted spoon, remove chorizo to paper towels, reserving 2 tablespoons drippings in pan.
2. In drippings, saute onion and red and poblano peppers over medium heat until tender, 8-10 minutes. Add garlic; cook and stir 1 minute. Stir in flour and seasonings until blended; cook and stir 3 minutes. Gradually stir in broth.
3. Add potatoes and corn; bring to a boil. Reduce heat; simmer, uncovered, until potatoes are tender, 10-15 minutes. Stir in sour cream and chorizo; heat through. Serve with cheese and cilantro.

Per 1⅓ cups: 304 cal., 15g fat (6g sat. fat), 41mg chol., 1095mg sodium, 27g carb. (4g sugars, 2g fiber), 16g pro.

**BLUE CHEESE CHICKEN
SALAD SANDWICHES**

BLUE CHEESE CHICKEN
SALAD SANDWICHES

*I'm a big fan of blue cheese dressing, so I
tried it in chicken salad instead of mayo.
So tangy! Serve the chicken mixture on a
bed of lettuce if you're in the mood for
salad instead.*
—Giovanna Kranenberg, Cambridge, MN

Start to Finish: 15 min.
Makes: 6 servings

- ⅔ cup chunky blue cheese salad
  dressing
- 1 celery rib, diced
- ½ cup seeded and diced cucumber
- ⅓ cup diced carrot
- 2 tablespoons finely chopped onion
- 1 garlic clove, minced
- ¼ teaspoon salt
- ¼ teaspoon pepper
- 2 cups shredded rotisserie chicken,
  chilled
- 12 slices sourdough bread
  Crumbled blue cheese, optional

Mix first eight ingredients; stir in chicken.
Spread over half of the bread slices. If

desired, sprinkle with blue cheese. Top
with remaining bread.
Per sandwich: 418 cal., 19g fat (4g sat.
fat), 50mg chol., 747mg sodium, 40g
carb. (5g sugars, 2g fiber), 22g pro.

COCONUT RED CURRY STEW

PICTURED ON P. 43
*This is a fragrant and flavorful dish that's
packed with all sorts of goodness. I like to
enjoy it with sticky rice on the side or a
leafy green salad.*
—Marly Chaland, Maple, ON

Prep: 20 min.
Cook: 50 min.
Makes: 4 servings

- 1 tablespoon canola oil
- 1 medium onion, chopped
- 1 garlic clove, minced
- 3 to 4 tablespoons red curry paste
- ½ teaspoon sugar
- 1 small eggplant, cut into 1-inch pieces
  (about 4 cups)
- 3 cups cubed peeled butternut squash
  (1 inch)
- 1 medium sweet red pepper, cut into
  1-inch pieces
- 1 medium green pepper, cut into
  1-inch pieces
- 1 can (15 ounces) chickpeas or
  garbanzo beans, rinsed and drained
- 1 carton (32 ounces) vegetable broth,
  divided
- 1 can (15 ounces) crushed tomatoes
- 1 can (13.66 ounces) coconut milk
  Chopped fresh cilantro
  Lime wedges and hot cooked rice,
  optional

1. In a 6-qt. stockpot, heat the oil over
medium-high heat; saute onion until lightly
browned, 3-4 minutes. Add garlic; cook
and stir 1 minute. Stir in the curry paste
and sugar.
2. Stir in vegetables, chickpeas, 3 cups
broth, tomatoes and coconut milk; bring
to a boil. Reduce heat; simmer, covered,
until vegetables are tender, 35-40 minutes.
3. Stir in remaining broth; heat through.
Serve with cilantro and, if desired, lime
wedges and rice.
Per 1½ cups: 457 cal., 22g fat (16g sat.
fat), 0 chol., 1364mg sodium, 59g carb.
(20g sugars, 14g fiber), 11g pro.

FETA-DILL CHICKEN BURGERS

I found fresh ground chicken at the butcher and gave it a whirl on our new grill. The result was these saucy burgers. Everybody went nuts—including my sister-in-law, an amazing cook!
—Wendy Boughton, Victoria, BC

Start to Finish: 25 min.
Makes: 4 servings

- 1 large egg, lightly beaten
- 1 large shallot, minced
- 2 tablespoons crushed Ritz crackers
- 2 tablespoons minced fresh dill
- 3 garlic cloves, minced
- ¼ teaspoon salt
- ¼ teaspoon pepper
- 1 pound ground chicken
- ½ cup finely crumbled feta cheese
- 2 tablespoons canola oil
- 4 hamburger buns, split
    Refrigerated tzatziki sauce and sliced tomato, optional

1. Combine first seven ingredients. Add chicken; mix lightly but thoroughly. Gently stir in cheese.
2. Shape into four ½-in. thick patties (mixture will be soft). Brush patties with oil. Grill, covered, over medium heat until a thermometer reads 165°, 5-6 minutes per side. Serve on buns. If desired, top with tzatziki sauce and tomato.
Per burger: 414 cal., 22g fat (5g sat. fat), 129mg chol., 608mg sodium, 27g carb. (4g sugars, 2g fiber), 27g pro.

GRILLED CHEESE & PEPPER SANDWICHES

Here's a yummy and wholesome sandwich that quickly comes together for one or two. It's a nice twist on traditional grilled cheese, a bit filling and especially good with rye bread.
—Arline Hofland, Deer Lodge, MT

Start to Finish: 20 min.
Makes: 2 servings

- 1 tablespoon olive oil
- ½ cup chopped onion
- ½ cup chopped green pepper
- ½ cup chopped sweet red pepper
- 2 teaspoons chopped seeded jalapeno pepper
- 4 slices rye bread with caraway seeds
- ¾ cup shredded Monterey Jack cheese
- 1 tablespoon butter, softened

1. In a skillet, heat oil over medium-high heat; saute onion and peppers until tender. Divide between two bread slices. Top with cheese and remaining bread. Spread the outsides of sandwiches with butter.
2. In a large skillet, toast sandwiches over medium heat until golden brown and cheese is melted, 2-3 minutes per side.
Per sandwich: 470 cal., 28g fat (13g sat. fat), 53mg chol., 690mg sodium, 39g carb. (7g sugars, 6g fiber), 17g pro.

LEMONY CHICKEN SOUP

While living in California, I enjoyed a delicious chicken-lemon soup at a local restaurant. When I returned to Texas, I just knew I had to try re-creating it. I experimented with many versions before landing on this one.
—Brenda Tollett, San Antonio, TX

Start to Finish: 25 min.
Makes: 8 servings (2 quarts)

- ⅓ cup butter, cubed
- ¾ cup all-purpose flour
- 6 cups chicken broth
- 1 cup whole milk
- 1 cup half-and-half cream
- 1½ cups cubed cooked chicken
- 1 tablespoon lemon juice
- ½ teaspoon salt
- ⅛ teaspoon pepper
    Dash ground nutmeg
    Lemon wedges

1. In a large heavy saucepan, melt butter. Stir in flour until smooth; gradually whisk in broth, milk and cream. Bring to a boil; cook and stir until thickened, about 2 minutes.
2. Stir in chicken, lemon juice and seasonings; heat through over medium heat, stirring occasionally. Serve with lemon wedges.
Per cup: 231 cal., 14g fat (8g sat. fat), 66mg chol., 994mg sodium, 12g carb. (3g sugars, 0 fiber), 12g pro.

FETA-DILL CHICKEN BURGERS

PULLED PORK GRILLED CHEESE

3 medium potatoes (about 1⅓ pounds), peeled and quartered
1 cup fresh mushrooms, halved
1 medium onion, cut into eight wedges
2 medium carrots, cut into 1-inch pieces
2 celery ribs, cut into ½-inch pieces
Additional water, optional

1. Preheat oven to 350°. Toss beef with flour and salt to coat lightly; shake off excess. In an ovenproof Dutch oven, heat 2 teaspoons oil over medium heat. Brown beef in batches, adding additional oil as needed. Remove from pan.
2. Add bouillon, herbs, 2 cups water and wine to same pan; bring to a boil, stirring to loosen browned bits from pan. Add beef; return to a boil. Transfer to oven; bake, covered, 1 hour.
3. Stir in vegetables and, if desired, thin with additional water. Bake, covered, until beef and vegetables are tender, 45-60 minutes.
Per 1½ cups: 419 cal., 15g fat (5g sat. fat), 106mg chol., 949mg sodium, 33g carb. (5g sugars, 4g fiber), 37g pro.

FAST FIX ▶
PULLED PORK GRILLED CHEESE

When my family combined two of our favorite things, pulled pork and grilled cheese, I knew we had a keeper. This recipe is super fast and easy when you use store-bought pulled pork.
—Crystal Jo Bruns, Iliff, CO

Start to Finish: 30 min.
Makes: 4 servings

1 carton (16 ounces) refrigerated fully cooked barbecued shredded pork
1 garlic clove, minced
8 slices country white bread
6 ounces sliced Manchego cheese or 8 slices Monterey Jack cheese
1 small red onion, thinly sliced
¼ cup mayonnaise

1. Heat shredded pork according to package directions. Stir in garlic. Layer four slices of bread with cheese, onion, pork mixture and remaining bread. Spread outsides of sandwiches with mayonnaise.

---

2. In a large nonstick skillet, toast the sandwiches in batches over medium-low heat until golden brown and cheese is melted, 2-3 minutes per side.
Per sandwich: 605 cal., 29g fat (13g sat. fat), 74mg chol., 1406mg sodium, 53g carb. (22g sugars, 2g fiber), 29g pro.

SLOW-SIMMERED BURGUNDY BEEF STEW
My mother-in-law shared this recipe with me almost 25 years ago. Ever since then, it's been a go-to whenever I need a lot of food without a lot of fuss.
—Mary Lou Timpson, Colorado City, AZ

Prep: 30 min. • **Bake:** 1¾ hours
Makes: 4 servings

1½ pounds beef stew meat (1¼-inch pieces)
3 tablespoons all-purpose flour
¾ teaspoon salt
2 to 4 teaspoons canola oil, divided
2 teaspoons beef bouillon granules
2 teaspoons dried parsley flakes
1½ teaspoons Italian seasoning
2 cups water
1 cup Burgundy wine or beef stock

FAST FIX ▶
CURRIED EGG SALAD
With curry and ginger, my take on egg salad is a tasty departure from the norm. We eat these open-faced sandwiches often in the summer.
—Joyce McDowell, West Union, OH

Start to Finish: 15 min.
Makes: 6 servings

½ cup mayonnaise
½ teaspoon ground curry
½ teaspoon honey
Dash ground ginger
6 hard-boiled large eggs, coarsely chopped
3 green onions, sliced
6 slices whole wheat bread
Tomato slices and cracked pepper, optional

Mix first four ingredients; stir in the eggs and green onions. Spread on bread. If desired, top with tomato and sprinkle with pepper.
Per open-faced sandwich: 273 cal., 20g fat (4g sat. fat), 188mg chol., 284mg sodium, 14g carb. (2g sugars, 2g fiber), 10g pro.

CREAMY TURKEY NOODLE SOUP

I was honored when my firefighter son-in-law asked to add this recipe to the firehouse's cookbook. You can prepare parts of this turkey soup ahead of time and then assemble when ready. Serve with crunchy-crusted bread.
—Carol Perkins, Washington, MO

Start to Finish: 30 min.
Makes: 8 servings (2 quarts)

⅓ cup butter, cubed
1 medium carrot, shredded
1 celery rib, finely chopped
⅓ cup all-purpose flour
1 carton (32 ounces) chicken broth
½ cup half-and-half cream
½ cup 2% milk
1 cup uncooked kluski or other egg noodles
2 cups cubed cooked turkey
1½ cups shredded cheddar cheese
¼ teaspoon salt
¼ teaspoon pepper

1. In a large saucepan, heat the butter over medium-high heat; saute carrot and celery until tender, 3-5 minutes. Stir in flour until blended; gradually add broth, cream and milk. Bring to a boil, stirring constantly; cook and stir until thickened, 1-2 minutes.
2. Stir in noodles. Reduce heat; simmer, uncovered, until noodles are al dente, 7-10 minutes, stirring occasionally. Add the remaining ingredients; cook and stir until the turkey is heated through and the cheese is melted.

Per cup: 285 cal., 18g fat (11g sat. fat), 92mg chol., 823mg sodium, 11g carb. (2g sugars, 1g fiber), 18g pro.

CREAMY TURKEY NOODLE SOUP

SESAME CHICKEN VEGGIE WRAPS

I'm always on the lookout for fast, nutritious recipes that will appeal to my three little kids. They happen to love edamame, so this is a great choice for those on-the-go days.
—Elisabeth Larsen, Pleasant Grove, UT

Start to Finish: 30 min.
Makes: 8 servings

1 cup frozen shelled edamame
DRESSING
2 tablespoons orange juice
2 tablespoons olive oil
1 teaspoon sesame oil
½ teaspoon ground ginger
¼ teaspoon salt
⅛ teaspoon pepper
WRAPS
2 cups fresh baby spinach
1 cup thinly sliced cucumber
1 cup fresh sugar snap peas, chopped
½ cup shredded carrots
½ cup thinly sliced sweet red pepper
1 cup chopped cooked chicken breast
8 whole wheat tortillas (8 inches), room temperature

1. Cook edamame according to package directions. Drain; rinse with cold water and drain well. Whisk together dressing ingredients.
2. In a large bowl, combine remaining vegetables, chicken and edamame; toss with dressing. Place about ½ cup mixture on each tortilla. Fold bottom and sides of tortilla over filling and roll up.

Per wrap: 214 cal., 7g fat (1g sat. fat), 13mg chol., 229mg sodium, 28g carb. (2g sugars, 5g fiber), 12g pro.
Diabetic Exchanges: 2 starch, 1 lean meat, 1 fat.

HAM, POTATO & PEPPER CHOWDER

PICTURED ON P. 43

I've been serving this chowder for years now. When I need to make it dairy-free for guests, I switch out butter for oil, and coconut milk or soy creamer for heavy cream, and it still turns out great!
—Eileen Stefanski, Wales, WI

Prep: 20 min. • **Cook:** 30 min.
Makes: 6 servings (2 quarts)

- 1½ pounds potatoes (about 2 large), peeled and cut into 1-inch cubes
- 1 carton (32 ounces) chicken broth, divided
- 2 tablespoons butter
- 1 large sweet red pepper, coarsely chopped
- 1 large green pepper, coarsely chopped
- 1 large onion, finely chopped
- 1 large carrot, chopped
- 1½ cups cubed fully cooked ham (about 8 ounces)
- 2 tablespoons chopped seeded jalapeno pepper
- ¼ teaspoon white pepper
- ¼ teaspoon cayenne pepper
- 1 large egg yolk
- ¼ cup heavy whipping cream
  Optional toppings: shredded cheddar cheese, cooked and crumbled bacon, minced fresh chives and sour cream

1. Place potatoes and 2 cups broth in a Dutch oven; bring to a boil. Reduce heat; simmer, covered, until the potatoes are tender, 10-15 minutes. Cool slightly. Transfer to a food processor; cover and process until smooth.
2. In same pan, heat butter over medium heat; saute red and green peppers, onion and carrot until the carrot is tender, 8-10 minutes. Add the ham, jalapeno and seasonings; cook and stir 1 minute.
3. Stir in pureed potatoes and remaining broth; bring just to a boil. In a small bowl, whisk a small amount of hot soup into egg yolk and cream; return all to the pan, whisking constantly. Bring to a gentle boil; cook and stir until thickened, 1-2 minutes. Serve with toppings as desired.
Per 1⅓ cups: 226 cal., 10g fat (6g sat. fat), 76mg chol., 1124mg sodium, 23g carb. (6g sugars, 3g fiber), 11g pro.

SWEET POTATO & CRAB SOUP

SWEET POTATO & CRAB SOUP

This sweet and savory soup is quick and easy to prepare. You can substitute butternut squash or pumpkin for the sweet potatoes, depending on what you have on hand.
—Judy Armstrong, Prairieville, LA

Prep: 15 min. • **Cook:** 35 min.
Makes: 8 servings (2 quarts)

- 4 tablespoons butter, divided
- 2 medium leeks (white portion only), finely chopped
- 3 garlic cloves, minced
- 4 cups cubed peeled sweet potatoes (about 1½ pounds)
- 1 teaspoon salt, divided
- ½ teaspoon ground cinnamon
- ½ teaspoon cayenne pepper
- 5 cups vegetable stock
- 2 cups heavy whipping cream
- 4 teaspoons fresh thyme leaves, divided
- 12 ounces lump crabmeat, drained
  Croutons, optional

1. In a Dutch oven, heat 2 tablespoons butter over medium heat; saute leeks and garlic until leeks are tender, 4-6 minutes.
2. Stir in sweet potatoes, ¾ teaspoon salt, cinnamon, cayenne and stock; bring to a boil. Reduce heat; simmer, covered, until potatoes are tender, 15-20 minutes.
3. Puree the soup using an immersion blender. Or, cool slightly and puree soup in batches in a blender; return to pan. Stir in cream and 2 teaspoons thyme; bring to a boil. Reduce heat; simmer, uncovered, 5 minutes.
4. Meanwhile, in a large skillet, melt the remaining butter over medium heat. Add crab and the remaining salt and thyme; cook 5 minutes, stirring gently to combine. Top servings with crab mixture and, if desired, croutons.
Per cup: 370 cal., 28g fat (18g sat. fat), 124mg chol., 994mg sodium, 20g carb. (5g sugars, 3g fiber), 11g pro.

✳
TEST KITCHEN TIP

Toasted pumpkin seeds or pepitas make a great change-of-pace topping for the Sweet Potato & Crab Soup.

FAST FIX ▶
THAI CHICKEN WRAPS

Thanks to quick-cooking chicken, convenient broccoli slaw mix and an easy peanut sauce, you can wrap up this dinner idea in 25 minutes.
—Trudy Williams, Shannonville, ON

Start to Finish: 25 min.
Makes: 6 servings

- ¼ cup sugar
- ¼ cup creamy peanut butter
- 3 tablespoons soy sauce
- 2 to 3 tablespoons water
- 2 garlic cloves, minced
- ¾ pound boneless skinless chicken breasts, cut into thin strips
- ½ teaspoon garlic salt
- ¼ teaspoon pepper
- 2 tablespoons canola oil, divided
- 4 cups broccoli coleslaw mix
- 1 medium red onion, halved and thinly sliced
- 1 teaspoon minced fresh gingerroot
- 6 flour tortillas (8 inches), warmed

1. Whisk the first five ingredients until blended. Toss chicken with garlic salt and pepper.
2. In a large nonstick skillet, heat 1 tablespoon oil over medium-high heat; stir-fry the chicken until no longer pink, 3-4 minutes. Remove from the pan; keep warm.
3. In same pan, heat remaining oil over medium-high heat; stir-fry coleslaw mix, onion and ginger until broccoli is crisp-tender, 2-3 minutes. Stir in peanut butter mixture. Serve chicken and vegetable mixture in tortillas.

Per wrap: 389 cal., 15g fat (3g sat. fat), 31mg chol., 935mg sodium, 44g carb. (12g sugars, 4g fiber), 21g pro.

FREEZE IT
SPICED APPLE CHILI

Nothing says fall like chili and apples. I use smoked paprika to give my slightly sweet chili a smoky kick.
—Joyce Moynihan, Lakeville, MN

Prep: 15 min. • **Cook:** 1 hour
Makes: 6 servings (2 quarts)

- 1 pound ground beef
- 1 large onion, chopped
- 1 can (6 ounces) tomato paste
- 3 teaspoons chili powder
- 3 teaspoons smoked paprika
- 2 teaspoons ground cumin
- 1 teaspoon ground cinnamon
- 2 garlic cloves, minced
- 2 tablespoons cider vinegar
- 3 cups beef broth
- 2 large Granny Smith apples, peeled and chopped
- 1 can (15 ounces) chili beans, undrained
- ½ teaspoon salt
- ¼ teaspoon pepper
- Optional toppings: shredded white cheddar cheese and diced red onion

1. In a Dutch oven, cook and crumble beef with onion over medium-high heat until no longer pink, 5-7 minutes; drain.
2. Add tomato paste, spices and garlic; cook and stir over medium heat 5 minutes. Stir in vinegar and broth until blended. Add remaining ingredients; bring to a boil. Simmer, covered, until apples are tender and flavors are blended, about 45 minutes, stirring occasionally. Serve with toppings as desired.

Freeze option: Freeze cooled chili in freezer containers. To use, partially thaw in refrigerator overnight. Heat through in a saucepan, stirring occasionally.

Per 1⅓ cups: 284 cal., 10g fat (4g sat. fat), 47mg chol., 945mg sodium, 31g carb. (11g sugars, 7g fiber), 21g pro.

THAI CHICKEN WRAPS

**SPINACH & SAUSAGE
LENTIL SOUP**

SPINACH & SAUSAGE LENTIL SOUP

During cooler months of the year, this soup makes regular appearances on our dinner table. It is approved by all, including my very picky 6-year-old.
—Kalyn Gensic, Ardmore, OK

Prep: 5 min. • **Cook:** 45 min.
Makes: 6 servings (2 quarts)

1 pound bulk spicy pork sausage
1 cup dried brown lentils, rinsed
1 can (15 ounces) cannellini or white kidney beans, rinsed and drained
1 carton (32 ounces) reduced-sodium chicken broth
1 cup water
1 can (14½ ounces) fire-roasted diced tomatoes, undrained
6 cups fresh spinach (about 4 ounces)
   Crumbled goat cheese, optional

1. In a Dutch oven, cook and crumble sausage over medium heat until no longer pink, 5-7 minutes; drain.
2. Stir in lentils, beans, broth and water; bring to a boil. Reduce heat; simmer, covered, until lentils are tender, about 30 minutes. Stir in tomatoes; heat through.
3. Remove from heat; stir in spinach until wilted. If desired, serve with goat cheese.
Freeze option: Freeze cooled soup in freezer containers. To use, partially thaw in refrigerator overnight. Heat through in a saucepan, stirring occasionally.
Per 1⅓ cups: 390 cal., 17g fat (5g sat. fat), 41mg chol., 1242mg sodium, 37g carb. (3g sugars, 8g fiber), 22g pro.

★ ★ ★ ★ ★ **READER REVIEW**

"This recipe was easy and tasty. We used regular sausage instead of spicy, because we were feeding our 2-year-old, and it still had plenty of flavor. I will make this again."

DELICIOUSLYRESOURCEFUL_GINA
TASTEOFHOME.COM

SOUTHERN FRIED BLT

SOUTHERN FRIED BLT

I'm really not big on tomatoes—but I do like them green and fried, so I decided to try them in a sandwich. It was a smash! If you must have cheese, add a slice of sharp cheddar to this indulgent twist on the traditional BLT.
—Stacy King, Rome, GA

Start to Finish: 30 min.
Makes: 4 servings

½ cup cornmeal
3 tablespoons all-purpose flour
   Dash pepper
2 medium green tomatoes, sliced ¼ in. thick
   Oil for frying
8 slices whole wheat bread, toasted
½ cup mayonnaise
12 cooked bacon strips
   Iceberg lettuce leaves

1. In a shallow bowl, mix the cornmeal, flour and pepper. Dip tomato slices in cornmeal mixture to coat both sides; shake off excess.
2. In a large skillet, heat ¼ in. of oil until hot. In batches, fry tomato slices until browned, 2-3 minutes per side. Drain on paper towels.
3. To serve, spread each slice of toast with mayonnaise. Layer half of the slices with bacon, fried tomatoes and lettuce; top with remaining slices.
Per sandwich: 634 cal., 45g fat (8g sat. fat), 36mg chol., 985mg sodium, 37g carb. (5g sugars, 4g fiber), 20g pro.

SOUPS & SANDWICHES

BRATWURST SOUP

I came up with this recipe one day when I had some leftover bratwurst. It's been a favorite of my husband's ever since and is requested whenever the guys are hanging out at our house.
—Anna Miller, Churdan, IA

Prep: 10 min. • **Cook:** 25 min.
Makes: 8 servings (2 quarts)

- 1 pound uncooked bratwurst links, casings removed
- ½ cup chopped onion
- 1 medium carrot, chopped
- 2 cans (15½ ounces each) navy beans, rinsed and drained
- ¼ cup pickled jalapeno slices, chopped
- ½ teaspoon pepper
- 2 cups reduced-sodium chicken broth
- ¼ cup all-purpose flour
- 1½ cups 2% milk, divided
- 12 slices process American cheese

1. In a Dutch oven, crumble bratwurst and cook with the onion and carrot over medium heat until no longer pink, 5-7 minutes; drain.
2. Stir in beans, jalapeno, pepper and broth; bring to a boil. Whisk together flour and ½ cup milk until smooth; stir into soup. Bring to a boil, stirring constantly; cook and stir until thickened, about 5 minutes. Gradually stir in remaining milk. Add cheese; cook and stir over low heat until melted.
Per cup: 468 cal., 25g fat (11g sat. fat), 53mg chol., 1322mg sodium, 33g carb. (5g sugars, 6g fiber), 25g pro.

SPICY PEANUT CHICKEN CHILI

FREEZE IT FAST FIX
SPICY PEANUT CHICKEN CHILI

After spending time in the Southwest, I discovered Mexican peanut chicken and thought it would be fun to make it into a chili. Chipotle peppers give it a nice spice that's extra warming on a very cold day.
—Crystal Schlueter, Babbitt, MN

Start to Finish: 30 min.
Makes: 6 servings

- 1 can (15 ounces) pinto beans, rinsed and drained
- 1 can (14½ ounces) Mexican diced tomatoes, undrained
- 1 can (14½ ounces) no-salt-added diced tomatoes, undrained
- 1 can (14½ ounces) reduced-sodium chicken broth
- 1 package (12 ounces) frozen Southwestern corn
- 3 tablespoons creamy peanut butter
- 1 to 2 tablespoons minced chipotle peppers in adobo sauce
- 2 teaspoons chili powder
- ½ teaspoon ground cinnamon
- 3 cups coarsely shredded rotisserie chicken
- 6 tablespoons reduced-fat sour cream
  Minced fresh cilantro, optional

1. Place first nine ingredients in a 6-qt. stockpot; bring to a boil. Reduce heat; simmer, covered, until flavors are blended, about 15 minutes.
2. Stir in chicken; heat through. Serve with sour cream and, if desired, cilantro.
Freeze option: Freeze cooled chili in freezer containers. To use, partially thaw in refrigerator overnight. Heat through in a saucepan, stirring occasionally and adding a little broth if necessary.
Per 1⅓ cups soup with 1 tablespoon sour cream: 368 cal., 13g fat (3g sat. fat), 67mg chol., 797mg sodium, 33g carb. (11g sugars, 6g fiber), 30g pro.

TURKEY DIJON MELTS

I like making these cheesy melts when I'm craving comfort food, but don't have the time or energy for a big meal. It works well with deli or leftover turkey.
—Sarah Marshall, Creedmoor, NC

Start to Finish: 25 min.
Makes: 2 servings

- 4 slices whole wheat bread
- 4 teaspoons mayonnaise
- ¼ pound thinly sliced cooked turkey
- 2 slices Monterey Jack cheese
- ¼ cup thinly sliced onion
   Dash salt and pepper
- 1 tablespoon honey Dijon salad dressing
- 1 tablespoon butter, softened

1. Spread two slices of bread with mayonnaise. Layer with turkey, cheese and onion; sprinkle with salt and pepper. Spread remaining slices of bread with the salad dressing; place over onion. Spread outsides of sandwiches with butter.

2. In a large skillet, toast sandwiches over medium heat until golden brown and cheese is melted, 4-5 minutes per side.
Per sandwich: 265 cal., 15g fat (7g sat. fat), 56mg chol., 400mg sodium, 14g carb. (3g sugars, 2g fiber), 17g pro.

SLOPPY CHEESESTEAKS

Sloppy joes are a great go-to dish for busy families, but my spin adds some melty provolone, green pepper and onions. What a fun, unexpected twist on a classic!
—Mandy Rivers, Lexington, SC

Start to Finish: 20 min.
Makes: 6 servings

- 1 pound ground beef
- 1 medium green pepper, chopped
- 1 medium onion, chopped
- 1 teaspoon garlic powder
- ½ teaspoon salt
- ½ teaspoon pepper
- 6 French rolls
- 6 slices provolone cheese
   Mayonnaise, optional

1. Preheat broiler. In a large skillet, cook and crumble beef with pepper and onion over medium-high heat until no longer pink, 5-7 minutes; drain. Stir in seasonings.

2. Cut rolls horizontally in half. Place bottoms on a baking sheet; broil 3-4 in. from heat until toasted, about 30 seconds. Top with beef mixture, then with cheese. Broil until the cheese is melted, 45-60 seconds.

3. Place roll tops on a baking sheet; broil 3-4 in. from heat until toasted, about 30 seconds. If desired, spread with mayonnaise. Close sandwiches.

Freeze option: Freeze cooled beef mixture in freezer containers. To use, partially thaw in refrigerator overnight. Microwave, covered, on high in a microwave-safe dish until heated through, stirring occasionally.
Per sandwich: 417 cal., 19g fat (9g sat. fat), 66mg chol., 798mg sodium, 34g carb. (2g sugars, 2g fiber), 27g pro.

SLOPPY CHEESESTEAKS

FAST FIX ▶

HOT ANTIPASTO SUBS

Hot or cold, these loaded sandwiches are always a family hit. They blend all the robust flavors of antipasto into an easy-to-eat bun.
—Sharlene Landers, Lake Placid, FL

Start to Finish: 30 min.
Makes: 4 servings

- ¼ cup horseradish mustard
- 3 tablespoons mayonnaise
- ½ teaspoon dried oregano
- 4 hoagie buns, split
- 1 cup fresh arugula or baby spinach
- 4 slices provolone cheese
- ¼ pound thinly sliced deli ham
- ¼ pound thinly sliced hard salami
- 1 jar (7½ ounces) marinated quartered artichoke hearts, drained
- ¼ cup roasted sweet red pepper strips
- ¼ cup sliced ripe olives

1. Preheat oven to 400°. Mix mustard, mayonnaise and oregano; spread on buns.
2. Layer remaining ingredients on bun bottoms; close sandwiches and wrap in foil. Bake on a baking sheet until heated through, 12-15 minutes.

Per sandwich: 623 cal., 39g fat (11g sat. fat), 57mg chol., 1861mg sodium, 43g carb. (10g sugars, 2g fiber), 26g pro.

HEALTH TIP This deli-quality sub tastes amazing, but it's a bit high in sodium. Condiments, deli meat, cheese and bread are all typically high in salt. Cut back by replacing some of the canned veggies with fresh, half of the deli meat with leftover cooked chicken or turkey and drizzling with olive oil and vinegar instead of spreading with mayonnaise and mustard.

QUICK CREAM OF MUSHROOM SOUP

FAST FIX ▶

QUICK CREAM OF MUSHROOM SOUP

My daughter-in-law, a gourmet cook, served this soup as the first course for Thanksgiving dinner. She'd gotten the recipe from her mom and graciously shared it with me. Now I'm happy to share it with my own friends and family.
—Anne Kulick, Phillipsburg, NJ

Start to Finish: 30 min.
Makes: 6 servings

- 2 tablespoons butter
- ½ pound sliced fresh mushrooms
- ¼ cup chopped onion
- 6 tablespoons all-purpose flour
- ½ teaspoon salt
- ⅛ teaspoon pepper
- 2 cans (14½ ounces each) chicken broth
- 1 cup half-and-half cream

1. In a large saucepan, heat butter over medium-high heat; saute mushrooms and onion until tender.
2. Mix flour, salt, pepper and one can broth until smooth; stir into mushroom mixture. Stir in remaining broth. Bring to a boil; cook and stir until thickened, about 2 minutes. Reduce heat; stir in cream. Simmer, uncovered, until flavors are blended, about 15 minutes, stirring occasionally.

Per cup: 136 cal., 8g fat (5g sat. fat), 33mg chol., 842mg sodium, 10g carb. (3g sugars, 1g fiber), 4g pro.

ASIAN LONG NOODLE SOUP

This flavorful soup is perfect when you want something warm and filling in a flash. If you can't find long noodles, angel hair pasta is a good substitute.
—Carol Emerson, Aransas Pass, TX

Start to Finish: 30 min.
Makes: 6 servings (2 quarts)

- 6 ounces uncooked Asian lo mein noodles
- 1 pork tenderloin (¾ pound), cut into thin strips
- 2 tablespoons soy sauce, divided
- ⅛ teaspoon pepper
- 2 tablespoons canola oil, divided
- 1½ teaspoons minced fresh gingerroot
- 1 garlic clove, minced
- 1 carton (32 ounces) chicken broth
- 1 celery rib, thinly sliced
- 1 cup fresh snow peas, halved diagonally
- 1 cup coleslaw mix
- 2 green onions, sliced diagonally
  Fresh cilantro leaves, optional

1. Cook noodles according to package directions. Drain and rinse with cold water; drain well.

2. Meanwhile, toss the pork with 1 tablespoon soy sauce and pepper. In a 6-qt. stockpot, heat 1 tablespoon oil over medium-high heat; saute pork until lightly browned, 2-3 minutes. Remove from pot.

3. In same pot, heat remaining oil over medium-high heat; saute ginger and garlic until fragrant, 20-30 seconds. Stir in broth and remaining soy sauce; bring to a boil. Add celery and snow peas; return to a boil. Simmer; uncovered, until crisp-tender, 2-3 minutes. Stir in pork and coleslaw mix; cook just until cabbage begins to wilt. Add noodles; remove from heat. Top with green onions and, if desired, cilantro.

Per 1⅓ cups: 227 cal., 7g fat (1g sat. fat), 35mg chol., 1078mg sodium, 23g carb. (2g sugars, 1g fiber), 16g pro.

ASIAN LONG NOODLE SOUP

FAVORITE WILD RICE SOUP

I'm crazy about homemade soup during the fall and winter months. This wild rice soup is one of my all-time-best cool-weather experiments.
—Deborah Williams, Peoria, AZ

Prep: 10 min. • **Cook:** 50 min.
Makes: 6 servings

- 2 cups water
- ⅓ cup uncooked wild rice
- ¾ teaspoon salt, divided
- ¼ cup butter, cubed
- 1 medium onion, finely chopped
- 2 celery ribs, finely chopped
- ¼ cup all-purpose flour
- ¼ teaspoon freshly ground pepper
- 5 cups 2% milk
- 1 teaspoon chicken bouillon granules

1. In a small saucepan, bring water to a boil. Stir in wild rice and ¼ teaspoon salt. Reduce heat; simmer, covered, until kernels are puffed open, 40-45 minutes.

2. In a large heavy saucepan, heat butter over medium heat; saute onion and celery until tender, 5-7 minutes. Stir in flour, pepper and remaining salt until blended; gradually stir in milk and bouillon. Bring to a boil, stirring constantly; cook and stir until thickened, 2-3 minutes.

3. Drain the rice; add to soup. Cook, uncovered, over medium heat 5 minutes, stirring occasionally.

Per cup: 231 cal., 12g fat (7g sat. fat), 37mg chol., 604mg sodium, 23g carb. (11g sugars, 1g fiber), 9g pro.

✳

TEST KITCHEN TIP

Unlike long grain rice, wild rice doesn't always absorb all of the water; you may need to drain excess cooking liquid before adding it to the soup. If you only have bouillon cubes, add one cube to equal one teaspoon of granules. You can also stir in leftover chicken, ham or turkey to make this a meal.

CHEESY CHICKEN WAFFLEWICHES

⑤INGREDIENTS

CHEESY CHICKEN WAFFLEWICHES

I've had lots of fun experimenting with my new waffle maker. I once decided to use shredded meat, cheese and veggies for a savory twist. Make sure the griddle is hot before adding the sandwiches.
—Marietta Slater, Justin, TX

Prep: 25 min. • **Cook:** 5 min./batch
Makes: 8 servings

- 1 tablespoon olive oil
- ½ cup chopped onion
- ½ cup chopped fresh mushrooms
- 1 cup shredded rotisserie chicken
- 1 cup shredded Swiss cheese
- 1 package (17.3 ounces) frozen puff pastry, thawed

1. In a large skillet, heat oil over medium heat; saute the onion until softened, 3-4 minutes. Reduce heat to medium-low; cook until caramelized, 6-8 minutes, stirring occasionally. Add mushrooms; cook and stir until tender, 2-3 minutes.

Cool slightly. Stir in chicken and cheese.
2. Preheat a four-square waffle maker. Unfold one puff pastry sheet onto a lightly floured surface; cut into four squares. Top each square with ¼ cup filling; bring up corners over filling and pinch firmly to seal. Refrigerate until ready to cook. Repeat with remaining pastry and filling.
3. In batches, place one pastry bundle in each section of the waffle maker. Bake until golden brown and crisp, 5-7 minutes.
Per sandwich: 405 cal., 24g fat (7g sat. fat), 28mg chol., 243mg sodium, 36g carb. (1g sugars, 5g fiber), 13g pro.

EAT SMART ⑤INGREDIENTS
PEA SOUP WITH QUINOA
This soup is low in fat, high in fiber, has a fantastically fresh flavor and a wonderful texture. Plus, it's so simple to make!
—Jane Hacker, Milwaukee, WI

Prep: 10 min. • **Cook:** 25 min.
Makes: 6 servings

- 1 cup water
- ½ cup quinoa, rinsed
- 2 teaspoons canola oil
- 1 medium onion, chopped

- 2½ cups frozen peas (about 10 ounces)
- 2 cans (14½ ounces each) reduced-sodium chicken broth or vegetable broth
- ½ teaspoon salt
- ¼ teaspoon pepper
  Optional toppings: plain yogurt, croutons, shaved Parmesan cheese and cracked pepper

1. In a small saucepan, bring water to a boil. Add quinoa. Reduce heat; simmer, covered, until the water is absorbed, 12-15 minutes.
2. Meanwhile, in a large saucepan, heat oil over medium-high heat; saute onion until tender. Stir in peas and broth; bring to a boil. Reduce heat; simmer, uncovered, until peas are tender, about 5 minutes.
3. Puree soup using an immersion blender. Or, cool slightly and puree soup in a blender; return to pan. Stir in quinoa, salt and pepper; heat through. Serve with toppings as desired.
Per cup: 126 cal., 3g fat (0 sat. fat), 0 chol., 504mg sodium, 19g carb. (4g sugars, 4g fiber), 7g pro.
Diabetic Exchanges: 1 starch, ½ fat.

BROCCOLI-CHEDDAR BEEF ROLLS

My grandma's recipe for beef rolls is easy to change up. Load them with ham, veggies, even olives. While they bake, I whip up au jus for dipping.
—Kent Call, Riverside, UT

....

Start to Finish: 30 min.
Makes: 6 servings

- ½ pound lean ground beef (90% lean)
- 2 cups chopped fresh broccoli
- 1 small onion, chopped
- ½ teaspoon salt
- ¼ teaspoon pepper
- 6 hard rolls
- 2 cups shredded cheddar cheese, divided

1. Preheat to 325°. In a large skillet, cook and crumble beef with broccoli and onion over medium heat until no longer pink, 4-6 minutes. Stir in salt and pepper.
2. Cut one-third off the top of each roll; discard or save for another use. Hollow out bottoms, leaving ½-in.-thick shells; place on a baking sheet.
3. Tear bread removed from centers into ½-in. pieces and place in a bowl. Stir in 1½ cups cheese and beef mixture. Spoon into bread shells. Sprinkle with remaining cheese. Bake until heated through and cheese is melted, 10-15 minutes.
Per serving: 394 cal., 18g fat (9g sat. fat), 61mg chol., 783mg sodium, 34g carb. (2g sugars, 2g fiber), 23g pro.

HAM CHEDDAR CHOWDER

Living in Wisconsin, I can't get enough cheese in my life, and this rich chowder is one of my favorite ways. It makes a great meal served with salad greens and rye rolls.
—Ruth Protz, Oshkosh, WI

....

Start to Finish: 30 min.
Makes: 8 servings (about 2 quarts)

- 3 cups cubed peeled potatoes (1 inch)
- 2 medium carrots, chopped
- 2 teaspoons salt
- 3 cups water
- 6 tablespoons butter
- 1 medium onion, chopped
- 2 celery ribs, chopped
- 6 tablespoons all-purpose flour
- ½ teaspoon pepper
- 4 cups whole milk
- 3 cups shredded cheddar cheese
- 1 cup cubed fully cooked ham (about 8 ounces)

1. Place first four ingredients in a large saucepan; bring to a boil. Reduce heat; cook, uncovered, until vegetables are tender, 10-15 minutes. Drain.
2. Meanwhile, in a Dutch oven, heat butter over medium heat; saute onion and celery until tender. Stir in flour and pepper until blended; gradually stir in milk. Bring to a boil, stirring occasionally; cook and stir until thickened, about 2 minutes. Remove from heat; stir in cheese until melted.
3. Stir in ham and potato mixture; heat through over low heat.
Per cup: 429 cal., 28g fat (16g sat. fat), 87mg chol., 690mg sodium, 27g carb. (8g sugars, 2g fiber), 19g pro.
HEALTH TIP This swap saves calories and fat in a lot of different recipes: Reduce the amount of cheese and switch to a more flavorful variety, like sharp cheddar in this case.

BROCCOLI-CHEDDAR BEEF ROLLS

30-Minute Dinners

Treat the family to fish tacos, Buffalo chicken or Indian curry without a trip to the restaurant. Savor old-time favorites such as Salisbury steak and chicken & dumplings, too. Best of all: Each amazing dinner in this chapter is table-ready in 30 minutes or less!

Sausage Cobb Salad Lettuce Wraps (p. 102) **Garlic Chicken with Herbs** (p. 80)
Sausage & Pasta Alfredo (p. 71) **Cheddar Bean Burritos** (p. 78) **Stuffed Peppers for Four** (p. 70)

ZUCCHINI BEEF SKILLET

FAST FIX ▶

ZUCCHINI BEEF SKILLET

Here's a go-to dish to use up your garden goodies: zucchini, tomatoes and peppers.
—Becky Calder, Kingston, MO

Start to Finish: 30 min.
Makes: 4 servings

- 1 pound ground beef
- 1 medium onion, chopped
- 1 small green pepper, chopped
- 2 teaspoons chili powder
- ¾ teaspoon salt
- ¼ teaspoon pepper
- 3 medium zucchini, cut into ¾-inch cubes
- 2 large tomatoes, chopped
- ¼ cup water
- 1 cup uncooked instant rice
- 1 cup shredded cheddar cheese

1. In a large skillet, cook and crumble the ground beef with onion and pepper over medium-high heat until no longer pink, 5-7 minutes; drain.

2. Stir in seasonings, vegetables, water and rice; bring to a boil. Reduce heat; simmer, covered, until rice is tender, 10-15 minutes. Sprinkle with cheese. Remove from heat; let stand until cheese is melted.
Per 2 cups: 470 cal., 24g fat (11g sat. fat), 98mg chol., 749mg sodium, 33g carb. (8g sugars, 4g fiber), 32g pro.

FAST FIX ▶

STUFFED PEPPERS FOR FOUR
PICTURED ON P. 69

Truly a meal in one, this quick supper has it all: veggies, meat, pasta and sauce, packed into tender peppers. It'll look so pretty on your table.
—*Taste of Home* Test Kitchen

Start to Finish: 30 min.
Makes: 4 servings

- ½ cup uncooked orzo pasta
- 4 medium sweet peppers (any color)
- ¼ cup water
- 1 pound ground beef
- ½ cup chopped onion
- 2 cups pasta sauce
- 1 cup frozen broccoli-cauliflower blend, thawed and chopped
- ½ cup grated Parmesan cheese, divided

1. Cook the orzo according to package directions; drain. Cut and discard tops from peppers; remove seeds. Place in a 3-qt. round microwave-safe dish. Add water; microwave, covered, on high until peppers are crisp-tender, 7-9 minutes.
2. In a large skillet, cook and crumble beef with onion over medium heat until no longer pink, 5-7 minutes; drain. Stir in pasta sauce, vegetables, ¼ cup cheese and orzo. Spoon into peppers. Sprinkle with remaining cheese.
3. Microwave, uncovered, on high until heated through, 1-2 minutes.
Note: This recipe was tested in a 1,100-watt microwave.
Per stuffed pepper: 448 cal., 18g fat (7g sat. fat), 79mg chol., 734mg sodium, 41g carb. (15g sugars, 6g fiber), 30g pro.

TILAPIA WITH JASMINE RICE

This tender, full-flavored tilapia with fragrant jasmine rice is absolutely to die for. And it gets better—each serving has only 5 grams of fat!
—Shirl Parsons, Cape Carteret, NC

Start to Finish: 25 min.
Makes: 2 servings

- ¾ cup water
- ½ cup uncooked jasmine rice
- 1½ teaspoons butter
- ¼ teaspoon ground cumin
- ¼ teaspoon seafood seasoning
- ¼ teaspoon pepper
- ⅛ teaspoon salt
- 2 tilapia fillets (6 ounces each)
- ¼ cup fat-free Italian salad dressing

1. In a small saucepan, combine water, rice and butter; bring to a boil. Reduce heat; simmer, covered, until the liquid is absorbed and the rice is tender, about 15-20 minutes.

2. Meanwhile, mix seasonings; sprinkle over tilapia. In a large skillet, heat salad dressing over medium heat until hot. Add fillets; cook until fish just begins to flake easily with a fork, 3-4 minutes per side. Serve with rice.

Per fillet with ¾ cup rice: 356 cal., 5g fat (3g sat. fat), 91mg chol., 743mg sodium, 41g carb. (2g sugars, 1g fiber), 35g pro.
Diabetic Exchanges: 4 lean meat, 3 starch, ½ fat.

TILAPIA WITH JASMINE RICE

SAUSAGE & PASTA ALFREDO
PICTURED ON P. 69

This skillet meal was born out of sheer necessity on a busy weeknight. I pulled together a package of turkey sausage links, some lasagna noodles, and a bag of frozen peas and went to work.
—Amy Freeze, Avon Park, FL

Start to Finish: 30 min.
Makes: 6 servings

- 8 ounces uncooked lasagna noodles (about 10 noodles), broken into 2-in. pieces
- 1 tablespoon olive oil
- 4 Italian turkey sausage links (about 1 pound), casings removed
- 1 small onion, chopped
- 1 garlic clove, minced
- 1 cup frozen peas
- ¼ teaspoon pepper
- 2 cups half-and-half cream
- ½ cup grated Parmesan cheese
  Additional grated Parmesan cheese, optional

1. Cook broken noodles according to package directions for al dente. Drain; rinse with water and drain again. Toss with oil to coat.

2. In a large skillet, cook sausage with onion over medium-high until no longer pink, 5-7 minutes, breaking up sausage into ¾-in. pieces. Add garlic; cook and stir 1 minute.

3. Stir in peas, pepper and cream; bring to a boil. Reduce heat; simmer, uncovered, until slightly thickened, 8-10 minutes. Stir in ½ cup cheese. Stir in noodles.

4. Serve immediately. If desired, serve with additional cheese.

Per cup: 386 cal., 17g fat (8g sat. fat), 73mg chol., 486mg sodium, 36g carb. (6g sugars, 2g fiber), 19g pro.

ASPARAGUS BEEF LO MEIN

SMOTHERED CHICKEN BREASTS

After trying this chicken in a restaurant, I decided to re-create it at home. Topped with bacon, caramelized onions and shredded cheese, it comes together in no time with what I keep on hand.
—Brenda Carpenter, Warrensburg, MO

Start to Finish: 30 min.
Makes: 4 servings

- 4 boneless skinless chicken breast halves (6 ounces each)
- ¼ teaspoon salt
- ¼ teaspoon lemon-pepper seasoning
- 1 tablespoon canola oil
- 8 bacon strips
- 1 medium onion, sliced
- ¼ cup packed brown sugar
- ½ cup shredded Colby-Monterey Jack cheese

1. Sprinkle chicken with salt and lemon pepper. In a large skillet, heat oil over medium heat; cook chicken until a thermometer reads 165°, 6-8 minutes per side. Remove from pan; keep warm.
2. In same skillet, cook bacon over medium heat until crisp. Remove the bacon to paper towels; pour off all but 2 tablespoons drippings.
3. In drippings, saute onion with brown sugar over medium heat until tender and golden brown. Top chicken with bacon, onion mixture and cheese.
Per serving: 560 cal., 34g fat (12g sat. fat), 143mg chol., 710mg sodium, 17g carb. (15g sugars, 0 fiber), 45g pro.

ASPARAGUS BEEF LO MEIN

This springtime beef stir-fry is as easy as it gets. Ramen noodles make it extra fun.
—Dottie Wanat, Modesto, CA

Start to Finish: 20 min.
Makes: 4 servings

- 1 beef top sirloin steak (1 pound), cut into thin strips
- 2 packages (3 ounces each) beef ramen noodles
- ⅔ cup hoisin sauce
- 2¼ cups water, divided
- 2 tablespoons olive oil, divided
- 1 pound fresh asparagus, trimmed and cut into 2½-inch pieces
- 1 small garlic clove, minced

1. Toss beef with ½ teaspoon seasoning from a ramen seasoning packet (discard remaining opened packet). In a small bowl, mix hoisin sauce and ¼ cup water.
2. In a saucepan, bring the remaining water to a boil. Add noodles and contents of the unopened seasoning packet; cook, uncovered, 3 minutes. Remove from the heat; let stand, covered, until the noodles are tender.
3. Meanwhile, in a large skillet, heat 1 tablespoon oil over medium-high heat; stir-fry beef until browned, 3-4 minutes. Remove from pan.
4. In same pan, heat remaining oil over medium-high heat; stir-fry asparagus with garlic until crisp-tender, 1-3 minutes. Stir in the hoisin sauce mixture; bring to a boil. Cook until slightly thickened. Stir in beef; heat through. Serve over noodles.
Per serving: 511 cal., 21g fat (7g sat. fat), 47mg chol., 1367mg sodium, 48g carb. (13g sugars, 3g fiber), 31g pro.

EASY BUFFALO CHICKEN LETTUCE WRAPS

One time when I made sloppy joes, I wanted mine spicy, so I doused the sandwich in hot sauce. After that, my mind went wild and I made my joes Buffalo-chicken style with ground chicken, diced celery and blue cheese crumbles. I've been making it this way and serving in lettuce wraps ever since.
—Jennifer Nielson, Spanish Fork, UT

Start to Finish: 25 min.
Makes: 6 servings

- 1½ pounds lean ground chicken
- 1 celery rib, diced
- ¼ teaspoon pepper
- ⅓ cup ketchup
- ¼ cup Louisiana-style hot sauce
- 3 tablespoons brown sugar
- 1 tablespoon cider vinegar
- 2 teaspoons yellow mustard
- 12 Bibb or Boston lettuce leaves
  Crumbled blue cheese, optional

1. In a large skillet, cook and crumble chicken over medium-high heat 3 minutes. Stir in celery and pepper; cook and stir until chicken is no longer pink and celery is crisp-tender, 2-3 minutes.
2. Stir in ketchup, hot sauce, brown sugar, vinegar and mustard; bring to a boil. Reduce heat; simmer, covered, until flavors are blended, about 5 minutes, stirring occasionally. Serve in lettuce leaves. If desired, top with cheese.
Freeze option: Freeze cooled chicken mixture in freezer containers. To use, partially thaw in refrigerator overnight. Heat through in a saucepan, stirring occasionally and adding a little broth or water if necessary.

Per 2 lettuce wraps: 198 cal., 6g fat (2g sat. fat), 81mg chol., 612mg sodium, 11g carb. (11g sugars, 1g fiber), 24g pro.
Diabetic Exchanges: 3 lean meat, 1 starch.

✳

TEST KITCHEN TIPS
Louisiana hot sauce is less spicy than other types. If you use a different kind, start with less. You can always add more.

This recipe doubles easily for a crowd. After making it, keep it warm on the buffet table in a slow cooker.

EASY BUFFALO CHICKEN LETTUCE WRAPS

TROPICAL SQUASH AND BLACK BEAN BURRITOS

(5) INGREDIENTS FAST FIX

BACON & CHEDDAR CHICKEN

Cheese and bacon don't usually come light. But this tasty recipe keeps the fat and calories low and flavor high. This family-friendly recipe can easily be doubled to serve a larger group.
—Trisha Kruse, Eagle, ID

Start to Finish: 30 min.
Makes: 4 servings

- 4 bacon strips, chopped
- 4 boneless skinless chicken breast halves (6 ounces each)
- ¼ teaspoon salt
- ¼ teaspoon pepper
- ⅔ cup barbecue sauce, divided
- ½ cup shredded cheddar cheese
  Thinly sliced green onions

1. Preheat oven to 350°. In an ovenproof skillet, cook bacon over medium heat until crisp, stirring occasionally. Using a slotted spoon, remove bacon to paper towels; reserve drippings.
2. Sprinkle chicken with salt and pepper. In same pan, brown chicken in drippings over medium heat, 3-4 minutes per side. Brush meat with ⅓ cup barbecue sauce. Transfer to oven; bake 8 minutes.
3. Spoon remaining sauce over chicken; sprinkle with cheese and bacon. Bake until the cheese is melted and a thermometer reads 165°, 4-6 minutes. Sprinkle with green onions.
Per 1 chicken breast half : 435 cal., 20g fat (8g sat. fat), 126mg chol., 973mg sodium, 19g carb. (15g sugars, 0 fiber), 41g pro.

EAT SMART FAST FIX

TROPICAL SQUASH & BLACK BEAN BURRITOS

The pineapple salsa in these hearty burritos gives you a taste of the tropics on a chilly day. Stuffed with black beans, butternut squash and spinach, they're a nutritious, delicious and fun dinner for any night.
—Deanna McDonald, Grand Rapids, MI

Start to Finish: 30 min.
Makes: 6 servings

- 1 small butternut squash (about 2½ pounds)
- 1 jar (16 ounces) pineapple salsa
- 1 can (15 ounces) black beans, rinsed and drained
- ½ teaspoon salt
- ½ teaspoon ground cumin
- ¼ teaspoon ground chipotle pepper
- 6 whole wheat tortillas (8 inches), warmed
- 2 cups fresh baby spinach

1. Halve squash lengthwise; remove the seeds. Place in a microwave-safe dish, cut side down. Microwave, covered, on high until soft, 15-20 minutes; cool slightly.
2. Meanwhile, in a saucepan, combine the salsa and beans; heat through over medium heat, stirring occasionally.
3. Scoop out squash pulp; place in a bowl. Mash until smooth; stir in the seasonings. Spoon squash and salsa mixtures onto center of tortillas; top with the spinach and roll up.
Note: This recipe was tested in a 1,100-watt microwave.
Per burrito: 290 cal., 1g fat (0 sat. fat), 0 chol., 692mg sodium, 62g carb. (13g sugars, 15g fiber), 10g pro.

✱
TEST KITCHEN TIPS

If you're short on time, use one 12-ounce package of frozen winter squash instead of a small butternut squash; heat it according to the package directions.

The black bean mixture can be heated in the microwave. For a subtle change in flavor, try mango salsa instead of pineapple salsa.

PORK MEDALLIONS WITH GARLIC-STRAWBERRY SAUCE

These crispy pork medallions are treated to a refreshing strawberry sauce that's ideal for a springtime or summer meal.
—*Taste of Home* Test Kitchen

Start to Finish: 25 min.
Makes: 4 servings

- 2 cups whole fresh strawberries
- ¼ cup water
- 1 teaspoon chicken bouillon granules
- ½ cup all-purpose flour
- 2 large eggs, lightly beaten
- ⅔ cup seasoned bread crumbs
- 1 pork tenderloin (1 pound)
- ¼ teaspoon salt
- ¼ teaspoon pepper
- 6 tablespoons butter, divided
- 1 teaspoon minced garlic
  Sliced fresh strawberries, optional

1. Place whole strawberries, water and bouillon in a food processor; process until blended. Place flour, eggs and bread crumbs in separate shallow bowls.
2. Cut pork into ½-in. slices; pound each with a meat mallet to ¼-in. thickness.

Sprinkle with salt and pepper. Dip the pork in the flour to coat both sides; shake off the excess. Dip in eggs, then in crumbs, patting to adhere.
3. In a large skillet, heat 2 tablespoons butter over medium-high heat. Add pork; cook until tender, 2-3 minutes per side. Remove from pan; keep warm.
4. In same pan, saute garlic in remaining butter 1 minute. Stir in the strawberry mixture; heat through. Serve pork with the sauce; if desired, top it with sliced strawberries.

Per serving: 422 cal., 25g fat (13g sat. fat), 203mg chol., 811mg sodium, 21g carb. (5g sugars, 2g fiber), 29g pro.

PEACH SALSA CHICKEN

Peachy sweetness mellows out the jalapeno kick in this homemade salsa. The whole meal is done in a half hour!
—Kristi Silk, Ferndale, WA

Start to Finish: 30 min.
Makes: 2 servings

- 1 large peach, peeled and chopped
- ½ cup chopped sweet onion
- ¼ cup salsa
- 1 small jalapeno pepper, seeded and minced
- 2 tablespoons finely chopped fresh cilantro
- 2 tablespoons lime juice
- 1 cup chicken broth
- ½ cup uncooked long grain rice
- 2 boneless skinless chicken breast halves (5 ounces each)
- ¼ teaspoon salt
- ¼ teaspoon pepper
- 1 tablespoon olive oil

1. Mix the first six ingredients. In a small saucepan, bring broth and ¼ cup peach mixture to a boil. Stir in rice; return to a boil. Reduce heat; simmer, covered, until liquid is absorbed and rice is tender, about 15-18 minutes.
2. Meanwhile, sprinkle chicken with salt and pepper. In a skillet, heat the oil over medium heat; brown chicken on both sides. Add remaining peach mixture; bring to a boil. Reduce heat; simmer, covered, until a thermometer inserted in chicken reads 165°, 7-9 minutes. Serve with rice.

Per serving: 467 cal., 11g fat (2g sat. fat), 78mg chol., 772mg sodium, 56g carb. (10g sugars, 3g fiber), 35g pro.

PORK MEDALLIONS WITH GARLIC-STRAWBERRY SAUCE

FAST FIX ▶

BLUE CHEESE PORK MEDALLIONS

This pork dish feels fancy thanks to the creamy blue cheese sauce. Guests go crazy over it, but they'd never guess how quickly it all comes together.
—Lynne German, Woodland Hills, CA

Start to Finish: 25 min.
Makes: 4 servings

- 1   pork tenderloin (1 pound)
- 2   teaspoons Montreal steak seasoning
- 2   tablespoons butter
- ½   cup heavy whipping cream
- ¼   cup crumbled blue cheese
- 1   tablespoon minced fresh parsley

1.   Cut pork into 12 slices; sprinkle with steak seasoning. In a large skillet, heat butter over medium heat. Add pork; cook, covered, until pork is tender, 3-5 minutes per side. Remove from pan; keep warm.
2.   Add cream to skillet; bring to a boil, stirring to loosen browned bits from pan. Cook until cream is slightly thickened, 2-3 minutes. Stir in cheese until melted. Serve with pork. Sprinkle with parsley.

Per 3 medallions with 2 tablespoons sauce: 317 cal., 23g fat (13g sat. fat), 126mg chol., 539mg sodium, 1g carb. (1g sugars, 0 fiber), 25g pro.

CHICKEN & GOAT CHEESE SKILLET

EAT SMART FAST FIX ▶

CHICKEN & GOAT CHEESE SKILLET

My husband was completely bowled over by this on-a-whim skillet meal. I can't wait to make it again very soon!
—Ericka Barber, Eureka, CA

Start to Finish: 20 min.
Makes: 2 servings

- ½   pound boneless skinless chicken breasts, cut into 1-inch pieces
- ¼   teaspoon salt
- ⅛   teaspoon pepper
- 2   teaspoons olive oil
- 1   cup cut fresh asparagus (1-inch pieces)
- 1   garlic clove, minced
- 3   plum tomatoes, chopped
- 3   tablespoons 2% milk
- 2   tablespoons herbed fresh goat cheese, crumbled

Hot cooked rice or pasta
Additional goat cheese, optional

1.   Toss chicken with salt and pepper. In a large skillet, heat oil over medium-high heat; saute chicken until no longer pink, 4-6 minutes. Remove chicken from pan; keep warm.
2.   Add asparagus to skillet; cook and stir over medium-high heat 1 minute. Add garlic; cook and stir 30 seconds. Stir in tomatoes, milk and 2 tablespoons cheese; cook, covered, over medium heat until cheese begins to melt, 2-3 minutes. Stir in chicken. Serve with rice. If desired, top with additional cheese.

Per 1½ cups chicken mixture: 251 cal., 11g fat (3g sat. fat), 74mg chol., 447mg sodium, 8g carb. (5g sugars, 3g fiber), 29g pro.
Diabetic Exchanges: 4 lean meat, 2 fat, 1 vegetable.

BEEF & MUSHROOMS WITH SMASHED POTATOES

I was inspired to make this recipe after I couldn't stop thinking of a similar dish that was served in my elementary school cafeteria more than 50 years ago! I like the fact that it's so quick to make, and everyone from my husband to my grandchildren just loves it.

—Ronna Farley, Rockville, MD

Start to Finish: 30 min.
Makes: 4 servings

- 1½ pounds red potatoes (about 6 medium), cut into 1½-inch pieces
- 1 pound ground beef
- ½ pound sliced fresh mushrooms
- 1 medium onion, halved and sliced
- 3 tablespoons all-purpose flour
- ¾ teaspoon pepper, divided
- ½ teaspoon salt, divided
- 1 can (14½ ounces) beef broth
- 2 tablespoons butter, softened
- ½ cup half-and-half cream
- ½ cup french-fried onions

1. Place potatoes in a large saucepan; add water to cover. Bring to a boil. Reduce heat to medium; cook, uncovered, until tender, 10-15 minutes.

2. Meanwhile, in a large skillet, cook and crumble beef with mushrooms and onion over medium-high heat until no longer pink, 6-8 minutes; drain. Stir in the flour, ½ teaspoon pepper and ¼ teaspoon salt until blended. Gradually stir in the broth; bring to a boil. Reduce the heat; simmer, uncovered, until thickened, for about 5 minutes, stirring occasionally.

3. Drain potatoes; return to pan. Mash potatoes to desired consistency, adding butter, cream and the remaining salt and pepper. Spoon into bowls; top with beef mixture. Sprinkle with fried onions.

Per serving: 517 cal., 26g fat (12g sat. fat), 100mg chol., 896mg sodium, 40g carb. (5g sugars, 4g fiber), 28g pr

✱
TEST KITCHEN TIPS

If you have time, cook the mushrooms separately from the ground beef. The beef will brown a bit more and the mushroom juices will stay with the mushrooms, creating even more flavor.

After returning the drained potatoes to the pan, heat them over low heat for 1-2 minutes before adding the butter and half-and-half. Any water will evaporate, leaving a richer flavor.

Try this approach: Spoon portions into individual ramekins. Top with your favorite cheese and french-fried onions. Bake at 350° for 5-7 minutes or until the cheese is melted. Yum!

BEEF & MUSHROOMS
WITH SMASHED POTATOES

CHEDDAR BEAN BURRITOS

PICTURED ON P. 69

My family goes meatless several nights a week, and this recipe is one of our favorites. I usually puree a can or two of chipotles in adobo and freeze in ice cube trays so I can use a small amount when I need it.
—Amy Bravo, Ames, IA

Start to Finish: 25 min.
Makes: 6 servings

- 2 teaspoons canola oil
- 1 tablespoon minced chipotle pepper in adobo sauce
- 2 garlic cloves, minced
- 2 teaspoons chili powder
- 1 teaspoon ground cumin
- ⅛ teaspoon salt
- 2 cans (15 ounces each) black beans, rinsed and drained
- 2 tablespoons water
- ½ cup pico de gallo
- 6 flour tortillas (8 inches), warmed
- 1 cup shredded cheddar or Monterey Jack cheese
- ½ cup sour cream
  Additional pico de gallo and sour cream, optional

1. In a large skillet, heat oil over medium heat; saute chipotle pepper, garlic and seasonings 2 minutes. Stir in beans and water; bring to a boil. Reduce the heat; simmer, uncovered, until the flavors are blended, 5-7 minutes, stirring occasionally.
2. Coarsely mash bean mixture; stir in pico de gallo. Spoon onto tortillas; top with cheese and sour cream and roll up. If desired, serve with additional pico de gallo and sour cream.
Freeze option: Cool the filling before making burritos. Individually wrap the burritos in paper towels and foil; freeze in a resealable plastic freezer bag. To use, remove foil; place a paper towel-wrapped burrito on a microwave-safe plate. Microwave on high until heated through, 4-6 minutes, turning once. Let stand 2 minutes.
Per burrito: 410 cal., 16g fat (7g sat. fat), 23mg chol., 726mg sodium, 50g carb. (2g sugars, 8g fiber), 16g pro.

EASY CHANA MASALA

EASY CHANA MASALA

I love this quick, healthy Indian-inspired dish so much I always make sure to stock the ingredients in my pantry. It makes weeknight dinners feel a bit more special.
—Janeen Judah, Houston, TX

Start to Finish: 30 min.
Makes: 4 servings

- 1 tablespoon canola oil
- ½ cup finely chopped onion
- 1 tablespoon minced fresh gingerroot
- 2 garlic cloves, minced
- 1 jalapeno pepper, seeded and finely chopped, optional
- ½ teaspoon salt
- 1 teaspoon garam masala
- ½ teaspoon ground coriander
- ½ teaspoon ground cumin
- 1 can (15 ounces) diced tomatoes, undrained
- 1 can (15 ounces) garbanzo beans or chickpeas, rinsed and drained
- 3 cups hot cooked brown rice
- ¼ cup plain yogurt
  Minced fresh cilantro

1. In a large skillet, heat oil over medium heat. Add the onion, ginger, garlic and, if desired, jalapeno; cook and stir until the onion is softened and lightly browned, 4-5 minutes. Add salt and spices; cook and stir 1 minute.
2. Stir in tomatoes and garbanzo beans; bring to a boil. Reduce the heat; simmer, covered, until flavors are blended, 12-15 minutes, stirring occasionally. Serve with rice. Top with yogurt and cilantro.
Freeze option: Freeze cooled chickpea mixture in freezer containers. To use, partially thaw in refrigerator overnight. Heat through in a saucepan, stirring occasionally and adding a little water if necessary.
Per ¾ cup chickpea mixture with ¾ cup rice: 359 cal., 8g fat (1g sat. fat), 2mg chol., 616mg sodium, 64g carb. (8g sugars, 9g fiber), 10g pro.

✱

TEST KITCHEN TIP

This is a quick version of a popular Indian and Pakistani dish. Chana refers to the chickpeas. Basmati or regular long grain white rice would also be great with this curry.

FAST FIX ▶

SKILLET HAM & RICE

Ham, rice and mushrooms make a tasty combination in this homey stovetop dish. It goes from start to finish in less than half an hour.
—Susan Zivec, Regina, SK

Start to Finish: 25 min.
Makes: 2 servings

- 1 teaspoon olive oil
- 1 medium onion, chopped
- 1 cup sliced fresh mushrooms
- 1 cup cubed fully cooked ham
- ⅛ teaspoon pepper
- ½ cup reduced-sodium chicken broth
- ¼ cup water
- ¾ cup uncooked instant rice
- 2 green onions, sliced
- ¼ cup shredded Parmesan cheese

1. In a large nonstick skillet, heat the oil over medium-high heat; saute onion and mushrooms until tender. Stir in the ham, pepper, broth and water; bring to a boil. Stir in rice. Reduce heat; simmer, covered, until rice is tender, about 5 minutes.
2. Fluff with a fork. Top with green onions and cheese.

Per 1¼ cups: 322 cal., 8g fat (3g sat. fat), 49mg chol., 1168mg sodium, 38g carb. (4g sugars, 2g fiber), 24g pro.

EAT SMART FAST FIX ▶

SPICY TURKEY QUESADILLAS

Here's a creative use of leftover turkey and cranberries from Thanksgiving.
—*Taste of Home* Test Kitchen

Start to Finish: 25 min.
Makes: 2 servings

- 3 ounces fat-free cream cheese
- ¼ cup chopped fresh or frozen cranberries, thawed
- 1 tablespoon canned chopped green chilies
- 1½ teaspoons honey
- 1 teaspoon Louisiana-style hot sauce
- 4 flour tortillas (6 inches)
- 1 cup diced cooked turkey breast

1. Combine first five ingredients; spread over tortillas. Top two tortillas with turkey, then remaining tortillas, pressing lightly.
2. In a large skillet, cook quesadillas over medium heat until lightly browned and heated through, 2-3 minutes per side.

Per quesadilla: 391 cal., 9g fat (3g sat. fat), 61mg chol., 870mg sodium, 43g carb. (8g sugars, 4g fiber), 33g pro. **Diabetic Exchanges:** 3 lean meat, 2 starch, 1 fat.

FAST FIX ▶

CREAMY PAPRIKA PORK

When I was little, I would ask my mom to make "favorite meat." She knew what I was really requesting: this homey pork recipe. It's been in my family for more than 30 years and is still a favorite!
—Alexandra Barnett, Forest, VA

Start to Finish: 30 min.
Makes: 4 servings

- 1 pork tenderloin (1 pound), cut into 1-inch cubes
- 1 teaspoon all-purpose flour
- 4 teaspoons paprika
- ¾ teaspoon salt
- ¼ teaspoon pepper
- 1 tablespoon butter
- ¾ cup heavy whipping cream
  Hot cooked egg noodles or rice
  Minced fresh parsley, optional

1. Toss pork with flour and seasonings. In a large skillet, heat butter over medium heat; saute pork until lightly browned, about 4-5 minutes.
2. Add cream; bring to a boil, stirring to loosen browned bits from pan. Cook, uncovered, until the cream is slightly thickened, about 5-7 minutes. Serve with noodles. If desired, sprinkle with parsley.

Per ¾ cup pork: 320 cal., 23g fat (14g sat. fat), 122mg chol., 524mg sodium, 3g carb. (1g sugars, 1g fiber), 24g pro.

SKILLET HAM & RICE

ONE-PAN TUSCAN RAVIOLI

FAST FIX ▶
ONE-PAN TUSCAN RAVIOLI

Sometimes I use chickpeas instead of cannellini beans, grated Asiago or provolone instead of Parmesan, and all zucchini if I don't have eggplant. The recipe is very flexible!
—Sonya Labbe, West Hollywood, CA

Start to Finish: 25 min.
Makes: 4 servings

- 1 tablespoon olive oil
- 2 cups cubed eggplant (½ inch)
- 1 can (14½ ounces) Italian diced tomatoes, undrained
- 1 can (14½ ounces) reduced-sodium chicken broth
- 1 medium zucchini, halved lengthwise and cut into ½-inch slices
- 1 package (9 ounces) refrigerated cheese ravioli
- 1 can (15 ounces) cannellini beans, rinsed and drained
  Shredded Parmesan cheese
  Thinly sliced fresh basil

1. In a large skillet, heat oil over medium heat; saute eggplant until lightly browned, 2-3 minutes.

2. Stir in tomatoes, broth and zucchini; bring it to a boil. Add the ravioli; cook, uncovered, over medium heat until ravioli are tender, about 7-9 minutes, stirring occasionally. Stir in beans; heat through. Sprinkle with cheese and basil.
Per 1½ cups: 376 cal., 10g fat (4g sat. fat), 36mg chol., 1096mg sodium, 56g carb. (11g sugars, 8g fiber), 16g pro.

EAT SMART **FAST FIX ▶**
GARLIC CHICKEN WITH HERBS
PICTURED ON P. 69

Pan-roasting garlic cloves turns them into rich, creamy deliciousness. This chicken is fantastic with crusty Italian bread or mashed potatoes on the side.
—Kathy Fleming, Lisle, IL

Start to Finish: 30 min.
Makes: 4 servings

- 4 boneless skinless chicken thighs (about 1 pound)
- ½ teaspoon salt
- ¼ teaspoon pepper
- 1 tablespoon butter
- 10 garlic cloves, peeled and halved
- ¼ cup white wine or chicken broth
- 1½ teaspoons minced fresh rosemary
- ½ teaspoon minced fresh sage
- 1 cup chicken broth
  Hot cooked rice of your choice

1. Sprinkle chicken with salt and pepper. In a large skillet, heat butter over medium-high heat; brown chicken on both sides. Remove from pan, reserving drippings.
2. In same skillet, saute garlic in drippings over medium-high heat until light golden brown. Add wine and herbs; bring to a boil, stirring to loosen browned bits from pan. Cook until the mixture is almost evaporated. Add broth and chicken; bring to a boil. Reduce heat; simmer, covered, until a thermometer inserted in chicken reads at least 170°, 10-12 minutes.
3. To serve, spoon pan juices over chicken. Serve with rice.
Per serving: 214 cal., 12g fat (3g sat. fat), 76mg chol., 487mg sodium, 3g carb. (0 sugars, 0 fiber), 22g pro.
Diabetic Exchanges: 3 lean meat, ½ fat.

✳
TEST KITCHEN TIP
To easily peel garlic clove, gently crush it with the flat side of a large knife blade to loosen the peel. If you don't have a large knife, you can crush the garlic with a small can. The peel will come right off.

ONE-PAN CHICKEN RICE CURRY

I've been loving the subtle spice from curry lately, so I incorporated it into this saucy chicken and rice dish. It's a one-pan meal that's become a go-to dinnertime favorite.
—Mary Lou Timpson, Colorado City, AZ

....

Start to Finish: 30 min.
Makes: 4 servings

- 2 tablespoons butter, divided
- 1 medium onion, halved and thinly sliced
- 2 tablespoons all-purpose flour
- 3 teaspoons curry powder
- ½ teaspoon salt
- ½ teaspoon pepper
- 1 pound boneless skinless chicken breasts, cut into 1-inch pieces
- 1 can (14½ ounces) reduced-sodium chicken broth
- 1 cup uncooked instant rice
   Chopped fresh cilantro leaves, optional

1. Using a large nonstick skillet, heat 1 tablespoon butter over medium-high heat; saute onion until tender and lightly browned, 3-5 minutes. Remove from pan.
2. Mix flour and seasonings; toss with chicken. In same pan, heat remaining butter over medium-high heat. Add chicken; cook just until no longer pink, 4-6 minutes, turning occasionally.
3. Stir in broth and onion; bring to a boil. Stir in rice. Remove from heat; let stand, covered, 5 minutes (mixture will be saucy). If desired, sprinkle with cilantro.
Per cup: 300 cal., 9g fat (4g sat. fat), 78mg chol., 658mg sodium, 27g carb. (2g sugars, 2g fiber), 27g pro.
Diabetic Exchanges: 3 lean meat, 2 starch, 1½ fat.

STEAK & MUSHROOM STROGANOFF

This homey recipe of steak and egg noodles in a creamy sauce is just like what we had at my gran's house when we'd visit. It's one of my favorite-memory meals, as I like to call them.
—Janelle Shank, Omaha, NE

....

Start to Finish: 30 minutes
Makes: 6 servings

- 6 cups uncooked egg noodles (about 12 ounces)
- 1 beef top sirloin steak (1½ pounds), cut into 2x½-in. strips
- 1 tablespoon canola oil
- ½ teaspoon salt
- ½ teaspoon pepper
- 2 tablespoons butter
- 1 pound sliced fresh mushrooms
- 2 shallots, finely chopped
- ½ cup beef broth
- 1 tablespoon snipped fresh dill
- 1 cup sour cream

1. Cook noodles according to package directions; drain.
2. Meanwhile, toss beef with oil, salt and pepper. Place a large skillet over medium-high heat; saute half of the beef until browned, 2-3 minutes. Remove from pan; repeat with remaining beef.
3. In same pan, heat butter over medium-high heat; saute mushrooms until lightly browned, 4-6 minutes. Add shallots; cook and stir until tender, 1-2 minutes. Stir in broth, dill and beef; heat through. Reduce heat to medium; stir in sour cream until blended. Serve with noodles.
Per serving: 455 cal., 19g fat (10g sat. fat), 115mg chol., 379mg sodium, 34g carb. (4g sugars, 2g fiber), 34g pro.
HEALTH TIP A simple switch to reduced-fat sour cream will save 40 calories and 5g fat .

ONE-PAN CHICKEN RICE CURRY

WEEKNIGHT PASTA SKILLET

This zesty pasta dish is ideal for busy weeknights. It requires relatively few ingredients, is easy to prepare, and tastes so comforting when the weather cools down. A salad on the side makes it a meal.
—Stacey Brown, Spring, TX

Start to Finish: 30 min.
Makes: 8 servings

- 1 package (19½ ounces) Italian turkey sausage links, casings removed
- 1 can (28 ounces) whole plum tomatoes with basil
- 1 can (14½ ounces) no-salt-added whole tomatoes
- 4 cups uncooked spiral pasta (about 12 ounces)
- 1 can (14½ ounces) reduced-sodium chicken broth
- ¼ cup water
- ½ cup crumbled goat or feta cheese

1. In a Dutch oven, cook and crumble sausage over medium-high heat until no longer pink, 5-7 minutes. Meanwhile, coarsely chop tomatoes, reserving juices.
2. Add tomatoes and reserved juices to sausage; stir in pasta, broth and water. Bring to a boil. Reduce heat to medium; cook, uncovered, until pasta is al dente, 15-18 minutes, stirring occasionally. Top with cheese.

Per 1½ cups: 278 cal., 7g fat (2g sat. fat), 34mg chol., 622mg sodium, 38g carb. (5g sugars, 4g fiber), 16g pro.
Diabetic Exchanges: 2½ starch, 2 medium-fat meat.

EAT SMART **FAST FIX**

PARMESAN CHICKEN WITH LEMON RICE

I like the challenge of inventing recipes with ingredients I have on hand. This easy-peasy meal is an example.
—Colleen Doucette, Truro, NS

Start to Finish: 30 min.
Makes: 4 servings

- 2 cups reduced-sodium chicken broth
- 2 tablespoons lemon juice
- 1 cup uncooked long grain rice
- ½ cup chopped onion
- 1 large egg
- 2 tablespoons fat-free milk
- ¾ cup panko (Japanese) bread crumbs
- ⅔ cup grated Parmesan cheese, divided
- 1 teaspoon dried oregano
- 1 pound boneless skinless chicken breasts
- 2 tablespoons olive oil
- 1 cup frozen peas (about 4 ounces), thawed
- ¼ teaspoon grated lemon peel
  Freshly ground pepper, optional

1. In a saucepan, bring broth and lemon juice to a boil. Stir in rice and onion; return to a boil. Reduce heat; simmer, covered, until liquid is almost absorbed and rice is tender, 15-20 minutes.
2. Meanwhile, in a shallow bowl, whisk together egg and milk. In another bowl, toss bread crumbs with ⅓ cup cheese and oregano. Pound chicken breasts with a meat mallet to ¼-in. thickness. Dip in egg mixture, then in crumb mixture to coat both sides.
3. In a large skillet, heat oil over medium heat. Cook chicken until no longer pink, 2-3 minutes per side.
4. When rice is cooked, gently stir in peas; cook, covered, until heated through, about 1-2 minutes. Stir in lemon peel and remaining cheese. Slice chicken; serve with rice. If desired, sprinkle with pepper.

Per 3 ounces cooked chicken with ¾ cup rice: 500 cal., 14g fat (4g sat. fat), 96mg chol., 623mg sodium, 55g carb. (4g sugars, 3g fiber), 36g pro.

FAST FIX

SPICY PEANUT CHICKEN & NOODLES

This simple recipe tastes like I spent hours making it. Everybody says it has the perfect levels of heat and spice.
—Sharon Collison, Newark, DE

Start to Finish: 30 min.
Makes: 4 servings

- 1 package (10.8 ounces) frozen broccoli, carrot and sugar snap pea blend
- ¾ cup reduced-sodium chicken broth
- ⅓ cup creamy peanut butter
- ¼ cup teriyaki sauce
- ¼ teaspoon pepper
- ¼ teaspoon cayenne pepper
- 1 cup coarsely shredded rotisserie chicken
- 1 package (8.8 ounces) thick rice noodles
- 3 green onions, thinly sliced on a diagonal
  Additional chicken broth, optional

1. Microwave frozen vegetables according to package directions.
2. Place broth, peanut butter, teriyaki sauce, pepper and cayenne in a large skillet; cook and stir over medium heat until blended. Stir in chicken; heat through. Stir in vegetables.
3. Prepare noodles according to package directions. Drain and immediately add to chicken mixture, tossing to combine. Sprinkle with green onions. If desired, moisten with additional broth. Serve it immediately.

Per serving: 489 cal., 14g fat (3g sat. fat), 31mg chol., 971mg sodium, 68g carb. (8g sugars, 4g fiber), 22g pro.

★ ★ ★ ★ ★ **READER REVIEW**

"We love Thai food, and I have been making my version of this for years. I used frozen veggies as indicated. Usually I use fresh veggies and saute lightly. Both are great."
MS11145 TASTEOFHOME.COM

SPICY PEANUT CHICKEN & NOODLES

<5> INGREDIENTS | FAST FIX >

PIEROGI CHICKEN SUPPER

This change-of-pace dish combines chicken, cheese and onion with frozen pierogies for a complete meal in just 30 minutes.
—Barbara Scott, Walkersville, MD

Start to Finish: 30 min.
Makes: 4 servings

- 1 package (16 ounces) frozen pierogies
- 1 pound boneless skinless chicken breasts, cut into 2x½-inch strips
- ¼ teaspoon salt
- ⅛ teaspoon pepper
- 2 tablespoons butter, divided
- ½ large sweet onion, thinly sliced
- ½ cup shredded cheddar cheese

1. Cook pierogies according to package directions; drain. Meanwhile, toss chicken with salt and pepper. In a large nonstick skillet, heat 1 tablespoon butter over medium-high heat; saute chicken and onion until chicken is no longer pink. Remove from pan.
2. In same pan, heat remaining butter over medium heat; saute pierogies until lightly browned. Stir in chicken mixture; sprinkle with cheese. Cover; remove from heat and let stand until cheese is melted.

Per cup: 444 cal., 16g fat (8g sat. fat), 101mg chol., 762mg sodium, 40g carb. (10g sugars, 3g fiber), 33g pro.

JEZEBEL CHICKEN THIGHS

FAST FIX >

JEZEBEL CHICKEN THIGHS

On busy weeknights, this sweet and spicy chicken is our standby.
—Judy Armstrong
Prairieville, LA

Start to Finish: 25 min.
Makes: 4 servings

- 4 bone-in chicken thighs
- ½ teaspoon salt
- ½ teaspoon paprika
- ¼ teaspoon pepper
- 1 tablespoon olive oil
- 1 shallot, finely chopped
- 2 garlic cloves, minced
- ½ cup apricot preserves
- ¼ cup chicken broth
- 1 to 2 tablespoons horseradish sauce
- 4 green onions, sliced, divided

1. Sprinkle chicken with seasonings. In a large nonstick skillet, heat the oil over medium-high heat; brown chicken on both sides, beginning skin side down. Remove from pan, reserving drippings.
2. In same pan, saute shallot and garlic in drippings over medium-high heat until tender, 1-2 minutes. Stir in preserves, broth, horseradish sauce and half of the green onions. Add chicken; cook, covered, over medium heat until a thermometer reads 170°-175°, 10-12 minutes.
3. To serve, spoon sauce over chicken; sprinkle with remaining green onions.

Per chicken thigh with 2 tablespoons sauce: 380 cal., 19g fat (5g sat. fat), 82mg chol., 474mg sodium, 30g carb. (19g sugars, 1g fiber), 23g pro.

TANGY PARMESAN TILAPIA

I was looking around for a fish coating that didn't have bread crumbs or flour. Don't forget the lime juice—it really perks up the dish.
—Deborah Purdue, Westland, MI

Start to Finish: 15 min.
Makes: 4 servings

¼ cup grated Parmesan cheese
2 tablespoons reduced-fat mayonnaise
1 tablespoon butter, softened
1 tablespoon lime juice
⅛ teaspoon garlic powder
⅛ teaspoon dried basil
⅛ teaspoon pepper
Dash onion powder
4 tilapia fillets (5 ounces each)
¼ teaspoon salt

1. Preheat broiler. Mix the first eight ingredients until blended.
2. Line a 15x10x1-in. baking pan with foil; coat foil with cooking spray. Place tilapia in pan; sprinkle with salt.
3. Broil 3-4 in. from heat 2-3 minutes per side. Spread cheese mixture over fillets. Broil until topping is golden brown and fish just begins to flake easily with a fork, about 1-2 minutes.

Per fillet: 191 cal., 8g fat (4g sat. fat), 84mg chol., 359mg sodium, 2g carb. (0 sugars, 0 fiber), 28g pro.
Diabetic Exchanges: 4 lean meat, 1½ fat

POTATO KIELBASA SKILLET

Smoky kielbasa steals the show in this hearty meal. It adds instant coziness to chilly fall nights.
—*Taste of Home* Test Kitchen

Start to Finish: 30 min.
Makes: 4 servings

1 pound red potatoes (3-4 medium), cut into 1-inch pieces
3 tablespoons water
2 tablespoons brown sugar
2 tablespoons cider vinegar
1 tablespoon Dijon mustard
1½ teaspoons minced fresh thyme or ½ teaspoon dried thyme
¼ teaspoon pepper
1 tablespoon olive oil
½ cup chopped onion
¾ pound smoked kielbasa or Polish sausage, cut into ¼-inch slices
4 cups fresh baby spinach
5 bacon strips, cooked and crumbled

1. Place the potatoes and water in a microwave-safe dish. Microwave, covered, on high until the potatoes are tender, 3-4 minutes; drain.
2. Meanwhile, mix brown sugar, vinegar, mustard, thyme and pepper. In a large skillet, heat oil over medium-high heat; saute the onion and kielbasa until the onion is tender.
3. Add potatoes; cook and stir until lightly browned, 3-5 minutes. Stir in brown sugar mixture; bring to a boil. Reduce heat; simmer, uncovered, 2 minutes, stirring occasionally. Stir in spinach until wilted. Stir in the bacon.

Per 1½ cups: 472 cal., 31g fat (10g sat. fat), 66mg chol., 873mg sodium, 31g carb. (10g sugars, 3g fiber), 17g pro.

TANGY PARMESAN TILAPIA

FAST FIX ▶

CHICKEN CORDON
BLEU SKILLET

*Here is a hearty supper. If I have fresh
mushrooms on hand, I slice them and toss
them in the skillet. You could add cooked
veggies like broccoli or cauliflower, too.*
—Sandy Harz, Spring Lake, MI

Start to Finish: 25 min.
Makes: 4 servings

- 8 ounces uncooked medium egg
  noodles (about 5 cups)
- 1 pound boneless skinless chicken
  breasts, cut in 1-inch pieces
- ½ teaspoon pepper
- 1 tablespoon butter
- 1 can (10¾ ounces) condensed cream
  of chicken soup, undiluted
- ½ cup shredded Swiss cheese
- ½ cup cubed fully cooked ham
- ¼ cup water
  Minced fresh parsley

1. Cook noodles according to package
directions; drain.
2. Meanwhile, sprinkle chicken with
pepper. In a large skillet, heat butter over
medium-high heat; saute chicken just until
browned, 3-5 minutes. Stir in the soup,
cheese, ham and water; cook, covered,

over medium heat until cheese is melted
and chicken is no longer pink, 6-8 minutes,
stirring occasionally. Stir in noodles.
Sprinkle with parsley.
Per 1½ cups: 516 cal., 18g fat (8g sat.
fat), 147mg chol., 878mg sodium, 47g
carb. (2g sugars, 3g fiber), 40g pro.

EAT SMART FAST FIX ▶

TURKEY QUESADILLAS
WITH CRANBERRY SALSA

*These quesadillas stuffed
with turkey and cheese
get amped up when you
add sweet-tart cranberry
salsa. You might want to
make extra; the salsa goes great with
chicken or pork, too!*
—Jodi Kristensen, Macomb, MI

Start to Finish: 30 min.
Makes: 4 servings

- ¾ cup fresh or frozen cranberries
- 2 tablespoons sugar
- ¼ cup water
- 1 small pear, chopped
- ¼ cup chopped red onion
- 1 jalapeno pepper, seeded and
  chopped
- 3 tablespoons chopped celery
- 2 teaspoons grated lemon peel

- 1 tablespoon lemon juice
- ½ teaspoon ground cumin
- 4 flour tortillas (6 inches)
- 2 cups cubed cooked turkey breast
- 1 cup shredded reduced-fat white
  or yellow cheddar cheese

1. For salsa, in a small saucepan, combine
cranberries, sugar and water; bring to a
boil. Reduce the heat to medium; cook,
uncovered, until the berries pop, about
10 minutes, stirring occasionally. Remove
from heat; cool slightly. Stir in the pear,
onion, jalapeno, celery, lemon peel and
juice, and cumin.
2. Preheat griddle over medium heat. Top
one half of each tortilla with ½ cup turkey;
sprinkle with ¼ cup cheese. Fold tortilla to
close. Cook on griddle until golden brown
and the cheese is melted, 1-2 minutes per
side. Serve with salsa.
Note: Wear disposable gloves when
cutting hot peppers; the oils can burn
skin. Avoid touching your face.
Per quesadilla with ⅓ cup salsa:
321 cal., 10g fat (4g sat. fat), 80mg chol.,
449mg sodium, 27g carb. (12g sugars,
2g fiber), 32g pro.
Diabetic Exchanges: 3 lean meat,
1½ starch, 1 fat, ½ fruit.

FAST FIX ▶

EASY CHICKEN & DUMPLINGS

Perfect for fall nights, my simple one-dish version of chicken and dumplings is low in fat as well as speedy and delicious.
—Nancy Tuck, Elk Falls, KS

Start to Finish: 30 min.
Makes: 6 servings

3 celery ribs, chopped
2 medium carrots, sliced
3 cans (14½ ounces each) reduced-sodium chicken broth
3 cups cubed cooked chicken breast
½ teaspoon poultry seasoning
⅛ teaspoon pepper
1⅔ cups reduced-fat biscuit/baking mix
⅔ cup fat-free milk

1. In a Dutch oven coated with cooking spray, cook and stir celery and carrots over medium heat until tender, about 5 minutes. Stir in broth, chicken and seasonings. Bring to a boil; reduce heat to a gentle simmer.
2. For dumplings, mix the biscuit mix and milk until a soft dough forms. Drop by tablespoonfuls on top of the simmering liquid. Reduce the heat to low; cover and cook 10-15 minutes or until a toothpick inserted in dumplings comes out clean (don't lift cover during first 10 minutes).
Per cup: 260 cal., 4g fat (1g sat. fat), 54mg chol., 1039mg sodium, 28g carb. (6g sugars, 2g fiber), 27g pro.

EASY CHICKEN & DUMPLINGS

FAST FIX ▶

SPAGHETTI & MEATBALL SKILLET SUPPER

I developed this one-skillet spaghetti to cut down on cooking time for busy nights. The beans, artichokes and tomatoes bump up the nutrition, while lemon and parsley make it pop with brightness.
—Roxanne Chan, Albany, CA

Start to Finish: 30 min.
Makes: 6 servings

1 tablespoon olive oil
1 package (12 ounces) refrigerated fully cooked Italian turkey meatballs
1 can (28 ounces) whole tomatoes, undrained, broken up
1 can (15 ounces) cannellini beans, rinsed and drained
1 can (14 ounces) water-packed quartered artichoke hearts, drained
½ teaspoon Italian seasoning
1 can (14½ ounces) reduced-sodium chicken broth
4 ounces uncooked spaghetti, broken into 2-inch pieces (about 1⅓ cups)
¼ cup chopped fresh parsley
1 tablespoon lemon juice
   Grated Parmesan cheese

1. Using a large skillet, heat the oil over medium heat; add meatballs and brown, turning occasionally.
2. Add tomatoes, beans, artichoke hearts, Italian seasoning and broth; bring to a boil. Add spaghetti; return to boil. Reduce heat; simmer, covered, until spaghetti is tender, 10-12 minutes, stirring occasionally.
3. Stir in parsley and lemon juice. Serve with cheese.
Per 1⅓ cups: 330 cal., 10g fat (2g sat. fat), 43mg chol., 1051mg sodium, 38g carb. (5g sugars, 6g fiber), 20g pro.

✳

TEST KITCHEN TIPS
With one-pan pasta dishes, the sauce is always a little starchier than usual from cooking the pasta.

Because they are a major part of this recipe, high-quality crushed tomatoes are a must. It's worth splurging on San Marzano.

If your kiddos are squeamish about tomatoes, switch to two 14-ounce cans of diced tomatoes so the pieces are smaller.

CLASSIC CHICKEN & WAFFLES

FAST FIX ▶

CLASSIC CHICKEN & WAFFLES

A down-home diner special quickly gets weeknight-easy with the help of rotisserie chicken. Want 'em even faster? Make the waffles ahead of time and freeze till dinnertime.
—Lauren Reiff, East Earl, PA

Start to Finish: 30 min.
Makes: 6 servings

- 3 tablespoons butter
- 3 tablespoons all-purpose flour
- ½ teaspoon salt
- ¼ teaspoon pepper
- ½ cup chicken broth
- 1¼ cups 2% milk
- 2 cups coarsely shredded rotisserie chicken

WAFFLES

- 2 cups all-purpose flour
- 2 tablespoons sugar
- 4 teaspoons baking powder
- ½ teaspoon salt
- 2 large eggs
- 1½ cups 2% milk
- 5 tablespoons butter, melted
  Sliced green onions, optional

1. In a large saucepan, melt butter over medium heat. Stir in flour, salt and pepper until smooth; gradually whisk in broth and milk. Bring to a boil, stirring constantly; cook and stir until thickened, 1-2 minutes. Stir in chicken; heat through. Keep warm.
2. Preheat waffle maker. Whisk together flour, sugar, baking powder and salt. In another bowl, whisk together eggs, milk and melted butter; add to dry ingredients, stirring just until moistened.
3. Bake the waffles according to the manufacturer's directions until golden brown. Top waffles with chicken mixture and, if desired, green onions.
Per 2 waffles with ⅔ cup chicken mixture: 488 cal., 23g fat (13g sat. fat), 154mg chol., 981mg sodium, 45g carb. (10g sugars, 1g fiber), 24g pro.

EAT SMART FAST FIX ▶

SEARED SALMON WITH STRAWBERRY BASIL RELISH

Take a sweet new approach to salmon by topping it off with a relish of strawberries, basil, honey and pepper.
—Stacy Mullens, Gresham, OR

Start to Finish: 20 min.
Makes: 6 servings

- 6 salmon fillets (4 ounces each)
- 1 tablespoon butter, melted
- ¼ teaspoon salt
- ⅛ teaspoon freshly ground pepper

RELISH

- 1¼ cups finely chopped fresh strawberries
- 1 tablespoon minced fresh basil
- 1 tablespoon honey
  Dash freshly ground pepper

1. Brush the fillets with melted butter; sprinkle with salt and pepper. Heat a large skillet over medium-high heat. Add fillets, skin side up, in batches if necessary; cook 2-3 minutes on each side or until fish just begins to flake easily with a fork.
2. In a small bowl, toss strawberries with basil, honey and pepper. Serve salmon with relish.
Per salmon fillet with 3 tablespoons relish: 215 cal., 12g fat (3g sat. fat), 62mg chol., 169mg sodium, 6g carb. (5g sugars, 1g fiber), 19g pro.
Diabetic Exchanges: 3 lean meat, ½ starch, ½ fat.

❋
TEST KITCHEN TIP
Salmon and other oily types of fish such as whitefish, mackerel and lake trout may be frozen for up to 3 months. Lean types of fish such as cod, tilapia, catfish and haddock may be frozen for up to 6 months. Wrap fish in freezer paper, heavy-duty plastic bags or heavy-duty foil before freezing.

GREEN PEPPER STEAK

This easy beef stir-fry dinner has loads of flavor, and with all those beautiful veggies, it's a good-for-you dinner you can feel good about any night of the week.
—Emmalee Thomas, Laddonia, MO

Start to Finish: 30 min.
Makes: 4 servings

- 1 tablespoon cornstarch
- ¼ cup reduced-sodium soy sauce
- ¼ cup water
- 2 tablespoons canola oil, divided
- 1 pound beef top sirloin steak, cut into ¼-in.-thick strips
- 2 small onions, cut into thin wedges
- 2 celery ribs, sliced diagonally
- 1 medium green pepper, cut into 1-inch pieces
- 2 medium tomatoes, cut into wedges
  Hot cooked rice

1. Mix cornstarch, soy sauce and water until smooth. In a large skillet, heat 1 tablespoon oil over medium-high heat; stir-fry beef until browned, 2-3 minutes. Remove from pan.
2. Stir-fry onions, celery and pepper in remaining oil 3 minutes. Stir cornstarch mixture; add to pan. Bring to a boil; cook and stir until thickened and bubbly, 1-2 minutes. Stir in tomatoes and beef; heat through. Serve with rice.
Per serving: 259 cal., 12g fat (2g sat. fat), 46mg chol., 647mg sodium, 10g carb. (4g sugars, 2g fiber), 27g pro.

SALISBURY STEAK DELUXE

I've always liked Salisbury steak, but I had to search a long time to find a recipe this tasty. It's handy, too because it can be prepared ahead, kept in the refrigerator and warmed up later.
—Denise Barteet, Shreveport, LA

Start to Finish: 30 min.
Makes: 6 servings

- 1 can (10¾ ounces) condensed cream of mushroom soup, undiluted
- 1 tablespoon prepared mustard
- 2 teaspoons Worcestershire sauce
- 1 teaspoon prepared horseradish
- 1 large egg
- ¼ cup dry bread crumbs
- ¼ cup finely chopped onion
- ½ teaspoon salt
  Dash pepper
- 1½ pound ground beef
- 1 to 2 tablespoons canola oil
- ½ cup water
- 2 tablespoons chopped fresh parsley

1. In a bowl, combine soup, mustard, Worcestershire sauce and horseradish. Set aside. In another bowl, lightly beat the egg. Add the bread crumbs, onion, salt, pepper and ¼ cup of the soup mixture. Crumble beef over mixture and mix well. Shape into six patties.
2. In a large skillet, brown patties in oil; drain. Combine remaining soup mixture with water; pour over top. Cover and cook over low heat 10-15 minutes or until meat is no longer pink. Sprinkle with parsley.
Per serving: 319 cal., 20g fat (7g sat. fat), 113mg chol., 706mg sodium, 9g carb. (1g sugars, 1g fiber), 25g pro.

GREEN PEPPER STEAK

SPICY SWEET SHRIMP WITH PINEAPPLE SALSA

I wanted to find a way to use pineapple salsa in a recipe. I came up with this simple, delicious and quick dish!
—Erin Schillo, Northfield, OH

Start to Finish: 30 min.
Makes: 8 servings

- 1½ cups uncooked basmati rice
- ¾ cup canned black beans, rinsed and drained
- 2 teaspoons canola oil
- ½ cup finely chopped onion
- 1½ cups unsweetened pineapple juice
- ¼ cup packed brown sugar
- 1 tablespoon Sriracha Asian hot chili sauce
- 3 cups cubed fresh pineapple
- 1 medium sweet red pepper, diced
- 1 cup chopped fresh cilantro
- 1 small red onion, finely chopped
- 2 tablespoons lime juice
- ¼ teaspoon salt
- ¼ teaspoon pepper
- 1½ pounds peeled and deveined shrimp (31-40 per pound)

1. Cook the rice according to package directions. Stir in the beans; cover and keep warm.
2. While rice cooks, heat oil in a large skillet over medium-high heat. Saute onion until tender, 3-4 minutes. Stir in pineapple juice, brown sugar and chili sauce; bring to a boil. Cook, uncovered, on high until liquid is reduced to ½ cup, 10-12 minutes.
3. For salsa, toss pineapple with red pepper, cilantro, red onion, lime juice, salt and pepper.
4. Once sauce has reduced, stir in shrimp and return just to a boil. Reduce heat; simmer, uncovered, until shrimp turns pink, 2-3 minutes. Serve with rice mixture and salsa.

Per serving: 356 cal., 3g fat (0 sat. fat), 129mg chol., 312mg sodium, 59g carb. (20g sugars, 3g fiber), 22g pro.

BUFFALO CHICKEN TENDERS

BUFFALO CHICKEN TENDERS

These chicken tenders get a spicy kick thanks to homemade Buffalo sauce. They taste like they're from a restaurant, but are so easy to make at home. Blue cheese dipping sauce takes them right over the top.
—Dahlia Abrams, Detroit, MI

Start to Finish: 20 min.
Makes: 4 servings

- 1 pound chicken tenderloins
- 2 tablespoons all-purpose flour
- ¼ teaspoon pepper
- 2 tablespoons butter, divided
- ⅓ cup Louisiana-style hot sauce
- 1¼ teaspoons Worcestershire sauce
- 1 teaspoon minced fresh oregano
- ½ teaspoon garlic powder
  Blue cheese salad dressing, optional

1. Toss chicken with flour and pepper. In a large skillet, heat 1 tablespoon butter over medium heat. Add chicken; cook until no longer pink, 4-6 minutes per side. Remove from pan.
2. Mix hot sauce, Worcestershire sauce, oregano and garlic powder. In same skillet, melt remaining butter; stir in the sauce mixture. Add the chicken; heat through, turning to coat. If desired, serve with blue cheese dressing.

Per serving: 184 cal., 7g fat (4g sat. fat), 71mg chol., 801mg sodium, 5g carb. (1g sugars, 0 fiber), 27g pro.
Diabetic Exchanges: 3 lean meat, 1½ fat.

CHICKEN & SPANISH CAULIFLOWER "RICE"

I learned about the paleo diet from some friends who now have tons of energy and are super fit. Since then, I've changed my eating habits, too. Everybody from my dad to my little nephew loves this riced cauliflower.

—Megan Schmoldt, Westminster, CO

Start to Finish: 30 min.
Makes: 4 servings

- 1 large head cauliflower
- 1 pound boneless skinless chicken breasts, cut into ½-inch cubes
- ½ teaspoon salt
- ½ teaspoon pepper
- 1 tablespoon canola oil
- 1 medium green pepper, chopped
- 1 small onion, chopped
- 1 garlic clove, minced
- ½ cup tomato juice
- ¼ teaspoon ground cumin
- ¼ cup chopped fresh cilantro
- 1 tablespoon lime juice

1. Core and cut cauliflower into 1-in. pieces. In batches, pulse cauliflower in a food processor until it resembles rice (do not overprocess).
2. Toss chicken with salt and pepper. In a large skillet, heat oil over medium-high heat; saute chicken until lightly browned, about 5 minutes. Add green pepper, onion and garlic; cook and stir 3 minutes.
3. Stir in tomato juice and cumin; bring to a boil. Add cauliflower; cook, covered, over medium heat until cauliflower is tender, 7-10 minutes, stirring occasionally. Stir in cilantro and lime juice.
Per 1½ cups: 227 cal., 7g fat (1g sat. fat), 63mg chol., 492mg sodium, 15g carb. (6g sugars, 5g fiber), 28g pro.
Diabetic Exchanges: 3 lean meat, 1 starch, ½ fat.

SOUTHWESTERN GOULASH

I had some extra cilantro in the fridge and didn't want to throw it away. Instead, I came up with a Southwest-inspired dish using ingredients I had on hand. The whole family loved it.

—Vikki Rebholz, West Chester, OH

Start to Finish: 25 min.
Makes: 6 servings

- 1 cup uncooked elbow macaroni
- 1 pound lean ground beef (90% lean)
- 1 medium onion, chopped
- 1 can (28 ounces) diced tomatoes, undrained
- 1 can (8 ounces) tomato sauce
- ⅔ cup frozen corn
- 1 can (4 ounces) chopped green chilies
- ½ teaspoon ground cumin
- ½ teaspoon pepper
- ¼ teaspoon salt
- ¼ cup minced fresh cilantro

1. Cook macaroni according to package directions; drain. Meanwhile, in a 6-qt. stockpot, cook and crumble beef with onion over medium heat until meat is no longer pink, 6-8 minutes; drain.
2. Stir in tomatoes, tomato sauce, corn, chilies and dry seasonings; bring to a boil. Reduce heat; simmer, uncovered, until flavors are blended, about 5 minutes. Stir in macaroni and cilantro.
Per 1⅓ cups: 224 cal., 6g fat (2g sat. fat), 37mg chol., 567mg sodium, 24g carb. (7g sugars, 4g fiber), 19g pro.
Diabetic Exchanges: 2 lean meat, 2 vegetable, 1 starch.

CHICKEN & SPANISH CAULIFLOWER "RICE"

FAST FIX

QUICK MOROCCAN SHRIMP SKILLET

When my niece was attending West Point, she was sent to Morocco for five months. I threw her a going-away party complete with Moroccan decorations, costumes and cuisine, including this saucy shrimp dish. Whenever I make it now, I think of her and I smile.
—Barbara Lento, Houston, PA

Start to Finish: 25 min.
Makes: 4 servings

- 1 tablespoon canola oil
- 1 small onion, chopped
- ¼ cup pine nuts
- 1 pound uncooked shrimp (16-20 per pound), peeled and deveined
- 1 cup uncooked pearl (Israeli) couscous
- 2 tablespoons lemon juice
- 3 teaspoons Moroccan seasoning (ras el hanout)
- 1 teaspoon garlic salt
- 2 cups hot water
  Minced fresh parsley, optional

1. In a large skillet, heat oil over medium-high heat; saute onion and pine nuts until onion is tender, 2-3 minutes. Stir in all remaining ingredients except parsley; bring just to a boil. Reduce heat; simmer, covered, until shrimp turn pink, about 4-6 minutes.
2. Remove from heat; let stand 5 minutes. If desired, top with parsley.
Per 1 cup: 335 cal., 11g fat (1g sat. fat), 138mg chol., 626mg sodium, 34g carb. (1g sugars, 1g fiber), 24g pro.

EAT SMART **FAST FIX**

CHICKEN ARTICHOKE SKILLET

This simple chicken recipe shows off some of my favorite Greek flavors. I like to change up the olives every and now and then—Greek, green, black or a mixture.
—Carol Latimore, Arvada, CO

Start to Finish: 25 min.
Makes: 4 servings

- 4 boneless skinless chicken breast halves (4 ounces each)
- ¼ teaspoon salt
- ¼ teaspoon pepper
- 2 teaspoons olive oil
- 1 can (14 ounces) water-packed quartered artichoke hearts, rinsed and drained
- ⅔ cup reduced-sodium chicken broth
- ¼ cup halved pimiento-stuffed olives
- ¼ cup halved pitted Greek olives
- 2 tablespoons minced fresh oregano or 2 teaspoons dried oregano
- 1 tablespoon lemon juice

1. Sprinkle chicken with salt and pepper. In a large skillet, heat oil over medium-high heat; brown chicken on both sides.
2. Add remaining ingredients; bring to a boil. Reduce heat; simmer, covered, until a thermometer inserted in chicken reads 165°, 4-5 minutes.
Per serving: 225 cal., 9g fat (1g sat. fat), 63mg chol., 864mg sodium, 9g carb. (0 sugars, 0 fiber), 26g pro.
Diabetic Exchanges: 3 lean meat, 1 vegetable.

BASIL PORK CHOPS

Just a few ingredients give these tender chops all the glazed goodness they need. Serve with your favorite roasted veggies.
—Lisa Gilliland, Fort Collins, CO

Start to Finish: 25 min.
Makes: 4 servings

- ¼ cup packed brown sugar
- 1½ teaspoons dried basil
- ½ teaspoon salt
- ½ teaspoon chili powder
- 2 tablespoons canola oil, divided
- 4 boneless pork loin chops (½ inch thick and 4 ounces each)

1. Mix first four ingredients; gradually stir in 1 tablespoon oil (mixture will be crumbly). Rub over both sides of the pork chops.
2. In a large skillet, heat the remaining oil over medium heat; cook the chops until a thermometer reads 145°, 4-6 minutes per side. Let stand 5 minutes before serving.

Per pork chop: 152 cal., 8g fat (1g sat. fat), 14mg chol., 312mg sodium, 14g carb. (13g sugars, 0 fiber), 6g pro.

TORTILLA CRUNCH TURKEY CUTLETS

I was inspired to create some more Southwestern-flavored foods by our many travels there. This is a great way to use leftover chips and salsa. Substitute chicken cutlets for turkey if you like.
—Lisa Varner, El Paso, TX

Start to Finish: 25 min.
Makes: 4 servings

- 2 large eggs
- 2 tablespoons water
- 3 teaspoons ground cumin
- 1 teaspoon garlic salt
- ½ teaspoon pepper
- 1¾ cups crushed tortilla chips
- 1 package (17.6 ounces) turkey breast cutlets
- 2 tablespoons canola oil
- ½ cup pico de gallo
  Sour cream and chopped fresh cilantro, optional

1. In a shallow bowl, whisk together first five ingredients. Place crushed chips in another shallow bowl. Dip cutlets in the egg mixture, then in the chips, pressing to help adhere.
2. In a large skillet, heat oil over medium-high heat. In batches, cook cutlets until golden brown, 2-3 minutes per side. Serve with pico de gallo and, if desired, sour cream and cilantro.

Per serving: 343 cal., 15g fat (2g sat. fat), 136mg chol., 603mg sodium, 17g carb. (1g sugars, 1g fiber), 34g pro.

✳
TEST KITCHEN TIP

A thrifty option to purchased garlic salt is to make your own: Just mix 1 teaspoon of garlic powder with 3 teaspoons of table salt or other fine-grained salt. The ratio works the same for onion salt, too.

TORTILLA CRUNCH TURKEY CUTLETS

SOUTHWESTERN FISH TACOS

CHICKEN WITH WHITE WINE SAUCE

My daughter calls this chicken dish with crunchy almonds "my favorite company recipe" because I love serving it to friends coming to dinner for the first time. They've always been impressed!
—Coralee Humphreys, New Hartford, NY

Start to Finish: 25 min.
Makes: 4 servings

- 1 teaspoon plus 2 tablespoons butter, divided
- ½ cup sliced almonds
- 2 tablespoons all-purpose flour
- ¾ teaspoon salt
- ½ teaspoon poultry seasoning
- ½ teaspoon pepper
- 4 boneless skinless chicken breast halves (6 ounces each)
- ½ cup white wine or reduced-sodium chicken broth

1. In a large skillet, melt 1 teaspoon butter over medium-high heat; saute almonds until lightly browned, 2-3 minutes. Remove from pan.
2. In a shallow bowl, mix the flour and seasonings. Dip chicken in mixture to coat lightly. In same pan, heat remaining butter over medium heat; cook chicken, covered, until browned, 3-4 minutes per side.
3. Add wine; bring to a boil. Reduce heat; simmer, covered, until a thermometer inserted in chicken reads 165°, about 4-6 minutes. Sprinkle with almonds.
Per serving: 344 cal., 16g fat (6g sat. fat), 112mg chol., 579mg sodium, 6g carb. (1g sugars, 2g fiber), 37g pro.

SOUTHWESTERN FISH TACOS

These bright tacos take me on an instant trip to sunny Southern California. This recipe has been on my family's most requested list for years.
—Joan Hallford, North Richland Hills, TX

Start to Finish: 20 min.
Makes: 2 servings

- ¼ cup mayonnaise
- ¼ cup sour cream
- 2 tablespoons minced fresh cilantro
- 4 teaspoons taco seasoning, divided
- ½ pound cod or haddock fillets, cut into 1-inch pieces
- 1 tablespoon lemon juice
- 1 tablespoon canola oil
- 4 taco shells
  Optional ingredients: shredded lettuce, chopped tomato and lime wedges

1. For sauce, mix mayonnaise, sour cream, cilantro and 2 teaspoons taco seasoning. In another bowl, toss cod with lemon juice and remaining taco seasoning.
2. In a skillet, heat oil over medium-high heat; saute cod just until it begins to flake easily with a fork, 4-6 minutes (fish may break apart as it cooks). Spoon into taco shells; serve with sauce and remaining ingredients as desired.
Per 2 tacos: 506 cal., 38g fat (8g sat. fat), 52mg chol., 852mg sodium, 20g carb. (1g sugars, 1g fiber), 20g pro.
HEALTH TIP Making a simple switch to reduced-fat mayo and sour cream in the sauce saves more than 100 calories and 10g fat.

FAST FIX ▶

TURKEY LINGUINE WITH TOMATO CREAM SAUCE

I love an easy weeknight meal! This meal comes together quickly and uses up that half block of cream cheese that ends up in the fridge.
—Amy Lents, Grand Forks, ND

Start to Finish: 30 min.
Makes: 6 servings

- ½ pound thick-sliced bacon strips, chopped
- 1 pound ground turkey
- 1 medium onion, chopped
- 2 garlic cloves, minced
- 1 carton (32 ounces) unsalted chicken stock
- 2 cans (14½ ounces each) diced tomatoes with basil, oregano and garlic, undrained
- ¼ teaspoon salt
- 12 ounces uncooked linguine
- 4 ounces cream cheese, cubed
- ½ cup chopped fresh parsley

1. In a Dutch oven, cook bacon over medium-high heat until crisp, stirring occasionally. Remove with a slotted spoon; drain on paper towels. Discard drippings.
2. In same pan, cook and crumble turkey with onion and garlic over medium-high heat until no longer pink, 5-7 minutes. Stir in stock, tomatoes and salt; bring to a boil. Stir in linguine and half of the bacon; bring to a boil. Reduce heat; simmer, covered, until linguine is al dente, 9-10 minutes.
3. Stir in cream cheese until melted; stir in parsley. Let stand 5 minutes. Sprinkle with remaining bacon.

Per 1⅓ cups: 510 cal., 18g fat (7g sat. fat), 79mg chol., 981mg sodium, 54g carb. (8g sugars, 5g fiber), 32g pro.

FAST FIX ▶

CREAMY RANCH MAC & CHEESE

I came up with the recipe for this creamy macaroni and cheese using a special ranch-flavored twist. My husband requests it often.
—Michelle Rotunno, Independence, MO

Start to Finish: 30 min.
Makes: 8 servings

- 1 package (16 ounces) elbow macaroni
- 1 cup 2% milk
- 2 tablespoons butter
- 4½ teaspoons ranch salad dressing mix
- 1 teaspoon garlic pepper blend
- 1 teaspoon lemon-pepper seasoning
- ½ teaspoon garlic powder
- 1 cup shredded Monterey Jack cheese
- 1 cup shredded Colby cheese
- 1 cup (8 ounces) reduced-fat sour cream
- ½ cup crushed saltines
- ⅓ cup grated Parmesan cheese

1. Cook macaroni according to package directions. Meanwhile, in a Dutch oven, combine the milk, butter, dressing mix and seasonings; heat through. Stir in Monterey Jack and Colby cheeses until melted. Stir in sour cream.
2. Drain the macaroni; stir into the cheese sauce with the crushed saltines. Sprinkle with Parmesan cheese.

Per cup: 433 cal., 17g fat (10g sat. fat), 49mg chol., 766mg sodium, 51g carb. (6g sugars, 2g fiber), 19g pro.

TURKEY LINGUINE WITH TOMATO CREAM SAUCE

FAST FIX

GINGER BEEF STIR-FRY

This stir-fry showcases tender slices of beef, while colorful carrots add crunch. For devoted meat-and-potatoes fans, replace the rice with mashed potatoes.
—*Taste of Home* Test Kitchen

Start to Finish: 25 min.
Makes: 4 servings

- 1 tablespoon plus 2 teaspoons cornstarch, divided
- 2 tablespoons water
- ¼ teaspoon salt
- 1½ pounds beef top sirloin steak, cut into ¼-inch-thick strips
- 1 cup beef broth
- 2 tablespoons soy sauce
- 4 teaspoons sugar
- 2 teaspoons grated orange peel
- 6 teaspoons canola oil, divided
- 2 medium carrots, diagonally cut into thin slices
- 1 tablespoon minced fresh gingerroot
- 2 garlic cloves, minced
- ½ teaspoon crushed red pepper flakes, optional
  Hot cooked rice

1. Mix 1 tablespoon cornstarch, water and salt; toss with beef. In a small bowl, mix broth, soy sauce, sugar, orange peel and remaining cornstarch until smooth.
2. In a large skillet, heat 2 teaspoons oil over medium-high heat; stir-fry half of the beef until browned, 2-3 minutes. Remove from the pan. Repeat with an additional 2 teaspoons oil and the remaining beef.
3. Stir-fry carrots in the remaining oil for 2 minutes. Add the ginger, garlic and, if desired, pepper flakes; cook and stir until fragrant, about 30 seconds. Stir broth mixture and add to pan; bring to a boil. Cook and stir until slightly thickened. Stir in beef; heat through. Serve with rice.
Per cup beef mixture: 334 cal., 14g fat (3g sat. fat), 69mg chol., 928mg sodium, 11g carb. (6g sugars, 1g fiber), 38g pro.

MAPLE-DIJON CHICKEN

EAT SMART **FAST FIX**

MAPLE-DIJON CHICKEN

Eating dinner as a family every night is really important to us, and this recipe is one that we all love. It's our favorite skillet chicken dish.
—Courtney Stultz, Weir, KS

Start to Finish: 30 min.
Makes: 4 servings

- 1 pound boneless skinless chicken breasts, cut into 1-inch-thick strips
- ½ teaspoon dried rosemary, crushed
- ½ teaspoon dried thyme
- ½ teaspoon pepper
- ¼ teaspoon salt
- 1 tablespoon coconut oil or olive oil
- ½ cup chopped onion
- 1 garlic clove, minced
- ⅓ cup Dijon mustard
- 3 tablespoons maple syrup

Toss chicken with seasonings. In a large skillet, heat oil over medium heat; saute chicken 10 minutes. Add onion and garlic; cook and stir 5 minutes. Stir in mustard and syrup; cook and stir until sauce is caramelized and chicken is no longer pink, 5-7 minutes.
Per serving: 221 cal., 6g fat (4g sat. fat), 63mg chol., 684mg sodium, 13g carb. (10g sugars, 1g fiber), 23g pro.
Diabetic Exchanges: 3 lean meat, 1 starch, ½ fat.

HERBED LEMON PORK CHOPS

You'll receive plenty of compliments on these tender and juicy pork chops. Mixed herbs and a final squeeze of lemon pack on the flavor in just 20 minutes!
—Billi Jo Sylvester, New Smyrna Beach, FL

Start to Finish: 20 min.
Makes: 2 servings

- 1 teaspoon salt-free garlic seasoning blend
- ½ teaspoon dried basil
- ½ teaspoon dried oregano
- ½ teaspoon dried parsley flakes
- ¼ teaspoon salt
- ¼ teaspoon garlic powder
- ¼ teaspoon dried rosemary, crushed
- 2 bone-in pork loin chops (6 ounces each)
- 1 teaspoon olive oil
- 1 tablespoon lemon juice

1. Mix seasonings; rub over both sides of chops. In a large nonstick skillet, heat oil over medium-high heat. Add the pork; cook until a thermometer reads 145°, 5-8 minutes per side.
2. Remove from heat; drizzle with lemon juice. Let it stand, covered, for 2 minutes before serving.
Per pork chop: 200 cal., 10g fat (3g sat. fat), 74mg chol., 350mg sodium, 1g carb. (0 sugars, 0 fiber), 26g pro.
Diabetic Exchanges: 4 lean meat, ½ fat.

HERBED LEMON PORK CHOPS

SWEET POTATO & TURKEY COUSCOUS

After the feast, we always have leftover turkey and sweet potatoes. I put them together in this quick, easy and nutritious main dish that satisfies with a simple green salad alongside.
—Roxanne Chan, Albany, CA

Start to Finish: 30 min.
Makes: 6 servings

- 1 pound sweet potatoes (about 2 medium), peeled and cut into ¾-inch cubes
- 1 tablespoon canola oil
- 1 package (8.8 ounces) uncooked pearl (Israeli) couscous
- ¼ cup chopped onion
- ¼ cup chopped celery
- ½ teaspoon poultry seasoning
- ½ teaspoon salt
- ½ teaspoon pepper
- 2 cans (14½ ounces each) chicken broth
- 2 cups chopped cooked turkey
- ¼ cup dried cranberries
- 1 teaspoon grated orange peel
  Chopped fresh parsley

1. Place sweet potatoes in a saucepan; add water to cover. Bring to a boil. Reduce heat; cook, uncovered, until tender, about 8-10 minutes. Drain.
2. Meanwhile, in a large skillet, heat oil over medium-high heat; saute couscous, onion and celery until couscous is lightly browned. Stir in seasonings and broth; bring to a boil. Reduce the heat; simmer, uncovered, until couscous is tender, about 10 minutes.
3. Stir in the turkey, cranberries, orange peel and potatoes; heat through. Sprinkle with parsley.
Per cup: 365 cal., 5g fat (1g sat. fat), 50mg chol., 848mg sodium, 59g carb. (13g sugars, 3g fiber), 21g pro.

FAST FIX ▶

GARLIC TILAPIA WITH MUSHROOM RISOTTO

Boxed risotto makes it quick; mushrooms, shallots and cheese make it tasty. Serve the risotto alongside seasoned fish for a healthy weeknight supper in a hurry.
—Lynn Moretti, Oconomowoc, WI

Start to Finish: 30 min.
Makes: 4 servings

- 1 package (5½ ounces) Parmesan risotto mix
- 1 cup sliced fresh mushrooms
- ¼ cup chopped shallots
- 1½ pounds tilapia fillets
- 1½ teaspoons seafood seasoning
- 4 tablespoons butter, divided
- 3 garlic cloves, sliced
- ¼ cup grated Parmesan cheese

1. Cook risotto according to package directions, adding mushrooms and shallots with the water.
2. Meanwhile, sprinkle tilapia with seafood seasoning. In a large nonstick skillet, heat 2 tablespoons butter over medium heat. In batches, cook tilapia with garlic until fish just begins to flake easily with a fork, about 5 minutes, turning the fillets halfway through.
3. Stir cheese and the remaining butter into risotto; remove from heat. Serve with tilapia.

Per serving: 1 serving: 432 cal., 18g fat (10g sat. fat), 118mg chol., 964mg sodium, 32g carb. (3g sugars, 1g fiber), 39g pro.

SHRIMP IN MANGO CHILI SAUCE

FAST FIX ▶

SHRIMP IN MANGO CHILI SAUCE

On-hand ingredients make a tasty shrimp entree in a matter of minutes! Try the shrimp over waffles or rice for another yummy option.
—Arlene Erlbach, Morton Grove, IL

Start to Finish: 30 min.
Makes: 4 servings

- ¾ cup frozen mango chunks
- ¾ cup chili sauce
- ¼ cup orange marmalade
- 3 tablespoons coconut milk
- 1 tablespoon lime juice
- 1 pound uncooked shrimp (31-40 per pound), peeled and deveined
- 2 green onions, chopped
- ⅓ cup coarsely chopped fresh cilantro
- ¼ cup chopped cashews
  Additional cilantro
  Warm corn bread, optional

1. Place first five ingredients in a large skillet; bring to a boil over medium heat, stirring frequently. Add shrimp and green onions; return to a boil. Reduce heat; simmer, uncovered, until shrimp turn pink, 6-8 minutes, stirring occasionally. Stir in ⅓ cup cilantro.
2. Sprinkle with cashews and additional cilantro. If desired, serve with corn bread.

Per ¾ cup shrimp mixture: 283 cal., 7g fat (3g sat. fat), 138mg chol., 895mg sodium, 36g carb. (27g sugars, 1g fiber), 20g pro.

EAT SMART **FAST FIX** ▶

CARAMELIZED PORK SLICES

This easy treatment for pork caught my eye when I was paging through a cookbook. The slightly sweet glaze is yummy. I like to serve this over noodles or rice...or with mashed potatoes.
—Elisa Lochridge, Beaverton, OR

Start to Finish: 25 min.
Makes: 4 servings

- 1 pork tenderloin (1 pound)
- 2 teaspoons canola oil, divided
- 2 garlic cloves, minced
- 2 tablespoons brown sugar
- 1 tablespoon orange juice
- 1 tablespoon molasses
- ½ teaspoon salt
- ¼ teaspoon pepper

1. Cut tenderloin into eight slices; pound each with a meat mallet to ½-in. thickness. In a nonstick skillet, heat 1 teaspoon oil over medium-high heat; brown pork on both sides. Remove from pan.

2. In same skillet, heat remaining oil over medium-high heat; saute garlic 1 minute. Stir in remaining ingredients. Add pork, turning to coat; cook, uncovered, until a thermometer reads 145°, 3-4 minutes. Let stand 5 minutes before serving.

Per 2 pork slices: 198 cal., 6g fat (2g sat. fat), 64mg chol., 344mg sodium, 12g carb. (11g sugars, 0 fiber), 23g pro.
Diabetic Exchanges: 3 lean meat, ½ starch.

CARAMELIZED PORK SLICES

EAT SMART **FAST FIX** ▶

ONE-POT STUFFED PEPPER DINNER

With its chili-like consistency and plenty of stuffed-pepper flavor, this dish will warm you up on chilly days.
—Charlotte Smith, McDonald, PA

Start to Finish: 30 min.
Makes: 4 servings

- 1 pound lean ground beef (90% lean)
- 3 medium green peppers, chopped (about 3 cups)
- 3 garlic cloves, minced
- 2 cans (14½ ounces each) Italian diced tomatoes, undrained
- 2 cups water
- 1 can (6 ounces) tomato paste
- 2 tablespoons shredded Parmesan cheese
- ¼ teaspoon pepper
- 1 cup uncooked instant rice

1. In a Dutch oven, cook and crumble beef with green peppers and garlic over medium-high heat until no longer pink and peppers are tender, 5-7 minutes; drain.

2. Stir in tomatoes, water, tomato paste, 2 tablespoons cheese and pepper; bring to a boil. Stir in rice; remove from heat. Let stand, covered, 5 minutes.

Per 2 cups: 415 cal., 10g fat (4g sat. fat), 72mg chol., 790mg sodium, 51g carb. (20g sugars, 5g fiber), 30g pro.
Diabetic Exchanges: 3 starch, 3 lean meat.

SAVORY BEER PORK CHOPS

(5)INGREDIENTS **FAST FIX**
SAVORY BEER PORK CHOPS

These tender chops in sauce are perfect for a hectic weeknight because they're so easy to prep and use only five ingredients! Try them with buttery noodles.
—Jana Christian, Farson, WY

Start to Finish: 20 min.
Makes: 4 servings

- 4 boneless pork loin chops (4 ounces each)
- ½ teaspoon salt
- ½ teaspoon pepper
- 1 tablespoon canola oil
- 3 tablespoons ketchup
- 2 tablespoons brown sugar
- ¾ cup beer or nonalcoholic beer

1. Sprinkle pork chops with salt and pepper. In a large skillet, heat oil over medium heat; brown chops on both sides.
2. Mix ketchup, brown sugar and beer; pour over chops. Bring to a boil. Reduce the heat; simmer, uncovered, until a thermometer inserted in pork reads 145°, 4-6 minutes. Let stand for 5 minutes before serving.
Per pork chop: 239 cal., 10g fat (3g sat. fat), 55mg chol., 472mg sodium, 11g carb. (11g sugars, 0 fiber), 22g pro.
Diabetic Exchanges: 3 lean meat, 1 fat, ½ starch.

EAT SMART **FAST FIX**
TILAPIA WITH LEMON CAPER SAUCE

My husband and I are always trying to increase the amount of fish in our diet. This recipe is fast, easy and enjoyable, even for non-fish lovers.
—Catherine Jensen, Blytheville, AR

Start to Finish: 25 min.
Makes: 4 servings

- 4 tilapia fillets (6 ounces each)
- ½ teaspoon salt
- ¼ teaspoon pepper
- 1 tablespoon all-purpose flour
- 1 tablespoon olive oil
- ½ cup reduced-sodium chicken broth
- 2 tablespoons lemon juice
- 1 tablespoon butter
- 1 tablespoon drained capers
  Lemon wedges, optional
  Hot cooked pasta, optional

1. Sprinkle tilapia with salt and pepper. Dust lightly with flour.
2. Using a large skillet, heat the oil over medium heat. Add tilapia; cook until lightly browned and fish just begins to flake easily with a fork, 3-5 minutes per side. Remove from pan; keep warm.
3. Add broth, lemon juice, butter and capers to same skillet; cook and stir until mixture is reduced by half, about 5 minutes. Spoon over tilapia. If desired, serve with pasta and lemon wedges.
Per fillet with 1 tablespoon sauce: 207 cal., 8g fat (3g sat. fat), 90mg chol., 500mg sodium, 2g carb. (0 sugars, 0 fiber), 32g pro.
Diabetic Exchanges: 5 lean meat, ½ fat.

GNOCCHI WITH PESTO SAUCE

Perk up gnocchi and vegetables with a flavorful pesto sauce. If you don't have pine nuts for the pesto, substitute any nut you like.
—*Taste of Home* Test Kitchen

Start to Finish: 25 min.
Makes: 4 servings

- 1 package (16 ounces) potato gnocchi
- 2 teaspoons olive oil
- 1 cup diced zucchini
- ½ cup chopped sweet yellow pepper
- ¼ cup prepared pesto
- 1 cup chopped tomatoes
   Toasted pine nuts, optional

1. Cook gnocchi according to package directions; drain.
2. Meanwhile, in a large skillet, heat oil over medium-high heat; saute zucchini and pepper until zucchini is tender.
3. Add pesto and gnocchi, stirring gently to coat. Stir in tomatoes. If desired, top with pine nuts.
Note: Look for potato gnocchi in the pasta or frozen foods section.
Per cup: 327 cal., 9g fat (2g sat. fat), 8mg chol., 682mg sodium, 52g carb. (10g sugars, 4g fiber), 9g pro.

ASIAN BEEF & NOODLES

I created this noodle dish on a whim to feed my hungry teenagers. It has since become a dinnertime staple. Two of my grandchildren now make it in their own kitchens.
—Judy Batson, Tampa, FL

Start to Finish: 25 min.
Makes: 4 servings

- 1 beef top sirloin steak (1 pound), cut into ¼-inch-thick strips
- 6 tablespoons reduced-sodium teriyaki sauce, divided
- 8 ounces uncooked whole grain thin spaghetti
- 2 tablespoons canola oil, divided
- 3 cups broccoli coleslaw mix
- 1 medium onion, halved and thinly sliced
   Chopped fresh cilantro, optional

1. Toss beef with 2 tablespoons teriyaki sauce. Cook the spaghetti according to package directions; drain.
2. In a large skillet, heat 1 tablespoon oil over medium-high heat; stir-fry beef until browned, 1-3 minutes. Remove from pan.
3. In same skillet, heat remaining oil over medium-high heat; stir-fry coleslaw mix and onion until crisp-tender, 3-5 minutes.

Add spaghetti and remaining teriyaki sauce; toss and heat through. Stir in beef. If desired, sprinkle with cilantro.
Per 2 cups: 462 cal., 13g fat (2g sat. fat), 46mg chol., 546mg sodium, 52g carb. (9g sugars, 8g fiber), 35g pro.

SPICY CAJUN SAUSAGE & RICE SKILLET

I created this easy skillet dish to use up the boil-in-a-bag rice in my cabinet. The result packs a lot of flavor.
—Sonali Ruder, New York, NY

Start to Finish: 30 min.
Makes: 4 servings

- 1 package (16 ounces) hot lean turkey breakfast sausage
- 1 large onion, chopped
- 1 medium green pepper, chopped
- 1 can (14½ ounces) diced tomatoes with garlic and onion, undrained
- 1 can (14½ ounces) reduced-sodium chicken broth
- 3 teaspoons Cajun seasoning
- ¼ teaspoon pepper
- 2 bags boil-in-bag white rice
   Louisiana-style hot sauce, optional

1. In a large nonstick skillet, cook and crumble sausage with onion and pepper over medium-high heat until no longer pink, 5-7 minutes.
2. Stir in tomatoes, broth, Cajun seasoning, pepper and contents of rice bags; bring to a boil. Reduce heat; simmer, covered, until liquid is absorbed and rice is tender, 8-10 minutes. If desired, serve with hot sauce.
Per 1½ cups: 461 cal., 12g fat (3g sat. fat), 122mg chol., 1816mg sodium, 52g carb. (6g sugars, 4g fiber), 35g pro.
HEALTH TIP Replace half of the sausage with lean ground turkey and use unsalted chicken broth to save almost 700mg sodium .

ASIAN BEEF & NOODLES

EAT SMART **FAST FIX** ▶

SPICY SHRIMP & PENNE PASTA

I created this creamy pasta when I needed to use up some marinara. Red pepper flakes give it a little heat, which my family loves. It's very versatile, so try it with chicken or stir in some fresh basil, too.
—Lorri Stout, Gaithersburg, MD

Start to Finish: 30 min.
Makes: 6 servings

- 3 cups uncooked penne pasta (about 12 ounces)
- 1 tablespoon butter, divided
- 1 tablespoon olive oil, divided
- 2 pounds uncooked shrimp (31-40 per pound), peeled and deveined, divided
- ½ teaspoon crushed red pepper flakes, divided
- 1 jar (24 ounces) marinara sauce
- ¾ cup half-and-half cream
- 4 cups chopped fresh spinach

1. In a 6-qt. stockpot, cook the pasta according to package directions; drain and return to pot.
2. In a large skillet, heat half of the butter and half of the oil over medium-high heat. Saute 1 pound shrimp with ¼ teaspoon pepper flakes until shrimp turns pink, 3-5 minutes; remove from pan. Repeat.
3. In same pan, heat marinara sauce and cream just to a boil over medium heat, stirring to blend. Stir in spinach until wilted; add to pasta. Stir in the shrimp; heat through.
Per 1⅔ cups: 395 cal., 12g fat (4g sat. fat), 206mg chol., 702mg sodium, 38g carb. (9g sugars, 4g fiber), 33g pro.
Diabetic Exchanges: 4 lean meat, 2 starch, 1 vegetable, 1 fat.

FAST FIX ▶

SAUSAGE COBB SALAD LETTUCE WRAPS

PICTURED ON P. 69
I substituted sausage for the bacon to make this lettuce roll-up your family and friends will adore. It's flavorful, crunchy and pretty on the plate.
—Devon Delaney, Westport, CT

Start to Finish: 25 min.
Makes: 6 servings

- ¾ cup ranch salad dressing
- ⅓ cup crumbled blue cheese
- ¼ cup watercress, chopped
- 1 pound bulk pork sausage
- 2 tablespoons minced fresh chives
- 6 large iceberg lettuce leaves, edges trimmed
- 1 medium ripe avocado, peeled and diced
- 4 hard-cooked large eggs, chopped
- 1 medium tomato, chopped

1. Mix the dressing, blue cheese and watercress. In a large skillet, cook and crumble sausage over medium heat until no longer pink, 5-7 minutes; drain. Stir in the chives.
2. To serve, spoon sausage into lettuce leaves. Top with avocado, eggs and tomato. Drizzle with dressing mixture.
Per serving: 433 cal., 38g fat (10g sat. fat), 174mg chol., 887mg sodium, 7g carb. (3g sugars, 3g fiber), 15g pro.

⑤ INGREDIENTS **FAST FIX** ▶

DIJON PORK CHOPS

A breadcrumb coating is all you need to turn pork chops into a wow-worthy family dinner. Try the breading on chicken breasts, too.
—Chris Rentmeister, Ripon, WI

Start to Finish: 30 min.
Makes: 6 servings

- 3 tablespoons Dijon mustard
- 6 boneless pork loin chops (8 ounces each and ¾ inch thick)
- ⅓ cup seasoned bread crumbs
  Dash pepper

1. Preheat oven to 375°. Spread mustard onto both sides of pork chops; place on a greased baking sheet. Mix bread crumbs with pepper; press onto chops.

2. Bake until lightly browned and a thermometer reads 145°, 20-25 minutes. Let stand 5 minutes before serving.
Per pork chop: 334 cal., 13g fat (5g sat. fat), 109mg chol., 347mg sodium, 4g carb. (0 sugars, 0 fiber), 44g pro.
HEALTH TIP If you're watching your calories, use 4- or 6-ounce chops and start checking whether they are done after just 15 minutes. You'll save 75-150 calories per serving.

FAST FIX ▶

SKILLET STEAK SUPPER

With all of the ingredients cooked in one skillet, this steak couldn't be quicker to prepare, or easier to clean up. The wine and mushroom sauce make it special.
—Sandra Fisher, Missoula, MT

Start to Finish: 20 min.
Makes: 2 servings

- 1 beef top sirloin steak (¾ pound)
- ½ teaspoon salt, divided
- ½ teaspoon pepper, divided
- 1 tablespoon olive oil
- 1 to 2 tablespoons butter
- ½ pound sliced fresh mushrooms
- 2 tablespoons white wine or chicken broth
- 3 tablespoons chopped green onions
- 1 tablespoon Worcestershire sauce
- 1 teaspoon Dijon mustard

1. Sprinkle steak with ¼ teaspoon each salt and pepper. In a skillet, heat oil over medium-high heat; cook the steak to the desired doneness (for medium-rare, a thermometer should read 145°; medium, 160°), 6-7 minutes per side. Remove from pan; keep warm.
2. In same skillet, heat the butter over medium-high heat; saute mushrooms until tender. Stir in wine; bring to a boil, stirring to loosen browned bits from pan. Stir in green onions, Worcestershire sauce, mustard and the remaining salt and pepper. Cut steak in half; serve with mushroom mixture.
Per serving: 368 cal., 20g fat (7g sat. fat), 85mg chol., 915mg sodium, 6g carb. (3g sugars, 2g fiber), 40g pro.

SKILLET STEAK SUPPER

Casseroles & Oven Dishes

What's not to love about bubbly casseroles, roasted chicken, homey potpie and handy sheet-pan suppers? When the weather turns crisp, turn to these recipes to warm you up!

DINNER POPPERS

FAST FIX ▶
EGGPLANT FLATBREAD PIZZAS
PICTURED ON P. 105

I loved to make these back in my home cooking days. Now I'm a chef!
—Christine Wendland
Browns Mills, NJ

Start to Finish: 30 min.
Makes: 4 servings

  3 tablespoons olive oil, divided
2½ cups cubed eggplant (½ inch)
  1 small onion, halved and thinly sliced
  ½ teaspoon salt
  ⅛ teaspoon pepper
  1 garlic clove, minced
  2 naan flatbreads
  ½ cup part-skim ricotta cheese
  1 teaspoon dried oregano
  ½ cup roasted garlic tomato sauce
  ½ cup loosely packed basil leaves
  1 cup shredded part-skim mozzarella cheese
  2 tablespoons grated Parmesan cheese
    Sliced fresh basil, optional

1. Preheat oven to 400°. In a large skillet, heat 1 tablespoon oil over medium-high heat; saute eggplant and onion with salt and pepper until the eggplant begins to soften, 4-5 minutes. Stir in garlic; remove from heat.
2. Place naan on a baking sheet. Spread with ricotta cheese; sprinkle with oregano. Spread with tomato sauce. Top with eggplant mixture and whole basil leaves. Sprinkle with mozzarella and Parmesan cheeses; drizzle top with the remaining oil.
3. Bake until crust is golden brown and cheese is melted, 12-15 minutes. If desired, top with sliced basil.
Per ½ pizza: 340 cal., 21g fat (7g sat. fat), 32mg chol., 996mg sodium, 25g carb. (5g sugars, 3g fiber), 14g pro.

DID YOU KNOW?
Naan flatbreads are tasty and durable, making them a great instant pizza crust. The breads are traditionally made using sourdough starter, and they're cooked by slapping each disk of dough against the wall of a hot tandoor oven. This gives the naan tiny charred bits and a slightly smoky taste.

DINNER POPPERS

I could eat jalapeno poppers all day long, but who wants to admit they had seven stuffed peppers for dinner? For this meal-in-one, I use poblanos for my husband and son and hotter peppers for my daughter and me.
—Sherri Jerzyk, tucson, AZ

Prep: 20 min. • **Bake:** 25 min.
Makes: 4 servings

    4 bacon strips
    4 chicken tenderloins
    ¼ teaspoon salt
    ⅛ teaspoon pepper
    2 teaspoons canola oil
    4 poblano peppers
  1½ cups shredded cheddar cheese, divided
    4 ounces cream cheese, cut into four strips

1. Preheat oven to 350°. In a large skillet, cook bacon over medium heat until partially cooked but not crisp. Remove to paper towels to drain.
2. Sprinkle chicken with salt and pepper. In a skillet, heat oil over medium-high heat; brown tenderloins on both sides. Cool slightly.
3. Carefully cut a slit down the side of each pepper and remove seeds. Fill each with a tenderloin and top with 2 tablespoons cheese and a strip of cream cheese. Close peppers; wrap with bacon and secure with toothpicks.
4. Place on a foil-lined baking sheet, slit side up. Top with remaining cheddar cheese; bake until browned and peppers are tender, 25-30 minutes. Remove toothpicks before serving.
Note: Wear disposable gloves when cutting hot peppers; the oils can burn skin. Avoid touching your face.
Per serving: 389 cal., 30g fat (15g sat. fat), 96mg chol., 682mg sodium, 9g carb. (4g sugars, 2g fiber), 23g pro.

SAGE CHICKEN CORDON BLEU

This savory chicken dish is an elegant surprise for the family during the week. I usually double the recipe so we can enjoy leftovers the next day.
—Martha Stine, Johnstown, PA

Prep: 20 min. • **Bake:** 40 min.
Makes: 6 servings

- 6 boneless skinless chicken breast halves (4 ounces each)
- ½ to ¾ teaspoon rubbed sage
- 6 slices thinly sliced deli ham
- 6 slices part-skim mozzarella cheese, halved
- 1 medium tomato, seeded and chopped
- ⅓ cup dry bread crumbs
- 2 tablespoons grated Parmesan cheese
- 2 tablespoons minced fresh parsley
- 4 tablespoons butter, divided

1. Preheat oven to 350°. Pound chicken breasts with a meat mallet to ⅛-in. thickness; sprinkle with sage. Place the ham, mozzarella cheese and tomato down the center of each; roll up chicken from a long side, tucking in ends. Secure with toothpicks.

2. In a shallow bowl, toss bread crumbs with Parmesan cheese and parsley. In a shallow microwave-safe dish, microwave 3 tablespoons butter until melted. Dip chicken in butter, then roll in the crumb mixture. Place in a greased 11x7-in. baking dish, seam side down. Melt remaining butter; drizzle over top.

3. Bake, uncovered, until chicken is no longer pink, 40-45 minutes. Discard toothpicks before serving.

Per serving: 328 cal., 17g fat (9g sat. fat), 112mg chol., 575mg sodium, 8g carb. (2g sugars, 1g fiber), 35g pro.

GRILLED CHEESE & TOMATO SOUP BAKE

This casserole brings together two classic comfort foods: grilled cheese sandwiches and tomato soup. There's no need for hands to get messy dipping into a bowl of hot soup. Best of all, my picky-eater husband devours every bite.
—Megan Kuns, Perrysburg, OH

Prep: 25 min.
Bake: 25 min. + standing
Makes: 6 servings

- 3 ounces reduced-fat cream cheese
- 1½ teaspoons dried basil, divided
- 12 slices Italian, sourdough or rye bread (½ inch thick)
- 6 slices part-skim mozzarella cheese
- 6 tablespoons butter, softened
- ½ cup tomato paste
- 1 garlic clove, minced
- ¼ teaspoon salt
- ¼ teaspoon pepper
- 1¾ cups 2% milk
- 2 large eggs
- 1 cup shredded Italian cheese blend or part-skim mozzarella cheese

1. Preheat oven to 350°. In a small bowl, mix cream cheese and 1 teaspoon basil until blended; spread onto six bread slices. Top with mozzarella cheese and remaining bread. Spread outsides of sandwiches with butter. Arrange in a greased 13x9-in. baking dish.

2. In a small saucepan, combine tomato paste, garlic, salt, pepper and remaining basil; cook and stir over medium heat 1 minute. Gradually whisk in the milk; bring to a boil. Reduce heat; simmer, uncovered, for 4-5 minutes or until thickened, stirring frequently. Remove from the heat.

3. Whisk eggs in a large bowl; gradually whisk in a third of the milk mixture. Stir in remaining milk mixture; pour over sandwiches. Sprinkle with cheese blend.

4. Bake, uncovered, 25-30 minutes or until golden brown and cheese is melted. Let stand 10 minutes before serving.

Per serving: 485 cal., 29g fat (17g sat. fat), 137mg chol., 918mg sodium, 33g carb. (7g sugars, 2g fiber), 23g pro.

SAGE CHICKEN CORDON BLEU

CHILI CHICKEN
ENCHILADAS

CRUMB-TOPPED SALMON

Here in the Northwest, we love our salmon, especially my family of fishermen. Whenever they come home with the fresh-caught fish, this crisp, lemony recipe is one of my favorite ways to use it up.
—Perlene Hoekema, Lynden, WA

Start to Finish: 30 min.
Makes: 4 servings

- 1½ cups soft bread crumbs
- 2 tablespoons minced fresh parsley
- 1 tablespoon minced fresh thyme or 1 teaspoon dried thyme
- 2 garlic cloves, minced
- 1 teaspoon grated lemon peel
- ½ teaspoon salt
- ¼ teaspoon lemon-pepper seasoning
- ¼ teaspoon paprika
- 1 tablespoon butter, melted
- 4 salmon fillets (6 ounces each)

1. Preheat oven to 400°. In a bowl, combine first eight ingredients. Toss with melted butter.
2. Place salmon in a 15x10x1-in. pan coated with cooking spray. Top with crumb mixture, patting gently. Bake until golden brown and fish just begins to flake with a fork, 12-15 minutes.
Note: To make soft bread crumbs, tear bread into pieces and place in a food processor or blender. Cover and pulse until crumbs form. One slice of bread yields ½ to ¾ cup crumbs.
Per fillet: 339 cal., 19g fat (5g sat. fat), 93mg chol., 507mg sodium, 9g carb. (1g sugars, 1g fiber), 31g pro.
Diabetic Exchanges: 4 lean meat, 1 fat, ½ starch.

CHILI CHICKEN ENCHILADAS

This meal is a terrific way to use up leftover cooked chicken, and a wonderful pick-me-up to take to friends who need a little help.
—Alicia Johnson, Hillsboro, OR

Prep: 20 min. • **Bake:** 25 min.
Makes: 4 servings

- 2 tablespoons all-purpose flour
- ¼ teaspoon ground coriander
- ⅛ teaspoon pepper
- 1 cup chicken broth
- 1 tablespoon butter
- ¼ cup chopped onion
- 2 garlic cloves, minced
- 1 can (4 ounces) chopped green chilies
- 1 cup shredded Monterey Jack cheese, divided
- ½ cup sour cream
- 2 cups chopped cooked chicken
- 4 flour tortillas (8 inches)
  Optional toppings: chopped tomatoes, sliced ripe olives and sliced green onions

1. Preheat oven to 350°. Mix first four ingredients until smooth.
2. In a small saucepan, heat butter over medium-high heat; saute onion until tender. Add the garlic; cook and stir 1 minute. Stir in chilies and flour mixture. Bring to a boil; cook and stir until thickened, about 1-2 minutes. Remove from heat; stir in ½ cup cheese and sour cream until cheese is melted.
3. In a bowl, mix the chicken with ¾ cup sauce. Place ½ cup of mixture on each tortilla; roll up and place the tortillas in a greased 11x7-in. baking dish, seam side down. Top with remaining sauce. Bake, uncovered, 20 minutes. Sprinkle with remaining cheese; bake until cheese is melted, 5-10 minutes. If desired, serve with toppings.
Per enchilada: 514 cal., 26g fat (13g sat. fat), 103mg chol., 855mg sodium, 35g carb. (2g sugars, 2g fiber), 34g pro.
HEALTH TIP To make a healthier version of this casserole, use just ½ cup cheese, reduced-fat sour cream, white meat chicken and whole wheat tortillas.
Per lighter enchilada: 355 cal., 13g fat (6g sat. fat), 78mg chol., 660mg sodium, 30g carb. (3g sugars, 4g fiber), 31g pro.

FAST FIX ▶
CRESCENT TURKEY CASSEROLE

How do you make a dinner of turkey and vegetables appealing to kids? You turn it into a pie, of course! My version tastes classic, but won't take any time at all.
—Daniela Essman, Perham, MN

Start to Finish: 30 min.
Makes: 4 servings

- ½ cup mayonnaise
- 2 tablespoons all-purpose flour
- 1 teaspoon chicken bouillon granules
- ⅛ teaspoon pepper
- ¾ cup 2% milk
- 2 cups frozen mixed vegetables (about 10 ounces), thawed
- 1½ cups cubed cooked turkey breast
- 1 tube (4 ounces) refrigerated crescent rolls

1. Preheat oven to 375°. In a saucepan, mix first four ingredients until smooth; gradually stir in milk. Bring to a boil over medium heat; cook and stir until thickened, about 2 minutes. Add the vegetables and turkey; cook and stir until heated through. Transfer to a greased 8-in. square baking pan.
2. Unroll crescent dough and separate into eight triangles; arrange over turkey mixture. Bake until heated through and topping is golden brown, 15-20 minutes.

Per serving: 453 cal., 28g fat (6g sat. fat), 48mg chol., 671mg sodium, 26g carb. (7g sugars, 3g fiber), 22g pro.

Turkey Biscuit Potpie: Combine thawed vegetables with turkey breast, one 10¾-ounce can condensed cream of chicken soup and ¼ teaspoon dried thyme. Place in a deep-dish 9-in. pie plate. Mix 1 cup biscuit/baking mix, ½ cup milk and 1 egg; spoon over top. Bake at 400° for 25-30 minutes.

Turkey Asparagus Casserole: Thaw a 10-ounce package of frozen cut asparagus; combine with turkey breast, one 10¾-ounce can condensed cream of chicken soup and ¼ cup water. Bake at 350° for 30 minutes, topping with a 2.8-ounce can of french-fried onions during last 5 minutes.

CRESCENT TURKEY CASSEROLE

EAT SMART FAST FIX ▶
CIDER-GLAZED PORK TENDERLOIN

This is a super recipe full of sweet fall flavor. The kiss of maple flavor really shines through.
—Susan Stetzel, Gainesville, NY

Start to Finish: 30 min.
Makes: 4 servings

- 1 pork tenderloin (1 pound)
- ¼ teaspoon salt
- ½ teaspoon pepper, divided
- 1 tablespoon olive oil
- ¾ cup apple cider or juice
- ¼ cup maple syrup
- 2 tablespoons cider vinegar

1. Preheat oven to 425°. Cut tenderloin in half to fit skillet; sprinkle with salt and ¼ teaspoon pepper. In a large skillet, heat oil over medium-high heat; brown pork on all sides. Transfer to a 15x10x1-in. pan. Roast until a thermometer reads 145°, about 12-15 minutes.
2. Meanwhile, in same skillet, bring cider, syrup, vinegar and remaining pepper to a boil, stirring to loosen browned bits from pan. Cook, uncovered, until mixture is reduced to a glaze consistency, about 5 minutes.
3. Remove pork from oven; let stand 5 minutes before slicing. Serve with the glaze.

Per 3 ounces cooked pork with 1 tablespoon glaze: 239 cal., 7g fat (2g sat. fat), 64mg chol., 200mg sodium, 19g carb. (17g sugars, 0 fiber), 23g pro.
Diabetic Exchanges: 3 lean meat, 1 starch, 1 fat.

CASSOULET FOR TODAY

Per serving: 1 serving: 394 cal., 14g fat (4g sat. fat), 91mg chol., 736mg sodium, 29g carb. (4g sugars, 8g fiber), 33g pro.
Diabetic Exchanges: 4 lean meat, 2 starch, ½ fat.

HEALTH TIP Adding pulses such as cannellini beans to a meat-based main dish bumps up the fiber and protein without adding saturated fat.

FAST FIX ▶

SIMPLE HERBED SCALLOPS
PICTURED ON P. 105

In Kansas, fresh seafood can be hard to come by. Luckily, frozen scallops aren't. This dish offers coastal flavor to those of us in the Midwest.
—Sarah Befort, Hays, KS

Start to Finish: 30 min.
Makes: 2 servings

- ½ to ¾ pound sea scallops
- 3 tablespoons butter, divided
- ¾ teaspoon lemon juice
- 1 teaspoon minced fresh parsley or ¼ teaspoon dried parsley
- 1½ teaspoons minced fresh chives or ½ teaspoon dried chives
- ¼ teaspoon minced fresh tarragon or ⅛ teaspoon dried tarragon
- ⅛ teaspoon garlic salt
  Dash pepper
- 2 tablespoons dry bread crumbs

1. Preheat oven to 350°. Place scallops in a greased 1-qt. baking dish. Mix 2 tablespoons melted butter, lemon juice, herbs, garlic salt and pepper; drizzle over scallops.
2. Mix bread crumbs with remaining melted butter; sprinkle over top. Bake, uncovered, until scallops are firm and opaque, 20-25 minutes.

Per serving: 260 cal., 18g fat (11g sat. fat), 73mg chol., 754mg sodium, 9g carb. (1g sugars, 1g fiber), 15g pro.

DID YOU KNOW?

Farmed scallops are becoming more common. Because scallops are filter-feeders that live on plankton, they don't require as much feed. Their low environmental impact makes farmed scallops a green choice.

FREEZE IT

CASSOULET FOR TODAY

Traditionally cooked for hours, this version of the rustic French cassoulet offers the same homey taste in less time. It's easy on the wallet, too.
—Virginia Anthony, Jacksonville, FL

Prep: 45 min. • **Bake:** 50 min.
Makes: 6 servings

- 6 boneless skinless chicken thighs (about 1½ pounds)
- ¼ teaspoon salt
- ¼ teaspoon coarsely ground pepper
- 3 teaspoons olive oil, divided
- 1 large onion, chopped
- 1 garlic clove, minced
- ½ cup white wine or chicken broth
- 1 can (14½ ounces) diced tomatoes, drained
- 1 bay leaf
- 1 teaspoon minced fresh rosemary or ¼ teaspoon dried rosemary, crushed
- 1 teaspoon minced fresh thyme or ¼ teaspoon dried thyme
- 2 cans (15 ounces each) cannellini beans, rinsed and drained
- ¼ pound smoked turkey kielbasa, chopped
- 3 bacon strips, cooked and crumbled

TOPPING
- ½ cup soft whole wheat bread crumbs
- ¼ cup minced fresh parsley
- 1 garlic clove, minced

1. Preheat oven to 325°. Sprinkle chicken with salt and pepper. In a broiler-safe Dutch oven, heat 2 teaspoons oil over medium heat; brown chicken on both sides. Remove from pan.
2. In same pan, saute onion in remaining oil over medium heat until crisp-tender. Add garlic; cook 1 minute. Add wine; bring to a boil, stirring to loosen browned bits from the pan. Add tomatoes, herbs and chicken; return to a boil.
3. Transfer to oven; bake, covered, for 30 minutes. Stir in beans and kielbasa; bake, covered, until chicken is tender, 20-25 minutes.
4. Remove from oven; preheat broiler. Discard bay leaf; stir in bacon. Toss bread crumbs with parsley and garlic; sprinkle over top. Place in oven so surface of cassoulet is 4-5 in. from heat; broil until crumbs are golden brown, 2-3 minutes.
Note: To make soft bread crumbs, tear bread into pieces and place in a food processor or blender. Cover and pulse until crumbs form. One slice of bread yields ½ to ¾ cup crumbs.

ROAST PORK WITH APPLES & ONIONS

The sweetness of the apples and onions really complements the pork in this dish. With crisp skin and savory-sweet flavor, this is my family's favorite weekend dinner.
—Lily Julow, Lawrenceville, GA

Prep: 30 min. **Bake:** 45 min. + standing
Makes: 8 servings

- 1 boneless pork loin roast (2 pounds)
- ¼ teaspoon salt
- ¼ teaspoon pepper
- 1 tablespoon olive oil
- 3 large Golden Delicious apples, cut into 1-inch wedges
- 2 large onions, cut into ¾-inch wedges
- 5 garlic cloves, peeled
- 1 tablespoon minced fresh rosemary or 1 teaspoon dried rosemary, crushed

1. Preheat oven to 350°. Sprinkle roast with salt and pepper. In a large nonstick skillet, heat oil over medium heat; brown roast on all sides. Transfer to a roasting pan coated with cooking spray. Place apples, onions and garlic around roast; sprinkle with rosemary.
2. Roast until a thermometer inserted in pork reads 145°, 45-55 minutes, turning apples, onion and garlic once. Remove from oven; tent with foil. Let stand for 10 minutes before slicing roast. Serve with apple mixture.
Per serving: 210 cal., 7g fat (2g sat. fat), 57mg chol., 109mg sodium, 14g carb. (9g sugars, 2g fiber), 23g pro.
Diabetic Exchanges: 3 lean meat, 1 starch, ½ fat.

MINI SAUSAGE PIES

The simple ingredients and family-friendly flavor of these little sausage cups make them a go-to dinner favorite. Everyone gets their own pie, and that makes them even better!
—Kerry Dingwall, Ponte Vedra, FL

Prep: 35 min. • **Bake:** 30 min.
Makes: 6 servings

- 1 package (17.3 ounces) frozen puff pastry, thawed
- 1 pound bulk sage pork sausage
- 6 green onions, chopped
- ½ cup chopped dried apricots
- ¼ teaspoon pepper
- ⅛ teaspoon ground nutmeg
- 1 large egg, lightly beaten

1. Preheat oven to 375°. On a lightly floured surface, unfold pastry sheets; roll each into a 16x12-in. rectangle. Using a floured cutter, cut twelve 4-in. circles from one sheet; press onto bottom and up sides of ungreased muffin cups. Using a floured cutter, cut twelve 3½-in. circles from remaining sheet.
2. Mix sausage, green onions, apricots and spices lightly but thoroughly. Place ¼ cup mixture into each pastry cup. Brush edges of pastry circles with egg; place over pies, pressing edges to seal. Brush with egg. Cut slits in top.
3. Bake pies until golden brown and a thermometer inserted in filling reads 160°, 30-35 minutes. Cool 5 minutes before removing from pan to a wire rack.
Freeze option: Cool baked pies and freeze in freezer containers. To use, partially thaw pies in the refrigerator overnight. Reheat on a baking sheet in a preheated 350° oven until heated through, 14-17 minutes.
Per 2 mini pies: 551 cal., 36g fat (10g sat. fat), 82mg chol., 784mg sodium, 42g carb. (5g sugars, 5g fiber), 16g pro.

ROAST PORK WITH APPLES & ONIONS

Lovin' Lasagna

Zip through the prep with a little know-how from a Virginia reader (and a box of no-cook noodles). Blair Lonergan turns an Italian classic into absolute amore.

Build the Ultimate Lasagna

1. Sauce
Cook sausage and onion; drain. Add garlic and tomato paste; cook and stir 1 minute. Stir in tomatoes, tomato sauce, basil, ½ teaspoon pepper and the salt. Simmer until slightly thickened.

2. Filling
Spread 1½ cups of the sauce onto the bottom of a greased 13x9-in. dish. Mix the egg, ricotta, 1¼ cups Parmesan and remaining pepper.

3. Layers
Place four noodles over the sauce. Top with 1½ cups ricotta blend, 1½ cups mozzarella and 1½ cups sauce. Repeat the layers. Top with the remaining noodles, sauce and cheeses.

4. Finale
Cover the lasagna with greased foil. Bake at 400° for 30 minutes. Uncover and bake until cheese is golden. Let the lasagna stand 15 minutes, then dig in.

SAUSAGE LASAGNA

The idea for this sausage lasagna recipe comes from my mother-in-law, who always makes it for my three boys on special holidays. I've put a personal twist on Carole's classic dish, and it's become one of my go-to dinners as well!
—Blair Lonergan, Rochelle, VA

Prep: 45 min.
Bake: 35 min. + standing
Makes: 12 servings

- 1 pound bulk Italian sausage
- 1 medium onion, chopped
- 2 garlic cloves, minced
- 1 can (6 ounces) tomato paste
- 1 can (28 ounces) crushed tomatoes
- 1 can (8 ounces) tomato sauce
- 3 teaspoons dried basil
- ¾ teaspoon pepper, divided
- ¼ teaspoon salt
- 1 large egg, lightly beaten
- 1 carton (15 ounces) whole-milk ricotta cheese
- 1½ cups grated Parmesan cheese, divided
- 12 no-cook lasagna noodles
- 4 cups shredded part-skim mozzarella cheese

Per serving: 416 cal., 23g fat (11g sat. fat), 83mg chol., 978mg sodium, 29g carb. (8g sugars, 3g fiber), 25g pro.

GINGER SALMON WITH GREEN BEANS

I developed this flavor-packed dinner for a busy friend who wants to eat clean.
—Nicole Stevens, Mount Pleasant, SC

....

Start to Finish: 30 min.
Makes: 2 servings

- ¼ cup lemon juice
- 2 tablespoons rice vinegar
- 3 garlic cloves, minced
- 2 teaspoons minced fresh gingerroot
- 2 teaspoons honey
- ⅛ teaspoon salt
- ⅛ teaspoon pepper
- 2 salmon fillets (4 ounces each)
- 1 medium lemon, thinly sliced

GREEN BEANS
- ¾ pound fresh green beans, trimmed
- 2 tablespoons water
- 2 teaspoons olive oil
- ½ cup finely chopped onion
- 3 garlic cloves, minced
- ⅛ teaspoon salt

1. Preheat oven to 325°. Mix the first seven ingredients.
2. Place each salmon fillet on an 18x12-in. piece of heavy-duty foil; fold up edges of foil to create a rim around the fish. Spoon lemon juice mixture over salmon; top with lemon slices. Carefully fold the foil around the fish, sealing tightly.
3. Place packets in a 15x10x1-in. pan. Bake until fish just begins to flake easily with a fork, 15-20 minutes. Open foil carefully to allow steam to escape.
4. Meanwhile, place green beans, water and oil in a large skillet; bring to a boil. Reduce heat; simmer, covered, 5 minutes. Stir in remaining ingredients; cook, uncovered, until beans are crisp-tender, stirring occasionally. Serve with salmon.

Per serving: 357 cal., 15g fat (3g sat. fat), 57mg chol., 607mg sodium, 35g carb. (18g sugars, 8g fiber), 24g pro.
Diabetic Exchanges: 3 lean meat, 1 starch, 1 vegetable, 1 fat.

⑤ INGREDIENTS

STUFFED CHICKEN WITH MARINATED TOMATOES

I invented this roast chicken to prove that goat cheese really is delish. I served it to my skeptical family without telling them, and they gobbled it up.
—Gilda Lester, Millsboro, DE

....

Prep: 15 min. + marinating • **Bake:** 20 min
Makes: 4 servings

- 4 boneless skinless chicken breast halves (6 ounces each)
- ¾ cup Italian salad dressing, divided
- 1 log (4 ounces) fresh goat cheese
- ¼ teaspoon salt
- ⅛ teaspoon pepper
- 2 cups grape tomatoes, quartered
- ½ cup thinly sliced fresh basil

1. Cut a pocket horizontally in the thickest part of each chicken breast; place in a bowl. Toss with ¼ cup dressing; refrigerate, covered, about 30 minutes.
2. Preheat oven to 425°. Crumble goat cheese; reserve ½ cup cheese for serving. Divide remaining cheese among chicken pockets; secure with toothpicks. Place in a greased 15x10x1-in. pan; sprinkle with salt and pepper.
3. Roast until a thermometer inserted in chicken reads 165°, 20-25 minutes. Toss tomatoes with the remaining dressing; let stand while chicken is cooking.
4. Add basil to tomato mixture; serve over chicken. Top with remaining cheese.

Per serving: 334 cal., 14g fat (4g sat. fat), 113mg chol., 797mg sodium, 7g carb. (5g sugars, 1g fiber), 38g pro.

GINGER SALMON WITH GREEN BEANS

BROWN SUGAR-GLAZED SALMON

BROWN SUGAR-GLAZED SALMON

Pop these protein-packed salmon fillets in the oven before whipping up a sweet basting sauce. This tangy entree cooks up in minutes, making it a perfect meal for busy families or unexpected guests.
—Debra Martin, Belleville, MI

Start to Finish: 25 min.
Makes: 4 servings

- 1 salmon fillet (1 pound)
- ¼ teaspoon salt
- ¼ teaspoon pepper
- 3 tablespoons brown sugar
- 4 teaspoons Dijon mustard
- 1 tablespoon reduced-sodium soy sauce
- 1 teaspoon rice vinegar

1. Preheat oven to 425°. Cut salmon into four portions; place in a foil-lined 15x10x1-in. pan. Sprinkle with salt and pepper. Roast 10 minutes. Remove from oven; preheat broiler.

2. In a small saucepan, mix remaining ingredients; bring just to a boil. Brush over salmon. Broil 6 in. from heat until the salmon just begins to flake easily with a fork, 1-2 minutes.

Per 3 ounces cooked fish: 225 cal., 10g fat (2g sat. fat), 57mg chol., 491mg sodium, 11g carb. (10g sugars, 0 fiber), 19g pro.
Diabetic Exchanges: 3 lean meat, 1 starch.

CRANBERRY CHICKEN & WILD RICE

This chicken in sweet-tart cranberry sauce is so simple to prepare. I love that I can do other things while it bakes.
—Evelyn Lewis, Independence, MO

Prep: 10 min. • **Bake:** 35 min
Makes: 6 servings

- 6 boneless skinless chicken breast halves (4 ounces each)
- 1½ cups hot water
- 1 package (6.2 ounces) fast-cooking long grain and wild rice mix
- 1 can (14 ounces) whole-berry cranberry sauce
- 1 tablespoon lemon juice
- 1 tablespoon reduced-sodium soy sauce
- 1 tablespoon Worcestershire sauce

1. Preheat oven to 350°. Place chicken in a 13x9-in. baking dish coated with cooking spray. In a bowl, mix hot water, rice mix and contents of seasoning packet; pour around chicken.

2. In a small bowl, mix the remaining ingredients; pour over chicken. Bake, covered, until a thermometer inserted in chicken reads 165°, 35-45 minutes.

Per chicken breast half with ½ cup rice mixture: 332 cal., 3g fat (1g sat. fat), 63mg chol., 592mg sodium, 50g carb. (19g sugars, 2g fiber), 26g pro.

APPLE-ONION TENDERLOIN

This slightly sweet and tender pork roast is quick enough to make for a weeknight, but I often serve it for special occasions. It tastes amazing served with mashed potatoes or over egg noodles.
—Trisha Kruse, Eagle, ID

Start to Finish: 30 min.
Makes: 4 servings

- 2 tablespoons canola oil, divided
- 1 pork tenderloin (1 pound), cut in half
- 3 tablespoons honey mustard
- 2 medium apples, thinly sliced
- 1 large onion, halved and thinly sliced
- ½ cup white wine or apple cider
- ⅛ teaspoon salt
- ⅛ teaspoon pepper

1. Preheat oven to 425°. In an ovenproof skillet, heat 1 tablespoon oil over medium-high heat. Brown tenderloin halves on all sides; remove pan from heat. Spread pork with mustard; roast in the oven until a thermometer reads 145°, 15-20 minutes.
2. Meanwhile, in another skillet, heat remaining oil over medium heat; saute apples and onion 7 minutes. Stir in the wine; bring to a boil. Reduce heat; simmer, uncovered, until apples and onion are tender, 5-8 minutes. Stir in salt and pepper.
3. Remove pork from oven; let stand for 5 minutes before slicing. Serve with the apple mixture.

Per 3 ounces cooked pork with ½ cup apple mixture: 294 cal., 12g fat (2g sat. fat), 64mg chol., 218mg sodium, 20g carb. (13g sugars, 3g fiber), 24g pro.
Diabetic Exchanges: 3 lean meat, 1½ fat, ½ starch, ½ fruit.

BUFFALO CHICKEN BISCUITS

These spicy, savory muffins are always a hit at parties. We love them as a simple snack on game day, too.
—Jasmin Baron, Livonia, NY

Prep: 20 min. • **Bake:** 25 min.
Makes: 6 servings

- 3 cups chopped rotisserie chicken
- ¼ cup Louisiana-style hot sauce
- 2 cups biscuit/baking mix
- ¼ teaspoon celery seed
- ⅛ teaspoon pepper
- 1 large egg
- ½ cup 2% milk
- ¼ cup ranch salad dressing
- 1½ cups shredded Colby-Monterey Jack cheese, divided
- 2 green onions, thinly sliced
  Additional ranch dressing and hot sauce, optional

1. Preheat oven to 400°. Toss chicken with hot sauce. In large bowl, whisk together baking mix, celery seed and pepper. In another bowl, whisk together egg, milk and dressing; add to dry ingredients, stirring just until moistened. Fold in 1 cup cheese, green onions and chicken mixture.
2. Spoon into 12 greased muffin cups. Sprinkle with remaining cheese. Bake until a toothpick inserted in center comes out clean, 25-30 minutes.
3. Cool 5 minutes before removing from pan to a wire rack. Serve warm. If desired, serve with additional dressing and hot sauce. Refrigerate leftovers.

Per 2 muffins: 461 cal., 24g fat (10g sat. fat), 121mg chol., 1180mg sodium, 29g carb. (3g sugars, 1g fiber), 31g pro.

APPLE-ONION TENDERLOIN

FAST FIX ▶

BAKED SAUCY PORK CHOPS

These cozy pork chops have a thick, maple sauce that we can't get enough of. It's the recipe I reach for when I want to feel cozy on a chilly day.
—Dorothy Toben, Blackwell, OK

Start to Finish: 30 min.
Makes: 2 servings

- 2 tablespoons butter
- 2 bone-in pork loin chops (¾ inch thick)
- ¼ cup chopped onion
- ¼ cup maple syrup
- 2 tablespoons water
- 1 tablespoon cider vinegar
- 2 teaspoons Worcestershire sauce
- 1 teaspoon chili powder
- ¼ teaspoon salt
- ¼ teaspoon pepper
- ⅛ teaspoon garlic powder

1. Preheat oven to 350°. In a large skillet, heat butter over medium heat. Brown pork chops on both sides. Transfer to a greased 11x7-in. baking dish; sprinkle with chopped onion.
2. In a bowl, mix remaining ingredients; pour over chops. Bake, covered, until a thermometer reads 145°, 15-20 minutes. Let stand 5 minutes before serving.
Per pork chop: 442 cal., 19g fat (7g sat. fat), 111mg chol., 472mg sodium, 31g carb. (26g sugars, 1g fiber), 37g pro.

BACON-WRAPPED
PESTO PORK TENDERLOIN

⑤ INGREDIENTS

BACON-WRAPPED PESTO PORK TENDERLOIN

I love to serve this family-favorite tenderloin—maybe because of all the compliments that come with it! When the weather warms up, we grill it instead.
—Megan Riofski, Frankfort, IL

Prep: 30 min. • **Bake:** 20 min.
Makes: 4 servings

- 10 bacon strips
- 1 pork tenderloin (1 pound)
- ¼ teaspoon pepper
- ½ cup prepared pesto
- 1 cup shredded Italian cheese blend
- 1 cup fresh baby spinach

1. Preheat oven to 425°. Arrange bacon strips lengthwise in a foil-lined 15x10x1-in. pan, overlapping slightly.

2. Cut tenderloin lengthwise through the center to within ½ in. of bottom. Open tenderloin flat; cover with plastic wrap. Pound with a meat mallet to ½-in thickness. Remove wrap; place tenderloin on center of bacon, perpendicular to the strips.
3. Sprinkle pepper over pork. Spread with pesto; layer with cheese and spinach. Close the tenderloin; wrap with bacon, overlapping the ends. Tie with kitchen string at 3-in. intervals. Secure ends with toothpicks.
4. In a 12-in. skillet, brown roast on all sides, about 8 minutes. Return to baking pan; roast in oven until a thermometer inserted in pork reads 145°, 17-20 minutes. Remove string and toothpicks; let stand 5 minutes before slicing.
Per serving: 402 cal., 25g fat (9g sat. fat), 104mg chol., 864mg sodium, 4g carb. (1g sugars, 1g fiber), 37g pro.

BAKED MAC & CHEESE

Even people who have had their own macaroni and cheese recipe for years ask for mine when they taste this crumb-topped version. Here's a winning tip: Make it with extra-sharp white cheddar cheese for even more flavor.
—Shelby Thompson, Dover, DE

Prep: 15 min. • **Bake:** 30 min.
Makes: 8 servings

- 1 package (16 ounces) uncooked elbow macaroni
- ⅓ cup plus ¼ cup butter, divided
- ¾ cup finely chopped onion
- 6 tablespoons all-purpose flour
- 1 teaspoon ground mustard
- ¾ teaspoon salt
- ¼ teaspoon pepper
- 4½ cups 2% milk
- 4 cups (16 ounces) shredded sharp cheddar cheese
- ¾ cup dry bread crumbs

1. Preheat oven to 350°. Cook macaroni according to the package directions for al dente; drain.

2. In a Dutch oven, heat ⅓ cup butter over medium heat; saute onion until tender. Stir in flour and seasonings until blended; gradually stir in milk. Bring to a boil, stirring constantly; cook and stir until thickened. Stir in cheese until melted. Stir in macaroni. Transfer to a greased 13x9-in. baking dish.

3. In a microwave, melt remaining butter; toss with bread crumbs. Sprinkle over casserole. Bake, uncovered, until heated through, 30-35 minutes.

Per cup: 689 cal., 37g fat (22g sat. fat), 104mg chol., 834mg sodium, 62g carb. (10g sugars, 3g fiber), 28g pro.

CLASSIC CHICKEN POTPIE

Our neighbors are always after me to make these yummy potpies. That's all the encouragement I need, since we love them, too!
—Ada-May Smith, Citrus Springs, FL

Prep: 20 min. • **Bake:** 20 min. + standing
Makes: 8 servings

- 3 cups frozen mixed vegetables (about 16 ounces), thawed

- 2¼ cups cubed cooked chicken
- 1 cup frozen pearl onions, thawed
- 1 jar (4½ ounces) sliced mushrooms, drained
- ¼ cup butter
- ¼ cup all-purpose flour
- ¾ teaspoon dried thyme
- 1 can (14½ ounces) chicken broth
- 2 teaspoons chicken bouillon granules
  Pastry for single-crust pie (9 inches)

1. Preheat oven to 450°. In a greased deep 2½-qt. baking dish, combine first four ingredients.

2. In a small saucepan, melt butter over medium heat. Stir in flour and thyme until blended; gradually whisk in broth and bouillon. Bring to a boil, stirring constantly; cook and stir until thickened, about 2 minutes. Pour over vegetable mixture.

3. Roll pastry dough to fit top of dish; place over filling. Trim and flute edge. Cut slits in top. Bake until golden brown and filling is heated through, 18-20 minutes. Let stand 5 minutes before serving.

Pastry for single-crust pie (9 inches):
Combine 1¼ cups all-purpose flour and ¼ teaspoon salt; cut in ½ cup cold butter until crumbly. Gradually add 3-5 tablespoons ice water, tossing with a fork until dough holds together when pressed. Wrap in plastic and refrigerate for 1 hour.

Per serving: 363 cal., 21g fat (12g sat. fat), 82mg chol., 757mg sodium, 28g carb. (4g sugars, 4g fiber), 16g pro.

BAKED MAC & CHEESE

**LEMON-DIJON PORK
SHEET PAN SUPPER**

HERBED TURKEY BREAST

Like many of you, I always serve turkey for our family's Thanksgiving meal. But instead of roasting a whole bird, I opt for a turkey breast since most of us prefer white meat. The herb butter basting sauce keeps it so moist and tender.
—Ruby Williams, Bogalusa, LA

Prep: 10 min. • **Bake:** 1½ hours + standing
Makes: 12 servings

- ½ cup butter, cubed
- ¼ cup lemon juice
- 2 tablespoons reduced-sodium soy sauce
- 2 tablespoons finely chopped green onions
- 1 tablespoon rubbed sage
- 1 teaspoon dried thyme
- 1 teaspoon dried marjoram
- ¼ teaspoon pepper
- 1 bone-in turkey breast (5½ to 6 pounds)

1. In a small saucepan, combine the first eight ingredients; bring to a boil. Remove from the heat. Place turkey in a shallow roasting pan; drizzle with butter mixture.
2. Bake, uncovered, at 325° for 1½ to 2 hours or until a thermometer reads 165°, basting every 30 minutes. Let stand for 10 minutes before carving.

Per 5 ounces cooked turkey: 291 cal., 11g fat (3g sat. fat), 112mg chol., 192mg sodium, 1g carb. (0 sugars, 0 fiber), 44g pro.

EAT SMART **FAST FIX** ▶

LEMON-DIJON PORK SHEET PAN SUPPER

Most nights, I need something that gets on the table with minimal effort and delicious results. Sheet pan suppers like this one have become an all-time favorite, not only because of the bright flavors, but also because of the speedy clean-up time!
—Elisabeth Larsen, Pleasant Grv, UT

Start to Finish: 30 min.
Makes: 4 servings

- 4 teaspoons Dijon mustard
- 2 teaspoons grated lemon peel
- 1 garlic clove, minced
- ½ teaspoon salt
- 2 tablespoons canola oil
- 1½ pounds sweet potatoes (about 3 medium), cut into ½-inch cubes
- 1 pound fresh Brussels sprouts (about 4 cups), quartered
- 4 boneless pork loin chops (6 ounces each)
  Coarsely ground pepper, optional

1. Preheat oven to 425°. In a large bowl, mix first four ingredients; gradually whisk in oil. Remove 1 tablespoon mixture for brushing pork. Add vegetables to the remaining mixture; toss to coat.
2. Place pork chops and vegetables in a 15x10x1-in. pan coated with cooking spray. Brush chops with reserved mustard mixture. Roast 10 minutes.
3. Turn chops and stir vegetables; roast until a thermometer inserted in pork reads 145° and vegetables are tender, 10-15 minutes. If desired, sprinkle with pepper.

Per pork chop with 1¼ cups vegetables: 516 cal., 17g fat (4g sat. fat), 82mg chol., 505mg sodium, 51g carb. (19g sugars, 9g fiber), 39g pro.
Diabetic Exchanges: 5 lean meat, 3 starch, 1½ fat, 1 vegetable.

✳

TEST KITCHEN TIPS

Cutting the Brussels sprouts and potatoes fairly small means they'll be perfectly tender by the time the pork is cooked.

Switch to spicy brown mustard for a little more zing.

Use silicone brushes for basting, because they can go right into the dishwasher.

TACO NOODLE DISH

While we were housebound during a snowstorm one winter, I used ingredients I had on hand to create a hearty casserole. Later, I modified it so it has less fat and fewer calories.
—Judy Munger, Warren, MN

....

Start to Finish: 30 min.
Makes: 6 servings

- 3 cups uncooked wide egg noodles
- 2 pounds lean ground turkey
- 1 envelope reduced-sodium taco seasoning
- 1 teaspoon onion powder
- 1 teaspoon chili powder
- ½ teaspoon garlic powder
- 1 can (8 ounces) tomato sauce
- 1 can (4 ounces) chopped green chilies
- ½ cup water
- 1 cup shredded cheddar cheese

TOPPINGS

- 2 cups shredded lettuce
- 2 medium tomatoes, chopped
- ⅓ cup sliced ripe olives
- ½ cup taco sauce
- ½ cup fat-free sour cream

1. Preheat oven to 350°. Cook noodles according to the package directions for al dente; drain.
2. Meanwhile, in a large nonstick skillet, cook and crumble turkey over medium-high heat until no longer pink, for 6-8 minutes; drain. Stir in the seasonings, tomato sauce, chilies and water; bring to a boil. Reduce heat; simmer, uncovered, 5 minutes.
3. Spread noodles in a 11x7-in. baking dish coated with cooking spray. Top with turkey mixture; sprinkle with cheese. Bake, uncovered, until cheese is melted, about 10-15 minutes.
4. Top casserole with lettuce, tomatoes, olives and taco sauce. Serve with sour cream.
Per serving: 455 cal., 20g fat (7g sat. fat), 140mg chol., 954mg sodium, 27g carb. (7g sugars, 3g fiber), 40g pro.

TACO NOODLE DISH

EAT SMART FAST FIX ▸

LEMON-PARSLEY TILAPIA

I like to include seafood in our weekly dinner rotation but don't want to bother with anything complicated (and it had better taste good or the family will riot). This herbed fish does the trick.
—Trisha Kruse, Eagle, ID

....

Start to Finish: 20 min.
Makes: 4 servings

- 4 tilapia fillets (about 4 ounces each)
- 2 tablespoons lemon juice
- 1 tablespoon butter, melted
- 2 tablespoons minced fresh parsley
- 2 garlic cloves, minced
- 2 teaspoons grated lemon peel
- ½ teaspoon salt
- ¼ teaspoon pepper

1. Preheat oven to 375°. Place tilapia in a parchment paper-lined 15x10x1-in. pan. Drizzle the fillets with lemon juice, then melted butter.
2. Bake until fish just begins to flake easily with a fork, 11-13 minutes. Meanwhile, mix remaining ingredients. Remove fish from oven; sprinkle with parsley mixture.
Per fillet: 124 cal., 4g fat (2g sat. fat), 63mg chol., 359mg sodium, 1g carb. (0 sugars, 0 fiber), 21g pro.
Diabetic Exchanges: 3 lean meat, 1 fat.

Lightened-Up Classics

From tacos and pizza to chicken nuggets and moo shu, turn here for light takes on classic dishes. Enjoy these family favorites and feel good about what you're serving. It's easy eating right!

Mediterranean Bulgur Spinach Bowl (p. 128) **Green Curry Salmon with Green Beans** (p. 126)
Seasoned Chicken Strips (p. 129) **Chickpea Mint Tabbouleh** (p. 137) **Glazed Pork Chops** (p. 125)

ASIAN CHICKEN
RICE BOWL

EAT SMART **FAST FIX**

ASIAN CHICKEN RICE BOWL

This super flavorful, nutrient-packed dish makes use of supermarket conveniences like coleslaw mix and rotisserie chicken. It's easy to double or triple the recipe for large families.
—Christianna Gozzi, Astoria, NY

Start to Finish: 20 min.
Makes: 4 servings

- ¼ cup rice vinegar
- 1 green onion, minced
- 2 tablespoons reduced-sodium soy sauce
- 1 tablespoon toasted sesame seeds
- 1 tablespoon sesame oil
- 1 tablespoon honey
- 1 teaspoon minced fresh gingerroot
- 1 package (8.8 ounces) ready-to-serve brown rice
- 4 cups coleslaw mix (about 9 ounces)
- 2 cups shredded rotisserie chicken, chilled
- 2 cups frozen shelled edamame, thawed

1. For dressing, whisk together first seven ingredients. Cook rice according to package directions. Divide rice among four bowls.

2. In a large bowl, toss coleslaw mix and chicken with half of the dressing. Serve edamame and slaw mixture over rice; drizzle with remaining dressing.

Per serving: 429 cal., 15g fat (2g sat. fat), 62mg chol., 616mg sodium, 38g carb. (13g sugars, 5g fiber), 32g pro.
Diabetic Exchanges: 3 lean meat, 2 starch, 1 vegetable, 1 fat.

EAT SMART **FAST FIX**

EGGPLANT FRIES

Coated with Italian seasoning, Parmesan cheese and garlic salt, these veggie sticks are broiled, not fried, so there's no guilt when you crunch into them.
—Mary Murphy, Atwater, CA

Start to Finish: 20 min.
Makes: 6 servings

- 2 large eggs
- ½ cup grated Parmesan cheese
- ½ cup toasted wheat germ
- 1 teaspoon Italian seasoning
- ¾ teaspoon garlic salt
- 1 medium eggplant (about 1¼ pounds)
  Cooking spray
- 1 cup meatless pasta sauce, warmed

1. Preheat broiler. In a shallow bowl, whisk together eggs. In another shallow bowl, mix cheese, wheat germ and seasonings.

2. Trim ends of eggplant; cut eggplant lengthwise into ½-in.-thick slices. Cut slices lengthwise into ½-in. strips. Dip eggplant in eggs, then coat with cheese mixture. Place on a baking sheet coated with cooking spray.

3. Spritz eggplant with additional cooking spray. Broil 4 in. from heat 3 minutes. Turn eggplant; spritz with additional cooking spray. Broil until golden brown, about 1-2 minutes. Serve immediately with pasta sauce.

Per serving: 135 cal., 5g fat (2g sat. fat), 68mg chol., 577mg sodium, 15g carb. (6g sugars, 4g fiber), 9g pro.
Diabetic Exchanges: 1 medium-fat meat, 1 vegetable, ½ starch.

DELICIOUS OVEN BARBECUED CHICKEN

A friend made this juicy chicken for us when we had our first child. I pared down the recipe to make it a little healthier. It's now a family favorite, and even the kids ask for it.
—Marge Wagner, Roselle, IL

Prep: 20 min. • **Bake:** 35 min.
Makes: 6 servings

- 6 bone-in chicken breast halves (8 ounces each)
- ⅓ cup chopped onion
- ¾ cup ketchup
- ½ cup water
- ⅓ cup white vinegar
- 3 tablespoons brown sugar
- 1 tablespoon Worcestershire sauce
- 1 teaspoon ground mustard
- ¼ teaspoon salt
- ⅛ teaspoon pepper

1. Preheat oven to 350°. In a nonstick skillet coated with cooking spray, brown chicken over medium heat. Transfer to a 13x9-in. baking dish coated with cooking spray.
2. Recoat skillet with cooking spray. Add the onion; cook and stir over medium heat until tender. Stir in the remaining ingredients; bring to a boil. Reduce heat; simmer, uncovered, 15 minutes. Pour over chicken.
3. Bake, uncovered, until a thermometer inserted in chicken reads 170°, about 35-45 minutes.

Per serving: 324 cal., 10g fat (3g sat. fat), 111mg chol., 602mg sodium, 16g carb. (15g sugars, 0 fiber), 39g pro.
Diabetic Exchanges: 5 lean meat, 1 starch.

DELICIOUS OVEN BARBECUED CHICKEN

SHRIMP SCAMPI SPINACH SALAD

My husband and I really enjoy shrimp scampi and fresh spinach salad, so I put the two together. My oldest son loves it, too, and he's only 3!
—Jamie Porter, Garnett, KS

Start to Finish: 20 min.
Makes: 4 servings

- 2 tablespoons butter
- 1 pound uncooked shrimp (31-40 per pound), peeled and deveined
- 3 garlic cloves, minced
- 2 tablespoons chopped fresh parsley
- 6 ounces fresh baby spinach (about 8 cups)
- 1 cup cherry tomatoes, halved
  Lemon halves
- ⅛ teaspoon salt
- ⅛ teaspoon coarsely ground pepper
- ¼ cup sliced almonds, toasted
  Shredded Parmesan cheese, optional

1. In a large skillet, heat butter over medium heat; saute shrimp and garlic until shrimp turn pink, 3-4 minutes. Stir in parsley; remove from heat.
2. To serve, place spinach and tomatoes in a serving dish; top with shrimp mixture. Squeeze lemon juice over salad; sprinkle with salt and pepper. Sprinkle with almonds and, if desired, cheese.

Note: To toast nuts, cook in a skillet over low heat until lightly browned, stirring occasionally.

Per serving: 201 cal., 10g fat (4g sat. fat), 153mg chol., 291mg sodium, 6g carb. (1g sugars, 2g fiber), 21g pro.
Diabetic Exchanges: 3 lean meat, 1½ fat, 1 vegetable.

JERK CHICKEN WITH
TROPICAL COUSCOUS

PINEAPPLE SHRIMP FRIED RICE

My husband often ordered pineapple fried rice at Thai restaurants, so I tweaked recipes until I got to this version. I like to use jasmine rice. The garnish of green onions and chopped peanuts really completes the dish.
—Bonnie Brien, Pacific Grove, CA

Start to Finish: 30 min.
Makes: 4 servings

- 2 tablespoons reduced-sodium soy sauce
- 1 teaspoon curry powder
- ½ teaspoon sugar
- 2 tablespoons peanut or canola oil, divided
- 1 pound uncooked shrimp (31-40 per pound), peeled and deveined
- 2 teaspoons minced fresh gingerroot
- 1 garlic clove, minced
- 1 medium sweet red pepper, chopped
- 1 medium carrot, finely chopped
- ½ cup chopped onion
- 1 can (20 ounces) unsweetened pineapple tidbits, drained
- 2 cups cooked rice, at room temperature
- 6 green onions, chopped
- ½ cup finely chopped salted peanuts
  Lime wedges

1. Mix soy sauce, curry powder and sugar. In a large skillet, heat 1 tablespoon oil over medium-high heat; stir-fry shrimp until it turns pink, 2-3 minutes. Remove from pan.
2. In same pan, heat remaining oil over medium-high heat. Add ginger and garlic; cook just until fragrant, about 10 seconds. Add pepper, carrot and onion; stir-fry 2 minutes. Stir in pineapple and shrimp. Add rice and soy sauce mixture; heat through over medium heat, tossing to combine and break up any clumps of rice. Stir in green onions. Sprinkle with peanuts; serve with lime wedges.
Per 1½ cups: 491 cal., 18g fat (3g sat. fat), 138mg chol., 513mg sodium, 54g carb. (22g sugars, 5g fiber), 28g pro.
HEALTH TIP Swap tamari for soy sauce to make this dish gluten-free. And make sure your peanuts have been processed in a gluten-free facility.

JERK CHICKEN WITH TROPICAL COUSCOUS

Caribbean cuisine brightens up our weeknights thanks to its bold colors and flavors. Done in less than 30 minutes, this chicken is one of my go-to easy meals.
—Jeanne Holt, Mendota Heights, MN

Start to Finish: 25 min.
Makes: 4 servings

- 1 can (15.25 ounces) mixed tropical fruit
- 1 pound boneless skinless chicken breasts, cut into 2½-in. strips
- 3 teaspoons Caribbean jerk seasoning
- 1 tablespoon olive oil
- ½ cup chopped sweet red pepper
- 1 tablespoon finely chopped seeded jalapeno pepper
- ⅓ cup thinly sliced green onions (green portion only)
- 1½ cups reduced-sodium chicken broth
- 3 tablespoons chopped fresh cilantro, divided
- 1 tablespoon lime juice
- ¼ teaspoon salt
- 1 cup uncooked whole wheat couscous
  Lime wedges

1. Drain mixed fruit, reserving ¼ cup syrup. Chop fruit.
2. Toss chicken with jerk seasoning. In a large skillet, heat oil over medium-high heat; saute chicken until no longer pink, 4-5 minutes. Remove from pan, reserving the drippings.
3. In same pan, saute peppers and green onions in drippings 2 minutes. Add broth, 1 tablespoon cilantro, lime juice, salt, reserved syrup and chopped fruit; bring to a boil. Stir in couscous; reduce heat to low. Place chicken on top; cook, covered, until liquid is absorbed and chicken is heated through, 3-4 minutes. Sprinkle with remaining cilantro. Serve with lime.
Per 1½ cups: 411 cal., 7g fat (1g sat. fat), 63mg chol., 628mg sodium, 57g carb. (19g sugars, 7g fiber), 31g pro.

JERK CHICKEN WITH TROPICAL COUSCOUS

GLAZED PORK CHOPS
PICTURED ON P. 121

When I was a new mom, I needed good, healthy meals that were fast to fix. These juicy chops are perfect. Since this is a one-pan dish, cleanup's quick, too.
—Kristin Tanis, Hatfield, PA

Start to Finish: 30 min.
Makes: 4 servings

- 4 bone-in pork loin chops (¾ inch thick and 7 ounces each)
- ⅓ cup plus 1 tablespoon cider vinegar, divided
- 3 tablespoons soy sauce
- 3 garlic cloves, minced
- 1½ teaspoons cornstarch

1. In a large nonstick skillet, brown pork chops over medium heat, about 2 minutes per side. Mix ⅓ cup vinegar, soy sauce and garlic; pour over chops. Bring to a boil. Reduce heat; simmer, covered, until a thermometer inserted in pork reads 145°, 7-9 minutes.

2. Mix cornstarch and remaining vinegar until smooth; stir into pan. Bring to a boil; cook and stir until sauce is thickened, about 1 minute.

Per 1 pork chop with 2 tablespoons sauce: 224 cal., 8g fat (3g sat. fat), 86mg chol., 754mg sodium, 2g carb. (0 sugars, 0 fiber), 32g pro.
Diabetic Exchanges: 4 lean meat.

TOMATO BAGUETTE PIZZA

When my tomatoes ripen all at once, I use them up in simple recipes like this one. Cheesy baguette pizzas, served with a salad, make an ideal lunch—and they're great for appetizers, too.
—Lorraine Caland, Shuniah, ON

Prep: 25 min. • **Bake:** 10 min.
Makes: 6 servings

- 2 teaspoons olive oil
- 8 ounces sliced fresh mushrooms
- 2 medium onions, halved and sliced
- 2 garlic cloves, minced
- ½ teaspoon Italian seasoning
- ¼ teaspoon salt
  Dash pepper
- 1 French bread baguette (10½ ounces), halved lengthwise
- 1½ cups shredded part-skim mozzarella cheese, divided
- ¾ cup thinly sliced fresh basil leaves, divided
- 3 medium tomatoes, sliced

1. Preheat oven to 400°. In a large skillet, heat oil over medium-high heat; saute mushrooms and onions until tender. Add the garlic and seasonings; cook and stir 1 minute.

2. Place baguette halves on a baking sheet, cut side up; sprinkle with half of the cheese and ½ cup basil. Top with mushroom mixture, tomatoes and remaining cheese.

3. Bake until cheese is melted, about 10-15 minutes. Sprinkle with remaining basil. Cut each half into three portions.
Per piece: 260 cal., 7g fat (4g sat. fat), 18mg chol., 614mg sodium, 36g carb. (5g sugars, 3g fiber), 13g pro.
Diabetic Exchanges: 2 starch, 1 medium-fat meat, 1 vegetable.

TOMATO BAGUETTE PIZZA

GREEN CURRY SALMON WITH GREEN BEANS

PICTURED ON P. 121

Like a lot of people here in the beautiful Pacific Northwest, my boyfriend, Michael, loves to fish. When we have an abundance of fresh salmon on hand, this is one way we cook it.
—Amy Paul Maynard, Albany, OR

Start to Finish: 30 min.
Makes: 4 servings

4	salmon fillets (4 ounces each)
1	cup light coconut milk
2	tablespoons green curry paste
1	cup uncooked instant brown rice
1	cup reduced-sodium chicken broth
⅛	teaspoon pepper
¾	pound fresh green beans, trimmed
1	teaspoon sesame oil
1	teaspoon sesame seeds, toasted
	Lime wedges

1. Preheat oven to 400°. Place salmon in an 8-in. square baking dish. Whisk together coconut milk and curry paste; pour over salmon. Bake, uncovered, until fish just begins to flake easily with a fork, 15-20 minutes.
2. Meanwhile, in a small saucepan, combine rice, broth and pepper; bring to a boil. Reduce heat; simmer, covered, 5 minutes. Remove from heat; let stand 5 minutes.
3. In a large saucepan, place steamer basket over 1 in. of water. Place green beans in basket; bring water to a boil. Reduce heat to maintain a simmer; steam, covered, until beans are crisp-tender, 7-10 minutes. Toss with sesame oil and sesame seeds.
4. Serve salmon with rice, beans and lime wedges. Spoon coconut sauce over top as desired.

Note: This recipe was tested with Thai Kitchen Green Curry Paste.

Per serving: 366 cal., 17g fat (5g sat. fat), 57mg chol., 340mg sodium, 29g carb. (5g sugars, 4g fiber), 24g pro.
Diabetic Exchanges: 3 lean meat, 2 starch, 1 fat.

HEALTH TIP This nutrition-packed complete meal is gluten-free, heart-smart and diabetic-friendly.

CHICKEN TOSTADA CUPS

CHICKEN TOSTADA CUPS

Several years ago I tried a version of these cups at a restaurant in Santa Fe, and I wanted to make my own spin. These are great for gatherings where you can let everyone add their own favorite toppings.
—Marla Clark, Moriarty, NM

Prep: 25 min. • **Bake:** 15 min.
Makes: 6 servings

12	corn tortillas (6 inches), warmed
	Cooking spray
2	cups shredded rotisserie chicken
1	cup salsa
1	can (16 ounces) refried beans
1	cup shredded reduced-fat Mexican cheese blend
	Optional toppings: shredded lettuce, reduced-fat sour cream, sliced ripe olives, sliced green onions, chopped cilantro, sliced radishes, diced avocado and additional salsa

1. Preheat oven to 425°. Press warm tortillas into 12 muffin cups coated with cooking spray, pleating sides as needed. Spritz with additional cooking spray.
2. Bake until lightly browned, 5-7 minutes. Toss chicken with salsa. Layer each cup with beans, chicken mixture and cheese.
3. Bake until heated through, about 9-11 minutes. Serve tostada cups with toppings as desired.

Per 2 tostada cups: 338 cal., 11g fat (4g sat. fat), 52mg chol., 629mg sodium, 35g carb. (2g sugars, 6g fiber), 25g pro.
Diabetic Exchanges: 3 lean meat, 2 starch, 1 fat.

★ ★ ★ ★ ★ **READER REVIEW**

"We absolutely loved these! I mixed everything in the skillet to warm except the cheese. No need to layer at all. Great flavor!"

PAJAMAANGEL TASTEOFHOME.COM

BLACKENED TILAPIA WITH ZUCCHINI NOODLES

I love quick and bright meals like this one-skillet wonder. Homemade pico de gallo is easy to make the night before.
—Tammy Brownlow, Dallas, TX

Start to Finish: 30 min.
Makes: 4 servings

- 2 large zucchini (about 1½ pounds)
- 1½ teaspoons ground cumin
- ¾ teaspoon salt, divided
- ½ teaspoon smoked paprika
- ½ teaspoon pepper
- ¼ teaspoon garlic powder
- 4 tilapia fillets (6 ounces each)
- 2 teaspoons olive oil
- 2 garlic cloves, minced
- 1 cup pico de gallo

1. Trim ends of zucchini. Using a spiralizer, cut zucchini into thin strands.

2. Mix cumin, ½ teaspoon salt, smoked paprika, pepper and garlic powder; sprinkle generously onto both sides of tilapia. In a large nonstick skillet, heat oil over medium-high heat. In batches, cook tilapia until fish just begins to flake easily with a fork, 2-3 minutes per side. Remove from pan; keep warm.

3. In same pan, cook zucchini with garlic over medium-high heat until slightly softened, 1-2 minutes, tossing constantly with tongs (do not overcook). Sprinkle with remaining salt. Serve with tilapia and pico de gallo.

Note: If a spiralizer is not available, zucchini may also be cut into ribbons using a vegetable peeler. Saute as directed, increasing time as necessary.

Per serving: 203 cal., 4g fat (1g sat. fat), 83mg chol., 522mg sodium, 8g carb. (5g sugars, 2g fiber), 34g pro.
Diabetic Exchanges: 5 lean meat, 1 vegetable, ½ fat.

GREEK PASTA TOSS

I developed this bright pasta dish with my husband, tossing in our favorite Greek ingredients like olives, feta cheese and sun-dried tomatoes. Try it with shrimp or chicken, too!
—Terri Gilson, Calgary, AB

Start to Finish: 30 min.
Makes: 4 servings

- 3 cups uncooked whole wheat spiral pasta (about 7 ounces)
- ¾ pound Italian turkey sausage links, casings removed
- 2 garlic cloves, minced
- 4 ounces fresh baby spinach (about 5 cups)
- ½ cup pitted Greek olives, halved
- ⅓ cup julienned oil-packed sun-dried tomatoes, drained and chopped
- ¼ cup crumbled feta cheese
   Lemon wedges, optional

1. In a 6-qt. stockpot, cook pasta according to package directions; drain and return to pot.

2. Meanwhile, in a large skillet, cook and coarsely crumble sausage over medium-high heat until no longer pink, 4-6 minutes. Add garlic; cook and stir 1 minute. Add to the pasta.

3. Stir in spinach, olives and tomatoes; heat through, allowing spinach to wilt slightly. Stir in cheese. If desired, serve with lemon wedges.

Per 2 cups: 335 cal., 13g fat (3g sat. fat), 35mg chol., 742mg sodium, 36g carb. (1g sugars, 6g fiber), 19g pro.
Diabetic Exchanges: 2 starch, 2 lean meat, 2 fat, 1 vegetable.

BLACKENED TILAPIA WITH ZUCCHINI NOODLES

EAT SMART `FAST FIX` ▶

SESAME CRUSTED TUNA WITH ASIAN SLAW

This is a healthy, light dinner perfect for a hot summer night. Even better, it can be on the table in 20 minutes!
—Jackie Campbell, Stanhope, NJ

Start to Finish: 20 min.
Makes: 4 servings

- 1 package (10 ounces) shredded red cabbage (about 4 cups)
- 1 medium pear, peeled and julienned
- 1 medium Granny Smith apple, julienned
- 1 small sweet red pepper, julienned
- ½ cup julienned carrot
- 2 tablespoons chopped sweet onion
- 1 cup sesame ginger salad dressing, divided
- ¼ teaspoon salt
- ½ cup sesame seeds
- 4 tuna steaks (6 ounces each)

1. Place first six ingredients in a large bowl. Toss with ¼ cup dressing and salt.

2. Place remaining dressing and sesame seeds in separate shallow bowls. Dip tuna in dressing, then in sesame seeds to coat both sides.

3. In a large skillet, cook tuna over medium-high heat until medium-rare to slightly pink in center, 2-3 minutes per side. Serve with slaw.

Per serving: 534 cal., 24g fat (4g sat. fat), 66mg chol., 707mg sodium, 35g carb. (22g sugars, 7g fiber), 46g pro.

EAT SMART `FAST FIX` ▶

MEDITERRANEAN BULGUR SPINACH BOWL

PICTURED ON P. 121
You can transform this tasty bowl into an Italian version with mozzarella, pesto, tomatoes, spinach and basil.
—Renata Smith, Brookline, MA

Start to Finish: 30 min.
Makes: 4 servings

- 1 cup bulgur
- ½ teaspoon ground cumin
- ¼ teaspoon salt
- 2 cups water
- 1 can (15 ounces) chickpeas or garbanzo beans, rinsed and drained
- 6 ounces fresh baby spinach (about 8 cups)
- 2 cups cherry tomatoes, halved
- 1 small red onion, halved and thinly sliced
- ½ cup crumbled feta cheese
- ¼ cup hummus
- 2 tablespoons chopped fresh mint
- 2 tablespoons lemon juice

1. In a 6-qt. stockpot, combine first four ingredients; bring to a boil. Reduce heat; simmer, covered, 10-12 minutes until tender. Stir in chickpeas; heat through.

2. Remove from heat; stir in spinach. Let stand, covered, until spinach is wilted, about 5 minutes. Stir in the remaining ingredients. Serve warm or cold.

Per 2 cups: 311 cal., 7g fat (2g sat. fat), 8mg chol., 521mg sodium, 52g carb. (6g sugars, 12g fiber), 14g pro.

HEALTH TIP Between the spinach, tomatoes and feta cheese, this dish supplies all the daily vitamin A you need.

CHILI-LIME MUSHROOM TACOS

I used to make this dish with beef, but substituting portobello mushrooms turned it into my family's vegetarian favorite. It's quick, nutritious, low in fat and tasty.
—Greg Fontenot, The Woodlands, TX

Start to Finish: 25 min.
Makes: 4 servings

- 4 large portobello mushrooms (about ¾ pound)
- 1 tablespoon olive oil
- 1 medium sweet red pepper, cut into strips
- 1 medium onion, halved and thinly sliced
- 2 garlic cloves, minced
- 1½ teaspoons chili powder
- ½ teaspoon salt
- ½ teaspoon ground cumin
- ¼ teaspoon crushed red pepper flakes
- 1 teaspoon grated lime peel
- 2 tablespoons lime juice
- 8 corn tortillas (6 inches), warmed
- 1 cup shredded pepper jack cheese

1. Remove stems from mushrooms; if desired, remove gills using a spoon. Cut mushrooms into ½-in. slices.
2. In a large skillet, heat oil over medium-high heat; saute mushrooms, red pepper and onion until mushrooms are tender, 5-7 minutes. Stir in garlic, seasonings, lime peel and lime juice; cook and stir 1 minute. Serve in tortillas; top with cheese.
Per 2 tacos: 300 cal., 14g fat (6g sat. fat), 30mg chol., 524mg sodium, 33g carb. (5g sugars, 6g fiber), 13g pro.
Diabetic Exchanges: 2 vegetable, 1½ starch, 1 medium-fat meat, ½ fat.
HEALTH TIP Making these tacos with lean ground beef will add almost 4g saturated fat . That's a good reason for a meatless Taco Tuesday!

EAT SMART **FAST FIX**
PARMESAN BAKED COD

This is a goof-proof way to keep oven-baked cod moist and flavorful. My mom shared this recipe with me years ago and I've been loving it ever since.
—Mary Jo Hoppe, Pewaukee, WI

Start to Finish: 25 min.
Makes: 4 servings

- 4 cod fillets (4 ounces each)
- ⅔ cup mayonnaise
- 4 green onions, chopped
- ¼ cup grated Parmesan cheese
- 1 teaspoon Worcestershire sauce

1. Preheat oven to 400°. Place cod in an 8-in. square baking dish coated with cooking spray. Mix remaining ingredients; spread over fillets.
2. Bake, uncovered, until fish just begins to flake easily with a fork, 15-20 minutes.
Per 1 fillet: 247 cal., 15g fat (2g sat. fat), 57mg chol., 500mg sodium, 7g carb. (2g sugars, 0 fiber), 20g pro.
Diabetic Exchanges: 3 lean meat, 3 fat.

EAT SMART **FAST FIX**
SEASONED CHICKEN STRIPS
PICTURED ON P. 121

I made these crisp chicken strips for my kids, but they're tasty enough for company, too. They're juicy, flavorful and would also be a great salad topper.
—Becky Oliver, Fairplay, CO

Start to Finish: 25 min.
Makes: 4 servings

- ⅓ cup egg substitute or 1 large egg
- 1 tablespoon prepared mustard
- 1 garlic clove, minced
- ¾ cup dry bread crumbs
- 2 teaspoons dried basil
- 1 teaspoon paprika
- ½ teaspoon salt
- ¼ teaspoon pepper
- 1 pound chicken tenderloins

1. Preheat oven to 400°. In a shallow bowl, whisk together egg substitute, mustard and garlic. In another shallow bowl, toss bread crumbs with seasonings. Dip chicken in egg mixture, then coat with crumb mixture.
2. Place on a baking sheet coated with cooking spray. Bake until golden brown and chicken is no longer pink, about 10-15 minutes.
Per 3 ounces cooked chicken: 194 cal., 2g fat (0 sat. fat), 56mg chol., 518mg sodium, 14g carb. (1g sugars, 1g fiber), 31g pro.
Diabetic Exchanges: 3 lean meat, 1 starch.

CHILI-LIME MUSHROOM TACOS

CASHEW CHICKEN WITH GINGER

EAT SMART **FAST FIX**

VEGGIE TACOS

These vegetarian tacos are stuffed with a blend of sauteed cabbage, peppers and black beans that is so filling you won't miss the meat. Top with avocado, cheese or a dollop of sour cream.
—*Taste of Home* Test Kitchen

Start to Finish: 30 min.
Makes: 4 servings

  2 **tablespoons canola oil**
  3 **cups shredded cabbage**
  1 **medium sweet red pepper, julienned**
  1 **medium onion, halved and sliced**
  2 **teaspoons sugar**
  1 **can (15 ounces) black beans, rinsed and drained**
  1 **cup salsa**
  1 **can (4 ounces) chopped green chilies**
  1 **teaspoon minced garlic**
  1 **teaspoon chili powder**
  ¼ **teaspoon ground cumin**
  8 **taco shells, warmed**
  ½ **cup shredded cheddar cheese**
  1 **medium ripe avocado, peeled and sliced**

1. In a large skillet, heat oil over medium-high heat; saute cabbage, pepper and onion until crisp-tender, about 5 minutes. Sprinkle with sugar.
2. Stir in beans, salsa, chilies, garlic, chili powder and cumin; bring to a boil. Reduce heat; simmer, covered, until flavors are blended, about 5 minutes.
3. Serve in taco shells. Top with cheese and avocado.
Per 2 tacos: 430 cal., 22g fat (5g sat. fat), 14mg chol., 770mg sodium, 47g carb. (8g sugars, 10g fiber), 12g pro.

EAT SMART **FAST FIX**

CASHEW CHICKEN WITH GINGER

There are lots of recipes for cashew chicken, but my family thinks this one stands alone. We love the flavor from the fresh ginger and the crunch of the cashews. Plus, it's easy to prepare.
—Oma Rollison, El Cajon, CA

Start to Finish: 30 min.
Makes: 6 servings

  2 **tablespoons cornstarch**
  1 **tablespoon brown sugar**
  1¼ **cups chicken broth**
  2 **tablespoons soy sauce**
  3 **tablespoons canola oil, divided**
  1½ **pounds boneless skinless chicken breasts, cut into 1-inch pieces**
  ½ **pound sliced fresh mushrooms**
  1 **small green pepper, cut into strips**
  1 **can (8 ounces) sliced water chestnuts, drained**
  1½ **teaspoons grated fresh gingerroot**
  4 **green onions, sliced**
  ¾ **cup salted cashews**
      Hot cooked rice

1. Mix first four ingredients until smooth. In a large skillet, heat 2 tablespoons oil over medium-high heat; stir-fry chicken until no longer pink. Remove from pan.
2. In same pan, heat remaining oil over medium-high heat; stir-fry mushrooms, pepper, water chestnuts and ginger until pepper is crisp-tender, 3-5 minutes. Stir broth mixture and add to pan with green onions; bring to a boil. Cook and stir until sauce is thickened, 1-2 minutes.
3. Stir In chicken and cashews; heat through. Serve with rice.
Per ¾ cup chicken mixture: 349 cal., 19g fat (3g sat. fat), 64mg chol., 650mg sodium, 18g carb. (6g sugars, 2g fiber), 28g pro.
Diabetic Exchanges: 3 lean meat, 3 fat, 1 starch.

TANDOORI CHICKEN PITA PIZZAS

My family and I are big picnickers, and I'm always looking for new dishes to try in the great outdoors. The amazing flavors at our favorite Indian restaurant inspired these mini pizzas.
—Angela Spengler, Tampa, FL

Start to Finish: 25 min.
Makes: 4 servings

- 1 cup plain Greek yogurt, divided
- 2 tablespoons chopped fresh cilantro
- ½ teaspoon ground coriander
- ½ teaspoon ground cumin
- ½ teaspoon ground ginger
- ½ teaspoon ground turmeric
- ½ teaspoon paprika
- ½ teaspoon cayenne pepper
- ¾ pound boneless skinless chicken breasts, cut into ½-inch-thick strips
- 4 whole wheat pita breads (6 inches)
- ⅔ cup crumbled feta cheese
- ⅓ cup chopped seeded tomato
- ⅓ cup chopped fresh Italian parsley

1. For sauce, mix ½ cup yogurt and cilantro. In a large bowl, mix spices and remaining yogurt; stir in chicken to coat.
2. Place chicken on an oiled grill rack over medium heat; grill, covered, until no longer pink, 2-3 minutes per side. Grill the pita breads until warmed, about 1 minute per side.
3. Spread pitas with sauce. Top with chicken, cheese, tomato and parsley.
Per pizza: 380 cal., 12g fat (6g sat. fat), 72mg chol., 598mg sodium, 41g carb. (5g sugars, 5g fiber), 29g pro.
Diabetic Exchanges: 3 lean meat, 2½ starch.

DID YOU KNOW?

Yogurt is a classic chicken marinade in Greek, Indian, North African and Middle Eastern cuisines. Its relatively gentle acidity (compared with lemon juice or vinegar) means it won't make the meat fibers tough from over-marinating the way that stronger acids can. The lactic acid in yogurt penetrates deeply into the meat without breaking down muscle fibers. It works much like buttermilk, which is another classic dairy-based dip, mildly acidic, that's perfect for fried chicken.

HOISIN TURKEY LETTUCE WRAPS

I'm married to a marathon runner, which means dinners need to be healthy but flavor-packed. These low-carb wraps are quick and easy. He loves the health aspect, and I love the taste!
—Melissa Pelkey Hass, Waleska, GA

Start to Finish: 30 min.
Makes: 4 servings

- 1 pound lean ground turkey
- ½ pound sliced fresh mushrooms
- 1 medium sweet red pepper, diced
- 1 medium onion, finely chopped
- 1 medium carrot, shredded
- 1 tablespoon sesame oil
- ¼ cup hoisin sauce
- 2 tablespoons balsamic vinegar
- 2 tablespoons reduced-sodium soy sauce
- 1 tablespoon minced fresh gingerroot
- 2 garlic cloves, minced
- 8 Bibb or Boston lettuce leaves

1. In a large skillet, cook and crumble turkey with vegetables in sesame oil over medium-high heat until turkey is no longer pink, 8-10 minutes, breaking up turkey into crumbles.
2. Stir in hoisin sauce, vinegar, soy sauce, ginger and garlic; cook and stir over medium heat until the sauce is slightly thickened, about 5 minutes. Serve in lettuce leaves.
Per 2 wraps: 292 cal., 13g fat (3g sat. fat), 79mg chol., 629mg sodium, 19g carb. (11g sugars, 3g fiber), 26g pro.
Diabetic Exchanges: 3 lean meat, 1 starch, 1 vegetable, 1 fat.

HOISIN TURKEY LETTUCE WRAPS

EAT SMART **FAST FIX** ▶

SAUSAGE-STUFFED BUTTERNUT SQUASH

Load butternut squash shells with a mixture of Italian turkey sausage and squash for a quick and easy meal. Even better, it's surprisingly low in calories.
—Katia Slinger, West Jordan, UT

Start to Finish: 30 min.

Makes: 4 servings

- 1 medium butternut squash (about 3 pounds)
- 1 pound Italian turkey sausage links, casings removed
- 1 medium onion, finely chopped
- 4 garlic cloves, minced
- ½ cup shredded Italian cheese blend
  Crushed red pepper flakes, optional

1. Preheat broiler. Cut squash lengthwise in half; discard seeds. Place squash in a large microwave-safe dish, cut side down; add ½ in. of water. Microwave, covered, on high until soft, 20-25 minutes. Cool slightly.
2. Meanwhile, in a large nonstick skillet, cook and crumble sausage with onion over medium-high heat until no longer pink, about 5-7 minutes. Add garlic; cook and stir 1 minute.
3. Leaving ½-in.-thick shells, scoop pulp from squash and stir into sausage mixture. Place squash shells on a baking sheet; fill with the sausage mixture. Sprinkle with cheese blend.
4. Broil 4-5 in. from heat until cheese is melted, 1-2 minutes. If desired, sprinkle with pepper flakes. To serve, cut each half into two portions.
Note: This recipe was tested in a 1,100-watt microwave.
Per serving: 325 cal., 10g fat (4g sat. fat), 52mg chol., 587mg sodium, 44g carb. (10g sugars, 12g fiber), 19g pro.
Diabetic Exchanges: 3 starch, 3 lean meat.
HEALTH TIP Butternut squash is an excellent source of vitamin A in the form of beta-carotene. It's important for normal vision and a healthy immune system, and it helps the heart, lungs and kidneys function properly.

ZINGY BAKED CHICKEN NUGGETS

EAT SMART **FAST FIX** ▶

ZINGY BAKED CHICKEN NUGGETS

These crispy chicken nuggets have just the right amount of spice. Yogurt makes them extra tender.
—Lee Evans, Queen Creek, AZ

Start to Finish: 30 min.

Makes: 6 servings

- ¼ cup plain yogurt
- 1 tablespoon lemon juice
- 1½ teaspoons seasoned salt
- 1 teaspoon garlic powder
- 1 teaspoon ground coriander
- ½ to ¾ teaspoon cayenne pepper
- 1½ pounds boneless skinless chicken breasts, cut into 1½-inch pieces
- 2 cups whole wheat or regular panko (Japanese) bread crumbs
  Honey mustard, optional

1. Preheat oven to 400°. Mix first six ingredients; stir in chicken to coat.
2. Place bread crumbs in a shallow bowl; add chicken, one piece at a time, and toss to coat. Place 1 in. apart on a greased baking sheet.
3. Bake until lightly browned and chicken is no longer pink, 18-20 minutes. If desired, serve with honey mustard.
Per serving: 222 cal., 4g fat (1g sat. fat), 64mg chol., 481mg sodium, 19g carb. (2g sugars, 2g fiber), 26g pro.
Diabetic Exchanges: 3 lean meat, 1 starch.

EAT SMART **FAST FIX** ▶

BROILED COD

This is the easiest and tastiest fish you'll serve. Even finicky eaters who think they don't like fish will love the beautiful and flaky results.
—Kim Russell, North Wales, PA

Start to Finish: 30 min.

Makes: 2 servings

- ¼ cup fat-free Italian salad dressing
- ½ teaspoon sugar
- ⅛ teaspoon salt
- ⅛ teaspoon garlic powder
- ⅛ teaspoon curry powder
- ⅛ teaspoon paprika
- ⅛ teaspoon pepper
- 2 cod fillets (6 ounces each)
- 2 teaspoons butter

1. Preheat broiler. In a shallow bowl, mix first seven ingredients; add cod, turning to coat. Let stand 10-15 minutes.
2. Place fillets on a greased rack of a broiler pan; discard remaining marinade. Broil 3-4 in. from heat until fish just begins to flake easily with a fork, 10-12 minutes. Top with butter.
Per 1 fillet: 168 cal., 5g fat (3g sat. fat), 75mg chol., 365mg sodium, 2g carb. (2g sugars, 0 fiber), 27g pro.
Diabetic Exchanges: 4 lean meat, 1 fat.

APRICOT-GINGER ACORN SQUASH

It's a real treat digging into tender baked squash with a buttery apricot sauce. Natural fruit preserves add sweetness, and ginger makes it savory without loading on unwanted calories.
—Trisha Kruse, Eagle, ID

Prep: 10 min. • **Bake:** 1 hour
Makes: 2 servings

- 1 small acorn squash
- 2 tablespoons apricot preserves
- 4 teaspoons butter, melted
- 1½ teaspoons reduced-sodium soy sauce
- ¼ teaspoon ground ginger
- ¼ teaspoon pepper

1. Preheat oven to 350°. Cut squash lengthwise in half; remove seeds. Cut a thin slice from bottoms to level if desired. Place in a greased 11x7-in. baking dish, cut side up.
2. Mix remaining ingredients; spoon over squash. Bake, covered, 45 minutes. Uncover; bake until tender, 15-20 minutes.
Per ½ squash: 234 cal., 8g fat (5g sat. fat), 20mg chol., 221mg sodium, 43g carb. (15g sugars, 4g fiber), 3g pro.

BRAISED PORK LOIN CHOPS

An easy herb rub gives sensational taste to these boneless pork loin chops, which can be cooked on the stovetop in minutes. The meat turns out tender and delicious.
—Marilyn Larsen, Port Orange, FL

Start to Finish: 30 min.
Makes: 4 servings

- 1 garlic clove, minced
- 1 teaspoon rubbed sage
- 1 teaspoon dried rosemary, crushed
- ½ teaspoon salt
- ⅛ teaspoon pepper
- 4 boneless pork loin chops (½ inch thick and 4 ounces each)
- 1 tablespoon butter
- 1 tablespoon olive oil
- ¾ cup dry white wine or apple juice
- 1 tablespoon minced fresh parsley

1. Mix first five ingredients; rub over both sides of pork chops. In a large nonstick skillet, heat butter and oil over medium-high heat; brown chops on both sides. Remove from pan.
2. In same pan, bring wine to a boil, stirring to loosen browned bits from pan. Cook, uncovered, until liquid is reduced to ½ cup. Add chops; return to a boil. Reduce heat; simmer, covered, until pork is tender, 6-8 minutes. Sprinkle with parsley.
Per pork chop with 2 tablespoons sauce: 218 cal., 13g fat (5g sat. fat), 62mg chol., 351mg sodium, 3g carb. (2g sugars, 0 fiber), 22g pro.
Diabetic Exchanges: 3 lean meat, 1½ fat.

Kickin' Cauliflower

You can eat your veggies...or you can devour them. These Buffalo cauliflower bites—roasted till golden and doused with wing sauce—are your new not-so-guilty pleasure.

✳ Cut up a head of cauliflower; toss with 1 Tbsp. oil. Roast at 400° for 25 minutes, stirring once. Toss with ½ cup wing sauce; serve with blue cheese dressing.

CREAMY DIJON CHICKEN

EAT SMART FAST FIX >
CREAMY DIJON CHICKEN

This chicken dish is extremely fast and economical. It makes a nice sauce that works well over brown rice or wide noodles. If you want extra sauce for leftovers, double the recipe.
—Irene Boffo, Fountain Hills, AZ

Start to Finish: 25 min.
Makes: 4 servings

- ½ cup half-and-half cream
- ¼ cup Dijon mustard
- 1 tablespoon brown sugar
- 4 boneless skinless chicken breast halves (6 ounces each)
- ¼ teaspoon salt
- ¼ teaspoon pepper
- 2 teaspoons olive oil
- 2 teaspoons butter
- 1 small onion, halved and very thinly sliced
  Minced fresh parsley

1. Whisk together cream, mustard and brown sugar. Pound chicken breasts with a meat mallet to even thickness; sprinkle with salt and pepper.
2. In a large skillet, heat oil and butter over medium-high heat; brown chicken on both sides. Reduce heat to medium. Add the onion and cream mixture; bring to a boil. Reduce the heat; simmer, covered, for 10-12 minutes until a thermometer inserted in chicken reads 165°. Sprinkle with minced parsley.

Per chicken breast half with 3 tablespoons sauce: 295 cal., 11g fat (5g sat. fat), 114mg chol., 621mg sodium, 6g carb. (5g sugars, 0 fiber), 36g pro.
Diabetic Exchanges: 5 lean meat, 1 fat, ½ starch.

EAT SMART FAST FIX >
BLUSHING PENNE PASTA

I reworked this recipe from an original that called for vodka and heavy whipping cream. My friends and family hardly believe a sauce this rich, flavorful and creamy could be light.
—Margaret Wilson, San Bernardino, CA

Start to Finish: 30 min.
Makes: 8 servings

- 1 package (16 ounces) penne pasta
- 2 tablespoons butter
- 1 medium onion, halved and thinly sliced
- 2 tablespoons minced fresh thyme or
- 2 teaspoons dried thyme
- 2 tablespoons minced fresh basil or
- 2 teaspoons dried basil
- 1 teaspoon salt
- 1½ cups half-and-half cream, divided
- ½ cup white wine or reduced-sodium chicken broth
- 1 tablespoon tomato paste
- 2 tablespoons all-purpose flour
- ½ cup shredded Parmigiano-Reggiano cheese, divided

1. In a 6-qt. stockpot, cook the pasta according to package directions. Drain; return to pot.
2. Meanwhile, in a large nonstick skillet, heat butter over medium heat; saute onion until lightly browned, 8-10 minutes. Add herbs and salt; cook and stir 1 minute. Add 1 cup cream, wine and tomato paste; cook and stir until blended.
3. Mix flour and remaining cream until smooth; gradually stir into onion mixture. Bring sauce to a boil; cook and stir until thickened, about 2 minutes. Stir in ¼ cup cheese. Stir into pasta. Serve with remaining cheese.

Per cup: 335 cal., 10g fat (6g sat. fat), 34mg chol., 431mg sodium, 47g carb. (4g sugars, 2g fiber), 12g pro.

EAT SMART FAST FIX

HEALTHIER-THAN-EGG ROLLS

Frying anything at home is a little intimidating for me, but I love egg rolls. With this recipe, I've figured out a way to get the best part of the egg roll—without the mess. This can be used to stuff egg roll wrappers, but we love it on its own, too.
—Sue Mitchell, Kerrville, TX

Start to Finish: 25 min.
Makes: 4 servings

- 1 pound lean ground chicken
- 1½ cups sliced fresh mushrooms
- 1 medium onion, chopped
- 2 garlic cloves, minced
- 1 teaspoon minced fresh gingerroot
- 2 tablespoons reduced-sodium soy sauce
- 1 package (14 ounces) coleslaw mix
- 1 tablespoon sesame oil
- 3 cups hot cooked brown rice
- ½ cup sweet-and-sour sauce
  Wonton strips, optional

1. In a large skillet, cook and crumble chicken with mushrooms, onion, garlic and ginger over medium-high heat until no longer pink, 6-8 minutes; drain. Stir in the soy sauce.
2. Add coleslaw mix; cook and stir until wilted, 3-4 minutes. Stir in sesame oil. Serve with rice and sweet-and-sour sauce. If desired, top with wonton strips.
Per 1¼ cups chicken mixture with ¾ cup rice: 451 cal., 11g fat (3g sat. fat), 81mg chol., 591mg sodium, 58g carb. (13g sugars, 6g fiber), 30g pro.

❉
TEST KITCHEN TIPS

Sesame oil adds a nutty flavor that makes this dish taste a lot like an egg roll. It's available in small bottles and makes a great addition to any pantry.

Use instant brown rice to make this dish fast. Or make it faster with ready-to-eat brown rice, which just needs to be heated in the microwave.

EAT SMART FAST FIX

NAKED FISH TACOS

This is one of my husband's all-time favorite meals. I've even converted some friends to fish after eating this. I serve it with fresh melon when it's in season to balance the subtle heat of the cabbage mixture.
—Elizabeth Bramkamp, Gig Harbor, WA

Start to Finish: 25 min.
Makes: 2 servings

- 1 cup coleslaw mix
- ¼ cup chopped fresh cilantro
- 1 green onion, sliced
- 1 teaspoon chopped seeded jalapeno pepper
- 4 teaspoons canola oil, divided
- 2 teaspoons lime juice
- ½ teaspoon ground cumin
- ½ teaspoon salt, divided
- ¼ teaspoon pepper, divided
- 2 tilapia fillets (6 ounces each)
- ½ medium ripe avocado, peeled and sliced

1. Place first four ingredients in a bowl; toss with 2 teaspoons oil, lime juice, cumin, ¼ teaspoon salt and ⅛ teaspoon pepper. Refrigerate until serving.
2. Pat fillets dry with paper towels; sprinkle with the remaining salt and pepper. In a large nonstick skillet, heat remaining oil over medium-high heat; cook tilapia until fish just begins to flake easily with a fork, 3-4 minutes per side. Top with slaw and avocado.
Per serving: 293 cal., 16g fat (2g sat. fat), 83mg chol., 663mg sodium, 6g carb. (1g sugars, 3g fiber), 33g pro.
Diabetic Exchanges: 5 lean meat, 3 fat, 1 vegetable.
HEALTH TIP If you're following a low-carb diet, this dish is for you! If not, pair it up with a whole grain side like brown rice pilaf or corn and pepper saute.

HEALTHIER-THAN-EGG ROLLS

EAT SMART **FAST FIX** ▶

SHRIMP PUTTANESCA

I throw together these bold ingredients for a feisty seafood pasta.
—Lynda Balslev, Sausalito, CA

Start to Finish: 30 min.
Makes: 4 servings

- 2 tablespoons olive oil, divided
- 1 pound uncooked shrimp (31-40 per pound), peeled and deveined
- ¾ to 1 teaspoon crushed red pepper flakes, divided
- ¼ teaspoon salt
- 1 small onion, chopped
- 2 to 3 anchovy fillets, finely chopped
- 3 garlic cloves, minced
- 2 cups grape tomatoes
- ½ cup dry white wine or vegetable broth
- ⅓ cup pitted Greek olives, coarsely chopped
- 2 teaspoons drained capers
  Sugar to taste
  Chopped fresh Italian parsley
  Hot cooked spaghetti, optional

1. In a large skillet, heat 1 tablespoon oil; saute shrimp with ½ teaspoon pepper flakes until shrimp turn pink, 2-3 minutes. Stir in salt; remove from pan.
2. In same pan, heat remaining oil over medium heat; saute onion until tender, about 2 minutes. Add anchovies, garlic and remaining pepper flakes; cook and stir until fragrant, about 1 minute. Stir in the tomatoes, wine, olives and capers; bring to a boil. Reduce heat; simmer, uncovered, until tomatoes are softened and mixture is thickened, 8-10 minutes.
3. Stir in shrimp and sugar; sprinkle with parsley. If desired, serve with spaghetti.

Per cup: 228 cal., 12g fat (2g sat. fat), 140mg chol., 579mg sodium, 8g carb. (3g sugars, 1g fiber), 20g pro.

SAUSAGE & VEGETABLE SKILLET DINNER

EAT SMART **FAST FIX** ▶

SAUSAGE & VEGETABLE SKILLET DINNER

I whipped up this recipe one night trying to use up produce before going out of town. Who knew it was going to be such a hit! Now it's a go-to recipe that I use when I don't have much time to cook or wash dishes.
—Elizabeth Kelley, Chicago, IL

Start to Finish: 30 min.
Makes: 4 servings

- 1 tablespoon olive oil
- 1 package (12 ounces) fully cooked Italian chicken sausage links, cut into 1-inch pieces
- 1 large onion, chopped
- 3 garlic cloves, minced
- ¼ teaspoon crushed red pepper flakes
- 1½ pounds red potatoes (about 5 medium), thinly sliced
- 1 package (10 ounces) frozen corn
- ¼ teaspoon pepper
- 1¼ cups vegetable broth
- 2 cups fresh baby spinach

1. In a 12-in. skillet, heat oil over medium-high heat; saute sausage and onion until onion is tender. Add garlic and pepper flakes; cook and stir 1 minute.
2. Add potatoes, corn, pepper and broth; bring to a boil. Reduce heat to medium; cook, covered, until potatoes are tender, 15-20 minutes. Stir in spinach until wilted.

Per 1½ cups: 371 cal., 11g fat (3g sat. fat), 65mg chol., 715mg sodium, 48g carb. (6g sugars, 5g fiber), 22g pro.
Diabetic Exchanges: 3 starch, 3 lean meat, 1 fat.

HEALTH TIP Italian chicken sausage has less than half the fat of regular. It's lean, but adds a lot of flavor.

SUMMERTIME ORZO & CHICKEN

This easy-as-can-be main dish is likely to become a summer staple at your house. It's that good! If you prefer, grill the chicken breasts instead of cooking in a skillet.

—Fran MacMillan, West Melbourne, FL

Start to Finish: 30 min.
Makes: 4 servings

- ¾ cup uncooked orzo pasta
- 1 pound boneless skinless chicken breasts, cut into 1-inch pieces
- 1 medium cucumber, chopped
- 1 small red onion, chopped
- ¼ cup minced fresh parsley
- 2 tablespoons lemon juice
- 1 tablespoon olive oil
- 1 teaspoon salt
- ¼ teaspoon pepper
- ¼ cup crumbled reduced-fat feta cheese

1. Cook pasta according to package directions; drain.
2. Meanwhile, in a large skillet coated with cooking spray, cook and stir chicken over medium heat until no longer pink, about 6-8 minutes. Transfer to a large bowl.

3. Add cucumber, onion, parsley and pasta. In a small bowl, mix lemon juice, oil, salt and pepper; toss with chicken mixture. Serve immediately or refrigerate and serve cold. Top with cheese before serving.
Per 1¼ cups: 320 cal., 7g fat (2g sat. fat), 65mg chol., 742mg sodium, 32g carb. (3g sugars, 2g fiber), 30g pro.
Diabetic Exchanges: 3 lean meat, 2 starch, 1 fat.

HEALTH TIP Make this salad heart-healthier: A simple switch to whole wheat orzo will add nearly 3g fiber.

EAT SMART **FAST FIX**

CHICKPEA MINT TABBOULEH

PICTURED ON P. 121
You'll love this healthy salad warm or chilled. For variety, add feta cheese. Also try this as a filling for stuffed tomatoes or mushrooms.

—Bryan Kennedy, Kaneohe, HI

Start to Finish: 30 min.
Makes: 4 servings

- 1 cup bulgur
- 2 cups water
- 1 cup fresh or frozen peas (about 5 ounces), thawed
- 1 can (15 ounces) chickpeas or garbanzo beans, rinsed and drained
- ½ cup minced fresh parsley
- ¼ cup minced fresh mint
- ¼ cup olive oil
- 2 tablespoons julienned soft sun-dried tomatoes (not packed in oil)
- 2 tablespoons lemon juice
- ½ teaspoon salt
- ¼ teaspoon pepper

1. In a large saucepan, combine bulgur and water; bring to a boil. Reduce heat; simmer, covered, 10 minutes. Stir in fresh or frozen peas; cook, covered, until bulgur and peas are tender, about 5 minutes.
2. Transfer to a large bowl. Stir in the remaining ingredients. Serve warm or cold.
Note: This recipe was tested with soft sun-dried tomatoes that do not need to be soaked before use.
Per 1 cup: 380 cal., 16g fat (2g sat. fat), 0 chol., 450mg sodium, 51g carb. (6g sugars, 11g fiber), 11g pro.
Diabetic Exchanges: 3 starch, 3 fat, 1 lean meat.

HEALTH TIP Bulgur is made from whole wheat kernels that are boiled, dried and cracked. Since it's made from the whole kernel, it's always a whole grain. It has more fiber than quinoa, oats and corn.

SUMMERTIME ORZO & CHICKEN

SPICY MONGOLIAN BEEF SALAD

This light and loaded beef salad even satisfies my husband, who loves meat for dinner. You won't believe how quickly it comes together.

—Marla Clark, Albuquerque, NM

Start to Finish: 30 min.
Makes: 4 servings

- ¼ cup olive oil
- 2 tablespoons rice vinegar
- 1 tablespoon reduced-sodium soy sauce
- 1 tablespoon sesame oil
- 2 teaspoons minced fresh gingerroot
- 1 small garlic clove, minced
- 1 teaspoon sugar

BEEF
- 1 tablespoon reduced-sodium soy sauce
- 2 garlic cloves, minced
- 2 teaspoons sugar
- 1 to 2 teaspoons crushed red pepper flakes
- 1 teaspoon sesame oil
- 1 beef top sirloin steak (1 pound), cut into ¼-inch strips
- 1 tablespoon olive oil

SALAD
- 8 cups torn mixed salad greens
- 1 cup shredded carrots
- ½ cup thinly sliced cucumber
- 4 radishes, thinly sliced

1. For dressing, whisk together first seven ingredients.
2. Mix the first five beef ingredients; toss with beef strips. In a large skillet, heat olive oil over medium-high heat; stir-fry beef mixture until browned, 2-3 minutes. Remove from pan.
3. Combine salad ingredients; divide among four plates. Top with beef. Drizzle with dressing.

Per serving: 396 cal., 26g fat (5g sat. fat), 46mg chol., 550mg sodium, 15g carb. (7g sugars, 3g fiber), 27g pro.

LOADED CHICKEN CARBONARA CUPS

LOADED CHICKEN CARBONARA CUPS

Spaghetti cupcakes with a chicken carbonara twist make for a tasty, fun family dinner. Whole wheat pasta and reduced-fat ingredients make these quick and easy little pasta cakes nutritional winners, too.

—Jeanne Holt, Mendota Heights, MN

Prep: 30 min. • **Bake:** 15 min.
Makes: 6 servings

- 4 ounces uncooked whole wheat spaghetti
- 1 large egg, lightly beaten
- 5 ounces frozen chopped spinach, thawed and squeezed dry (about ½ cup)
- ½ cup 2% cottage cheese
- ½ cup shredded Parmesan cheese, divided
- ¼ teaspoon lemon-pepper seasoning
- 6 bacon strips, cooked and crumbled, divided
- ½ cup reduced-fat reduced-sodium condensed cream of chicken soup, undiluted
- ¼ cup reduced-fat spreadable chive and onion cream cheese
- 1 cup chopped cooked chicken breast
- ⅓ cup shredded part-skim mozzarella cheese
- ¼ cup finely chopped oil-packed sun-dried tomatoes

1. Preheat oven to 350°. In a large saucepan, cook spaghetti according to package directions; drain, reserving ⅓ cup pasta water.
2. In a large bowl, mix the egg, spinach, cottage cheese, ¼ cup Parmesan cheese, lemon pepper and half of the bacon. Add spaghetti; toss to combine. Divide among 12 greased muffin cups. Using a greased tablespoon, make an indentation in the center of each.
3. In a large bowl, whisk together soup, cream cheese and reserved pasta water. Stir in chicken, mozzarella cheese and tomatoes; spoon into cups. Sprinkle with remaining bacon and Parmesan cheese.
4. Bake until set, about 15 minutes. Cool 5 minutes before removing from pan.

Per 2 pasta cups: 266 cal., 12g fat (5g sat. fat), 74mg chol., 553mg sodium, 20g carb. (4g sugars, 3g fiber), 21g pro.
Diabetic Exchanges: 2 lean meat, 1½ fat, 1 starch.

TORTILLA PIE

My husband and I especially like this delicious dinner pie because it's lighter tasting than traditional lasagnas made with pasta. Even our two young daughters get excited when I bring this to the table!
—Lisa King, Caledonia, MI

Start to Finish: 30 min.
Makes: 4 servings

- ½ pound lean ground beef (90% lean)
- ½ cup chopped onion
- 2 garlic cloves, minced
- 1 teaspoon chili powder
- ½ teaspoon ground cumin
- 1 can (14½ ounces) Mexican diced tomatoes, drained
- ¾ cup reduced-fat ricotta cheese
- ¼ cup shredded part-skim mozzarella cheese
- 3 tablespoons minced fresh cilantro, divided
- 4 whole wheat tortillas (8 inches)
- ½ cup shredded cheddar cheese

1. Preheat oven to 400°. In a large skillet, cook and crumble beef with onion and garlic over medium heat until no longer pink, 4-6 minutes. Stir in spices and tomatoes. Bring to a boil; remove from heat. In a small bowl, mix the ricotta, mozzarella and 2 tablespoons cilantro.
2. Place one tortilla in a 9-in. round baking pan coated with cooking spray. Layer with half of the meat sauce, one tortilla, ricotta mixture, another tortilla and remaining meat sauce. Top with remaining tortilla; sprinkle with cheddar cheese and the remaining cilantro.
3. Bake, covered, until heated through, 15-20 minutes.

Per serving: 356 cal., 14g fat (6g sat. fat), 65mg chol., 574mg sodium, 32g carb. (7g sugars, 5g fiber), 25g pro.
Diabetic Exchanges: 3 medium-fat meat, 2 starch.

TORTILLA PIE

SKINNY COBB SALAD

This skinny version of Cobb salad has all the taste and creaminess with half the fat and calories. You can skip the coleslaw mix and do all lettuce, but I like the crunch you get with cabbage.
—Taylor Kiser, Brandon, FL

Start to Finish: 25 min.
Makes: 4 servings

- ¼ cup fat-free plain Greek yogurt
- 2 tablespoons reduced-fat ranch salad dressing
- 1 to 2 teaspoons cold water

SALAD
- 3 cups coleslaw mix
- 3 cups chopped lettuce
- 1 large apple, chopped
- ½ cup crumbled reduced-fat feta or blue cheese
- 1 cup cubed cooked chicken breast
- 2 green onions, chopped
- 4 turkey bacon strips, chopped and cooked
- 1 can (15 ounces) garbanzo beans or chickpeas, rinsed and drained
- 1 small ripe avocado, peeled and cubed

1. Mix yogurt and dressing; thin with water as desired. Toss coleslaw mix with lettuce; divide among four plates.
2. Arrange remaining ingredients in rows over top. Drizzle with yogurt mixture.

Per serving: 324 cal., 13g fat (3g sat. fat), 48mg chol., 646mg sodium, 31g carb. (11g sugars, 9g fiber), 23g pro.
Diabetic Exchanges: 2 lean meat, 2 fat, 1½ starch, 1 vegetable.

HEALTH TIP Combining classic Cobb salad flavors with healthy ingredients—like Greek yogurt, chopped apple and garbanzo beans—makes this main-dish salad a win-win.

HONEY CHICKEN STIR-FRY

I'm a new mom, and my schedule is very dependent upon our young son. So I like meals that can be ready in as little time as possible. This chicken stir-fry with a hint of sweetness from honey is a major time-saver.
—Caroline Sperry, Allentown, MI

Start to Finish: 30 min.
Makes: 4 servings

- 2 teaspoons cornstarch
- 1 tablespoon cold water
- 3 teaspoons olive oil, divided
- 1 pound boneless skinless chicken breasts, cut into 1-inch pieces
- 1 garlic clove, minced
- 3 tablespoons honey
- 2 tablespoons reduced-sodium soy sauce
- ⅛ teaspoon salt
- ⅛ teaspoon pepper
- 1 package (16 ounces) frozen broccoli stir-fry vegetable blend
  Hot cooked rice

1. Mix cornstarch and water until smooth. In a large nonstick skillet, heat 2 teaspoons oil over medium-high heat; stir-fry chicken and garlic 1 minute. Add honey, soy sauce, salt and pepper; cook and stir until chicken is no longer pink, 2-3 minutes. Remove from pan.

2. In same pan, stir-fry vegetable blend in remaining oil just until tender, 4-5 minutes. Return chicken to pan. Stir cornstarch mixture and add to pan; bring to a boil. Cook and stir until thickened, about 1 minute. Serve with rice.

Per cup stir-fry: 249 cal., 6g fat (1g sat. fat), 63mg chol., 455mg sodium, 21g carb. (15g sugars, 3g fiber), 25g pro.
Diabetic Exchanges: 3 lean meat, 2 vegetable, ½ starch.

MOO SHU LETTUCE CUPS

I took ordinary ground beef and turned it into a healthy new classic with sweet and savory flavors. We love the meat mixture served in flour tortillas, too!
—Christine Keating, Norwalk, CA

Prep: 25 min. • **Cook:** 3 hours
Makes: 4 servings

- ¼ cup apricot preserves
- 3 tablespoons hoisin sauce
- 2 tablespoons soy sauce
- 1 tablespoon honey
- ½ teaspoon sesame oil
- ¼ teaspoon crushed red pepper flakes, optional
- 1 pound lean ground beef (90% lean)
- ½ cup chopped onion
- 3 garlic cloves, minced
- 1 teaspoon minced fresh gingerroot
- 1 cup sliced fresh mushrooms
- 1 medium carrot, diced
- 1 celery rib, diced
- ½ cup chopped sweet red pepper
- 12 Bibb lettuce leaves
  Diagonally sliced green onions

1. Mix first five ingredients and, if desired, pepper flakes. In a large skillet, cook and crumble beef with onion, garlic and ginger over medium heat until no longer pink, 5-7 minutes. Transfer to a 3- or 4-qt. slow cooker. Add mushrooms, carrot, celery and pepper; stir in sauce mixture.

2. Cook, covered, on low until vegetables are tender and flavors are blended, for 3-4 hours. Serve in lettuce leaves; sprinkle with green onions.

Per 3 filled lettuce cups: 311 cal., 11g fat (4g sat. fat), 71mg chol., 744mg sodium, 29g carb. (19g sugars, 2g fiber), 25g pro.

HONEY CHICKEN STIR-FRY

CURRIED SHRIMP PASTA

This light and spicy shrimp dish comes together easily. My favorite pasta to use is capellini, but angel hair works fine as well.
—Thomas Faglon, Somerset, NJ

Start to Finish: 25 min.
Makes: 4 servings

- 8 ounces uncooked angel hair pasta
- 8 ounces fresh sugar snap peas (about 2 cups), halved diagonally
- 2 tablespoons olive oil
- 1 pound uncooked shrimp (26-30 per pound), peeled and deveined
- 3 teaspoons curry powder
- 1 teaspoon ground cumin
- ¾ teaspoon salt
- 6 green onions, diagonally sliced

1. Cook pasta according to package directions, adding snap peas during the last 1-2 minutes of cooking. Drain, reserving ½ cup pasta water.
2. In a large skillet, heat oil over medium-high heat; saute shrimp 2 minutes. Add seasonings and green onions; cook and stir until shrimp turns pink, 1-2 minutes. Add pasta and peas; heat through, tossing to combine and adding reserved pasta water if desired.

Per 1⅓ cups: 404 cal., 10g fat (1g sat. fat), 138mg chol., 588mg sodium, 50g carb. (4g sugars, 5g fiber), 28g pro.
Diabetic Exchanges: 3 starch, 3 lean meat, 1½ fat.

BLACK BEAN & SWEET POTATO RICE BOWLS

BLACK BEAN & SWEET POTATO RICE BOWLS

With three hungry boys in my house, dinners need to be quick and filling and it helps to get in some veggies, too. This one is a favorite because it's hearty and fun to tweak with different ingredients.
—Kim Van Dunk, Caldwell, NJ

Start to Finish: 30 min.
Makes: 4 servings

- ¾ cup uncooked long grain rice
- ¼ teaspoon garlic salt
- 1½ cups water
- 3 tablespoons olive oil, divided
- 1 large sweet potato, peeled and diced
- 1 medium red onion, finely chopped
- 4 cups chopped fresh kale (tough stems removed)
- 1 can (15 ounces) black beans, rinsed and drained
- 2 tablespoons sweet chili sauce

Lime wedges, optional
Additional sweet chili sauce, optional

1. Place rice, garlic salt and water in a large saucepan; bring to a boil. Reduce heat; simmer, covered, until water is absorbed and the rice is tender, about 15-20 minutes. Remove from heat; let stand 5 minutes.
2. Meanwhile, in a large skillet, heat 2 tablespoons oil over medium-high heat; saute sweet potato 8 minutes. Add onion; cook and stir until sweet potato is tender, 4-6 minutes. Add kale; cook and stir until tender, 3-5 minutes. Stir in beans; heat through.
3. Gently stir 2 tablespoons chili sauce and remaining oil into rice; add to potato mixture. If desired, serve with lime wedges and additional chili sauce.

Per 2 cups: 435 cal., 11g fat (2g sat. fat), 0 chol., 405mg sodium, 74g carb. (15g sugars, 8g fiber), 10g pro.
HEALTH TIP Sweet potato + kale + black beans = nearly ⅓ of the daily value for fiber!

Cooking For Kids

Whether you're cooking for kids or grandkids—or planning a family get-together—turn here for wholesome foods that children love. Find muffin-cup dinners, after-school snacks and even PB&J milk shakes.

QUICK CHILI MAC

FAST FIX ▶

QUICK CHILI MAC

This yummy skillet dinner combines my chili recipe with an easy pasta dish. It's a great meal for company or potlucks. Add taco seasoning and black beans for a flavor twist.

—Lee Steinmetz, Lansing, MI

Start to Finish: 20 min.
Makes: 6 servings

- 1 cup uncooked elbow macaroni
- 1 pound ground beef
- 1 small green pepper, chopped
- 1 small onion, chopped
- 2 cans (15 ounces each) chili with beans
- 1 can (11 ounces) whole kernel corn, drained
- 1 cup shredded cheddar cheese

1. Cook macaroni according to package directions; drain. Meanwhile, in a large skillet, cook and crumble beef with pepper and onion over medium heat until no longer pink, 5-7 minutes; drain.

2. Stir in chili, corn and macaroni; heat through. Sprinkle with cheese.

Per 1⅓ cups: 422 cal., 21g fat (9g sat. fat), 89mg chol., 898mg sodium, 27g carb. (6g sugars, 4g fiber), 30g pro.

TUNA NOODLE CUPS

Older kids can get a jump on preparing dinner by stirring up these miniature tuna casseroles. Or serve them for brunch with fresh fruit, a tossed salad and rolls.

—Marlene Pugh, Fort McMurray, AB

Prep: 25 min. • **Bake:** 30 min.
Makes: 9 servings

- 8 ounces uncooked medium egg noodles (about 4 cups)
- 2 cans (5 ounces each) light tuna in water, drained
- 2 cups frozen peas and carrots (about 10 ounces), thawed
- 1 small onion, finely chopped
- 2 cups shredded cheddar cheese, divided
- 3 large eggs
- 1 can (12 ounces) evaporated milk
- ½ cup water
- 1 teaspoon garlic salt
- ¼ teaspoon pepper

1. Preheat oven to 350°. In a 6-qt. stockpot, cook noodles according to package directions; drain and return to pot. Add tuna, peas and carrots, onion and 1 cup cheese.

2. Whisk together eggs, milk, water and seasonings; toss with noodle mixture. Divide among 18 well-greased muffin cups. Sprinkle with remaining cheese.

3. Bake until heated through, 30-35 minutes. Cool 5 minutes. Loosen edges with a knife before removing from pans.

Per 2 noodle cups: 316 cal., 14g fat (7g sat. fat), 131mg chol., 549mg sodium, 27g carb. (5g sugars, 2g fiber), 21g pro.

FAST FIX ▶

SPANISH NOODLES & GROUND BEEF

Bacon adds flavor to this comforting stovetop supper that my mom frequently made when we were growing up. And now I prepare it for my family.
—Kelli Jones, Peris, CA

Start to Finish: 25 min.
Makes: 4 servings

- 1 pound ground beef
- 1 small green pepper, chopped
- ⅓ cup chopped onion
- 3¼ cups uncooked medium egg noodles (about 6 ounces)
- 1 can (14½ ounces) diced tomatoes, undrained
- 1½ cups water
- ¼ cup chili sauce
- ¼ teaspoon salt
- ⅛ teaspoon pepper
- 4 bacon strips, cooked and crumbled

1. In a large skillet, cook and crumble the beef with green pepper and onion over medium heat until no longer pink, for 5-7 minutes; drain.

2. Stir in noodles, tomatoes, water, chili sauce, salt and pepper; bring to a boil. Reduce heat; simmer, covered, until the noodles are tender, for 15-20 minutes, stirring frequently. Top with bacon.

Per 1½ cups: 409 cal., 18g fat (6g sat. fat), 104mg chol., 756mg sodium, 33g carb. (8g sugars, 3g fiber), 28g pro.

PINEAPPLE-GLAZED CHICKEN THIGHS

EAT SMART **FAST FIX** ▶

PINEAPPLE-GLAZED CHICKEN THIGHS

These juicy chicken thighs taste so rich and delicious with a sweet pineapple-maple glaze. I love that I can reach in my pantry for ingredients and end up with this impressive weeknight meal.
—Trisha Kruse, Eagle, ID

Start to Finish: 30 min.
Makes: 4 servings

- 1 can (20 ounces) unsweetened pineapple tidbits
- 4 boneless skinless chicken thighs
- ¾ teaspoon salt
- ½ teaspoon lemon-pepper seasoning
- 2 teaspoons olive oil
- 1 tablespoon butter
- 2 tablespoons maple syrup
  Hot cooked brown rice

1. Drain pineapple well, reserving ¼ cup juice. Sprinkle chicken with seasonings. In a large skillet, heat oil over medium-high heat; brown thighs on both sides. Remove from pan.

2. In the same skillet, melt butter over medium heat. Add drained pineapple; cook and stir 5 minutes. Stir in maple syrup and reserved juice. Add chicken; cook, covered, until a thermometer inserted in chicken reads 170°, 5-7 minutes. Remove chicken to a serving plate; keep warm.

3. Increase heat to medium-high; cook and stir pineapple mixture until slightly thickened. Spoon over chicken; serve with rice.

Per chicken thigh with ¼ cup pineapple mixture: 328 cal., 14g fat (4g sat. fat), 83mg chol., 571mg sodium, 31g carb. (28g sugars, 2g fiber), 22g pro.
Diabetic Exchanges: 3 lean meat, 1 starch, 1 fruit, 1 fat.

SKILLET MAC & CHEESE

This super-creamy mac 'n' cheese is so simple it almost seems too easy! Kids really go for the rich, cheesy flavor, but I've never met an adult who didn't love it, either.
—Ann Bowers, Rockport, TX

Start to Finish: 25 min.
Makes: 4 servings

  2 cups uncooked elbow macaroni (about 8 ounces)
  2 tablespoons butter
  2 tablespoons all-purpose flour
  1½ cups half-and-half cream
  ¾ pound process cheese (Velveeta), cubed
     Optional toppings: crumbled cooked bacon, crushed cheddar cheese fish-shaped crackers, chopped fresh chives and freshly ground pepper

1. Cook macaroni according to package directions; drain.

2. Meanwhile, in a large nonstick skillet, melt butter over medium heat. Stir in flour until smooth; gradually whisk in cream. Bring to a boil, stirring constantly. Cook and stir until thickened, about 2 minutes. Reduce heat; stir in cheese until melted.

3. Add macaroni; cook and stir until heated through. Top as desired.
Per 1½ cups: 600 cal., 37g fat (23g sat. fat), 144mg chol., 1185mg sodium, 40g carb. (9g sugars, 1g fiber), 23g pro.

SCHOOLHOUSE CHILI
PICTURED ON P. 143

When I was a school cook, the students loved my chili because they thought it didn't have beans in it. They didn't know I puree the beans, tomatoes, onions and green pepper to create a tasty and nutritious chili!
—Mary Selner, Green Bay, WI

Prep: 10 min. • **Cook:** 70 min.
Makes: 6 servings

  1 can (14½ ounces) diced tomatoes, undrained
  1 can (16 ounces) mild chili beans, undrained
  ½ cup chopped onion
  ¼ cup chopped green pepper
  1 pound ground beef
  1½ teaspoons salt
  1 to 2 teaspoons chili powder
  1 teaspoon ground cumin
  ½ teaspoon pepper
     Hot cooked spaghetti, optional

1. In a blender, combine the tomatoes, beans, onion and green pepper; cover and puree until smooth.
2. In a large saucepan, cook beef over medium heat until no longer pink; drain. Add seasonings and pureed vegetables. Bring to a boil. Reduce heat; cover and simmer for 1 hour. Serve with spaghetti if desired.
Per cup: 243 cal., 10g fat (4g sat. fat), 50mg chol., 1048mg sodium, 17g carb. (3g sugars, 5g fiber), 19g pro.

SKILLET MAC & CHEESE

Roasted Pumpkin Seeds

Scoop up a buttery batch of fall's most addictive snack.

Cook Homemade Pumpkin Seeds

1. Scoop

Preheat oven to 250°. Cut the top off of a carving pumpkin. Scoop out the seeds and the stringy pulp.

2. Toss

Rinse the seeds, discarding the pulp. Pat them dry. Toss with melted butter, salt and Worcestershire sauce.

3. Spread

Evenly spread the seeds over the surface of a greased, foil-lined 15x10x1-in. pan.

4. Roast

Bake 45 minutes, stirring occasionally. Increase the temperature to 325°. Bake until lightly browned and dry, about 5 minutes. Serve your pumpkin seeds warm or at room temperature. Cool completely before storing in an airtight container.

EAT SMART **(5) INGREDIENTS**

ROASTED PUMPKIN SEEDS

To enjoy the seeds from a pumpkin you hollow out, spice 'em and bake 'em for a fun snack.

—Dawn Fagerstrom, Warren, MN

Prep: 20 min. • **Bake:** 50 min.
Makes: 2 cups

- 2 cups fresh pumpkin seeds
- 3 tablespoons butter, melted
- 1 teaspoon salt
- 1 teaspoon Worcestershire sauce

Per ¼ cup: 110 cal., 7g fat (3g sat. fat), 11mg chol., 339mg sodium, 9g carb. (0 sugars, 3g fiber), 3g pro.
Diabetic Exchanges: 1½ fat, ½ starch.

DID YOU KNOW?

Worcestershire sauce was originally considered a mistake. In 1835, an English lord commissioned two chemists to duplicate a sauce he had tried in India. The pungent batch was disappointing and wound up in their cellar. When the pair stumbled upon the aged concoction 2 years later, they were pleasantly surprised by its unique taste.

SWEET CHILI AND ORANGE CHICKEN

My husband loves this simple chicken dish so much he often requests it when he comes home from deployment. The sweet chili sauce adds just the right amount of heat—not too much for most kids— to the bright, citrusy entree.
—Jessica Eastman, Bremerton, WA

Start to Finish: 20 min.
Makes: 4 servings

- 1 pound boneless skinless chicken breasts, cut into 1-inch pieces
- ¼ teaspoon salt
- ¼ teaspoon pepper
- 2 tablespoons butter
- ¾ cup sweet chili sauce
- ⅓ cup thawed orange juice concentrate
   Hot cooked jasmine or other rice
   Minced fresh basil

1. Toss chicken with salt and pepper. In a large skillet, heat butter over medium-high heat; stir-fry chicken until no longer pink, 5-7 minutes. Remove from pan; keep warm.
2. Add chili sauce and juice concentrate to skillet; cook and stir until heated through. Stir in chicken. Serve with rice; sprinkle with basil.

Per ½ cup chicken mixture: 309 cal., 9g fat (4g sat. fat), 78mg chol., 1014mg sodium, 33g carb. (31g sugars, 1g fiber), 24g pro.

MEAT LOAF MUFFINS

Serve these tangy meat loaf muffins for dinner or slice them up for a take-along sandwich lunch. They're just as flavorful after freezing.
—Cheryl Norwood, Canton, GA

Start to Finish: 30 min.
Makes: 6 servings

- 1 large egg, lightly beaten
- ½ cup dry bread crumbs
- ½ cup finely chopped onion
- ½ cup finely chopped green pepper
- ¼ cup barbecue sauce
- 1½ pounds lean ground beef (90% lean)
- 3 tablespoons ketchup
   Additional ketchup, optional

1. Preheat oven to 375°. Mix first five ingredients. Add beef; mix lightly but thoroughly. Press about ⅓ cupfuls into each of 12 ungreased muffin cups.
2. Bake 15 minutes. Brush tops with 3 tablespoons ketchup; bake until a thermometer reads 160°, 5-7 minutes. If desired, serve with additional ketchup.

Freeze option: Bake meat loaves without ketchup; cover and freeze on a plastic wrap-lined baking sheet until firm. Transfer meat loaves to a resealable plastic freezer bag; return to freezer. To use, partially thaw in refrigerator overnight. Place meat loaves on a greased shallow baking pan. Spread with ketchup. Bake in a preheated 350° oven until heated through.

Per 2 mini meat loaves: 260 cal., 11g fat (4g sat. fat), 102mg chol., 350mg sodium, 15g carb. (7g sugars, 1g fiber), 24g pro.

SWEET CHILI AND ORANGE CHICKEN

MINI SHEPHERD'S PIES

SWEET & SALTY PEANUT BUTTER BITES

My son Micah and I love peanut butter cups, so we made them into a new treat. We entered them in a creative baking contest and won first place!
—Autumn Emigh, Gahanna, OH

Prep: 20 min. • **Cook:** 5 min. + standing
Makes: about 5 dozen

- ½ cup semisweet chocolate chips
- 4 peanut butter cups (¾ ounce each), chopped
- 1⅓ cups creamy peanut butter
- 1 cup sugar
- 1 cup light corn syrup
- ⅛ teaspoon salt
- 4 cups Rice Krispies
- 1 cup broken pretzels

1. Freeze chocolate chips and peanut butter cups until partially frozen, for about 15 minutes.
2. In a 6-qt. stockpot, combine peanut butter, sugar, corn syrup and salt. Cook and stir over low heat until blended.
3. Remove from heat; stir in Rice Krispies and pretzels until coated. Let stand 5 minutes; gently fold in chocolate chips and peanut butter cups until just combined. Drop by tablespoonfuls onto waxed paper; let stand until set.
Per cookie: 86 cal., 4g fat (1g sat. fat), 0 chol., 67mg sodium, 13g carb. (10g sugars, 0 fiber), 2g pro.

FREEZE IT
MINI SHEPHERD'S PIES

These savory little pies may be made with simple convenience items, but I'm just as confident serving them to drop-in company as I am to my husband and three boys.
—Ellen Osborne, Clarksville, TN

Prep: 30 min. • **Bake:** 20 min.
Makes: 5 servings

- 1 pound ground beef
- ¼ cup chopped onion
- 1 garlic clove, minced
- ⅓ cup chili sauce or ketchup
- 1 tablespoon cider vinegar
- 1¼ cups water
- 3 ounces cream cheese, cubed
- 3 tablespoons butter
- 1¼ cups mashed potato flakes
- 2 tubes (6 ounces each) small refrigerated buttermilk biscuits
- ½ cup crushed potato chips
  Paprika, optional

1. Preheat oven to 375°. In a large skillet, cook and crumble beef with onion and garlic over medium heat until no longer pink, 5-7 minutes; drain. Stir in chili sauce and vinegar.
2. In a small saucepan, combine water, cream cheese and butter; bring to a boil. Remove from heat; stir in potato flakes.
3. Separate biscuits; press each onto bottom and up sides of a greased muffin cup. Fill with beef mixture; top with mashed potatoes. Sprinkle with potato chips.
4. Bake until topping is golden brown, about 20-25 minutes. If desired, sprinkle with paprika.
Freeze option: Freeze cooled pies in a single layer in freezer containers. To use, partially thaw in refrigerator overnight. Reheat on a baking sheet in a preheated 375° oven until heated through, for 15-18 minutes.
Per 2 mini shepherd's pies: 612 cal., 36g fat (15g sat. fat), 92mg chol., 1094mg sodium, 49g carb. (11g sugars, 2g fiber), 24g pro.

LASAGNA CUPS

I love lasagna and garlic bread, so it only made sense to put them together in these fun little cups. Have one as an appetizer or two for a meal!
—Angelique Douglas, Maryville, IL

Prep: 40 min. • **Bake:** 15 min.
Makes: 8 servings

- 3 individual lasagna noodles
- ½ pound ground turkey or beef
- 1 cup meatless pasta sauce
- ⅓ cup 2% cottage cheese
- ¼ teaspoon garlic powder
- 2 tubes (8 ounces each) refrigerated crescent rolls
- 2 cups shredded Italian cheese blend or cheddar cheese
- 1 cup grape tomatoes, halved

1. Preheat oven to 375°. Cook lasagna noodles according to package directions. Drain and rinse with water; cut each noodle into six squares.
2. In a large skillet, cook and crumble turkey over medium heat until no longer pink, 5-7 minutes. Stir in sauce, cottage cheese and garlic powder; bring to a boil. Remove from heat.
3. Unroll both tubes of crescent dough; separate each into eight triangles. Press each triangle onto bottom and up sides of a greased muffin cup. Layer each with 1 tablespoon cheese, one noodle piece and 1 rounded tablespoon meat sauce (discard extra noodle pieces). Sprinkle with remaining cheese.
4. Bake on a lower oven rack until crust is golden brown, 15-20 minutes. Let stand 5 minutes before removing from pan. Top with tomatoes.

Per 2 lasagna cups: 412 cal., 21g fat (9g sat. fat), 39mg chol., 839mg sodium, 34g carb. (7g sugars, 1g fiber), 18g pro.

LASAGNA CUPS

FREEZE IT
DUTCH WAFFLE COOKIES

My mom taught me how to make these waffle iron cookies. Now I have my friends bring their waffle irons to my house, and we make big batches.
—Rachel Setala, Surrey, BC

Prep: 40 min. • **Cook:** 5 min./batch
Makes: about 6 dozen

- 1 cup butter, softened
- 1 cup sugar
- 2 large eggs
- ½ cup 2% milk
- 1 tablespoon vanilla extract
- 4 cups all-purpose flour
- 1¾ teaspoons baking powder
- ¾ teaspoon baking soda
  Confectioners' sugar, optional

1. In large bowl, beat butter and sugar until blended. Beat in eggs, milk and vanilla. In another bowl, whisk the flour, baking powder and baking soda; gradually beat into butter mixture.
2. Shape level tablespoons of dough into balls; place 2 in. apart on a preheated waffle iron coated with cooking spray. Bake on medium heat 3-4 minutes or until cookies are golden brown. Remove to wire racks to cool. If desired, dust with confectioners' sugar.

Freeze option: Freeze the cookies, layered between waxed paper, in freezer containers. To use, thaw in the covered containers. If desired, dust with additional confectioners' sugar.

Per cookie: 62 cal., 3g fat (2g sat. fat), 12mg chol., 46mg sodium, 8g carb. (3g sugars, 0 fiber), 1g pro.

Party Animals

Step right up and celebrate Animal Crackers Day (it's April 18) with a homemade circus treat.

> ✳ The greatest snack on earth! Mix popcorn, pastel marshmallows, Raisinets, peanuts, pretzels, and frosted and plain animal crackers.

EAT SMART **FAST FIX** ▸

DELICIOUS APPLE SALAD

PICTURED ON P. 143

This yummy fruit salad was a favorite of my great-grandmother's. My family always enjoys it, and I'm happy knowing it's good for them, too.
—Sue Gronholz, Beaver Dam, WI

Start to Finish: 15 min.
Makes: 6 servings

- 3   cups cubed apples (½ inch)
- 2   tablespoons lemon juice
- 1   cup chopped celery
- 1   cup miniature marshmallows
- ⅔   cup fat-free mayonnaise
- ½   cup chopped pecans or walnuts

In a large bowl, toss apples with lemon juice. Add celery and marshmallows. Stir in mayonnaise, then nuts. Serve immediately or refrigerate.
Per ¾ cup: 140 cal., 7g fat (1g sat. fat), 0 chol., 234mg sodium, 21g carb. (13g sugars, 3g fiber), 1g pro.
Diabetic Exchanges: 1 starch, 1 fat, ½ fruit.

EAT SMART **FAST FIX** ▸

HOMEMADE PEANUT BUTTER

PICTURED ON P. 143

We eat a lot of peanut butter, and so I decided to make my own. I checked the cost of my homemade spread against the price in stores around here and found mine to be much cheaper, with the added value of knowing what goes into it! Not to mention it's a whole lot tastier.
—Marge Austin, North Pole, AK

Start to Finish: 15 min.
Makes: about 1 cup

- 2   cups unsalted dry roasted peanuts
- ½   teaspoon salt
- 1   tablespoon honey

Process peanuts and salt in a food processor until desired consistency, about 5 minutes, scraping down sides as needed. Add honey; process just until blended. Store in an airtight container in refrigerator.
Per tablespoon: 111 cal., 9g fat (1g sat. fat), 0 chol., 75mg sodium, 5g carb. (2g sugars, 2g fiber), 4g pro.
Diabetic Exchanges: 2 fat.

---

⑤ INGREDIENTS **FAST FIX** ▸

PEANUT BUTTER & JELLY BREAKFAST SHAKE

My husband is a big kid who'll often whip up this tasty shake for a breakfast on the go. Your kids will love the flavor of a peanut butter and jelly sandwich in a glass.
—Loretta Levitz, Allston, MA

Start to Finish: 10 min.
Makes: 2 servings (2½ cups)

- 2   cups cold milk
- 1   ripe banana, sliced
- 2   tablespoons peanut butter
- 2   tablespoons jam, jelly or preserves (any flavor)
- ½   teaspoon vanilla extract

In a blender, place all ingredients; cover and process for 3 minutes or until smooth. Pour into chilled glasses; serve immediately.
Per 1¼ cups: 346 cal., 16g fat (6g sat. fat), 24mg chol., 173mg sodium, 41g carb. (32g sugars, 2g fiber), 13g pro.

SNACK MIX SQUARES

A fun snack mix pressed into chewy bars, this treat is popular with kids of all ages. Someone is always asking me for this quick and easy recipe.
—Lisa Byler, Millersburg, IN

Start to Finish: 30 min.
Makes: about 3 dozen

- 2½ cups halved pretzel sticks
- 2 cups Corn Chex
- 1½ cups M&M's
- ½ cup butter
- ⅓ cup creamy peanut butter
- 5 cups miniature marshmallows

1. In a large bowl, combine pretzels, cereal and M&M's. In a large saucepan over low heat, melt butter and peanut butter. Add marshmallows; cook and stir until the marshmallows are melted and mixture is smooth.
2. Pour over pretzel mixture; stir to coat. Press into a greased 13x9-in. pan. Cool until firm; cut into squares.

Per serving: 114 cal., 6g fat (3g sat. fat), 8mg chol., 107mg sodium, 15g carb. (9g sugars, 0 fiber), 2g pro.

STOVETOP BEEF & SHELLS

STOVETOP BEEF & SHELLS

I fix this sauced-up supper when I'm pressed for time, and lucky for my family, it's as tasty as it is fast. Team it up with salad, bread and fruit for a comforting meal.
—Donna Roberts, Manhattan, KS

Start to Finish: 30 min.
Makes: 4 servings

- 1½ cups uncooked medium pasta shells (about 4 ounces)
- 1 pound lean ground beef (90% lean)
- 1 medium onion, chopped
- 1 garlic clove, minced
- 1 can (15 ounces) crushed tomatoes
- 1 can (8 ounces) tomato sauce
- 1 teaspoon sugar
- ½ teaspoon salt
- ½ teaspoon pepper

1. Cook pasta according to package directions; drain.
2. Meanwhile, in a large skillet, cook and crumble beef with onion and garlic over medium-high heat until no longer pink, for 5-7 minutes. Stir in remaining ingredients; bring to a boil. Reduce the heat; simmer, uncovered, until the flavors are blended, 10-15 minutes.
3. Stir in pasta; heat through.

Per 1¼ cups: 344 cal., 11g fat (4g sat. fat), 71mg chol., 815mg sodium, 35g carb. (9g sugars, 4g fiber), 29g pro.
Diabetic Exchanges: 3 lean meat, 2 starch, 1 vegetable.

★ ★ ★ ★ ★ **READER REVIEW**
"My picky 3-year-old had three helpings of this. Need I say more?"
MVPHELAN TASTEOFHOME.COM

Breakfast & Brunch

Make any morning a great start when you prepare one of these tasty breakfasts. Bacony breakfast pizza, on-the-go mini crustless quiches, and a fluffy, fanciful German pancake are just some of the choices you'll find. Why skimp on breakfast when you have options like these?

Egg-Topped Wilted Salad (p. 159) **Sausage Cheese Squares** (p. 161)
Stuffed Ham & Egg Bread (p. 156) **Breakfast Pizza** (p. 164) **Spiced Apple Oatmeal** (p. 160)

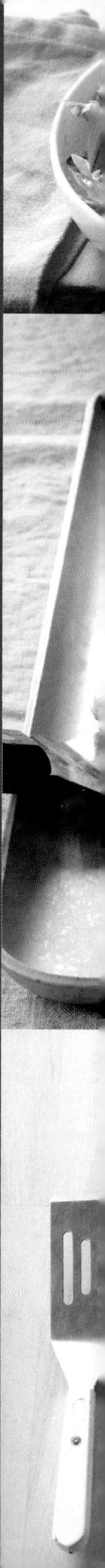

CINNAMON APPLE PANCAKES

CINNAMON APPLE PANCAKES

My family loves the apple and cinnamon flavor in these light and hearty pancakes. And best of all, they're sweet enough to enjoy even without syrup.
—Kim McConnell, Tulsa, OK

Start to Finish: 25 min.
Makes: 6 servings

- 2 **cups whole wheat flour**
- 4 **teaspoons baking powder**
- 1 **teaspoon ground cinnamon**
- ½ **teaspoon salt**
- 2 **large eggs**
- 2 **cups fat-free milk**
- 2 **tablespoons honey**
- 1 **tablespoon canola oil**
- 1 **medium apple, chopped**

1. In a bowl, whisk together first four ingredients. In another bowl, whisk together eggs, milk, honey and oil; add to the dry ingredients, stirring just until moistened. Stir in apple.
2. Preheat a lightly greased griddle over medium heat. Pour batter by ⅓ cupfuls onto griddle; cook until bubbles on top begin to pop and bottoms of pancakes are golden brown.
Per 2 pancakes: 241 cal., 5g fat (1g sat. fat), 64mg chol., 576mg sodium, 42g carb. (12g sugars, 5g fiber), 10g pro.
Diabetic Exchanges: 3 starch, 1 lean meat, ½ fat.
HEALTH TIP According to a study cited by the Harvard T. H. Chan School of Public Health, people who ate the most whole grains had a lower risk of cancer, heart disease and mortality compared to those who ate little or no whole grains.

⑤ INGREDIENTS

STUFFED HAM & EGG BREAD
PICTURED ON P. 155

My son, Gus, is a lover of all things ham-and-eggs, so I created this comforting stuffed bread with him in mind. I later added tomatoes, and he still gives it a big thumbs up.
—Karen Kuebler, Dallas, TX

Prep: 25 min. • **Bake:** 20 min.
Makes: 8 servings

- 2 **teaspoons canola oil**
- 1 **can (14½ ounces) diced tomatoes, drained**
- 6 **large eggs, lightly beaten**
- 2 **cups chopped fully cooked ham**
- 1 **tube (11 ounces) refrigerated crusty French loaf**
- 2 **cups shredded sharp cheddar cheese**

1. Preheat oven to 400°. In a large nonstick skillet, heat oil over medium heat. Add tomatoes; cook and stir until juices are evaporated, 12-15 minutes. Add eggs; cook and stir until they are thickened and no liquid egg remains, for 3-4 minutes. Remove from heat; stir in ham.
2. Unroll dough onto a greased baking sheet. Sprinkle cheese lengthwise down one half of the dough to within 1 in. of edges. Top with egg mixture. Fold dough over the filling, pinching to seal; tuck the ends under.
3. Bake until deep golden brown, about 17-20 minutes. Cut into slices.
Per piece: 321 cal., 17g fat (7g sat. fat), 188mg chol., 967mg sodium, 22g carb. (3g sugars, 1g fiber), 22g pro.

PUFF PASTRY DANISHES

Even though they're quite simple, these jam-filled pastries are right at home in a holiday brunch spread. They were my dad's favorite, so the recipe will always be close to my heart.
—Chellie Richardson, Sidney, OH

....

Prep: 30 min. • **Bake:** 15 min.
Makes: 1½ dozen

- 1 package (8 ounces) cream cheese, softened
- ¼ cup sugar
- 2 tablespoons all-purpose flour
- ½ teaspoon vanilla extract
- 2 large egg yolks, divided
- 1 tablespoon water
- 1 package (17.3 ounces) frozen puff pastry, thawed
- ⅔ cup seedless raspberry jam or jam of choice

1. Preheat oven to 425°. Beat the first four ingredients until smooth; beat in 1 egg yolk.
2. Mix water and remaining egg yolk. On a lightly floured surface, unfold each sheet of puff pastry; roll into a 12-in. square. Cut each into nine 4-in. squares; transfer to parchment paper-lined baking sheets.
3. Top each square with 1 tablespoon cream cheese mixture and 1 rounded teaspoon jam. Bring two opposite corners of pastry over filling, sealing with yolk mixture. Brush tops of the pastries with remaining yolk mixture.
4. Bake until golden brown, about 14-16 minutes. Serve warm. Refrigerate the leftovers.
Per pastry: 197 cal., 12g fat (4g sat. fat), 33mg chol., 130mg sodium, 20g carb. (3g sugars, 2g fiber), 3g pro.

PUFF PASTRY DANISHES

SUNRISE SAUSAGE ENCHILADAS

These delicious enchiladas are equally good made with cubed ham or sausage. Prepare ahead, refrigerate, and bake when you are ready for a convenient, hot, full-meal breakfast all in one pan.
—Deb LeBlanc, Phillipsburg, KS

....

Prep: 30 min. + chilling • **Bake:** 40 min.
Makes: 10 servings

- 1 pound bulk pork sausage
- 2 tablespoons canola oil
- 7 cups frozen shredded hash brown potatoes, thawed (20 ounces)
- ½ teaspoon salt
- ½ teaspoon chili powder
- ¼ teaspoon cayenne pepper
- ¼ teaspoon pepper
- 1 can (4 ounces) chopped green chilies
- 2 cups shredded cheddar cheese, divided
- 10 flour tortillas (6 inches)
- 2 cans (10 ounces each) green enchilada sauce

OPTIONAL TOPPINGS
   Chopped red onion
   Chopped sweet red pepper
   Chopped fresh cilantro

1. In a large skillet, cook and crumble sausage over medium heat until no longer pink, 5-7 minutes. Remove from pan with a slotted spoon; discard drippings.
2. In same pan, heat oil over medium-high heat; saute potatoes until lightly browned, 8-10 minutes. Remove from heat; stir in seasonings, chilies, sausage and ½ cup of cheese.
3. Place ½ cup filling on each tortilla; roll up the enchiladas and place in a greased 13x9-in. baking dish, seam side down. Top with sauce. Refrigerate, covered, several hours or overnight.
4. Preheat oven to 375°. Remove enchiladas from refrigerator while oven heats. Bake, covered, for 30 minutes. Sprinkle with remaining cheese. Bake, uncovered, until lightly browned and heated through, 10-15 minutes. If desired, serve with toppings.
Per enchilada: 398 cal., 25g fat (9g sat. fat), 48mg chol., 1116mg sodium, 30g carb. (2g sugars, 2g fiber), 14g pro.

French Toast for All

The trick to getting sleepyheads out of bed is a dash of vanilla, a quick dip and a sizzle on the griddle.

HOW-TO

Toast Up Golden Perfection

1. Mix Up The Custard

In a shallow dish, whisk the first five ingredients until well blended. Preheat a greased griddle over medium heat.

2. Let It Sink In

Place the bread in the egg mixture, allowing each slice to soak for 30 seconds per side. The bread should be saturated well, but not so soggy that it falls apart.

3. Get Ready To Toast

Remove bread from the egg mixture; allow excess liquid to drip back into the dish.

4. Sizzle Away

Toast the bread on the griddle until both sides are golden. Serve right away with your favorite toppings, or keep warm in a 200° oven until you're ready.

EAT SMART **FAST FIX**

VANILLA FRENCH TOAST

We discovered this recipe in Mexico. We couldn't figure out what made the French toast so delicious until we learned the secret was vanilla—one of Mexico's most popular flavorings. Since then, we've added a touch of vanilla to our waffle and pancake recipes, and it really does make all the difference.
—Joe and Bobbi Schott, Castroville, TX

Start to Finish: 15 min.
Makes: 6 servings

- 4 large eggs, lightly beaten
- 1 cup 2% milk
- 2 tablespoons sugar
- 2 teaspoons vanilla extract
- 1/8 teaspoon salt
- 12 slices day-old sandwich bread
  Optional toppings: butter, maple syrup, fresh berries and confectioners' sugar

Whole Wheat Cinnamon French Toast: Omit the vanilla. Substitute 1½ teaspoons honey for sugar and whole wheat bread for the day-old bread. Add ¼ teaspoon ground cinnamon to the milk mixture.

Per 2 slices: 218 cal., 6g fat (3g sat. fat), 127mg chol., 376mg sodium, 30g carb. (9g sugars, 1g fiber), 10g pro.
Diabetic Exchanges: 2 starch, 1 medium-fat meat.

EGG-TOPPED WILTED SALAD

PICTURED ON P. 155

Tossed with a bright champagne vinegar dressing and topped with maple-chipotle bacon and sunny eggs, this is the ultimate brunch salad. But it's so delicious I'd gladly enjoy it any time of any day!
—Courtney Gaylord, Columbus, IN

Prep: 20 min. • **Bake:** 25 min.
Makes: 4 servings

- 8 bacon strips
- 1 teaspoon packed brown sugar
- ¼ teaspoon ground chipotle pepper
- 1 small red onion, halved and thinly sliced
- 2 tablespoons champagne vinegar
- 1 teaspoon sugar
- ½ teaspoon pepper
- 4 large eggs
- ¼ teaspoon salt
- 8 cups spring mix salad greens (about 5 ounces)
- ½ cup crumbled feta cheese

1. Preheat oven to 350°. Place bacon on one half of a foil-lined 15x10x1-in. pan. Mix brown sugar and chipotle pepper; sprinkle evenly over bacon. Bake until bacon begins to shrink, about 10 minutes.

2. Using tongs, move bacon to other half of pan. Add onion to bacon drippings, stirring to coat. Return to oven; bake until bacon is crisp, about 15 minutes. Drain on paper towels, reserving 2 tablespoons of the drippings.

3. In a small bowl, whisk together vinegar, sugar, pepper and reserved drippings. Coarsely chop bacon.

4. Place a large nonstick skillet coated with cooking spray over medium-high heat. Break eggs, one at a time, into pan. Reduce heat to low; cook eggs until desired doneness, turning after whites are set if desired. Sprinkle with salt.

5. Toss greens with the dressing; divide among four plates. Top with bacon, onion, cheese and eggs. Serve immediately.

Per serving: 279 cal., 20g fat (8g sat. fat), 216mg chol., 730mg sodium, 10g carb. (3g sugars, 3g fiber), 17g pro.

YANKEE RANCHEROS

FAST FIX ▶ YANKEE RANCHEROS

After my in-laws began affectionately referring to me as a Yankee, I decided I needed to learn to make a few Mexican dishes. These rancheros are super easy and make my Tex-Mex-loving family happy—even if they do come from a Northerner.
—Darla Andrews, Schertz, TX

Start to Finish: 25 min.
Makes: 4 servings

- 5 cups frozen shredded hash brown potatoes (about 15 ounces)
- 1 cup refried beans
- ¼ cup salsa
- 2 naan flatbreads, halved
- 4 large eggs
- ½ cup shredded cheddar cheese or Mexican cheese blend
  Additional salsa, optional

1. Cook potatoes according to package directions for stovetop.

2. Meanwhile, in a microwave-safe bowl, mix beans and salsa. Microwave, covered, on high until heated through, 1-2 minutes, stirring once. In a large nonstick skillet, heat naan over medium-high heat until lightly browned, 2-3 minutes per side; remove from pan. Keep warm.

3. Coat same skillet with cooking spray; place over medium-high heat. Break eggs, one at a time, into pan; reduce heat to low. Cook until whites are set and yolks begin to thicken, turning once if desired.

4. To serve, spread bean mixture over naan. Top with potatoes, eggs and cheese. If desired, serve with additional salsa.

Per serving: 430 cal., 23g fat (6g sat. fat), 202mg chol., 703mg sodium, 40g carb. (4g sugars, 4g fiber), 16g pro.

✳
TEST KITCHEN TIPS
Bring the forks and knives to this "sandwich." It's a meal!

Chopped fresh cilantro, if you're a fan, makes for a perfect garnish.

> **"The crisp bacon, hard-cooked eggs and crunchy green onions make these special sandwiches look impressive when company drops by for lunch. Best of all, they're a snap to assemble."**
> —ANN FUEMMELER, GLASGOW, MO

BACON & EGG SANDWICHES

FAST FIX

BACON & EGG SANDWICHES

Start to Finish: 20 min.
Makes: 4 servings

- ½ cup sour cream
- 8 slices bread
- 4 green onions, chopped
- 4 slices process American cheese
- 2 hard-boiled large eggs, cut into ¼-inch slices
- 8 cooked bacon strips
- 2 tablespoons butter, softened

1. Spread sour cream over four bread slices; top with green onions, cheese, eggs, bacon and remaining bread. Spread outsides of sandwiches with butter.
2. Toast sandwiches until golden brown and cheese is melted, 2-3 minutes per side.
Per sandwich: 461 cal., 27g fat (13g sat. fat), 137mg chol., 887mg sodium, 32g carb. (6g sugars, 2g fiber), 19g pro.

SLOW COOKER

SPICED APPLE OATMEAL

PICTURED ON P. 155

These easy, appley oats let your family have a warm and cozy breakfast no matter how busy you are.
—Teri Rasey, Cadillac, MI

Prep: 15 min. • **Cook:** 4½ hours
Makes: 10 servings

- ½ cup packed brown sugar
- 2 tablespoons lemon juice
- 2 tablespoons molasses
- 3 teaspoons ground cinnamon
- 1 teaspoon ground nutmeg
- ½ teaspoon ground ginger
- ½ teaspoon ground allspice
- ¼ teaspoon salt
- 4 medium apples, peeled and cut into 1-inch slices
- 2 cups steel-cut oats
- 2 large eggs
- 2½ cups water
- 2 cups 2% milk
- 1 cup refrigerated vanilla dairy creamer
  Chopped pecans and additional milk, optional

1. Mix first eight ingredients. Place apples in a greased 4-qt. slow cooker. Top with brown sugar mixture, then with oats.
2. Whisk together eggs, water, milk and creamer; pour over oats. Cook, covered, on low until the oats are tender, 4½ to 5 hours. If desired, serve oatmeal with pecans and additional milk.
Per cup: 290 cal., 7g fat (3g sat. fat), 49mg chol., 109mg sodium, 53g carb. (30g sugars, 5g fiber), 7g pro.

MINI NUTELLA DOUGHNUTS

These crispy bites can be made in advance and refrigerated before frying. Pop them into your mouth still warm from the fryer for the best results.
—Renee Murphy, Smithtown, NY

Prep: 30 min. • **Cook:** 5 min./batch
Makes: 32 doughnuts

- 1 large egg
- 1 tablespoon water
- 1 tube (16.3 ounces) large refrigerated flaky biscuits (8 count)
- ⅔ cup Nutella
  Oil for deep-fat frying
  Confectioners' sugar

1. Whisk egg with water. On a lightly floured surface, roll each biscuit into a 6-in. circle; cut each into four wedges. Brush lightly with egg mixture; top each wedge with 1 teaspoon Nutella. Bring up corners over filling; pinch biscuit edges firmly to seal.

2. In an electric skillet or deep fryer, heat oil to 350°. In small batches, place doughnuts in hot oil, seam side down; fry until golden brown, 1-2 minutes per side. Drain on paper towels. Dust with confectioners' sugar; serve warm.
Per doughnut: 99 cal., 6g fat (1g sat. fat), 6mg chol., 142mg sodium, 10g carb. (5g sugars, 0 fiber), 2g pro.

FAST FIX ▶
SAUSAGE CHEESE SQUARES
PICTURED ON P. 155

My grandsons tried these savory morsels for the first time as youngsters and loved them. They're all grown-up now, and so instead of little appetizer squares, we make the servings breakfast-size pieces!
—Helen McFadden, Sierra Vista, AZ

Start to Finish: 30 min.
Makes: 12 servings

- 1 tube (8 ounces) refrigerated crescent rolls
- 1 package (8 ounces) frozen fully cooked breakfast sausage links, thawed and cut into ½-inch slices

MINI NUTELLA DOUGHNUTS

- 2 cups shredded Monterey Jack cheese
- 4 large eggs
- ¾ cup milk
- 2 tablespoons chopped green pepper
- ½ teaspoon salt
- ¼ teaspoon pepper

1. Unroll dough; place in an ungreased 13x9-in. baking dish. Press onto bottom and ½ in. up sides to form a crust. Top with sausage and cheese. Beat eggs in a bowl; add remaining ingredients. Carefully pour over cheese.
2. Bake, uncovered, at 425° for 20-25 minutes or until a knife inserted in the center comes out clean. Cut into 12 pieces (they will be rectangles).
Per piece: 252 cal., 19g fat (8g sat. fat), 92mg chol., 570mg sodium, 9g carb. (3g sugars, trace fiber), 11g pro.

⑤INGREDIENTS FAST FIX ▶
ZUCCHINI FRITTATA

When we travel by car, I use this as a sandwich filling. Make the frittata the night before, stuff it into pita bread in the morning, microwave for a minute or two and wrap in a towel to stay warm until you're ready to eat!
—Carol Blumenberg, Lehigh Acres, FL

Start to Finish: 20 min.
Makes: 2 servings

- 3 large eggs
- ¼ teaspoon salt
- 1 teaspoon canola oil
- ½ cup chopped onion
- 1 cup coarsely shredded zucchini
- ½ cup shredded Swiss cheese
  Coarsely ground pepper, optional

1. Preheat oven to 350°. Whisk together eggs and salt.
2. In an 8-in. ovenproof skillet coated with cooking spray, heat oil over medium heat; saute onion and zucchini until onion is crisp-tender. Pour in egg mixture; cook until almost set, 5-6 minutes. Sprinkle with cheese.
3. Bake, uncovered, until cheese is melted, 4-5 minutes. If desired, sprinkle with pepper.
Per serving: 261 cal., 18g fat (8g sat. fat), 304mg chol., 459mg sodium, 7g carb. (3g sugars, 1g fiber), 18g pro.

MAKE-AHEAD COFFEE CAKE

This coffee cake is a wonderful time-saver because it's assembled the night before. My kids think that the nutty topping, sweet glaze and from-scratch cake make it the ultimate treat.

—Cindy Harris, San Antonio, TX

Prep: 15 min. + chilling
Bake: 35 min. + cooling
Makes: 15 servings

- ¾ cup butter, softened
- 1 cup sugar
- 2 large eggs
- 2 cups all-purpose flour
- 1 teaspoon baking soda
- 1 teaspoon ground nutmeg
- ½ teaspoon salt
- 1 cup (8 ounces) sour cream
- ¾ cup packed brown sugar
- ½ cup chopped pecans or walnuts
- 1 teaspoon ground cinnamon

ICING
- 1 cup confectioners' sugar
- 1 to 2 tablespoons 2% milk

1. Cream butter and sugar until light and fluffy; beat in eggs, one at a time. In another bowl, whisk together flour, baking soda, nutmeg and salt; beat into creamed mixture alternately with sour cream. Spread into a greased 13x9-in. baking dish.
2. Mix the brown sugar, pecans and cinnamon; sprinkle over top. Refrigerate, covered, overnight.
3. Preheat oven to 350°. Remove coffee cake from refrigerator while oven heats. Bake, uncovered, until a toothpick inserted in center comes out clean, 35-40 minutes.
4. Cool on a wire rack 10 minutes. Mix icing ingredients; drizzle over the warm coffee cake.

Per piece: 336 cal., 16g fat (8g sat. fat), 53mg chol., 255mg sodium, 46g carb. (33g sugars, 1g fiber), 4g pro.

GERMAN PANCAKE

FAST FIX

GERMAN PANCAKE

Piping hot and puffy from the oven, this golden pancake made a pretty presentation for a skier's theme breakfast I hosted. Served with the homemade buttermilk syrup, it's an eye-opening treat. That easy syrup tastes great on waffles and French toast, too.

—Renae Moncur, Burley, ID

Start to Finish: 30 min.
Makes: 8 servings (2 cups syrup)

- 6 large eggs
- 1 cup 2% milk
- 1 cup all-purpose flour
- ½ teaspoon salt
- 2 tablespoons butter, melted

BUTTERMILK SYRUP
- ½ cup butter, cubed
- 1½ cups sugar
- ¾ cup buttermilk
- 2 tablespoons corn syrup
- 1 teaspoon baking soda
- 2 teaspoons vanilla extract
  Confectioners' sugar
  Fresh blueberries, optional

1. Preheat oven to 400°. Place the first four ingredients in a blender; process just until smooth.
2. Pour melted butter into a 13x9-in. baking dish; tilt dish to coat. Add batter; bake, uncovered, until puffed and golden brown, about 20 minutes.
3. Meanwhile, place butter, sugar, buttermilk, corn syrup and baking soda in a small saucepan; bring to a boil. Cook, uncovered, 7 minutes. Remove from heat; stir in vanilla.
4. Remove pancake from oven. Dust with confectioners' sugar; serve the pancake immediately with syrup and, if desired, fresh blueberries.

Per piece with ¼ cup syrup: 428 cal., 19g fat (11g sat. fat), 203mg chol., 543mg sodium, 56g carb. (42g sugars, 0 fiber), 8g pro.

HEALTH TIP The pancake itself is just 150 calories and 7g fat. For a nutritious spin, fill it with sauteed fresh fruit and a dusting of confectioners' sugar, or go savory with some leftover cubed turkey, gravy and herbs.

MAPLE SAUSAGE PATTIES

Maple syrup, sage and thyme give delightful flavor to these homemade sausage patties. It's such a treat to have homemade sausage, especially alongside pancakes or French toast.
—Margaret Eid, Huron, SD

Prep: 15 min. + chilling
Cook: 10 min.
Makes: 8 servings

- 1 tablespoon maple syrup
- ½ teaspoon salt
- ½ teaspoon onion powder
- ½ teaspoon rubbed sage
- ½ teaspoon dried thyme
- ½ teaspoon poultry seasoning
- ½ teaspoon ground nutmeg
- ¼ teaspoon cayenne pepper
- 1 to 2 teaspoons liquid smoke, optional
- 1 pound ground pork

1. In a large bowl, mix maple syrup, salt, spices and, if desired, liquid smoke. Add pork; mix lightly but thoroughly. Shape into eight 2½-in. patties. Refrigerate, covered, at least 1 hour.

2. In a large nonstick skillet coated with cooking spray, cook patties over medium heat until a thermometer reads 160°, 4-6 minutes per side.

Per patty: 128 cal., 8g fat (3g sat. fat), 38mg chol., 177mg sodium, 2g carb. (2g sugars, 0 fiber), 10g pro.

Turkey Maple Sausage Patties: Sub lean ground turkey for pork. The patties will be slightly more delicate to work with.

5 INGREDIENTS FAST FIX

SAUTEED APPLES

Here's a sweet side dish my family loves. It's wonderful on its own, but you can use it to top pancakes or French toast for breakfast, too.
—Shirley Heston, Pickerington, OH

Start to Finish: 30 min.
Makes: 6 servings

- ¼ cup butter, cubed
- 5 medium Golden Delicious apples, peeled and thinly sliced
- ¼ cup water
- ½ cup sugar
- ½ teaspoon ground cinnamon

In a large skillet, heat the butter over medium-high heat; saute apples for 1 minute. Add water; bring to a boil. Stir in sugar and cinnamon. Reduce heat; simmer, covered, until apples are tender, 10-12 minutes, stirring occasionally.

Per ⅔ cup: 185 cal., 8g fat (5g sat. fat), 20mg chol., 61mg sodium, 31g carb. (28g sugars, 2g fiber), 0 pro

MAPLE SAUSAGE PATTIES

CRANBERRY-APPLE FRENCH TOAST

My husband's breakfast club at work raves about this make-ahead French toast. Pop it in the oven in the morning to get your day off to a sweet, bubbly start.
—Mara Faulkner, Martinsburg, WV

Prep: 25 min. + chilling
Bake: 40 min + standing
Makes: 12 servings

- ⅔ cup packed light brown sugar
- ¼ cup maple syrup
- ¼ cup unsalted butter, melted
- ¼ teaspoon ground nutmeg
- 3 teaspoons ground cinnamon, divided
- 3 medium Granny Smith apples, peeled and thinly sliced
- ½ cup dried cranberries
- 6 large eggs
- 1½ cups whole milk
- 1 teaspoon vanilla extract
- 1 loaf (1 pound) challah or egg bread, cut into 1-inch slices

1. Mix the first four ingredients and 2 teaspoons cinnamon; toss with apples and cranberries. Transfer to a greased 13x9-in. baking dish.
2. In a large bowl, whisk together eggs, milk, vanilla and remaining cinnamon. Dip bread in egg mixture to moisten; place over fruit, overlapping or trimming slices to fit. Pour remaining egg mixture over bread. Refrigerate, covered, overnight.
3. Preheat oven to 375°. Remove baking dish from refrigerator while oven heats.

Bake, covered, for 30 minutes. Uncover; bake until bubbly and lightly browned, 10-15 minutes. Let stand 10 minutes before serving.
Per serving: 295 cal., 10g fat (4g sat. fat), 126mg chol., 197mg sodium, 45g carb. (25g sugars, 2g fiber), 8g pro.

⑤ INGREDIENTS FAST FIX

CARAMELIZED BACON TWISTS

My grandchildren get these sweet chewy bacon strips as a treat whenever they visit. Lining the pan with foil before baking helps cut down on cleanup.
—Jane Paschke, University Pk, FL

Start to Finish: 30 min.
Makes: about 3 dozen

- ½ cup packed brown sugar
- 2 teaspoons ground cinnamon
- 1 pound bacon strips

1. Preheat oven to 350°. Line a 15x10x1-in. pan with foil.
2. In a shallow bowl, mix brown sugar and cinnamon. Cut bacon strips crosswise in half; dip in sugar mixture to coat. Twist each piece two or three times, then place in prepared pan. Bake until browned and crisp, 15-20 minutes.

Freeze option: Freeze cooled bacon twists in freezer containers, separating layers with waxed paper. If desired, reheat in a microwave oven or on a foil-lined baking sheet in a preheated 350° oven before serving.
Per bacon twist: 35 cal., 2g fat (1g sat. fat), 5mg chol., 81mg sodium, 3g carb. (3g sugars, 0 fiber), 2g pro.

⑤ INGREDIENTS FAST FIX

BREAKFAST PIZZA

PICTURED ON P. 155

Pizza for breakfast? Yes, please! I used to make this for my morning drivers when I worked at a pizza delivery restaurant. It's a quick and easy eye-opener and a twist on scrambled eggs that appeals to all.
—Cathy Shortall, Easton, MD

Start to Finish: 30 min.
Makes: 8 servings

- 1 tube (13.8 ounces) refrigerated pizza crust

- 2 tablespoons olive oil, divided
- 6 large eggs
- 2 tablespoons water
- 1 package (3 ounces) bacon bits
- 1 cup shredded Monterey Jack cheese
- 1 cup shredded cheddar cheese

1. Preheat oven to 400°. Unroll and press dough onto bottom and ½ in. up sides of a greased 15x10x1-in. pan. Prick thoroughly with a fork; brush with 1 tablespoon oil. Bake until lightly browned, 7-8 minutes.
2. Meanwhile, whisk together eggs and water. In a nonstick skillet, heat remaining oil over medium heat. Add eggs; cook and stir just until thickened and no liquid egg remains. Spoon over crust. Sprinkle with bacon bits and cheeses.
3. Bake until cheese is melted, 5-7 minutes.
Per piece: 352 cal., 20g fat (8g sat. fat), 169mg chol., 842mg sodium, 24g carb. (3g sugars, 1g fiber), 20g pro.

FAST FIX

MUFFIN TIN QUICHE CUPS

Make this crustless quiche in muffin cups or in a regular-size pie tin. Either way, there's plenty of bacony, cheesy goodness to go around.
—Angela Lively, Conroe, TX

Start to Finish: 25 min.
Makes: 6 servings

- 1 cup chopped fresh broccoli
- 1 cup pepper jack cheese
- 6 large eggs, lightly beaten
- ¾ cup heavy whipping cream
- ½ cup bacon bits
- 1 shallot, minced
- ¼ teaspoon salt
- ¼ teaspoon pepper

1. Preheat oven to 350°. Divide broccoli pieces and cheese among 12 greased muffin cups.
2. Whisk together remaining ingredients; pour into cups. Bake until set, about 15-20 minutes.
Per 2 quiche cups: 291 cal., 24g fat (12g sat. fat), 243mg chol., 523mg sodium, 4g carb. (2g sugars, 0 fiber), 16g pro.
HEALTH TIP Swap half-and-half for whipped cream and save more than 60 calories and 6g saturated fat .

MUFFIN TIN QUICHE CUPS

Morning Sweetie

Fluff and stuff energy-boosting sweet potatoes for a stick-with-you breakfast that wins the day.

Pierce sweet 'taters and microwave 12-14 minutes. Slice open and top with apples, maple syrup, yogurt and coconut.

HAM & CHEESE EGG BAKE

This make-ahead egg casserole is just the thing when entertaining in the morning. It's loaded with hearty ham, cheese and mushrooms—or change it to suit you.
—Susan Miller, North Andover, MA

Prep: 25 min. + chilling • **Bake:** 35 min.
Makes: 10 servings

- 1½ cups shredded cheddar cheese
- 1½ cups shredded part-skim mozzarella cheese
- 2 tablespoons butter
- ½ pound sliced fresh mushrooms
- 1 medium sweet red pepper, chopped
- 6 green onions, chopped
- 1¾ cups cubed fully cooked ham
- 8 large eggs
- 1¾ cups 2% milk
- ¼ cup all-purpose flour
- ¼ teaspoon salt
- ¼ teaspoon pepper

1. Sprinkle cheeses into a greased 13x9-in. baking dish. In a large skillet, heat butter over medium-high heat; saute mushrooms, red pepper and green onions until tender. Stir in ham; spoon mixture over cheese.

2. In a large bowl, whisk together eggs, milk, flour, salt and pepper; pour over ham mixture. Refrigerate, covered, overnight.
3. Preheat oven to 350°. Remove the casserole from refrigerator while oven heats. Bake, uncovered, until a knife inserted in center comes out clean, for 35-45 minutes. Let dish stand 5 minutes before serving.
Per serving: 272 cal., 17g fat (9g sat. fat), 201mg chol., 678mg sodium, 8g carb. (4g sugars, 1g fiber), 21g pro.
HEALTH TIP If your guests don't eat meat, leave out the ham and toss in more veggies (you'll also save 300mg sodium).

OVERNIGHT BAKED OATMEAL

After making a few tweaks to an oatmeal recipe from the owners of a nearby bed-and-breakfast, I now bake this breakfast treat whenever I want to re-create those cozy weekend mornings.
—Jennifer Cramer, Lebanon, PA

Prep: 10 min. + chilling • **Bake:** 45 min.
Makes: 8 servings

- 2 large eggs, lightly beaten
- 3 cups 2% milk
- ¾ cup packed brown sugar
- ¼ cup canola oil
- 1½ teaspoons ground cinnamon
- 1 teaspoon salt
- 2 cups old-fashioned oats
- ¼ cup dried blueberries
- ¼ cup dried cherries
- ¼ cup sliced almonds

1. In a bowl, whisk first six ingredients. Stir in oats, blueberries and cherries. Transfer to a greased 8-in. square baking dish. Refrigerate, covered, 8 hours or overnight.
2. Preheat the oven to 350°. Remove oatmeal from refrigerator while oven heats. Stir oatmeal; sprinkle with almonds. Bake, uncovered, until golden brown and a thermometer reads 160°, 40-50 minutes.
Per serving: 331 cal., 13g fat (2g sat. fat), 54mg chol., 364mg sodium, 46g carb. (30g sugars, 4g fiber), 8g pro.

DID YOU KNOW?
Quaker Oats featured its first oatmeal cookie recipe on the package in 1908. The recipe used just three ingredients: oats, butter and eggs. Other ingredients we now take for granted were added to recipes later—sugar, vanilla, cinnamon, raisins, nuts and chocolate chips.

PUFFY APPLE OMELET

With all the eggs our chickens produce, I could make this omelet every day! It's a pretty festive-looking dish so I often make it for special occasions, but you could fix it anytime...including for a light supper.
—Melissa Davenport, Campbell, MN

Start to Finish: 30 min.
Makes: 2 servings

- 3 tablespoons all-purpose flour
- ¼ teaspoon baking powder
- ⅛ teaspoon salt, optional
- 2 large eggs, separated
- 3 tablespoons 2% milk
- 1 tablespoon lemon juice
- 3 tablespoons sugar

TOPPING

- 1 large apple, peeled if desired and thinly sliced
- 1 teaspoon sugar
- ¼ teaspoon ground cinnamon

1. Preheat oven to 375°. Mix flour, baking powder and, if desired, salt. In a small bowl, whisk together egg yolks, milk and lemon juice; stir into flour mixture.
2. In another bowl, beat egg whites on medium speed until foamy. Gradually add sugar, 1 tablespoon at a time, beating on high after each addition until stiff peaks form. Fold into flour mixture.
3. Pour into a 9-in. deep-dish pie plate coated with cooking spray. Arrange apple slices over top. Mix sugar and cinnamon; sprinkle over apple.
4. Bake, uncovered, until a knife inserted in the center comes out clean, 18-20 minutes. Serve immediately.

Per piece: 253 cal., 5g fat (2g sat. fat), 188mg chol., 142mg sodium, 44g carb. (32g sugars, 2g fiber), 9g pro.

HEALTH TIP Most puff pancakes are pretty lean, but satisfying even as breakfast for dinner. The filling often makes them unhealthy, but this recipe uses just a touch of sugar for sweetness.

PORTOBELLO MUSHROOMS FLORENTINE

Enjoy these bite-sized stuffed mushrooms as a savory take on breakfast.
—Sara Morris, Laguna beach, CA

Start to Finish: 25 min.
Makes: 2 servings

- 2 large portobello mushrooms, stems removed
  Cooking spray
- ⅛ teaspoon garlic salt
- ⅛ teaspoon pepper
- ½ teaspoon olive oil
- 1 small onion, chopped
- 1 cup fresh baby spinach
- 2 large eggs
- ⅛ teaspoon salt
- ¼ cup crumbled goat or feta cheese
  Minced fresh basil, optional

1. Preheat oven to 425°. Spritz mushrooms with cooking spray; place in a 15x10x1-in. pan, stem side up. Sprinkle with garlic salt and pepper. Bake, uncovered, until tender, about 10 minutes.
2. Meanwhile, in a nonstick skillet, heat oil over medium-high heat; saute onion until tender. Stir in spinach until wilted.
3. Whisk together eggs and salt; add to skillet. Cook and stir until the eggs are thickened and no liquid egg remains; spoon onto mushrooms. Sprinkle with cheese and, if desired, basil.

Per stuffed mushroom: 126 cal., 5g fat (2g sat. fat), 18mg chol., 472mg sodium, 10g carb. (4g sugars, 3g fiber), 11g pro.
Diabetic Exchanges: 2 vegetable, 1 lean meat, ½ fat.

PUFFY APPLE OMELET

Breads in a Jiffy

~

Think you don't have time to bake up buttery biscuits, aromatic breads and other over-the-top crowd pleasers? Let this heartwarming chapter show you how to easily turn your kitchen into a bakery.

**BREAD MACHINE
PUMPKIN MONKEY BREAD**

BREAD MACHINE PUMPKIN MONKEY BREAD

I love making this pumpkin bread straight from my bread machine. Leftovers reheat well on busy weekdays, and the sauce is good enough to make by itself as syrup for pancakes and waffles.
—Emily Main, Tonopah, AZ

Prep: 45 min. + rising
Bake: 20 min. + cooling
Makes: 18 servings

- 1 cup warm 2% milk (70° to 80°)
- ¾ cup canned pumpkin
- 2 tablespoons butter, softened
- ¼ cup sugar
- 1 teaspoon salt
- 1 teaspoon ground cinnamon
- ½ teaspoon ground ginger
- ¼ teaspoon ground cloves
- ¼ teaspoon ground nutmeg
- 4 to 4¼ cups all-purpose flour
- 2 teaspoons active dry yeast

SAUCE
- 1 cup butter, cubed
- 1 cup packed brown sugar
- 1 cup dried cranberries
- ¼ cup canned pumpkin
- 1 teaspoon ground cinnamon
- ½ teaspoon ground ginger
- ¼ teaspoon ground nutmeg
- ¼ teaspoon ground cloves

1. In bread machine pan, place the first 11 ingredients in order suggested by manufacturer. Select dough setting. Check dough after 5 minutes of mixing; add 1-2 tablespoons of water or flour if needed.
2. Meanwhile, in a large saucepan, combine sauce ingredients; cook and stir until blended. Remove from heat.
3. When dough cycle is completed, turn dough onto a lightly floured surface. Divide into 36 portions; shape into balls.
4. Arrange half of the balls in a greased 10-in. fluted tube pan; cover with half of the sauce. Repeat, being sure to thoroughly coat the top layer with sauce.
5. Let rise in a warm place until doubled, about 30 minutes. Preheat oven to 375°. Bake 20-25 minutes or until golden brown. Cover loosely with foil if the top browns too quickly.
6. Cool in pan 10 minutes before inverting onto a serving plate. Serve warm.

Note: We recommend you do not use a bread machine's time-delay feature for this recipe.

Per 2 pieces: 302 cal., 12g fat (8g sat. fat), 32mg chol., 234mg sodium, 46g carb. (22g sugars, 2g fiber), 4g pro.

POMEGRANATE CREAM CHEESE SURPRISE MUFFINS

I baked these muffins for the kids I babysit, and they couldn't get enough. Their favorite part? The filling, of course! Pomegranate seeds add a fun touch.
—Jodie Gharbi, Shreveport, LA

Prep: 30 min. • **Bake:** 20 min.
Makes: 16 muffins

- 1 package (8 ounces) cream cheese, softened
- ½ cup sugar
- ¾ teaspoon grated lemon peel
- ¼ teaspoon vanilla extract

MUFFINS
- 2 cups all-purpose flour
- ⅔ cup sugar
- 1 tablespoon baking powder
- 1 teaspoon grated lemon peel
- ½ teaspoon salt
- 1 large egg
- 1 cup 2% milk
- ¼ cup butter, melted
- 1¼ cups pomegranate seeds
- 2 teaspoons coarse sugar

1. Preheat oven to 400°. For filling, mix first four ingredients until blended.
2. In a large bowl, whisk together first five muffin ingredients. In another bowl, whisk together egg, milk and melted butter. Add to the dry ingredients, stirring just until moistened. Fold in pomegranate seeds.
3. Fill paper-lined muffin cups one-third full with batter. Drop the filling by tablespoonfuls into center of each muffin; cover with remaining batter. Sprinkle with coarse sugar.
4. Bake until top springs back when lightly touched, 18-22 minutes. Cool 5 minutes before removing from pans to wire racks. Serve warm. Refrigerate leftovers.

Per muffin: 211 cal., 9g fat (5g sat. fat), 35mg chol., 244mg sodium, 31g carb. (18g sugars, 1g fiber), 4g pro.

HEALTH TIP A simple sprinkling of coarse sugar on these muffins adds crunch and sweetness, like a streusel topping, without adding a lot of calories.

DID YOU KNOW?

The seeds and surrounding juice sacs (arils) are the only edible parts of the pomegranate. A medium pomegranate (about 8 ounces) yields roughly ¾ cup of the ruby red treasures.

POMEGRANATE CREAM CHEESE SURPRISE MUFFINS

(5) INGREDIENTS FAST FIX ▶

GARLIC CRESCENT ROLLS

Delicious rolls can embellish a dinner, and it only takes a minute to prepare them using convenient refrigerated items. With a little imagination, you can create several flavor combinations to complement your menu. I experimented and came up with a few touches that make these rolls a conversation piece!
—Pat Habiger, Spearville, KS

Start to Finish: 20 min.
Makes: 2 servings

- 1 package (4 ounces) refrigerated crescent rolls
- 2 teaspoons grated Parmesan cheese
- ¼ to ½ teaspoon garlic powder
- 1 large egg, beaten
- ½ teaspoon sesame and/or poppy seeds

1. Separate crescent dough into four triangles. Sprinkle with Parmesan cheese and garlic powder. Beginning at the wide end, roll up dough. Place with point down on a greased baking sheet.
2. Brush with egg; sprinkle with sesame and/or poppy seeds. Bake at 375° for 11-13 minutes or until golden brown. Serve warm.
Per roll: 272 cal., 15g fat (4g sat. fat), 108mg chol., 508mg sodium, 23g carb. (4g sugars, 0 fiber), 8g pro.

SMOKY ONION
BISCUIT SQUARES

SMOKY ONION BISCUIT SQUARES

Whip up a batch of my savory little biscuit squares to complete dinner. They're the perfect little bite when you need a yummy bit of comfort.
—Donna-Marie Ryan, Topsfield, MA

Prep: 20 min. • **Bake:** 20 min.
Makes: 16 servings

- 1 small onion, chopped
- 2 tablespoons butter
- ¼ teaspoon sugar
- 1 garlic clove, minced
- 1½ cups biscuit/baking mix
- ½ cup 2% milk
- 1 large egg
- ¼ pound smoked mozzarella cheese, shredded, divided
- 1 teaspoon salt-free Southwest chipotle seasoning blend

1. In a small skillet, cook onion in butter over medium heat until tender. Add sugar; cook 10-15 minutes longer or until golden brown. Add garlic; cook for 1 minute. Cool onion slightly.
2. In a small bowl, combine the biscuit mix, milk and egg. Fold in ½ cup cheese, seasoning blend and onion mixture. Transfer to an 8-in. square baking dish coated with cooking spray. Sprinkle with remaining cheese.
3. Bake at 400° for 18-22 minutes or until a toothpick inserted in the center comes out clean. Cut into squares; serve warm.
Per square: 91 cal., 5g fat (2g sat. fat), 22mg chol., 197mg sodium, 8g carb. (1g sugars, 0 fiber), 3g pro.
Diabetic Exchanges: 1 fat, ½ starch.

★ ★ ★ ★ ★ **READER REVIEW**

"Great with goulash. I used smoked Gouda instead of mozzarella. We will make this again!"

MEAGAN_TEAL TASTEOFHOME.COM

(5) INGREDIENTS FAST FIX ▶
PARMESAN SWEET CREAM BISCUITS

Sweet cream biscuits were the first kind I mastered. Since the ingredients are so simple, I can scale the recipe up or down. In fact, I've actually memorized it!
—Helen Nelander, Boulder Creek, CA

Start to Finish: 25 min.
Makes: about 1 dozen

- 2 cups all-purpose flour
- ⅓ cup grated Parmesan cheese
- 2 teaspoons baking powder
- ½ teaspoon salt
- 1½ cups heavy whipping cream

1. Preheat oven to 400°. Whisk together the first four ingredients. Add the cream; stir just until moistened.
2. Turn the dough onto a lightly floured surface; knead gently 6-8 times. Roll or pat dough to ½-in. thickness; cut with a floured 2¾-in. biscuit cutter. Place 1 in. apart on an ungreased baking sheet.
3. Bake until light golden brown, 12-15 minutes. Serve warm.

Per biscuit: 187 cal., 12g fat (7g sat. fat), 36mg chol., 227mg sodium, 17g carb. (1g sugars, 1g fiber), 4g pro.

CRANBERRY NUT BREAD

I created this bread years ago by combining a couple of recipes from my collection. There's a big burst of tart cranberry and lots of crunchy nuts in every piece. People also like the delicious hint of orange, making it perfect for holidays.
—Dawn E. Lowenstein, Huntingdon Valley, PA

Prep: 15 min. • **Bake:** 65 min. + cooling
Makes: 1 loaf (16 slices)

- 2 cups all-purpose flour
- 1 cup sugar
- 1½ teaspoons baking powder
- 1 teaspoon salt
- ½ teaspoon baking soda
- ¼ cup butter, cubed
- 1 large egg
- ¾ cup orange juice
- 1 tablespoon grated orange peel
- 1½ cups fresh or frozen cranberries
- ½ cup chopped walnuts

1. In a large bowl, combine the flour, sugar, baking powder, salt and baking soda. Cut in butter until mixture resembles coarse crumbs. In a small bowl, whisk the egg, orange juice and peel; stir into dry ingredients just until moistened. Fold in cranberries and walnuts.
2. Spoon batter into a greased and floured 8x4-in. loaf pan. Bake at 350° for 65-70 minutes or until a toothpick inserted in the center comes out clean. Cool in pan 10 minutes before removing to a wire rack to cool completely.

Per slice: 169 cal., 6g fat (2g sat. fat), 21mg chol., 258mg sodium, 27g carb. (14g sugars, 1g fiber), 3g pro.

PARMESAN SWEET CREAM BISCUITS

HONEY WHOLE WHEAT ROLLS

There's nothing quite like a warm yeast roll fresh from the oven.
—Celecia Stoup, Hobart, OK

Prep: 20 min. + rising • **Bake:** 20 min.
Makes: 15 rolls

- 2 packages (¼ ounce each) active dry yeast
- 1 cup warm water (110° to 115°)
- ¼ cup butter, melted
- ¼ cup honey
- 1 large egg
- ¾ cup whole wheat flour
- ½ cup old-fashioned oats
- 1 teaspoon salt
- 2½ to 3 cups all-purpose flour
  Additional melted butter, optional

1. In a small bowl, dissolve yeast in warm water. In a large bowl, combine butter, honey, egg, whole wheat flour, oats, salt, yeast mixture and 1 cup all-purpose flour; beat on medium speed until smooth. Stir in enough of the remaining flour to form a soft dough.
2. Turn dough onto a floured surface; knead until smooth and elastic, 6-8 minutes. Place in a greased bowl, turning once to grease the top. Cover with plastic wrap and let rise in a warm place until doubled, about 1 hour.
3. Punch down dough; shape into 15 balls. Place in a greased 13x9-in. pan. Cover with a kitchen towel; let rise in warm place until doubled, about 45 minutes. Preheat oven to 375°.
4. Bake until golden brown, about 20 minutes. If desired, brush with additional butter. Serve warm.

Per roll: 151 cal., 4g fat (2g sat. fat), 21mg chol., 188mg sodium, 25g carb. (5g sugars, 2g fiber), 4g pro.

(5) INGREDIENTS
ONE-BOWL CHOCOLATE CHIP BREAD

My family hops out of bed on Valentine's Day because they know I'm baking this quick bread for breakfast. They're major chocoholics, and our annual custom always hits the spot.
—Angela Lively, Conroe, TX

Prep: 20 min. • **Bake:** 65 minutes
Makes: 1 loaf (16 slices)

- 3 large eggs
- 1 cup sugar
- 2 cups (16 ounces) sour cream
- 3 cups self-rising flour
- 2 cups (12 ounces) semisweet chocolate chips

1. Preheat oven to 350°. Beat the eggs, sugar and sour cream until well blended. Gradually stir in flour. Fold in chocolate chips. Transfer mixture to a greased 9x5-in. loaf pan.
2. Bake until a toothpick comes out clean, 65-75 minutes. Cool in pan 5 minutes before removing to a wire rack to cool.
Note: As a substitute for 3 cups of self-rising flour, place 4½ teaspoons baking powder and 1½ teaspoons salt in a 1-cup measuring cup. Add all-purpose flour to measure 1 cup; combine with an additional 2 cups all-purpose flour.
Per slice: 306 cal., 13g fat (8g sat. fat), 42mg chol., 305mg sodium, 44g carb. (25g sugars, 2g fiber), 5g pro.

HONEY WHOLE WHEAT ROLLS

ONE-DISH
NO-KNEAD BREAD

CHOCOLATE BISCUIT PUFFS

I know my favorite snack is fun for kids to make and eat because I dreamed it up at age 9! The puffs are shaped to hide the chocolate inside for a tasty surprise.
—Joy Clark, Seabeck, WA

Start to Finish: 20 min.
Makes: 10 servings

- 1 tube (12 ounces) refrigerated buttermilk biscuits
- 1 milk chocolate candy bar (1.55 ounces)
- 2 teaspoons cinnamon sugar

1. Preheat oven to 450°. Flatten each biscuit into a 3-in. circle. Break candy bar into pieces; place a piece on each biscuit. Bring up edges to enclose candy and pinch to seal.

Place seam side down on an ungreased baking sheet. Sprinkle with cinnamon sugar. Bake 8-10 minutes or until puffs are golden brown.

Per puff: 127 cal., 5g fat (2g sat. fat), 1mg chol., 284mg sodium, 18g carb. (5g sugars, 0g fiber), 2g pro.

EAT SMART ⑤ INGREDIENTS
ONE-DISH NO-KNEAD BREAD

Here's an easy way to make homemade bread. Don't worry if you're new to baking. If you can stir, you can make this!
—Heather Chambers, Largo, FL

Prep: 15 min. + rising • **Bake:** 40 min.
Makes: 1 loaf (12 slices)

- 1 teaspoon active dry yeast
- 1½ cups warm water (110° to 115°)
- 2¾ cups all-purpose flour
- 2 tablespoons sugar
- 2 tablespoons olive oil
- 1½ teaspoons salt

1. In a large bowl, dissolve yeast in warm water. Stir in remaining ingredients to form a wet dough; transfer to a greased 2½-qt. baking dish. Cover; let stand in a warm place 1 hour.
2. Stir down dough. Cover; let stand 1 hour. Preheat oven to 425°.
3. Bake 20 minutes. Reduce oven setting to 350°. Bake until top is golden brown and a thermometer reads 210°, about 20 minutes.
4. Remove bread from baking dish to a wire rack to cool. Serve warm.

Per slice: 133 cal., 3g fat (0 sat. fat), 0 chol., 296mg sodium, 24g carb. (2g sugars, 1g fiber), 3g pro.
Diabetic Exchanges: 1½ starch, ½ fat.

HEALTH TIP Some packaged breads have more than 20 ingredients! This loaf includes just five easy-to-pronounce ones plus water—nothing artificial.

PUMPKIN BREAD

Every autumn, our farm becomes a large-scale operation when we harvest our pumpkins. Then we reap the rewards in recipes like this.
—Dorothy and Martin Schumacher
Barnesville, OH

Prep: 10 min. • **Bake:** 1¼ hours + cooling
Makes: 2 loaves (12 slices each)

- 3 cups sugar
- 1 can (15 ounces) solid-pack pumpkin
- 1 cup canola oil
- 4 large eggs
- ⅔ cup cold water
- 3½ cups all-purpose flour
- 2 teaspoons baking soda
- 1½ teaspoons salt
- 1½ teaspoons ground cinnamon
- 1 teaspoon ground nutmeg

1. Preheat oven to 325°. In a bowl, beat sugar, pumpkin, oil, eggs and water until well mixed. Combine the remaining ingredients; gradually add to pumpkin mixture and mix well.
2. Pour into two greased 8x4-in. loaf pans. Bake 75-80 minutes or until a toothpick inserted in center comes out clean. Cool 10 minutes before removing from pans to wire racks.

APPLE BREAD

APPLE BREAD

I got this recipe ages ago, and with a few tweaks it's become one of our all-time favorites. Everyone who's ever tasted this special quick bread has asked me for the recipe. It's lovely any time of year.
—Phyllis Herlocker, Farlington, KS

Prep: 20 min. • **Bake:** 50 min. + cooling
Makes: 2 loaves (12 slices each)

- 3 cups all-purpose flour
- 2 cups sugar
- 2 teaspoons ground cinnamon
- 1 teaspoon baking soda
- ½ teaspoon baking powder
- ½ teaspoon salt
- 4 large eggs
- 1 cup canola oil
- ½ teaspoon vanilla extract
- 2 cups chopped peeled apples (about 2 medium)
- 1 cup coarsely chopped walnuts

1. Preheat oven to 350° Line two greased 8x4-in. loaf pans with parchment paper; grease paper.
2. Whisk together first six ingredients. In another bowl, whisk together eggs, oil and vanilla; add to flour mixture, stirring just until moistened (batter will be thick). Fold in apples and walnuts.
3. Transfer to prepared pans. Bake until a toothpick inserted in center comes out clean, 50-55 minutes. Cool in pans 10 minutes before removing to wire racks to cool.

Freeze option: Securely wrap cooled loaves in plastic and foil, then freeze. To use, thaw at room temperature.
Per slice: 253 cal., 13g fat (1g sat. fat), 31mg chol., 124mg sodium, 31g carb. (18g sugars, 1g fiber), 3g pro.

STUFFED SPINACH LOAF

My mom made this recipe, and I always remembered how good it tasted. So I set out to make it myself from memory. Not only was it a success, but it was a big hit. Even folks who think they don't like spinach often go back for a second or third slice. You're in for a tasty surprise when you try it.
—Anita Harmala, Howell, MI

Prep: 15 min. • **Bake:** 25 min.
Makes: 10 servings

- 1 pound bulk Italian sausage
- ½ teaspoon salt
- ½ teaspoon dried basil
- 1 loaf (1 pound) frozen bread dough, thawed
- 1 package (10 ounces) frozen spinach, thawed and well-drained
- 2 cups shredded mozzarella cheese

1. In a large skillet, cook sausage over medium heat until no longer pink; drain. Sprinkle with salt and basil.
2. Roll out bread dough to a 13x10-in. rectangle. Sprinkle with meat mixture. Top with spinach; sprinkle with cheese. Roll up jelly-roll style, starting with a long side; pinch seams to seal and tuck ends under.
3. Place seam side down on a greased baking sheet. Bake at 350° for 25-30 minutes or until crust is golden brown. Serve warm. Refrigerate leftovers.
Per slice: 270 cal., 13g fat (5g sat. fat), 36mg chol., 688mg sodium, 25g carb. (2g sugars, 2g fiber), 15g pro.

OAT DINNER ROLLS

These delicious homemade rolls make a delightful addition to any special-occasion meal. They're so simple and only call for a few ingredients.
—Patricia Rutherford, Winchester, IL

Prep: 30 min. + rising • **Bake:** 20 min.
Makes: 2 dozen

2⅓ cups water, divided
1 cup quick-cooking oats
⅔ cup packed brown sugar
3 tablespoons butter
1½ teaspoons salt
2 packages (¼ ounce each) active dry yeast
5 to 5¾ cups all-purpose flour

1. In a large saucepan, bring 2 cups water to a boil. Stir in oats; reduce heat. Simmer, uncovered, for 1 minute. Stir in brown sugar, butter, salt and remaining water.
2. Transfer to a large bowl; let stand until mixture reaches 110°-115°. Stir in yeast. Add 3 cups flour; beat well. Add enough remaining flour to form a soft dough.
3. Turn onto a floured surface; knead until smooth and elastic, about 6-8 minutes. Place in a greased bowl; turn once to grease top. Cover and let rise in a warm place until doubled, about 1 hour.
4. Punch dough down; shape into 24 rolls. Place on greased baking sheets. Cover and let rise until doubled, about 30 minutes.
5. Bake at 350° for 20-25 minutes or until golden brown. Remove from pan and cool on wire racks.

Per roll: 132 cal., 1g fat (0 sat. fat), 0 chol., 150mg sodium, 28g carb. (6g sugars, 1g fiber), 3g pro.

BLUEBERRY CORNBREAD

BLUEBERRY CORN BREAD

My husband is a fourth-grade teacher, and he incorporates monthly baking projects into the curriculum. His recipe for blueberry corn bread is a class favorite.
—Jennifer Martin, Martinez, CA

Prep: 10 min. • **Bake:** 30 min.
Makes: 9 servings

1½ cups all-purpose flour
½ cup sugar
½ cup yellow cornmeal
1 tablespoon baking powder
½ teaspoon salt
2 large eggs
1¼ cups soy or 2% milk
⅓ cup canola oil
1 cup fresh or frozen blueberries

1. Preheat oven to 350°. Grease an 8-in. square baking pan.
2. Whisk together first five ingredients. In another bowl, whisk together eggs, milk and oil; add to dry ingredients, stirring just until moistened. Fold in blueberries. Transfer to prepared pan.
3. Bake until a toothpick inserted in center comes out clean, 30-35 minutes. Cool on a wire rack. Serve warm or at room temperature.

Note: If using frozen blueberries, use without thawing to avoid discoloring the batter.

Per piece: 264 cal., 10g fat (1g sat. fat), 41mg chol., 325mg sodium, 38g carb. (14g sugars, 1g fiber), 5g pro.

Slow-Cooked Sensations

Everyone loves the aroma of dinner waiting when they walk in the door! Ditto for waking up to a hot, hearty breakfast that's ready to dig into. Treat yourself to these best-loved dishes, plus soups, sandwiches, potluck favorites and more. They'll become your busy-day staples.

HEARTY BAKED POTATO SOUP

I got this recipe from my aunt, who's a great cook. Packed with bacon, cheese and chives, this soup tastes just like a loaded baked potato! My husband and I love it on chilly nights.
—Molly Seidel, Edgewood, NM

Prep: 25 min. • **Cook:** 6 hours
Makes: 10 servings (3½ quarts)

- 5 pounds baking potatoes, cut into ½-inch cubes (about 13 cups)
- 1 large onion, chopped
- ¼ cup butter
- 4 garlic cloves, minced
- 1 teaspoon salt
- ⅛ teaspoon pepper
- 3 cans (14½ ounces each) chicken broth
- 1 cup shredded sharp cheddar cheese
- 1 cup half-and-half cream
- 3 tablespoons minced fresh chives
  Optional toppings: shredded cheddar cheese, sour cream, crumbled cooked bacon and minced chives

1. Place first seven ingredients in a 6-qt. slow cooker. Cook, covered, on low until potatoes are very tender, 6-8 hours.
2. Mash potatoes slightly to break up and thicken soup. Add 1 cup cheese, cream and chives; heat through, stirring until blended. Serve with toppings as desired.
Freeze option: Freeze cooled soup in freezer containers. To use, partially thaw in refrigerator overnight. Heat through in a saucepan, stirring occasionally.
Per 1⅓ cups: 310 cal., 11g fat (7g sat. fat), 38mg chol., 906mg sodium, 43g carb. (4g sugars, 5g fiber), 9g pro.

✳

TEST KITCHEN TIP
Thinly sliced green onions are an economical substitute for fresh chives from the herb section.

PIZZA SOUP WITH GARLIC TOAST CROUTONS

PIZZA SOUP WITH GARLIC TOAST CROUTONS

This comforting soup satisfies our pizza cravings. It's super versatile, too, and I sometimes substitute light Italian sausage for the chicken or add a little Parmesan cheese. Go nuts and toss in all your favorite pizza toppings!
—Joan Hallford, North Richland Hills, TX

Prep: 10 min. • **Cook:** 6 hours
Makes: 10 servings (about 4 quarts)

- 1 can (28 ounces) diced tomatoes, drained
- 1 can (15 ounces) pizza sauce
- 1 pound boneless skinless chicken breasts, cut into 1-inch pieces
- 1 package (3 ounces) sliced pepperoni, halved
- 1 cup sliced fresh mushrooms
- 1 small onion, chopped
- ½ cup chopped green pepper
- ¼ teaspoon pepper
- 2 cans (14½ ounces each) chicken broth
- 1 package (11¼ ounces) frozen garlic Texas toast
- 1 package (10 ounces) frozen chopped spinach, thawed and squeezed dry
- 1 cup shredded part-skim mozzarella cheese

1. In a 6-qt. slow cooker, combine first nine ingredients. Cook, covered, on low until chicken is tender, 6-8 hours .
2. For croutons, cut Texas toast into cubes; bake according to package directions. Add spinach to soup; heat through, stirring occasionally. Top servings with cheese and warm croutons.
Freeze option: Freeze cooled soup in freezer containers. To use, partially thaw in refrigerator overnight. Heat through in a saucepan, stirring occasionally. Prepare croutons as directed. Top soup with cheese and croutons.
Per 1½ cups: 292 cal., 13g fat (5g sat. fat), 46mg chol., 1081mg sodium, 24g carb. (7g sugars, 4g fiber), 20g pro.
HEALTH TIP The cheese and garlic croutons put this soup over the top, but it's still amazing without them (and a lot leaner: just 150 calories and 6g fat).

SAUSAGE & KRAUT BUNS

This recipe has become a regular at our church potlucks. Let's just say I'm in trouble if I show up at a get-together without them! For a fun dinner spin, try the sausages and kraut over warm mashed potatoes.

—Patsy Unruh, Perryton, TX

Prep: 20 min. • **Cook:** 4 hours.
Makes: 12 servings

- 2 cans (14½ ounces each) no-salt-added diced tomatoes, drained
- 2 cans (14 ounces each) sauerkraut, rinsed and drained
- ½ pound sliced fresh mushrooms
- 1 large sweet pepper, thinly sliced
- 1 large onion, halved and thinly sliced
- 2 tablespoons brown sugar
- ½ teaspoon pepper
- 2 packages (14 ounces each) smoked sausage, sliced
- 12 pretzel sausage buns, warmed and split partway

SAUSAGE & KRAUT BUNS

1. In a 5- or 6-qt. slow cooker, combine first seven ingredients. In a large skillet, saute sausage over medium-high heat until lightly browned. Stir into tomato mixture.
2. Cook, covered, on low until vegetables are tender, 4-5 hours. Serve in buns.

Per 1 sandwich: 468 cal., 23g fat (8g sat. fat), 44mg chol., 1491mg sodium, 51g carb. (12g sugars, 4g fiber), 17g pro.

---

⑤INGREDIENTS **SLOW COOKER**

SLOW-COOKED MESQUITE RIBS

PICTURED ON P. 179

When we're missing the grill during winter, these tangy ribs give us that same smoky barbecue taste we love. They're so simple, and fall-off-the-bone delicious, too!

—Sue Evans, Marquette, MI

Prep: 10 min. • **Cook:** 6½ hours
Makes: 8 servings

- 1 cup water
- 2 tablespoons cider vinegar
- 1 tablespoon soy sauce
- 2 tablespoons mesquite seasoning
- 4 pounds pork baby back ribs, cut into serving-size portions.
- ½ cup barbecue sauce

1. In a 6-qt. slow cooker, mix water, vinegar and soy sauce. Rub ribs with mesquite seasoning; place in slow cooker.
2. Cook, covered, on low until tender, 6-8 hours. Remove ribs to a platter. Brush with barbecue sauce; return to the slow cooker. Cook, covered, on low until ribs are glazed, about 30 minutes.

Per serving: 314 cal., 21g fat (8g sat. fat), 81mg chol., 591mg sodium, 7g carb. (6g sugars, 0 fiber), 23g pro.

SLOW COOKER

TANDOORI CHICKEN PANINI

The tandoori-style spices in my slow-cooked chicken give it a bold flavor that's so hard to resist. It tastes incredible tucked between pieces of naan, then grilled for an Indian-inspired panini.

—Yasmin Arif, Manassas, VA

Prep: 25 min. • **Cook:** 3 hours
Makes: 6 servings

- 1½ pounds boneless skinless chicken breasts
- ¼ cup reduced-sodium chicken broth
- 2 garlic cloves, minced
- 2 teaspoons minced fresh gingerroot
- 1 teaspoon paprika
- ¼ teaspoon salt
- ¼ to ½ teaspoon cayenne pepper
- ¼ teaspoon ground turmeric
- 6 green onions, chopped
- 6 tablespoons chutney
- 6 naan flatbreads

1. Place first eight ingredients in a 3-qt. slow cooker. Cook, covered, on low until chicken is tender, 3-4 hours.
2. Shred chicken with two forks. Stir in green onions.
3. Spread chutney over one side of each naan. Top chutney side of three naan with chicken mixture; top with remaining naan, chutney side down.
4. Cook sandwiches on panini maker or grill, covered, until golden brown, 6-8 minutes. To serve, cut in half.

Per ½ panini: 351 cal., 6g fat (2g sat. fat), 68mg chol., 830mg sodium, 44g carb. (12g sugars, 2g fiber), 27g pro. **Diabetic Exchanges:** 3 starch, 3 lean meat.

SLOW COOKER 🍲

BISTRO BEEF BARBECUE SANDWICHES

These zippy barbecue sandwiches make for fun late-summer dinners and are perfect for potluck gatherings, too. The coleslaw topping adds the perfectly tangy crunch.
—Gilda Lester, Millsboro, DE

Prep: 25 min. • **Cook:** 8 hours
Makes: 16 servings

- 1½ cups ketchup
- ½ cup packed brown sugar
- ½ cup picante sauce
- ½ cup dry red wine
- ¼ cup balsamic vinegar
- 2 tablespoons Worcestershire sauce
- ½ teaspoon salt
- ½ teaspoon pepper
- ¼ teaspoon ground allspice
- 1 beef sirloin tip roast (4 pounds)
- 4 garlic cloves, sliced
- 16 kaiser rolls, split and toasted
- 2 cups deli coleslaw

1. Mix first nine ingredients. Cut roast in half; cut slits in roast and insert garlic. Place in a 5-qt. slow cooker. Pour sauce over top. Cook, covered, on low until tender, 8-10 hours.

2. Remove beef. Skim fat from cooking liquid. Shred meat with two forks; return to slow cooker and heat through. Serve on rolls with coleslaw.

Freeze option: Freeze cooled meat mixture and sauce in freezer containers. To use, partially thaw in refrigerator overnight. Heat through in a saucepan, stirring occasionally.

Per 1 sandwich: 411 cal., 11g fat (3g sat. fat), 76mg chol., 832mg sodium, 49g carb. (18g sugars, 2g fiber), 29g pro.

HEALTH TIP Beef sirloin tip roast is a lean cut that's usually more affordable than other lean roasts like beef tenderloin or top round roast.

BISTRO BEEF BARBECUE SANDWICHES

SLOW COOKER 🍲

SPICY SAUSAGE FETTUCCINE

PICTURED ON P. 179

One time, I accidentally bought hot Italian sausage but wanted to find a way to use it anyway. I tossed it in the slow cooker with mushrooms, tomatoes and wine, which helped to mellow out the heat. Now I buy the hot stuff on purpose!
—Judy Batson, Tampa, FL

Prep: 25 min. • **Cook:** 6 hours
Makes: 8 servings

- 2 teaspoons canola oil
- 8 hot Italian sausage links
- ½ pound sliced fresh mushrooms
- 1 small sweet onion, chopped
- 2 garlic cloves, minced
- 1 can (14½ ounces) diced tomatoes with mild green chilies, undrained
- ½ cup beef stock
- ½ cup dry white wine or additional stock
- 1 package (12 ounces) fettuccine or tagliatelle
  Grated Parmesan cheese, optional

1. In a large skillet, heat oil over medium heat; brown sausages on all sides. Transfer to a 3-qt. slow cooker, reserving drippings in pan.

2. In same skillet, saute mushrooms and onion in drippings over medium heat until tender, 4-5 minutes. Stir in garlic; cook and stir 1 minute. Stir in tomatoes, stock and wine; pour over sausages. Cook, covered, on low for 6-8 hours (a thermometer inserted in the sausages should read at least 160°).

3. To serve, cook fettuccine according to package directions; drain. Remove the sausages from slow cooker; cut into thick slices.

4. Skim fat from mushroom mixture. Add fettuccine and sausage; toss to combine. Serve in bowls. If desired, top with cheese.

Per 1⅓ cups: 448 cal., 25g fat (7g sat. fat), 57mg chol., 817mg sodium, 37g carb. (5g sugars, 3g fiber), 19g pro.

ITALIAN SAUSAGE SLOPPY JOES

My grandma absolutely loves Italian food, so I decided to make a twist on classic sloppy joe sandwiches just for her. The mozzarella and tomato sauce are classic; the red peppers make it fun!
—Kristen Heigl, Staten Island, NY

Prep: 20 min. • **Cook:** 4 hours
Makes: 8 servings

- 1 pound bulk Italian sausage
- 1 medium sweet red pepper, chopped
- 1 medium onion, chopped
- 1½ pounds lean ground beef (90% lean)
- 2 cans (8 ounces each) no-salt-added tomato sauce
- 1 can (6 ounces) tomato paste
- 1 teaspoon garlic powder
- 1 teaspoon liquid smoke, optional
- 16 slices smoked mozzarella cheese (about ¾ pound)
- 8 hoagie buns, split and toasted
  Pickled hot cherry peppers, optional

1. In a large skillet, cook and crumble sausage with red pepper and onion over medium-high heat until no longer pink, 5-7 minutes. Transfer mixture to a 3- or 4-qt. slow cooker.
2. In same pan, cook and crumble beef over medium-high heat until no longer pink, 5-7 minutes. Using a slotted spoon, add beef to slow cooker. Stir in tomato sauce, tomato paste, garlic powder and, if desired, liquid smoke. Cook, covered, on low until flavors are blended, 4-5 hours.
3. To serve, place cheese on bun bottoms; top with meat mixture and, if desired, peppers. Close sandwiches.
Freeze option: Freeze cooled meat mixture in freezer containers. To use, partially thaw in refrigerator overnight. Heat through in a saucepan, stirring occasionally and adding a little water if necessary.
Per 1 sandwich: 661 cal., 35g fat (14g sat. fat), 121mg chol., 1231mg sodium, 46g carb. (9g sugars, 3g fiber), 42g pro.

CABBAGE ROLL STEW

A head of cabbage seems like it never ends. Here's a delicious way to use it up. My husband is this stew's biggest fan.
—Pamela Kennemer, Sand Springs, OK

Prep: 25 min. • **Cook:** 5 hours
Makes: 8 servings (3 quarts)

- 2 cans (14½ ounces each) petite diced tomatoes, drained
- 1 can (14½ ounces) reduced-sodium beef broth
- 1 can (8 ounces) tomato sauce
- 1 tablespoon cider vinegar
- 1 tablespoon Worcestershire sauce
- 1 teaspoon garlic powder
- 1 teaspoon Cajun seasoning
- ½ teaspoon salt
- ½ teaspoon pepper
- 1 medium head cabbage (about 2 pounds), cut into 1½-inch pieces
- 1½ pounds ground beef
- ½ pound bulk Italian sausage
- 1 medium onion, chopped
- 3 garlic cloves, minced
  Hot cooked rice and chopped fresh parsley, optional

1. Mix first nine ingredients. Place cabbage in a 5- or 6-qt. slow cooker;
2. In a large skillet, cook and crumble beef and sausage with onion and garlic over medium-high heat until no longer pink, 7-9 minutes; drain. Spoon over cabbage; top with tomato mixture.
3. Cook, covered, on low until cabbage is tender and flavors are blended, 5-6 hours. If desired, serve stew with rice and sprinkle with parsley.
Freeze option: Freeze cooled meat mixture in freezer containers. To use, partially thaw in refrigerator overnight. Heat through in a saucepan, stirring occasionally.
Per 1½ cups: 195 cal., 11g fat (4g sat. fat), 46mg chol., 564mg sodium, 11g carb. (6g sugars, 4g fiber), 14g pro.
HEALTH TIP Cabbage is a low-calorie food that really adds body and volume to this stew. A generous serving of 1½ cups is less than 200 calories.

✳

TEST KITCHEN TIP
Using a combination of ground beef and Italian sausage gives this recipe a flavor boost. (And it's a great idea for perking up most ground beef meals.)

BBQ CHICKEN & SMOKED SAUSAGE

SLOW COOKER 🍲

BBQ CHICKEN & SMOKED SAUSAGE

My party-ready barbecue recipe works great on weeknights, too. With just a few minutes of prep time, you still get that low-and-slow flavor everybody craves (thanks, slow cooker!). Throw in minced jalapenos for extra oomph.
—Kimberly Young, Mesquite, TX

Prep: 30 min. • **Cook:** 4 hours
Makes: 8 servings

1 medium onion, chopped
1 large sweet red pepper, cut into 1-inch pieces
4 bone-in chicken thighs, skin removed
4 chicken drumsticks, skin removed
1 package (12 ounces) smoked sausage links, cut into 1-inch pieces
1 cup barbecue sauce
Sliced seeded jalapeno pepper, optional

1. Place first five ingredients in a 4 or 5-qt. slow cooker; top with barbecue sauce. Cook, covered, on low until chicken is tender and a thermometer inserted in chicken reads at least 170°-175°, about 4-5 hours.
2. Remove the chicken, sausage and vegetables from slow cooker; keep warm. Transfer cooking juices to a saucepan; bring to a boil. Reduce heat; simmer sauce, uncovered, until thickened, for 15-20 minutes, stirring occasionally.
3. Serve chicken, sausage and vegetables with sauce. If desired, top with jalapeno.

Per serving: 331 cal., 18g fat (6g sat. fat), 91mg chol., 840mg sodium, 17g carb. (13g sugars, 1g fiber), 24g pro.

HEALTH TIP Swap smoked turkey sausage for regular to lighten up this dish. Serve the meat with skinny smashed potatoes or rice and steamed green beans for a complete meal.

FREEZE IT **SLOW COOKER** 🍲

MOROCCAN POT ROAST

Prep: 25 min. • **Cook:** 7 hours
Makes: 8 servings

2 tablespoons olive oil
3 small onions, chopped
3 tablespoons paprika
1 tablespoon plus ½ teaspoon garam masala, divided
1¼ teaspoons salt, divided
¼ teaspoon cayenne pepper
2 tablespoons tomato paste
1 can (15 ounces) chickpeas or garbanzo beans, rinsed and drained
1 can (14½ ounces) beef broth
¼ teaspoon pepper
1 boneless beef chuck roast (3 pounds)
4 medium carrots, cut diagonally into ¾-inch pieces
1 small eggplant, cubed
2 tablespoons honey
2 tablespoons minced fresh mint
Hot cooked couscous or flatbreads, optional

1. In a large skillet, heat oil over medium heat; saute the onions with paprika, 1 tablespoon garam masala, ½ teaspoon salt and cayenne until tender, 4-5 minutes. Stir in tomato paste; cook and stir 1 minute. Stir in chickpeas and broth; transfer to a 5- or 6-qt. slow cooker.
2. Mix pepper and the remaining ½ teaspoon garam masala and ¾ teaspoon salt; rub over roast. Place in slow cooker. Add carrots and eggplant. Cook, covered, until the meat and vegetables are tender, 7-9 hours.
3. Remove roast from slow cooker; break into pieces. Remove vegetables with a slotted spoon; skim fat from cooking juices. Stir in honey. Return beef and vegetables to slow cooker and heat through. Sprinkle with mint. If desired, serve with couscous.

Freeze option: Freeze cooled beef and vegetable mixture in freezer containers. To use, partially thaw in refrigerator overnight. Microwave, covered, on high in a microwave-safe dish until heated through, stirring gently.

Per serving: 435 cal., 21g fat (7g sat. fat), 111mg chol., 766mg sodium, 23g carb. (10g sugars, 6g fiber), 38g pro.

"My husband loves meat and I love veggies, so we're both happy with this spiced twist on a beefy pot roast. With chickpeas, eggplant, honey and mint, it's like something you'd eat at a Marrakech bazaar."

—CATHERINE DEMPSEY, CLIFTON PARK, NY

SHORT RIB POUTINE

SLOW COOKER

SHORT RIB POUTINE

This dish combines the hearty, spicy flavors of my beloved slow cooker short ribs with my all-time favorite comfort food: fries and gravy. With a little prep in the morning, it's just about ready when I come home from work (plus, the kitchen smells amazing!). If you are sensitive to spice, simply reduce the amount of Sriracha chili sauce.
—Erin DeWitt, Long Beach, CA

Prep: 45 min. • **Cook:** 6 hours
Makes: 4 servings

- 1 **pound well-trimmed boneless beef short ribs**
- 3 **tablespoons all-purpose flour**
- ½ **teaspoon pepper**
- 2 **tablespoons olive oil**

- 1 **medium onion, coarsely chopped**
- 4 **garlic cloves, minced**
- 1½ **cups beef stock, divided**
- ¼ **cup Sriracha Asian hot chili sauce**
- 3 **tablespoons ketchup**
- 2 **tablespoons Worcestershire sauce**
- 1 **tablespoon packed brown sugar**
- 3 **cups frozen french-fried potatoes (about 11 ounces)**
- 1 **cup cheese curds or 4 ounces white cheddar cheese, broken into small chunks**

1. Toss short ribs with flour and pepper, shaking off excess; reserve remaining flour mixture. In a large skillet, heat oil over medium-high heat; brown ribs on all sides. Transfer to a 3-qt. slow cooker, reserving the drippings.

2. In same skillet, saute onion in the drippings over medium heat until tender, 2-3 minutes. Add garlic; cook and stir for 1 minute. Add 1 cup stock; bring to a boil, stirring to loosen browned bits from pan.

3. In a small bowl, whisk the reserved flour mixture, chili sauce, ketchup, Worcestershire sauce, brown sugar and remaining stock until smooth; stir into onion mixture. Pour over ribs.

4. Cook, covered, on low until ribs are tender, 6-8 hours. Remove ribs; shred with two forks and keep warm. Skim fat from onion mixture; puree using an immersion blender. (Or cool slightly and puree in a blender; return to the slow cooker and heat through.)

5. Cook potatoes according to package directions. Serve beef over potatoes; top with gravy and cheese.

Per serving: 560 cal., 31g fat (12g sat. fat), 80mg chol., 1453mg sodium, 39g carb. (15g sugars, 3g fiber), 28g pro.

SLOW COOKER GERMAN POTATO SALAD

Here's the dish everyone looks for at our parties, so we always double the recipe. It was handed down from my mother-in-law and has been a family favorite for years.
—Stacy Novak, Stafford, VA

Prep: 35 min. • **Cook:** 3 hours
Makes: 12 servings

- 3 pounds red potatoes (about 8 medium)
- 1 pound bacon strips, chopped
- 1 large onion, chopped
- 3 tablespoons all-purpose flour
- ⅔ cup sugar
- ⅓ cup packed light brown sugar
- 2½ teaspoons salt
- ½ teaspoon pepper
- ⅓ cup cider vinegar
- 2 cups water
  Minced fresh chives, optional

1. Place potatoes in a 6-qt. stockpot; add water to cover. Bring to a boil. Reduce heat; cook, uncovered, just until the potatoes are tender, about 15 minutes. Drain; cool slightly.

2. In a large skillet, cook bacon over medium heat until crisp, stirring occasionally. Using a slotted spoon, remove bacon to paper towels, reserving 3 tablespoons drippings.

3. For dressing, saute onion in drippings over medium-high heat until tender, 4-6 minutes. Stir in the flour until blended. Stir in sugars, salt and pepper. Gradually stir in vinegar and water; bring to a boil, stirring constantly. Cook and stir until slightly thickened, 4-6 minutes.

4. Slice the potatoes; place in a greased 5- or 6-qt. slow cooker. Top with dressing; sprinkle with bacon. Cook, covered, on low until heated through, 3-4 hours. If desired, sprinkle with chives.

Per ¾ cup: 318 cal., 15g fat (5g sat. fat), 25mg chol., 751mg sodium, 38g carb. (19g sugars, 2g fiber), 7g pro.

SLOW COOKER GERMAN POTATO SALAD

APPLE CHICKEN STEW

My husband and I enjoy visiting the apple orchards in nearby Nebraska City. We always make sure to buy extra cider to use in this sensational slow-cooked stew.
—Carol Mathias, Lincoln, NE

Prep: 35 min. • **Cook:** 3 hours
Makes: 8 servings

- 1½ teaspoons salt
- ¾ teaspoon dried thyme
- ½ teaspoon pepper
- ¼ to ½ teaspoon caraway seeds
- 1½ pounds potatoes (about 4 medium), cut into ¾-inch pieces
- 4 medium carrots, cut into ¼-inch slices
- 1 medium red onion, halved and sliced
- 1 celery rib, thinly sliced
- 2 pounds boneless skinless chicken breasts, cut into 1-inch pieces
- 2 tablespoons olive oil
- 1 bay leaf
- 1 large tart apple, peeled and cut into 1-inch cubes
- 1 tablespoon cider vinegar
- 1¼ cups apple cider or juice
  Minced fresh parsley

1. Mix first four ingredients. In a 5-qt. slow cooker, layer vegetables; sprinkle with half of the salt mixture.

2. Toss chicken with oil and remaining salt mixture. In a large skillet over medium-high heat, brown chicken in batches. Add to slow cooker. Top with bay leaf and apple. Add vinegar and cider.

3. Cook, covered, on high until chicken is no longer pink and vegetables are tender, 3 to 3½ hours. Discard bay leaf. Stir before serving. Sprinkle with parsley.

Per cup: 284 cal., 6g fat (1g sat. fat), 63mg chol., 533mg sodium, 31g carb. (9g sugars, 4g fiber), 26g pro.
Diabetic Exchanges: 3 lean meat, 2 starch, 1 fat.

FREEZE IT **SLOW COOKER**

SLOW COOKER POTLUCK BEANS

It was the morning of our family potluck and I still needed a dish to bring. I threw together this recipe while drinking my morning coffee. By the end of the party, the beans were all gone, and someone had even washed the crock for me!
—Mary Anne Thygesen, Portland, OR

Prep: 10 min. • **Cook:** 4 hours
Makes: 12 servings

- 1 cup brewed coffee
- ½ cup packed brown sugar
- ¼ cup spicy brown mustard
- 2 tablespoons molasses
- 2 cans (16 ounces each) butter beans
- 2 cans (16 ounces each) kidney beans
- 2 cans (16 ounces each) navy beans

In a greased 3- or 4-qt. slow cooker, mix first four ingredients. Rinse and drain beans; stir into coffee mixture. Cook, covered, on low until flavors are blended, 4-5 hours.

Freeze option: Freeze cooled beans in freezer containers. To use, partially thaw in refrigerator overnight. Heat through in a covered saucepan, stirring gently and adding a little water if necessary.

Per ½ cup: 243 cal., 0 fat (0 sat. fat), 0 chol., 538mg sodium, 50g carb. (13g sugars, 10g fiber), 14g pro.

FREEZE IT **SLOW COOKER**

SAUSAGE & CHICKEN GUMBO

This classic southern comfort food was the first thing I cooked for my girlfriend. It was simple to make but tasted gourmet. Lucky for me, it was love at first bite.
—Kael Harvey, Brooklyn, NY

Prep: 35 min. • **Cook:** 6 hours
Makes: 6 servings

- ¼ cup all-purpose flour
- ¼ cup canola oil
- 4 cups chicken broth, divided
- 1 package (14 ounces) smoked sausage, cut into ½-inch slices
- 1 cup frozen sliced okra, thawed
- 1 small green pepper, chopped
- 1 medium onion, chopped
- 1 celery rib, chopped
- 3 garlic cloves, minced
- ½ teaspoon pepper
- ¼ teaspoon salt
- ¼ teaspoon cayenne pepper
- 2 cups coarsely shredded cooked chicken
  Hot cooked rice

1. In a heavy saucepan over medium heat, cook and stir flour and oil until smooth and light brown, about 4 minutes. Reduce heat to medium-low; cook and stir until dark reddish brown, about 15 minutes (do not burn). Gradually stir in 3 cups broth; transfer to a 4- or 5-qt. slow cooker.
2. Stir in sausage, vegetables, garlic and seasonings. Cook, covered, on low until the flavors are blended, 6-8 hours. Stir in chicken and remaining broth; heat mixture through. Serve with rice.

Freeze option: Freeze cooled soup in freezer containers. Partially thaw in refrigerator overnight. Heat through in a saucepan, stirring occasionally.

Per cup: 427 cal., 31g fat (9g sat. fat), 89mg chol., 1548mg sodium, 11g carb. (4g sugars, 1g fiber), 25g pro.

SLOW COOKER

DEB'S MUSHROOM & BARLEY SOUP

Nothing is more wonderful than coming home to this rich soup! I prep all the ingredients the evening before and start the slow cooker on my way out the door.
—Debra Kamerman, New York, NY

Prep: 25 min. • **Cook:** 6 hours
Makes: 10 servings (3½ quarts)

- 1 pound sliced baby portobello mushrooms
- 3 medium carrots, finely chopped
- 3 celery ribs, finely chopped
- 1 medium onion, finely chopped
- 1 cup medium pearl barley
- 1 teaspoon dried thyme
- 1 teaspoon pepper
- 5 cups water
- 4 cups beef stock
- 3 teaspoons salt, divided
- 1 large egg, lightly beaten
- 1 pound ground turkey

1. Place the first nine ingredients and 2½ teaspoons of salt in a 6- or 7-qt. slow cooker.
2. In a large bowl, mix egg and remaining salt. Add turkey; mix lightly but thoroughly. Shape into 1¼-in. balls; drop gently into slow cooker. Cook soup, covered, on low until vegetables and barley are tender, 6-8 hours.

Per 1⅓ cups: 180 cal., 4g fat (1g sat. fat), 49mg chol., 967mg sodium, 22g carb. (4g sugars, 5g fiber), 15g pro.

SLOW COOKER POTLUCK BEANS

TURKEY SAUSAGE CABBAGE ROLLS

I practically grew up in my Polish grandmother's kitchen, watching Babci cook and listening to her stories. I made her cabbage roll recipe healthier with whole grains and turkey, but kept the same rich flavors I remember.
—Fay Moreland, Wichita Falls, TX

Prep: 50 min. • **Cook:** 7 hours
Makes: 12 servings

- 12 large plus 6 medium cabbage leaves
- 2 packets (3 ounces each) instant multigrain rice mix
- 1 medium onion, finely chopped
- ½ cup finely chopped sweet red pepper
- ¼ cup minced fresh parsley
- 3 teaspoons Italian seasoning
- 1¼ teaspoons salt
- 1 teaspoon garlic powder
- 1 teaspoon pepper
- 1½ pounds lean ground turkey
- 3 Italian turkey sausage links (about 4 ounces each), casings removed
- 1 bottle (46 ounces) V8 juice

PORK TACOS WITH MANGO SALSA

1. In batches, cook cabbage leaves in boiling water until crisp-tender, about 5 minutes. Drain; cool slightly.
2. In a large bowl, combine rice mix, onion, red pepper, parsley and seasonings. Add the turkey and sausage; mix lightly but thoroughly.
3. Line bottom of a 6-qt. slow cooker with medium cabbage leaves, overlapping as needed. Trim thick veins from bottom of large cabbage leaves, making V-shaped cuts. Top each with about ½ cup filling. Pull cut edges together to overlap, then fold over filling; fold in sides and roll up. Layer in slow cooker, seam side down. Pour vegetable juice over top.
4. Cook, covered, on low until cabbage is tender, 7-9 hours (a thermometer inserted in the filling should read at least 165°).
Note: This recipe was tested with Minute Brand Multi-Grain Medley.
Per cabbage roll with 3 tablespoons sauce: 202 cal., 7g fat (2g sat. fat), 49mg chol., 681mg sodium, 19g carb. (5g sugars, 3g fiber), 17g pro.
Diabetic Exchanges: 2 lean meat, 1 starch.

PORK TACOS WITH MANGO SALSA

I've made quite a few tacos in my day, but you can't beat the tender filling made in a slow cooker. These are by far the best pork tacos we've had—and we've tried plenty. Make the mango salsa from scratch if you have time! Yum.
—Amber Massey, Argyle, TX

Prep: 25 min. • **Cook:** 6 hours
Makes: 12 servings

- 2 tablespoons lime juice
- 2 tablespoons white vinegar
- 3 tablespoons chili powder
- 2 teaspoons ground cumin
- 1½ teaspoons salt
- ½ teaspoon pepper
- 3 cups cubed fresh pineapple
- 1 small red onion, coarsely chopped
- 2 chipotle peppers in adobo sauce
- 1 bottle (12 ounces) dark Mexican beer
- 3 pounds pork tenderloin, cut into 1-inch cubes
- ¼ cup chopped fresh cilantro
- 1 jar (16 ounces) mango salsa
  Corn tortillas (6 inches), warmed

OPTIONAL TOPPINGS
  Cubed fresh pineapple
  Cubed avocado
  Queso fresco

1. Puree first nine ingredients in a blender; stir in beer. In a 5- or 6-qt. slow cooker, combine pork and pineapple mixture. Cook, covered, on low until pork is very tender, 6-8 hours. Stir to break up the pork.
2. Stir cilantro into salsa. Using a slotted spoon, serve pork mixture in tortillas; add salsa and toppings as desired.
Freeze option: Freeze cooled meat mixture and cooking juices in freezer containers. To use, partially thaw in refrigerator overnight. Heat through in a saucepan, stirring occasionally.
Per ⅔ cup pork mixture with 2 tablespoons salsa: 178 cal., 4g fat (1g sat. fat), 64mg chol., 656mg sodium, 9g carb. (5g sugars, 2g fiber), 23g pro.
Diabetic Exchanges: 3 lean meat, ½ starch.

ROOT VEGETABLE POT ROAST

SLOW COOKER 🍲

ROOT VEGETABLE POT ROAST

During the hectic holiday season, I make this roast a lot. We've devoured it before and after shopping and while wrapping presents. Root vegetables and roast beef make everyone feel cozy and calm.
—Pat Dazis, Charlotte, NC

Prep: 30 min.
Cook: 7 hours
Makes: 8 servings

- 1 can (14½ ounces) reduced-sodium beef broth
- 2 chai black tea bags
- 2 medium potatoes (about 1 pound), cut into 1½-inch cubes
- 2 medium turnips (about 9 ounces), cut into 1½-inch pieces
- 4 medium carrots, cut into ½-inch pieces

- 2 medium parsnips, peeled and cut into ½-inch pieces
- 1 large onion, cut into 1-inch wedges
- 2 celery ribs, cut into ½-inch pieces
- 1 tablespoon olive oil
- 1 boneless beef chuck roast (about 3 pounds)
- 1 teaspoon salt
- ½ teaspoon pepper
- 1 medium lemon, thinly sliced
- 3 tablespoons cornstarch
- 3 tablespoons cold water

1. In a small saucepan, bring broth to a boil; remove from heat. Add tea bags; steep, covered, 3-5 minutes according to taste. Discard tea bags. Meanwhile, combine vegetables in a 6-qt. slow cooker.

2. In a large skillet, heat oil over medium-high heat; brown roast on all sides. Place over vegetables; pour tea-steeped broth over top. Sprinkle roast with salt and pepper; top with lemon slices. Cook,

covered, on low until beef and vegetables are tender, 7-9 hours.

3. Discard lemon. Remove roast and vegetables from slow cooker; keep warm.

4. Transfer cooking juices to a saucepan; skim fat. Bring juices to a boil. In a small bowl, mix cornstarch and water until smooth; stir into juices. Return to a boil, stirring constantly; cook and stir until thickened, 1-2 minutes. Serve with roast and vegetables.

Per serving: 421 cal., 18g fat (7g sat. fat), 112mg chol., 523mg sodium, 27g carb. (7g sugars, 5g fiber), 36g pro.

✱

TEST KITCHEN TIP
The flavor of chai tea varies quite a bit by brand. We tested this recipe with Twinings, and it added a subtle spiced flavor. If you want stronger chai flavor, use more tea bags rather than steeping longer. Too much steeping can turn the flavor bitter.

SLOW COOKER

SIMPLE SWEDISH MEATBALLS

When my husband packs these saucy slow-cooked meatballs in his lunch, all his work buddies wish they had their own! It's comfort food at its easiest.
—Christina Logan, Gun Barrel City, TX

Prep: 15 min. • **Cook:** 5¼ hours
Makes: 10 servings

- 1 tablespoon butter
- 1 pound sliced fresh mushrooms
- 1 can (14½ ounces) reduced-sodium beef broth
- 1 can (10¾ ounces) reduced-fat reduced-sodium condensed cream of chicken soup, undiluted
- 1 envelope Lipton beefy onion soup mix
- 1 package (24 ounces) frozen fully cooked Swedish meatballs or 1 package (26 ounces) frozen fully cooked homestyle meatballs
- ⅔ cup sour cream
- 2 tablespoons minced fresh parsley or 2 teaspoons dried parsley flakes
  Hot cooked noodles or mashed potatoes, optional

1. In a large skillet, heat butter over medium-high heat; saute mushrooms until tender, 4-5 minutes. Transfer to a 4-qt. slow cooker. Stir in the broth, cream of chicken soup and soup mix. Stir in the meatballs. Cook, covered, on low until flavors are blended, 5-6 hours.
2. Stir in sour cream and parsley. Cook, covered, until heated through, about 15 minutes. If desired, serve with noodles.
Per 1 cup meatballs and sauce: 295 cal., 22g fat (11g sat. fat), 46mg chol., 1045mg sodium, 11g carb. (3g sugars, 3g fiber), 14g pro.

SLOW COOKER

BACON CHEESEBURGER SOUP

This creamy recipe brings two of my absolute favorite foods together in one! The lettuce, tomato and crispy bacon toppers make this soup taste just like burger time.
—Geoff Bales, Hemet, CA

Prep: 20 min. • **Cook:** 4 hours
Makes: 6 servings

- 1½ pounds lean ground beef (90% lean)
- 1 large onion, chopped
- ⅓ cup all-purpose flour
- ½ teaspoon pepper
- 2½ cups chicken broth
- 1 can (12 ounces) evaporated milk
- 1½ cups shredded cheddar cheese
- 8 slices process American cheese, chopped
- 1½ cups shredded lettuce
- 2 medium tomatoes, chopped
- 6 bacon strips, cooked and crumbled

1. In a large skillet, cook and crumble the beef with onion over medium-high heat until no longer pink, 6-8 minutes; drain. Stir in the flour and pepper; transfer to a 5-qt. slow cooker.
2. Stir in broth and milk. Cook, covered, on low until flavors are blended, 4-5 hours. Stir in cheeses until melted. Top servings with remaining ingredients.
Per cup: 557 cal., 32g fat (17g sat. fat), 135mg chol., 1160mg sodium, 18g carb. (10g sugars, 1g fiber), 42g pro.

SLOW COOKER

CINNAMON SPICED APPLES

If you're feeling festive, scoop some vanilla ice cream over a bowl of my cinnamon spiced apples. They're homey, aromatic and just plain heavenly.
—Amie Powell, Knoxville, TN

Prep: 15 min. • **Cook:** 3 hours
Makes: 6 cups

- ⅓ cup sugar
- ¼ cup packed brown sugar
- 1 tablespoon cornstarch
- 3 teaspoons ground cinnamon
- ⅛ teaspoon ground nutmeg
- 6 large Granny Smith apples, peeled and cut into eighths
- ¼ cup butter, cubed

1. In a small bowl, mix the first five ingredients. Place apples in a greased 5-qt. slow cooker; add sugar mixture and toss to coat. Top with butter.
2. Cook, covered, on low 3-4 hours or until apples are tender, stirring halfway through cooking.
Per ¾ cup: 181 cal., 6g fat (4g sat. fat), 15mg chol., 48mg sodium, 34g carb. (29g sugars, 2g fiber), 0 pro.

SIMPLE SWEDISH MEATBALLS

ASIAN SHREDDED PORK SANDWICHES

CHEESY CHICKEN TACO DIP

We're huge college football fans (go Irish!), and my chicken taco dip hasn't missed a season opener in 14 years and counting. A slow cooker lets us keep the dip warm for the whole game—if it lasts that long!

—Deanna Garretson, Yucaipa, CA

Prep: 15 min. • **Cook:** 4 hours 10 min.
Makes: 8 cups

- 1 jar (16 ounces) salsa
- 1 can (30 ounces) refried beans
- 1½ pounds boneless skinless chicken breasts
- 1 tablespoon taco seasoning
- 2 cups shredded cheddar cheese
- 3 green onions, chopped
- 1 medium tomato, chopped
- ¼ cup chopped fresh cilantro
  Tortilla chips

1. In a greased 3- or 4-qt. slow cooker, mix salsa and beans. Top with chicken; sprinkle with taco seasoning. Cook, covered, on low until chicken is tender, 3-4 hours.
2. Remove chicken; shred finely using two forks. Return to the slow cooker; stir in cheese. Cook, covered, on low until the cheese is melted, 10-15 minutes, stirring mixture occasionally.
3. To serve, top with green onions, tomato and cilantro. Serve with chips.
Per ¼ cup: 82 cal., 3g fat (2g sat. fat), 19mg chol., 238mg sodium, 5g carb. (1g sugars, 1g fiber), 7g pro.
HEALTH TIP Skip the tortilla chips and serve with crunchy celery sticks for a lighter bite.

★ ★ ★ ★ ★ **READER REVIEW**

"Delicious! Will be a great addition to our party tables this year."
RENA 55 TASTEOFHOME.COM

FREEZE IT **SLOW COOKER**

ASIAN SHREDDED PORK SANDWICHES

On cool-weather weeknights, the slow cooker is our friend. The plums might surprise in these juicy pork sandwiches, but they add a little sweetness and make the meat extra tender.

—Holly Battiste, Barrington, NJ

Prep: 30 min. • **Cook:** 6 hours
Makes: 10 servings

- 1 can (15 ounces) plums, drained and pitted
- 1 tablespoon Sriracha Asian hot chili sauce
- 1 tablespoon hoisin sauce
- 1 tablespoon reduced-sodium soy sauce
- 1 tablespoon rice vinegar
- 1 tablespoon honey
- 2 garlic cloves, minced
- 1 teaspoon pepper
- 1 teaspoon sesame oil
- ½ teaspoon ground ginger
- ¼ teaspoon salt
- 2 tablespoons canola oil
- 1 boneless pork shoulder butt roast (3 pounds)
- 4 medium carrots, finely chopped
- 10 ciabatta rolls, split
  Shredded napa or other cabbage

1. Mix first 11 ingredients. In a large skillet, heat oil over medium-high heat. Brown roast on all sides.
2. Place carrots in a 4- or 5-qt. slow cooker. Add roast; pour plum mixture over top. Cook, covered, on low until pork is tender, 6-8 hours.
3. Remove pork; shred with two forks. Skim fat from carrot mixture; stir in pork and heat through. Serve pork on rolls; top with cabbage.
Freeze option: Freeze cooled pork mixture in freezer containers. To use, partially thaw in refrigerator overnight. Heat through in a covered saucepan, stirring gently and adding a little broth if necessary.
Per sandwich: 637 cal., 21g fat (6g sat. fat), 81mg chol., 864mg sodium, 85g carb. (17g sugars, 5g fiber), 34g pro.

RAISIN NUT OATMEAL

There's no better feeling than waking up to a hot, ready-to-eat breakfast. The oats, fruit and spices in this homey meal cook together while you sleep!
—Valerie Sauber, Adelanto, CA

Prep: 10 min. • **Cook:** 7 hours
Makes: 6 servings

3½ cups fat-free milk
1 large apple, peeled and chopped
¾ cup steel-cut oats
¾ cup raisins
3 tablespoons brown sugar
4½ teaspoons butter, melted
¾ teaspoon ground cinnamon
½ teaspoon salt
¼ cup chopped pecans

In a 3-qt. slow cooker coated with cooking spray, combine the first eight ingredients. Cover and cook on low for 7-8 hours or until liquid is absorbed. Spoon oatmeal into bowls; sprinkle with chopped pecans.
Note: You may substitute 1½ cups quick-cooking oats for the steel-cut oats and increase the fat-free milk to 4½ cups.
Per ¾ cup: 289 cal., 9g fat (3g sat. fat), 10mg chol., 282mg sodium, 47g carb. (28g sugars, 4g fiber), 9g pro.

SLOW COOKER
EASY SLOW COOKER MAC & CHEESE
PICTURED ON P. 179

My sons always cheer, "You're the best mom in the world!" whenever I make this creamy mac and cheese perfection.
—Heidi Fleek, Hamburg, PA

Prep: 25 min. • **Cook:** 1 hour
Makes: 8 servings

2 cups uncooked elbow macaroni
1 can (10¾ ounces) condensed cheddar cheese soup, undiluted
1 cup 2% milk
½ cup sour cream
¼ cup butter, cubed
½ teaspoon onion powder
¼ teaspoon white pepper
⅛ teaspoon salt
1 cup shredded cheddar cheese
1 cup shredded fontina cheese
1 cup shredded provolone cheese

CHICKEN FAJITA CHOWDER

1. Cook macaroni according to package directions for al dente. Meanwhile, in a large saucepan, combine soup, milk, sour cream, butter and seasonings; cook and stir over medium-low heat until blended. Stir in cheeses until melted.
2. Drain macaroni; transfer to a greased 3-qt. slow cooker. Stir in cheese mixture. Cook, covered, on low 1-2 hours or until heated through.
Per ¾ cup: 346 cal., 23g fat (14g sat. fat), 71mg chol., 712mg sodium, 20g carb. (4g sugars, 1g fiber), 15g pro.

FREEZE IT **SLOW COOKER**
CHICKEN FAJITA CHOWDER
This south-of-the-border chowder is one of my favorite slow recipes. We like it topped with fresh avocado, shredded cheddar cheese and corn chips.
—Nancy Heishman, Las Vegas, NV

Prep: 20 min. • **Cook:** 4 hours
Makes: 10 servings (3½ quarts)

3 large tomatoes, chopped
1 can (15 ounces) black beans, rinsed and drained
6 ounces fully cooked Spanish chorizo links, sliced
2 pounds boneless skinless chicken breasts, cut into 1-inch cubes
1 envelope fajita seasoning mix
1½ cups frozen corn, thawed
1 medium sweet red pepper, chopped
1 medium green pepper, chopped
6 green onions, chopped
¾ cup salsa
½ cup chopped fresh cilantro
2 cans (14½ ounces each) reduced-sodium chicken broth
1 can (10¾ ounces) condensed nacho cheese soup, undiluted
Cubed avocado and additional cilantro, optional

1. Place first twelve ingredients in a 6-qt. slow cooker. Cook, covered, on low until chicken is tender, 4-5 hours.
2. Stir in cheese soup; heat through. If desired, top servings with avocado and additional cilantro.
Freeze option: Freeze cooled soup in freezer containers. To use, partially thaw in refrigerator overnight. Heat through in a saucepan, stirring occasionally.
Per 1⅓ cups: 269 cal., 9g fat (3g sat. fat), 64mg chol., 1069mg sodium, 20g carb. (5g sugars, 4g fiber), 26g pro.

SLOW COOKER

LORA'S RED BEANS & RICE

My dear mother-in-law gave this simple recipe to me. With meats, beans and savory veggies that simmer all day, it's tasty, easy and economical, too!
—Carol Simms, Madison, MS

Prep: 15 min. + soaking • **Cook:** 8 hours
Makes: 10 servings

- 1 package (16 ounces) dried kidney beans (about 2½ cups)
- 2 cups cubed fully cooked ham (about 1 pound)
- 1 package (12 ounces) fully cooked andouille chicken sausage links or flavor of choice, sliced
- 1 medium green pepper, chopped
- 1 medium onion, chopped
- 2 celery ribs, chopped
- 1 tablespoon hot pepper sauce
- 2 garlic cloves, minced
- 1½ teaspoons salt
  Hot cooked rice

1. Place beans in a large bowl; add cool water to cover. Soak overnight.
2. Drain beans, discarding water; rinse with cool water. Place beans in a greased 6-qt. slow cooker. Stir in ham, sausage, vegetables, pepper sauce, garlic and salt. Add water to cover by 1 in.
3. Cook, covered, on low until beans are tender, 8-9 hours. Serve with rice.
Per cup: 249 cal., 5g fat (1g sat. fat), 43mg chol., 906mg sodium, 31g carb. (2g sugars, 7g fiber), 23g pro.

KOREAN PULLED PORK TACOS

FREEZE IT SLOW COOKER

KOREAN PULLED PORK TACOS

I created this surprising pulled pork recipe to replicate our favorite food truck tacos at home. They're a little sweet, a little spicy and totally delicious any time of year.
—Julie Orr, Fullerton, CA

Prep: 25 min. • **Cook:** 8 hours
Makes: 10 servings

- ½ cup reduced-sodium soy sauce
- ½ cup water
- 3 tablespoons brown sugar
- 2 tablespoons sesame oil
- 1 tablespoon baking cocoa
- 3 teaspoons chili powder
- 1 garlic clove, minced
- ¼ teaspoon ground ginger
- 1 boneless pork shoulder butt roast (4-5 pounds)

SLAW
- 3 tablespoons sugar
- 2 tablespoons reduced-sodium soy sauce
- 1 tablespoon Sriracha Asian hot chili sauce
- 2 teaspoons sesame oil
- 1 teaspoon rice vinegar
- 1 package (14 ounces) coleslaw mix
- 1 tablespoon toasted sesame seeds, optional

ASSEMBLY
- 20 flour tortillas (6 inches), warmed
  Thinly sliced green onions and additional chili sauce, optional

1. Whisk together first eight ingredients. Place roast in a 6-qt. slow cooker. Pour soy sauce mixture over top. Cook, covered, on low until pork is tender, 8-10 hours.
2. About 1 hour before serving, mix first five slaw ingredients until blended. Place coleslaw mix in a large bowl; toss with dressing and, if desired, sesame seeds. Refrigerate, covered, until serving.
3. Remove roast; skim fat from cooking juices. Shred pork with two forks; return to slow cooker and heat through. Serve in tortillas with slaw. If desired, serve with green onions and additional chili sauce.
Freeze option: Freeze cooled pork mixture in freezer containers. To use, partially thaw in refrigerator overnight. Heat through in a saucepan, stirring occasionally and adding a little water or broth if necessary.
Per 2 tacos: 603 cal., 29g fat (10g sat. fat), 108mg chol., 1177mg sodium, 46g carb. (11g sugars, 4g fiber), 37g pro.

SLOW COOKER 🍲
SLOW-COOKED MEATBALL SOUP

As a mother, I try to sneak as many veggies into my daughter's diet as I can. This savory soup with meatballs and pasta does the trick. The whole family loves it!
—Kymm Wills, Phoenix, AZ

Prep: 15 min. • **Cook:** 5¼ hours
Makes: 10 servings (3½ quarts)

- 3 medium carrots, sliced
- 2 celery ribs, sliced
- 1 small onion, chopped
- 1 bay leaf
- 1 teaspoon Italian seasoning
- ¼ teaspoon pepper
- 1 package (24 ounces) frozen fully cooked Italian meatballs, thawed
- 1 carton (32 ounces) beef broth
- 2 cans (14½ ounces each) Italian diced tomatoes, undrained
- 2 cups water
- ¾ cup dry red wine or additional water
- ¾ cup ditalini or other small pasta
- 4 cups fresh baby spinach (about 5 ounces)
  Grated Parmesan cheese

1. Place first eleven ingredients in a 6-qt. slow cooker. Cook, covered, on low until vegetables are tender and flavors are blended, 5-6 hours.
2. Stir in pasta; cook, covered, on high until pasta is tender, 15-20 minutes. Discard bay leaf; stir in spinach until wilted. Serve with cheese.
Note: This recipe was tested with Johnsonville Classic Italian Style Meatballs.
Per 1⅓ cups: 288 cal., 16g fat (7g sat. fat), 33mg chol., 1173mg sodium, 23g carb. (7g sugars, 3g fiber), 15g pro.

SLOW COOKER 🍲
CHICKEN & VEGETABLE WILD RICE SOUP

This go-to weeknight recipe is one I tweaked over and over again till it was just right. It has morphed from a labor-intensive wintry bowl to a steamy, comforting, slow-cooked favorite that our family loves.
—Courtney Riggin, Hatchechubbee, AL

Prep: 20 min. • **Cook:** 6½ hours
Makes: 8 servings (3 quarts)

- 1 pound boneless skinless chicken thighs, trimmed and cut into 1-inch pieces
- 2 cups frozen corn (about 10 ounces), thawed
- 1 package (6 ounces) long grain and wild rice mix
- 1 medium sweet red pepper, finely chopped
- 2 medium carrots, finely chopped
- 1 medium leek (white portion only), finely chopped
- 1 celery rib, finely chopped
- 3 bacon strips, cooked and crumbled
- 1 tablespoon minced fresh thyme or 1 teaspoon dried thyme
- ½ teaspoon salt
- 6 cups reduced-sodium chicken broth
- ⅓ cup dry sherry or additional broth
- 1 cup sour cream
- 1 tablespoon all-purpose flour
- 1 cup cut fresh asparagus (1-inch pieces)
  Chopped green onions, optional

1. Place the first 12 ingredients in a 5- or 6-qt. slow cooker; stir to combine. Cook, covered, on low until the chicken and vegetables are tender, 6-8 hours.
2. Mix sour cream and flour until smooth; stir into soup. Stir in asparagus. Cook, covered, on high until soup is thickened and asparagus is tender, 20-25 minutes. If desired, serve with green onions.
Per 1½ cups: 310 cal., 12g fat (5g sat. fat), 48mg chol., 1060mg sodium, 32g carb. (5g sugars, 3g fiber), 19g pro.

SLOW-COOKED MEATBALL SOUP

FREEZE IT **SLOW COOKER**

TOMATO BALSAMIC CHICKEN

I came up with this saucy chicken during a particularly busy holiday season. As new parents, my husband and I both appreciate having a go-to dinner that's easy, homemade and delicious.
—Anne Colvin, Chicago, IL

Prep: 25 min. • **Cook:** 6 hours
Makes: 6 servings

- 2 medium carrots, chopped
- ½ cup thinly sliced shallots
- 2 pounds bone-in chicken thighs, skin removed
- 1 tablespoon all-purpose flour
- ½ cup reduced-sodium chicken broth
- 1 can (14½ ounces) petite diced tomatoes, undrained
- ¼ cup balsamic vinegar
- 1 tablespoon olive oil
- 2 garlic cloves, minced
- 1 bay leaf
- ½ teaspoon Italian seasoning
- ½ teaspoon salt
- ¼ teaspoon pepper
  Hot cooked orzo

1. Place carrots and shallots in a 3- or 4-qt. slow cooker; top with chicken. In a bowl, whisk flour and broth until smooth; stir in tomatoes, vinegar, oil, garlic and seasonings. Pour over chicken. Cook, covered, on low until chicken and carrots are tender, 6-8 hours.
2. Remove chicken; cool slightly. Discard bay leaf and, if desired, skim fat from carrot mixture.
3. Remove chicken from bones; shred slightly with two forks. Return to slow cooker and heat through. Serve with orzo.
Freeze option: Freeze cooled chicken mixture in freezer containers. To use, partially thaw in refrigerator overnight. Heat through in a saucepan, stirring occasionally.
Per ¾ cup chicken mixture: 235 cal., 11g fat (3g sat. fat), 77mg chol., 433mg sodium, 12g carb. (7g sugars, 2g fiber), 23g pro.
Diabetic Exchanges: 3 lean meat, 1 vegetable, ½ fat.

STRAWBERRY-BANANA
PUDDING CAKE

SLOW COOKER

STRAWBERRY-BANANA PUDDING CAKE

This luscious pudding cake is so easy to put together. Top it with ice cream and fresh fruit, and your family will be happy.
—Nadine Mesch, Mount Healthy, OH

Prep: 15 min. • **Cook:** 3½ hours + standing
Makes: 10 servings

- 1 package strawberry cake mix (regular size)
- 1 package (3.4 ounces) instant banana cream pudding mix
- 2 cups plain Greek yogurt
- 4 large eggs
- 1 cup water
- ¾ cup canola oil
- 2 tablespoons minced fresh basil
- 1 cup white baking chips
  Optional toppings: vanilla ice cream, sliced bananas, sliced strawberries and fresh basil

1. In a large bowl, combine first six ingredients; beat on low speed for 30 seconds. Beat on medium 2 minutes; stir in basil. Transfer to a greased 5-qt. slow cooker. Cook, covered, on low until edges of cake are golden brown (center will be moist), 3½ to 4 hours.
2. Turn off slow cooker; sprinkle cake with baking chips. Remove insert; let stand, uncovered, 10 minutes before serving. Serve warm with toppings as desired.
Per serving: 373 cal., 29g fat (8g sat. fat), 90mg chol., 239mg sodium, 23g carb. (21g sugars, 0 fiber), 5g pro.

SLOW COOKER

HEARTY MANHATTAN CLAM CHOWDER

Talk about hearty. This veggie-packed clam chowder really satisfies. Butter up some French bread and you have yourself a complete meal.
—Carol Bullick, Royersford, PA

Prep: 20 min. • **Cook:** 7 hours
Makes: 6 servings (about 2¼ quarts)

- 1½ pounds potatoes (about 3 medium), peeled and cut into ¾-inch cubes
- 1 large onion, chopped
- 2 medium carrots, shredded (about ¾ cup)
- 3 celery ribs, sliced
- 4 cans (6½ ounces each) chopped clams, undrained
- 5 bacon strips, cooked and crumbled
- 1 tablespoon dried parsley flakes
- 1 bay leaf
- 1½ teaspoons dried thyme
- ¼ teaspoon coarsely ground pepper
- 1 can (28 ounces) diced tomatoes, undrained

Place all ingredients in a 4- or 5-qt. slow cooker. Cook, covered, on low until the vegetables are tender, 7-9 hours. Remove bay leaf before serving.
Per 1½ cups: 203 cal., 4g fat (1g sat. fat), 50mg chol., 995mg sodium, 29g carb. (8g sugars, 5g fiber), 15g pro.

BUFFALO CHICKEN SLIDERS

I got the idea for these sliders from my mom and dad, who'd made a similar recipe for a family get-together. To make it special, I sometimes use several different styles of buffalo sauce and let guests mix and match their favorites.

—Christina Addison, Blanchester, OH

Prep: 20 min. • **Cook:** 3 hours
Makes: 6 servings

- 1 pound boneless skinless chicken breasts
- 2 tablespoons plus ⅓ cup Louisiana-style hot sauce, divided
- ¼ teaspoon pepper
- ¼ cup butter, cubed
- ¼ cup honey
- 12 Hawaiian sweet rolls, warmed
  Optional ingredients: lettuce leaves, sliced tomato, thinly sliced red onion and crumbled blue cheese

1. Place chicken in a 3-qt. slow cooker. Toss with 2 tablespoons hot sauce and pepper; cook, covered, on low until tender, 3-4 hours.
2. Remove chicken; discard cooking juices. In a small saucepan, combine butter, honey and remaining hot sauce; cook and stir over medium heat until blended. Shred chicken with two forks; stir into sauce and heat through. Serve on rolls with optional ingredients as desired.
Freeze option: Freeze cooled chicken mixture in freezer containers. To use, partially thaw in refrigerator overnight. Microwave, covered, on high in a microwave-safe dish until heated through, stirring occasionally and adding a little water or broth if necessary.
Per 2 sliders: 396 cal., 15g fat (8g sat. fat), 92mg chol., 873mg sodium, 44g carb. (24g sugars, 2g fiber), 24g pro.

DID YOU KNOW?

For easy cleanup, spritz the measuring cup with a little cooking spray before measuring sticky ingredients like honey and molasses.

BUFFALO CHICKEN SLIDERS

SLOW COOKER CHICKEN ENCHILADA MELTS

After tasting a similar recipe at a sandwich shop, I knew I had to try my own version at home. Personally, I like mine even more! I like to mix equal parts salsa and ranch dressing to make a tasty sauce for these sandwiches.

—Blair Lonergan, Rochelle, VA

Prep: 25 min. • **Cook:** 4 hours
Makes: 6 servings

- 1½ pounds boneless skinless chicken breasts
- 1 jar (16 ounces) salsa
- 1 envelope reduced-sodium taco seasoning
- 4 medium tomatoes, seeded and chopped
- ½ cup minced fresh cilantro
- 12 diagonally sliced French bread slices (1-inch thick)
- 1 cup shredded cheddar cheese
  Sliced ripe olives and additional chopped tomatoes, optional

1. In a greased 3-qt. slow cooker, combine chicken, salsa and taco seasoning. Cook, covered, on low until chicken is tender, 4-5 hours.
2. To serve, preheat broiler. Shred chicken with two forks; stir in tomatoes and cilantro.
3. Place bread on ungreased baking sheets; broil 2-3 in. from heat until tops are lightly browned. Using tongs, place rounded ⅓ cup chicken mixture on each toast. Sprinkle with cheese. Broil until cheese is melted, 2-3 minutes. If desired, top with olives and additional tomatoes.
Freeze option: Cool chicken mixture without tomatoes and cilantro; freeze in freezer containers. To use, partially thaw in refrigerator overnight. Heat through in a saucepan, stirring occasionally; stir in tomatoes and cilantro. Serve as directed.
Per 2 open-faced sandwiches: 377 cal., 10g fat (5g sat. fat), 81mg chol., 1082mg sodium, 36g carb. (7g sugars, 2g fiber), 32g pro.

CHICKPEA & POTATO CURRY

CHICKPEA & POTATO CURRY

I make chana masala, the classic Indian dish, in my slow cooker. Browning the onion, ginger and garlic first really makes the sauce amazing.
—Anjana Devasahayam, San Antonio, TX

Prep: 25 min. • **Cook:** 6 hours
Makes: 6 servings

- 1 tablespoon canola oil
- 1 medium onion, chopped
- 2 garlic cloves, minced
- 2 teaspoons minced fresh gingerroot
- 2 teaspoons ground coriander
- 1 teaspoon garam masala
- 1 teaspoon chili powder
- ½ teaspoon salt
- ½ teaspoon ground cumin
- ¼ teaspoon ground turmeric
- 1 can (15 ounces) crushed tomatoes
- 2 cans (15 ounces each) chickpeas, rinsed and drained
- 1 large baking potato, peeled and cut into ¾-inch cubes
- 2½ cups vegetable stock
- 1 tablespoon lime juice
  Chopped fresh cilantro
  Hot cooked rice
  Sliced red onion, optional
  Lime wedges, optional

1. In a large skillet, heat oil over medium-high heat; saute onion until tender, 2-4 minutes. Add garlic, ginger and dry seasonings; cook and stir 1 minute. Stir in the tomatoes; transfer to a 3- or 4-qt. slow cooker.

2. Stir in chickpeas, potato and stock. Cook, covered, on low until the potato is tender and flavors are blended, 6-8 hours.

3. Stir in lime juice; sprinkle with cilantro. Serve with rice and, if desired, red onion and lime wedges.

Per 1¼ cups chickpea mixture: 240 cal., 6g fat (0 sat. fat), 0 chol., 767mg sodium, 42g carb. (8g sugars, 9g fiber), 8g pro.

SLOW COOKER PEACH CRUMBLE

I look forward to going on our beach vacation every year, but I don't always relish the time spent cooking for everybody. This slow cooker dessert (or breakfast!) gives me more time to lie in the sun and enjoy the waves. Melty ice cream is a must.
—Colleen Delawder, Herndon, VA

Prep: 20 min. • **Cook:** 3 hours
Makes: 8 servings

- 1 tablespoon butter, softened
- 6 large ripe peaches, peeled and sliced (about 6 cups)
- 2 tablespoons light brown sugar
- 1 tablespoon lemon juice
- 1 tablespoon vanilla extract
- 2 tablespoons coconut rum, optional

TOPPING
- 1 cup all-purpose flour
- ¾ cup packed light brown sugar
- 1½ teaspoons baking powder
- 1 teaspoon ground cinnamon
- ½ teaspoon baking soda
- ⅛ teaspoon salt
- 1 cup old-fashioned oats
- 6 tablespoons cold butter, cubed

1. Grease a 6-qt. oval slow cooker with 1 tablespoon softened butter. Toss peaches with brown sugar, lemon juice, vanilla and, if desired rum; spread evenly in slow cooker.

2. Whisk together first six topping ingredients; stir in oats. Cut in butter until crumbly; sprinkle over peaches. Cook, covered, on low until peaches are tender, 3-4 hours.

Per ¾ cup: 339 cal., 11g fat (7g sat. fat), 27mg chol., 293mg sodium, 57g carb. (36g sugars, 4g fiber), 4g pro.

SQUASH & LENTIL LAMB STEW

My family lived in New Zealand many years ago. Every Sunday, my mother made a lamb stew. It was Dad's favorite! I changed the recipe to suit my own family's more modern palates, but it seems just as exotic and delicious.
—Nancy Heishman, Las Vegas, NV

Prep: 30 min. • **Cook:** 6 hours
Makes: 8 servings (2½ quarts)

- 1 can (13.66 ounces) coconut milk
- ½ cup creamy peanut butter
- 2 tablespoons red curry paste
- 1 tablespoon hoisin sauce
- 1 teaspoon salt
- ½ teaspoon pepper
- 1 can (14½ ounces) chicken broth
- 3 teaspoons olive oil, divided
- 1 pound lamb or beef stew meat (1- to 1½-inch pieces)
- 2 small onions, chopped
- 1 tablespoon minced fresh gingerroot
- 3 garlic cloves, minced
- 1 cup dried brown lentils, rinsed
- 4 cups cubed peeled butternut squash (about 1 pound)
- 2 cups chopped fresh spinach
- ¼ cup minced fresh cilantro
- ¼ cup lime juice

1. In a 5- or 6-qt slow cooker, whisk together first seven ingredients. In a large skillet, heat 2 teaspoons oil over medium heat; brown lamb in batches. Add meat to slow cooker.

2. In the same skillet, saute onions in remaining oil over medium heat until tender, 4-5 minutes. Add ginger and garlic; cook and stir 1 minute. Add to slow cooker. Stir in lentils and squash.

3. Cook, covered, on low until meat and lentils are tender, 6-8 hours. Stir in spinach until wilted. Stir in cilantro and lime juice.

Freeze option: Freeze cooled stew in freezer containers. To use, partially thaw in refrigerator overnight. Heat through in a saucepan, stirring occasionally and adding a little broth if necessary.

Per 1¼ cups: 411 cal., 21g fat (11g sat. fat), 38mg chol., 777mg sodium, 34g carb. (7g sugars, 6g fiber), 23g pro.

SQUASH & LENTIL LAMB STEW

SLOW-COOKED MEXICAN BEEF SOUP

My family loves this stew, and I'm happy to make it since it's so simple! You can serve it with corn bread instead of chips to make it even more satisfying.
—Angela Lively, Conroe, TX

Prep: 15 min. • **Cook:** 6 hours
Makes: 8 servings (2 quarts)

- 1 pound beef stew meat (1¼-inch pieces)
- ¾ pound potatoes (about 2 medium), cut into ¾-inch cubes
- 2 cups frozen corn (about 10 ounces), thawed
- 2 medium carrots, cut into ½-inch slices
- 1 medium onion, chopped
- 2 garlic cloves, minced
- 1½ teaspoons dried oregano
- 1 teaspoon ground cumin
- ½ teaspoon salt
- ¼ teaspoon crushed red pepper flakes
- 2 cups beef stock
- 1 can (10 ounces) diced tomatoes and green chilies, undrained
  Sour cream and tortilla chips, optional

In a 5- or 6-qt. slow cooker, combine first 12 ingredients. Cook, covered, on low until meat is tender, 6-8 hours. If desired, serve with sour cream and chips.

Per 1⅓ cups: 218 cal., 6g fat (2g sat. fat), 47mg chol., 602mg sodium, 24g carb. (5g sugars, 3g fiber), 19g pro.
Diabetic Exchanges: 2 lean meat, 1½ starch.

★ ★ ★ ★ ★ **READER REVIEW**

"This was very good! The tomatoes and chilies gave it a kick (I left out the red pepper flakes at my husband's request). I'll be making this one again!"

DIANEC23 TASTEOFHOME.COM

SLOW COOKER STUFFED PEPPER SOUP

I tweaked a recipe I got from one of my best friends, and I couldn't believe how much it really does taste like stuffed green peppers! With beef and brown rice, it makes a hearty meal on a cold day.
—Gina Baxter, Plainfield, IL

Prep: 15 min. • **Cook:** 5 hours
Makes: 12 servings (4 ½ quarts)

- 1 pound extra-lean ground beef (95% lean)
- 1 medium onion, chopped
- 2 medium green peppers, chopped
- 1 package (8.8 ounces) ready-to-serve brown rice
- 3 tablespoons packed brown sugar
- ½ teaspoon salt
- ½ teaspoon dried basil
- ½ teaspoon dried oregano
- 2 cans (15 ounces each) tomato sauce
- 2 cans (14½ ounces each) diced tomatoes, undrained
- 1 carton (32 ounces) beef broth

1. In a large skillet, cook and crumble beef with onion over medium heat until no longer pink, 5-7 minutes; transfer to a 6-qt. slow cooker. Stir in the remaining ingredients.
2. Cook, covered, on low until flavors are blended, 5-6 hours.
Freeze option: Freeze cooled soup in freezer containers. To use, partially thaw in refrigerator overnight. Heat through in

a saucepan, stirring occasionally and adding a little broth or water if necessary.
Per 1½ cups: 141 cal., 3g fat (1g sat. fat), 22mg chol., 852mg sodium, 18g carb. (8g sugars, 3g fiber), 11g pro.

SLOW-COOKED VEGETABLE CURRY

I love the fuss-free nature of the slow cooker, but I don't want to sacrifice flavor for convenience. This cozy, spiced-up dish has both.
—Susan Smith, Mead, WA

Prep: 35 min. • **Cook:** 5 hours.
Makes: 6 servings

- 1 tablespoon canola oil
- 1 medium onion, finely chopped
- 4 garlic cloves, minced
- 3 teaspoons ground coriander
- 1½ teaspoons ground cinnamon
- 1 teaspoon ground ginger
- 1 teaspoon ground turmeric
- ½ teaspoon cayenne pepper
- 2 tablespoons tomato paste
- 2 cans (15 ounces each) garbanzo beans or chickpeas, rinsed and drained
- 3 cups cubed peeled sweet potatoes (about 1 pound)
- 3 cups fresh cauliflower florets (about 8 ounces)
- 4 medium carrots, cut into ¾-inch pieces (about 2 cups)
- 2 medium tomatoes, seeded and chopped
- 2 cups chicken broth
- 1 cup light coconut milk
- ½ teaspoon pepper
- ¼ teaspoon salt
  Minced fresh cilantro
  Hot cooked brown rice
  Lime wedges
  Plain yogurt, optional

1. In a large skillet, heat oil over medium heat; saute onion until soft and lightly browned, 5-7 minutes. Add garlic and spices; cook and stir 1 minute. Stir in tomato paste; cook 1 minute. Transfer to a 5- or 6-qt. slow cooker.
2. Mash 1 can of beans until smooth; add to slow cooker. Stir in remaining beans, vegetables, broth, coconut milk, pepper and salt.

3. Cook, covered, on low until vegetables are tender, 5-6 hours. Sprinkle with cilantro. Serve with rice, lime wedges and, if desired, yogurt.
Per 1⅔ cups curry: 304 cal., 8g fat (2g sat. fat), 2mg chol., 696mg sodium, 49g carb. (12g sugars, 12g fiber), 9g pro.
HEALTH TIP Chickpeas are a smart way to add a dose of protein to a meatless main. They are also a good source of fiber, folate and vitamin B6.

MOIST ITALIAN TURKEY BREAST

This recipe makes some of the juiciest turkey I've ever eaten. High in lean protein, it's a smart entree for a special occasion.
—Jessica Kunz, Springfield, IL

Prep: 25 min. • **Cook:** 5 hours + standing
Makes: 12 servings

- 1 pound carrots, cut into 2-inch pieces
- 2 medium onions, cut into wedges
- 3 celery ribs, cut into 2-inch pieces
- 1 can (14½ ounces) chicken broth
- 1 bone-in turkey breast (6 to 7 pounds), thawed and skin removed
- 2 tablespoons olive oil
- 1½ teaspoons seasoned salt
- 1 teaspoon Italian seasoning
- ½ teaspoon pepper

1. Place vegetables and broth in a 6- or 7-qt. slow cooker; top with turkey breast. Brush turkey with oil; sprinkle with seasonings.
2. Cook, covered, on low until a thermometer inserted in turkey reads at least 170°, 5-6 hours. Remove turkey from slow cooker; let stand, covered, for 15 minutes before carving. Serve with vegetables. If desired, strain cooking juices and thicken for gravy.
Per serving: 360 cal., 15g fat (4g sat. fat), 123mg chol., 477mg sodium, 6g carb. (3g sugars, 2g fiber), 48g pro.

MOIST ITALIAN TURKEY BREAST

CINNAMON BLUEBERRY FRENCH TOAST

SLOW COOKER

HAM & CHEDDAR BREAKFAST CASSEROLE

PICTURED ON P. 179

This easy, cheesy casserole has made appearances at holiday breakfasts, potlucks and even my daughter's college apartment to feed her happy-to-be-fed roommates. It's my go-to recipe for action-packed mornings.

—Patty Bernhard, Greenville, OH

Prep: 20 min. + chilling
Cook: 4 hours + standing
Makes: 12 servings

- 12 large eggs
- 1 cup 2% milk
- 1 teaspoon salt
- ½ teaspoon pepper
- 1 package (30 ounces) frozen shredded hash brown potatoes, thawed
- 2 cups cubed fully cooked ham (about 1 pound)
- 1 medium onion, chopped
- 4 cups shredded cheddar cheese

1. Whisk together first four ingredients. Place a third of the potatoes in a greased 5- or 6-qt. slow cooker; layer with a third of each of the following: ham, onion and cheese. Repeat layers twice. Pour egg mixture over the top. Refrigerate, covered, overnight.

2. Cook, covered, on low until set and edges begin to brown, 4-5 hours. Turn off slow cooker. Remove insert; let stand, uncovered, 30 minutes before serving.

Per serving: 324 cal., 19g fat (9g sat. fat), 239mg chol., 822mg sodium, 17g carb. (3g sugars, 1g fiber), 22g pro.

EAT SMART SLOW COOKER

CINNAMON BLUEBERRY FRENCH TOAST

I like to prep this breakfast in the afternoon, let it chill, and put into the slow cooker before I go to bed. When we wake up in the morning, it's done just right for us to dig in.

—Angela Lively, Conroe, TX

Prep: 15 min. • **Cook:** 3 hours
Makes: 6 servings

- 3 large eggs
- 2 cups 2% milk
- ¼ cup sugar
- 1 teaspoon ground cinnamon
- 1 teaspoon vanilla extract
- ¼ teaspoon salt
- 9 cups cubed French bread (about 9 ounces)
- 1 cup fresh or frozen blueberries, thawed
  Maple syrup

1. Whisk together first six ingredients. Layer half of the bread in a greased 5-qt. slow cooker; top with ½ cup blueberries and half of the milk mixture. Repeat layers. Refrigerate, covered, 4 hours or overnight.

2. Cook, covered, on low until a knife inserted in the center comes out clean, 3-4 hours. Serve warm with syrup.

Per cup: 265 cal., 6g fat (2g sat. fat), 100mg chol., 430mg sodium, 42g carb. (18g sugars, 2g fiber), 11g pro.

HEALTH TIP Swap whole wheat for white French bread to increase fiber. If you have leftover 100% whole wheat buns, cube and use those.

FREEZE IT SLOW COOKER

GAME-STOPPER CHILI

This hearty chili with sausage, beef, beans and barley is perfect for the half-time food rush. People actually cheer when they see me coming with my slow cooker!
—Barbara Lento, Houston, PA

Prep: 25 min. • **Cook:** 6 hours
Makes: 12 servings (4 quarts)

- 1 can (28 ounces) diced tomatoes, undrained
- 1 can (15 ounces) black beans, rinsed and drained
- 1 can (15 ounces) kidney beans, rinsed and drained
- 1 pound boneless beef chuck steak, cut into 1-inch cubes
- 1 pound bulk spicy pork sausage, cooked and drained
- 2 medium onions, chopped
- 1 medium sweet red pepper, chopped
- 1 medium green pepper, chopped
- 1 cup hot chunky salsa
- ⅓ cup medium pearl barley
- 2 tablespoons chili powder
- 2 teaspoons jarred roasted minced garlic
- 1 teaspoon salt
- 1 teaspoon ground cumin
- 4 cups beef stock
- 2 cups shredded Mexican cheese blend
  Corn chips

1. Place all ingredients except the cheese and chips in a 6-qt. slow cooker. Cook, covered, on low until the beef is tender, 6-8 hours.

2. Stir in cheese until melted. Serve chili with chips.

Freeze option: Freeze cooled chili in freezer containers. To use, partially thaw in refrigerator overnight. Heat through in a saucepan, stirring occasionally.

Per 1⅓ cups: 359 cal., 18g fat (7g sat. fat), 62mg chol., 1062mg sodium, 26g carb. (6g sugars, 6g fiber), 23g pro.

GAME-STOPPER CHILI

FREEZE IT SLOW COOKER

SLOW COOKER SWEET POTATO SOUP

I love that I can top this creamy soup with anything my heart desires, which means I can eat it several days in a row without ever having to have it the same way twice. You can substitute fresh onions and celery in this recipe if you prefer, but using the dried version makes it easy to throw together on a weekday morning.
—Colleen Delawder, Herndon, VA

Prep: 15 min. • **Cook:** 5 hours
Makes: 8 servings (2½ quarts)

- 3 pounds sweet potatoes, peeled and cut into 1-inch cubes (about 8 cups)
- 2 tablespoons butter
- 1 tablespoon Worcestershire sauce
- 1 teaspoon dried minced onion
- 1 teaspoon dried celery flakes, optional
- ½ teaspoon salt
- ½ teaspoon pepper
- ¼ teaspoon dried thyme
- ⅛ teaspoon ground chipotle pepper
- 6 cups reduced-sodium chicken broth
  Sour cream and pepitas, optional

1. In a 4- or 5-qt. slow cooker, combine all ingredients except the sour cream and pepitas. Cook, covered, on low until the potatoes are tender, 5-6 hours.

2. Puree soup using an immersion blender. Or cool slightly and puree soup in batches in a blender; return to slow cooker and heat through. If desired, top servings with sour cream and pepitas.

Freeze option: Freeze cooled soup in freezer containers. To use, partially thaw in refrigerator overnight. Heat through in a saucepan, stirring occasionally and adding a little broth or water if necessary.

Per 1¼ cups: 215 cal., 3g fat (2g sat. fat), 8mg chol., 637mg sodium, 43g carb. (18g sugars, 5g fiber), 5g pro.

✳

TEST KITCHEN TIP

Use 1 medium onion and 2 celery ribs, chopped, if you want to use fresh vegetables in the recipe instead of reaching into the spice cabinet for the dry versions. Chipotle pepper adds a little smoky heat, but it can be omitted.

TROPICAL CRANBERRY COBBLER

SLOW COOKER 🍲

TROPICAL CRANBERRY COBBLER

The sunny island flavors of pineapple and orange go so well with the tart cranberries in this Hawaiian-inspired dessert. A scoop of vanilla ice cream makes it a creamy treat.
—Jeanne Holt, Mendota Heights, MN

Prep: 20 min. • **Cook:** 4 hours + standing
Makes: 12 servings

- 2 cups fresh or frozen cranberries, thawed
- 1 can (20 ounces) unsweetened pineapple tidbits, drained
- ¾ cup sweetened shredded coconut
- ¾ cup orange marmalade
- ½ cup packed light brown sugar
- 6 tablespoons butter, melted

TOPPING

- 1 package yellow cake mix (regular size)
- 1 package (3.4 ounces) instant coconut cream pudding mix
- 4 large eggs
- ¾ cup pineapple-orange juice
- ½ cup butter, melted
- ¼ cup packed light brown sugar
- 1 teaspoon vanilla extract
  Whipped cream, optional
- ¼ cup sweetened shredded coconut, toasted

1. In a greased 6-qt. oval slow cooker, layer cranberries, pineapple and ¾ cup coconut. In a bowl, mix marmalade, brown sugar and melted butter; spoon evenly over fruit.

2. In a large bowl, combine first seven topping ingredients; beat on low speed for 1 minute. Beat on medium for 2 minutes. Pour over filling.

3. Cook, covered, on low until top springs back when lightly touched, about 4 hours. Turn off slow cooker. Remove insert; let stand 15 minutes before serving. If desired, serve cobbler with whipped cream. Sprinkle with toasted coconut.

Per serving: 514 cal., 22g fat (13g sat. fat), 98mg chol., 508mg sodium, 78g carb. (59g sugars, 2g fiber), 5g pro.

✳ TEST KITCHEN TIPS

If you don't have pineapple-orange juice on hand, use apple, grape, plain orange or pineapple juice.

This is a cross between a cobbler, dump cake and upside-down cake. The cake layer is more substantial than it is in a typical cobbler.

Adding a package of pudding mix makes the cake layer extra tender and moist. Be sure to look for instant pudding mix, not cook-and-serve.

SLOW COOKER STUFFED SHELLS

There's no need to precook the shells in this simple pasta dish. It's almost like magic when you open the lid and find the deliciousness waiting in the slow cooker. Add garlic bread, and you're golden!
—Sherry Day, Pinckney, MI

Prep: 30 min. • **Cook:** 4 hours
Makes: 10 servings

- 1 carton (15 ounces) part-skim ricotta cheese
- 1 package (10 ounces) frozen chopped spinach, thawed and squeezed dry
- 2½ cups shredded Italian cheese blend
- ½ cup diced red onion
- ½ teaspoon garlic powder
- 2 teaspoons dried basil
- ½ teaspoon dried oregano
- ½ teaspoon dried thyme
- 2 jars (24 ounces each) roasted garlic Parmesan pasta sauce
- 1 package (12 ounces) jumbo pasta shells
- 2 cups water
  Additional shredded Italian cheese blend and sliced fresh basil

1. Mix first eight ingredients (mixture will be stiff). In a greased 6-qt. slow cooker, mix one jar pasta sauce with water. Fill shells with ricotta mixture; layer in slow cooker. Top shells with remaining jar of pasta sauce.
2. Cook, covered, on low until pasta is tender, 4-5 hours. If desired, serve with additional cheese and fresh basil.

Per 4 stuffed shells: 303 cal., 10g fat (6g sat. fat), 34mg chol., 377mg sodium, 34g carb. (4g sugars, 3g fiber), 17g pro.
Diabetic Exchanges: 2 starch, 2 medium-fat meat.

HEALTH TIP Relative to other cheeses, ricotta is especially high in calcium. Just ¼ cup of it provides almost 20% of the recommended daily value.

LAMB PITAS WITH YOGURT SAUCE

PICTURED ON P. 179

The spiced lamb in these stuffed pita pockets goes perfectly with cool cucumber and yogurt. It's like having your own Greek gyro stand in the kitchen!
—Angela Leinenbach, Mechanicsville, VA

Prep: 35 min. • **Cook:** 6 hours
Makes: 8 servings

- 2 tablespoons olive oil
- 2 pounds lamb stew meat (¾-inch pieces)
- 1 large onion, chopped
- 1 garlic clove, minced
- ⅓ cup tomato paste
- ½ cup dry red wine
- 1¼ teaspoons salt, divided
- 1 teaspoon dried oregano
- ½ teaspoon dried basil
- 1 medium cucumber
- 1 cup (8 ounces) plain yogurt
- 16 pita pocket halves, warmed
- 4 plum tomatoes, sliced

1. In a large skillet, heat oil over medium-high heat; brown lamb in batches. Transfer lamb to a 3- or 4-qt. slow cooker, reserving drippings in skillet.
2. In drippings, saute onion over medium heat until tender, 4-6 minutes. Add garlic and tomato paste; cook and stir 2 minutes. Stir in wine, 1 teaspoon salt, oregano and basil. Add to lamb. Cook, covered, on low until lamb is tender, 6-8 hours.
3. To serve, dice enough cucumber to measure 1 cup; thinly slice remaining cucumber. Combine diced cucumber with yogurt and remaining salt. Fill pitas with lamb mixture, tomatoes, sliced cucumbers and yogurt mixture.
Freeze option: Freeze cooled lamb mixture in freezer containers. To use, partially thaw in refrigerator overnight. Heat through in a saucepan, stirring occasionally and adding a little broth or water if necessary.
Per 2 filled pita halves: 383 cal., 11g fat (3g sat. fat), 78mg chol., 766mg sodium, 39g carb. (5g sugars, 3g fiber), 31g pro.
Diabetic Exchanges: 3 lean meat, 2½ starch, 1 fat.

SLOW COOKER STUFFED SHELLS

Hot Off the Grill

When you want dinner in a hurry, why not head outdoors for sizzling fare that's ready in a flash? These simple recipes keep the kitchen clean and cool and the whole family satisfied.

GRILLED APPLE TOSSED SALAD

⑤ INGREDIENTS ▸ FAST FIX ▸
CONTEST-WINNING BARBECUED PORK CHOPS
PICTURED ON P. 207

Sherry, honey, barbecue and steak sauces combine to give these chops a beautiful glaze and dressed-up flavor. The sauce works well on chicken breasts, too.
—LaJuana Kay Holland, Amarillo, TX

Start to Finish: 20 min.
Makes: 6 servings

- ⅓ cup hickory smoke-flavored barbecue sauce
- ⅓ cup A.1. steak sauce
- ⅓ cup sherry or unsweetened apple juice
- 2 tablespoons honey
- 6 bone-in pork loin chops (¾ inch thick and 8 ounces each)
- ¾ teaspoon salt
- ½ teaspoon pepper

1. Mix first four ingredients; reserve ⅓ cup sauce for serving.
2. Sprinkle pork chops with salt and pepper. Place on an oiled grill rack over medium heat. Grill, covered, until a thermometer reads 145°, 4-6 minutes per side, brushing frequently with remaining sauce after turning. Let stand 5 minutes before serving. Serve with reserved sauce.

Per pork chop with 2 teaspoons sauce: 299 cal., 10g fat (4g sat. fat), 98mg chol., 771mg sodium, 16g carb. (14g sugars, 0 fiber), 35g pro.

GRILLED APPLE TOSSED SALAD

The grilled apples in this salad combine so well with the blue cheese, walnuts and balsamic dressing. I like to serve it on pink Depression glass dessert plates from my great-grandmother.
—Paul Soska, Toledo, OH

Prep: 15 min. + marinating • **Grill:** 10 min.
Makes: 6 servings

- 6 tablespoons olive oil
- ¼ cup minced fresh cilantro
- ¼ cup orange juice
- ¼ cup white or regular balsamic vinegar
- 2 tablespoons honey
- 1 garlic clove, minced
- ½ teaspoon salt
- ½ teaspoon Sriracha Asian hot chili sauce
- 2 large apples, cut into ½-inch wedges
- 1 package (5 ounces) spring mix salad greens
- 1 cup walnut halves, toasted
- ½ cup crumbled blue cheese

1. For dressing, whisk together first eight ingredients. In a bowl, toss the apples with ¼ cup dressing.
2. Place apple slices on a grill rack over medium heat; reserve dressing left in bowl. Grill apples, covered, until tender and lightly browned, 3-4 minutes per side, brushing with reserved marinade.
3. To serve, toss greens with remaining dressing. Top with grilled apples, walnuts and cheese.

Note: To toast nuts, bake in a shallow pan in a 350° oven for 5-10 minutes or cook in a skillet over low heat until lightly browned, stirring occasionally.
Per serving: 341 cal., 28g fat (5g sat. fat), 8mg chol., 360mg sodium, 22g carb. (16g sugars, 3g fiber), 6g pro.

HEALTH TIP Lighten this salad by leaving off the walnuts and blue cheese. You'll save 150 calories, but the grilled apples and homemade dressing will still make it taste like it came from a restaurant.

GRILLED BEAN BURGERS

These burgers have major flavor thanks to cumin, garlic and a little chili powder. They hold their own against any veggie burger you'd buy at the supermarket.
—Marguerite Shaeffer, Sewell, NJ

Prep: 25 min. • **Grill:** 10 min.
Makes: 8 servings

- 1 tablespoon olive oil
- 1 large onion, finely chopped
- 4 garlic cloves, minced
- 1 medium carrot, shredded
- 1 to 2 teaspoons chili powder
- 1 teaspoon ground cumin
- ¼ teaspoon pepper
- 1 can (15 ounces) pinto beans, rinsed and drained
- 1 can (15 ounces) black beans, rinsed and drained
- 2 tablespoons Dijon mustard
- 2 tablespoons reduced-sodium soy sauce
- 1 tablespoon ketchup
- 1½ cups quick-cooking oats
- 8 whole wheat hamburger buns, split
- 8 lettuce leaves
- ½ cup salsa

1. In a large nonstick skillet, heat oil over medium-high heat; saute onion 2 minutes. Add garlic; cook and stir 1 minute. Stir in carrot and spices; cook and stir until the carrot is tender, 2-3 minutes. Remove from heat.

2. In a large bowl, mash pinto and black beans using a potato masher. Stir in mustard, soy sauce, ketchup and carrot mixture. Add oats, mixing well. Shape into eight 3½-in. patties.

3. Place burgers on an oiled grill rack over medium heat or on a greased rack of a broiler pan. Grill, covered, or broil 4 in. from heat until lightly browned and heated through, 4-5 minutes per side. Serve on buns with lettuce and salsa.

Per burger: 305 cal., 5g fat (1g sat. fat), 0 chol., 736mg sodium, 54g carb. (8g sugars, 10g fiber), 12g pro.
Diabetic Exchanges: 3½ starch, 1 lean meat.

GRILLED BEAN BURGERS

TERIYAKI SHISH KABOBS
PICTURED ON P. 207

When I was a teenager, my father worked for an airline, and my family lived on the island of Guam in the South Pacific. A friend of my mother gave her this tangy-sweet recipe, and we enjoyed it often. Now I make it for my family, who have become big fans, as well.
—Suzanne Pelegrin, Ocala, FL

Prep: 20 min. + marinating • **Grill:** 15 min.
Makes: 8 servings

- 1 cup sugar
- 1 cup reduced-sodium soy sauce
- 1 cup ketchup
- 2 teaspoons garlic powder
- 2 teaspoons ground ginger
- 2 pounds beef top sirloin steak, cut into 1½-inch cubes
- 2 to 3 small zucchini, cut into 1-inch slices
- ½ pound medium fresh mushrooms
- 1 large green or sweet red pepper, cut into 1-inch pieces
- 1 small onion, cut into 1-inch pieces
- 2 cups cubed fresh pineapple

1. For marinade, mix first five ingredients. Place beef and half of the marinade in a large resealable plastic bag; seal bag and turn to coat. Cover and reserve remaining marinade. Refrigerate beef and marinade overnight.

2. On metal or soaked wooden skewers, thread vegetables and, on separate skewers, thread beef with pineapple. Discard remaining marinade in bag. Grill kabobs, covered, over medium heat until vegetables are tender and beef reaches desired doneness, 12-15 minutes, turning the kabobs occasionally.

3. In a small saucepan, bring reserved marinade to a boil, stirring occasionally; cook for 1 minute. Remove vegetables, pineapple and beef from skewers before serving. Serve with sauce.

Per serving: 306 cal., 5g fat (2g sat. fat), 46mg chol., 1203mg sodium, 38g carb. (32g sugars, 2g fiber), 27g pro.

POTATO-SAUSAGE FOIL PACKS

We had these smoky campfire bundles at a friend's house for dinner and loved the simplicity of this great summer meal. Now we make it often for summer weeknight dinners.
—Alissa Keith, Forest, VA

Prep: 20 min. • **Grill:** 30 min.
Makes: 4 servings

1 medium green pepper
1 medium sweet red pepper
1 medium sweet yellow pepper
1 package (14 ounces) smoked turkey kielbasa, sliced
2 large potatoes, cut into wedges
1 medium onion, chopped
4 teaspoons lemon juice
4 teaspoons olive oil
½ teaspoon garlic powder
½ teaspoon pepper
Lemon wedges, optional

1. Cut peppers into 1-in. pieces; place in a large bowl. Toss with remaining ingredients. Divide mixture among four double-thickness rectangles of heavy-duty foil (about 18x12 in.). Fold foil around mixture, sealing tightly.
2. Grill, covered, over medium heat until potatoes are tender, 30-35 minutes. Open foil carefully to allow steam to escape. If desired, serve with lemon wedges.
Per serving: 344 cal., 10g fat (2g sat. fat), 62mg chol., 990mg sodium, 42g carb. (8g sugars, 6g fiber), 21g pro.

ASIAN NOODLE & BEEF SALAD

EAT SMART **FAST FIX**
ASIAN NOODLE & BEEF SALAD

My Asian-inspired pasta salad is crunchy, tangy and light. If you have fresh herbs, such as basil or cilantro, on hand simply add them to the mix.
—Kelsey Casselbury, Odenton, MD

Start to Finish: 30 min.
Makes: 4 servings

¼ cup reduced-sodium soy sauce
¼ cup lime juice
2 tablespoons sugar
2 tablespoons rice vinegar
1 tablespoon grated fresh gingerroot
1 tablespoon sesame oil
1 beef top sirloin steak (1 pound)
¼ teaspoon pepper
6 ounces thin rice noodles
1 cup julienned zucchini
2 medium carrots, thinly sliced
1 celery rib, sliced

1. For dressing, mix first six ingredients. Sprinkle steak with pepper. Grill, covered, over medium heat until meat reaches desired doneness (for medium-rare, a thermometer should read 135°; medium, 140°), 6-8 minutes per side. Let stand 5 minutes before slicing.
2. Meanwhile, prepare rice noodles according to package directions. Drain; rinse with cold water and drain again. In a large bowl, combine noodles, vegetables and steak; toss with dressing.
Note: Salad can be made ahead, refrigerated and served cold.
Per 1½ cups: 399 cal., 8g fat (2g sat. fat), 46mg chol., 855mg sodium, 50g carb. (11g sugars, 2g fiber), 29g pro.

GINGERED HONEY SALMON

Ginger, garlic and green onion blend nicely in an easy marinade that gives a big flavor boost to salmon. We also like to use this versatile mixture when grilling chicken.
—Dan Strumberger, Farmington, MN

Prep: 10 min. + marinating • **Grill:** 15 min.
Makes: 6 servings

- ⅓ cup orange juice
- ⅓ cup reduced-sodium soy sauce
- ¼ cup honey
- 1 green onion, chopped
- 1 teaspoon ground ginger
- 1 teaspoon garlic powder
- 1 salmon fillet (1½ pounds and ¾ inch thick)

1. For marinade, mix first six ingredients. In a shallow bowl, combine salmon and ⅔ cup marinade; refrigerate 30 minutes, turning occasionally. Reserve remaining marinade for basting.

2. Place salmon on an oiled grill rack over medium heat, skin side down; discard marinade remaining in bowl. Grill salmon, covered, until it just begins to flake easily with a fork, 15-18 minutes, basting with reserved marinade during last 5 minutes.

Per 3 ounces cooked fish: 237 cal., 10g fat (2g sat. fat), 57mg chol., 569mg

sodium, 15g carb. (13g sugars, 0 fiber), 20g pro.
Diabetic Exchanges: 3 lean meat, 1 starch.

ZESTY GRILLED HAM

If it's ham, my kids will eat it, and they like this spiced-up recipe best of all. Even the small ones eat adult-sized portions, so be sure to make plenty.
—Mary Ann Lien, Tyler, TX

Start to Finish: 15 min.
Makes: 4 servings

- ⅓ cup packed brown sugar
- 2 tablespoons prepared horseradish
- 4 teaspoons lemon juice
- 1 fully cooked bone-in ham steak (1 to 2 pounds)

1. Place brown sugar, horseradish and lemon juice in a small saucepan; bring to a boil, stirring constantly. Brush over both sides of ham.

2. Place ham on an oiled grill rack over medium heat. Grill, covered, until glazed and heated through, 7-10 minutes, turning occasionally.

Per serving: 180 cal., 5g fat (2g sat. fat), 44mg chol., 845mg sodium, 20g carb. (19g sugars, 0 fiber), 14g pro.

GRILLED CHICKEN & MANGO SKEWERS

This recipe was inspired by eating charbroiled chicken skewers while strolling along Calle Ocho in Miami on Sunday afternoons.
—Wolfgang Hanau, West Palm Beach, FL

Start to Finish: 30 min.
Makes: 4 servings

- 3 medium ears sweet corn
- 1 tablespoon butter
- ⅓ cup plus 3 tablespoons sliced green onions, divided
- 1 pound boneless skinless chicken breasts, cut into 1-inch cubes
- ½ teaspoon salt
- ¼ teaspoon pepper
- 1 medium mango, peeled and cut into 1-inch cubes
- 1 tablespoon extra virgin olive oil
  Lime wedges, optional

1. Cut corn from cobs. In a large skillet, heat butter over medium-high heat; saute corn until crisp-tender, about 5 minutes. Stir in ⅓ cup green onions. Keep warm.

2. Toss chicken with salt and pepper. Thread chicken and mango onto four metal or soaked wooden skewers; brush with oil.

3. Grill, covered, over medium heat or broil 4 in. from heat until chicken is no longer pink, 10-12 minutes, turning occasionally. Serve with corn mixture; sprinkle with remaining green onions. If desired, serve with lime wedges.

Per skewer with ½ cup corn mixture: 297 cal., 10g fat (3g sat. fat), 70mg chol., 387mg sodium, 28g carb. (16g sugars, 3g fiber), 26g pro.
Diabetic Exchanges: 3 lean meat, 2 starch, 1½ fat.

GINGERED HONEY SALMON

GRILLED BRATS WITH SRIRACHA MAYO

I am a Sriracha fanatic, so that's what inspired this dish. For added flavor, you can boil the brats in your favorite beer before grilling, or spread garlic butter on lightly toasted buns. If you want less sodium, cut out the relish and use half the spicy mayo mix.
—Quincie Ball, Olympia, WA

Start to Finish: 20 min.
Makes: 4 servings

- ½ cup mayonnaise
- ⅓ cup minced roasted sweet red peppers
- 3 tablespoons Sriracha Asian hot chili sauce
- 1 teaspoon hot pepper sauce
- 4 fully cooked bratwurst links
- 4 brat buns or hot dog buns, split
- ½ cup dill pickle relish
- ½ cup finely chopped red onion
  Ketchup, optional

Mix the first four ingredients. Grill bratwursts, covered, over medium-low heat until browned and heated through, 7-10 minutes, turning occasionally. Serve in buns with mayonnaise mixture, relish, onion and, if desired, ketchup.
Per serving: 742 cal., 49g fat (13g sat. fat), 65mg chol., 2020mg sodium, 54g carb. (10g sugars, 2g fiber), 20g pro.

GRILLED PINEAPPLE CHIMICHURRI CHICKEN

PICTURED ON P. 207

Put a Hawaiian twist on classic chimichurri by adding sweet pineapple and crunchy macadamia nuts. For a spicier version, you can substitute red serrano pepper for the bell pepper.
—Naylet LaRochelle, Miami, FL

Start to Finish: 30 min.
Makes: 4 servings

- ½ small sweet red pepper, stemmed and seeded
- 2 slices fresh pineapple (½-inch)
- ⅔ cup fresh cilantro leaves
- ⅔ cup parsley sprigs (stems removed)
- 4 teaspoons lime juice
- ¼ cup canola oil
- ¼ cup island teriyaki sauce
- 1 tablespoon minced fresh gingerroot
- 4 boneless skinless chicken breast halves (6 ounces each)
  Hot cooked couscous, optional
- 2 green onions, sliced
- ¼ cup chopped macadamia nuts, toasted

1. Place pepper and pineapple on an oiled grill rack over medium heat; grill, covered, until lightly browned, 3-4 minutes per side.
2. For chimichurri, place cilantro, parsley and lime juice in a food processor; pulse until finely chopped. Continue processing while slowly adding oil. Chop pepper and pineapple; stir into the herb mixture.
3. Mix teriyaki sauce and ginger. Place chicken on an oiled grill rack over medium heat; grill, covered, until a thermometer reads 165°, 5-7 minutes per side. Brush with some of the teriyaki mixture during the last 4 minutes.
4. Brush chicken with remaining teriyaki mixture before serving. If desired, serve with couscous. Top with chimichurri, green onions and macadamia nuts.
Note: To toast nuts, cook in a skillet over low heat until lightly browned, stirring occasionally.
Per chicken breast half with about ¼ cup sauce: 428 cal., 24g fat (3g sat. fat), 94mg chol., 686mg sodium, 19g carb. (13g sugars, 2g fiber), 37g pro.

BARBECUED CHICKEN PIZZAS

Prep: 25 min. • **Grill:** 10 min.
Makes: 2 pizzas (4 pieces each)

- 2 boneless skinless chicken breast halves (6 ounces each)
- ¼ teaspoon pepper
- 1 cup barbecue sauce, divided
- 1 tube (13.8 ounces) refrigerated pizza crust
- 2 teaspoons olive oil
- 2 cups shredded Gouda cheese
- 1 small red onion, halved and thinly sliced
- ¼ cup minced fresh cilantro

1. Sprinkle chicken with pepper; place on an oiled grill rack over medium heat. Grill, covered, until a thermometer reads 165°, 5-7 minutes per side, basting frequently with ½ cup barbecue sauce during the last 4 minutes. Cool slightly. Cut into cubes.
2. Divide dough in half. On a well-greased large sheet of heavy-duty foil, press each portion of dough into a 10x8-in. rectangle; brush lightly with oil. Invert dough onto grill rack; peel off foil. Grill, covered, over medium heat until the bottom is lightly browned, 1-2 minutes.
3. Remove from grill. Spread grilled sides with remaining barbecue sauce. Top with cheese, chicken and onion. Grill, covered, until bottom is lightly browned and cheese is melted, for 2-3 minutes. Sprinkle pizzas with cilantro.
Per piece: 339 cal., 12g fat (6g sat. fat), 56mg chol., 956mg sodium, 39g carb. (15g sugars, 1g fiber), 20g pro.

GRILLED BRATS WITH SRIRACHA MAYO

BARBECUED
CHICKEN PIZZAS

"So fast and so easy with
refrigerated pizza crust, these saucy,
smoky pizzas make quick fans with
their hot-off-the-grill, rustic flavor.
They're perfect for spur-of-the-
moment cookouts and summer
dinners on the patio."

—ALICIA TREVITHICK, TEMECULA, CA

LEMON GARLIC MUSHROOMS

I baste mushrooms with lemony sauce for this simple side. Using skewers or a basket makes it easy to turn them as they grill.
—Diane Hixon, Niceville, FL

Start to Finish: 15 min.
Makes: 4 servings

- ¼ cup lemon juice
- 3 tablespoons minced fresh parsley
- 2 tablespoons olive oil
- 3 garlic cloves, minced
  Pepper to taste
- 1 pound large fresh mushrooms

1. For dressing, whisk together first five ingredients. Toss the mushrooms with 2 tablespoons dressing.
2. Grill mushrooms, covered, over medium-high heat until tender, 5-7 minutes per side. Toss with remaining dressing before serving.

Per serving: 94 cal., 7g fat (1g sat. fat), 0mg chol., 2mg sodium, 6g carb. (0g sugars, 0g fiber), 3g pro.
Diabetic Exchanges: 1 vegetable, 1½ fat.

CASHEW MANGO GRILLED CHICKEN

This sweet and nutty chicken hits all the right spots for taste, speed and family appeal. On a rainy day, you can bake it, then finish it under the broiler.
—Trisha Kruse, Eagle, ID

Start to Finish: 25 min.
Makes: 8 servings

- ¼ cup mango chutney, chopped
- ¼ cup cashew butter
- 2 tablespoons reduced-sodium soy sauce
- 2 tablespoons rice vinegar
- 8 boneless skinless chicken thighs
- ½ teaspoon salt
- ½ teaspoon crushed red pepper flakes
- 1 large mango, peeled and thinly sliced
- ⅓ cup lightly salted cashews, chopped
  Additional mango chutney, optional

1. Combine first four ingredients.
2. Sprinkle chicken with salt and pepper flakes; place on an oiled grill rack over medium heat. Grill, covered, until a thermometer reads 170°, 6-8 minutes per side, brushing with chutney mixture during the last 5 minutes. Serve with mango slices; top with cashews and, if desired, additional chutney.

Per serving: 308 cal., 16g fat (4g sat. fat), 76mg chol., 537mg sodium, 18g carb. (12g sugars, 1g fiber), 24g pro.
Diabetic Exchanges: 3 lean meat, 2½ fat, 1 starch.

GARLIC & HERB ARTICHOKE SALMON

If you're new to cooking fish (or even if you're a pro), this no-fail salmon recipe is a must-make. It's easy enough for everyday, but also wows at dinner parties.
—Margee Berry, White Salmon, WA

Start to Finish: 25 min.
Makes: 4 servings

- 4 salmon fillets (6 ounces each)
- 2 teaspoons grated lemon peel
- ¼ teaspoon salt
- ¼ teaspoon pepper
- 2 green onions, white and green portions separated and sliced
- ¼ cup marinated quartered artichoke hearts
- 1 tablespoon lemon juice
- ⅓ cup garlic-herb spreadable cheese (about half of a 6.5-oz. package)

1. Place fillets on one large piece of heavy-duty foil (about 18x12-in.), skin side down. Sprinkle with lemon peel, salt and pepper; top with white portion of green onions. Fold foil around fish, sealing tightly. Grill, covered, over medium-high heat until fish just begins to flake easily with a fork, 7-9 minutes.
2. Meanwhile, place artichoke hearts, lemon juice and cheese in a food processor; process until smooth. To serve, open the foil carefully to allow steam to escape. Remove salmon to serving plates, leaving skin on the foil. Top fillets with artichoke mixture; sprinkle with remaining green onion.

Per serving: 379 cal., 27g fat (10g sat. fat), 109mg chol., 409mg sodium, 3g carb. (1g sugars, 0 fiber), 30g pro.

CASHEW MANGO GRILLED CHICKEN

ASIAN SLAW WITH STEAK

Main-dish salads are perfect for summer, especially this one with its Asian-inspired dressing. The crunchy slaw and juicy steak make a breezy weeknight dinner.
—Roxanne Chan, Albany, CA

Start to Finish: 30 min.
Makes: 4 servings

- ⅓ cup rice vinegar
- 3 tablespoons minced fresh mint
- 3 tablespoons sesame oil
- ⅓ cup miso paste
- 1 beef top sirloin steak (1 inch thick and 1 pound)
- 1 package (12 ounces) broccoli coleslaw mix
- 1 medium mango, peeled and diced
- 1 cup frozen shelled edamame, thawed
- ¼ cup sliced radishes
- ¼ cup minced fresh cilantro
- 1 green onion, sliced
  Grated lime peel, optional

1. For dressing, place the first four ingredients in a blender; cover and process until blended. Set aside ½ cup dressing for slaw. Brush remainder onto both sides of steak; let stand while preparing slaw.
2. Place coleslaw mix, mango, edamame, radishes, cilantro and green onion in a large bowl. Toss with reserved dressing.
3. Grill steak, covered, over medium heat until desired doneness (for medium-rare, a thermometer should read 135°; medium, 140°), 5-7 minutes per side. Let stand 5 minutes before slicing. Serve with slaw. If desired, sprinkle with lime peel.
Note: Look for miso paste in natural food or Asian markets.
Per serving: 423 cal., 18g fat (3g sat. fat), 46mg chol., 1370mg sodium, 32g carb. (24g sugars, 5g fiber), 34g pro.

GRILLED CHICKEN SALAD WITH BLUEBERRY VINAIGRETTE

GRILLED CHICKEN SALAD WITH BLUEBERRY VINAIGRETTE

We love adding grilled chicken to our salads in the summer, but the real star here is the vinaigrette made with blueberry preserves and maple syrup. It goes great with a fresh baguette and a frosty glass of minted lemonade.
—Susan Gauthier, Falmouth, ME

Prep: 20 min. + marinating
Grill: 10 min.
Makes: 4 servings

- 2 boneless skinless chicken breast halves (6 ounces each)
- 1 tablespoon olive oil
- 1 garlic clove, minced
- ¼ teaspoon salt
- ¼ teaspoon pepper

VINAIGRETTE
- ¼ cup olive oil
- ¼ cup blueberry preserves
- 2 tablespoons balsamic vinegar
- 2 tablespoons maple syrup
- ¼ teaspoon ground mustard
- ⅛ teaspoon salt
  Dash pepper

SALADS
- 1 package (10 ounces) ready-to-serve salad greens
- 1 cup fresh blueberries
- ½ cup canned mandarin oranges
- 1 cup crumbled goat cheese

1. Toss chicken with oil, garlic, salt and pepper; refrigerate, covered, 30 minutes. In a small bowl, whisk together vinaigrette ingredients; refrigerate mixture, covered, until serving.
2. Grill chicken, covered, over medium heat until a thermometer reads 165°, 5-7 minutes per side. Let stand 5 minutes before slicing.
3. Place greens on a serving plate; top with chicken, blueberries and mandarin oranges. Whisk vinaigrette again; drizzle over salad. Top with cheese.
Per serving: 455 cal., 26g fat (7g sat. fat), 82mg chol., 460mg sodium, 36g carb. (27g sugars, 4g fiber), 24g pro.

FAST FIX ▸

APRICOT TURKEY

You see a lot of steak, chicken and chops at cookouts, but how about something different? With its zesty apricot glaze, this juicy turkey is one of our picnic faves.
—Wendy Moylan, Crystal Lake, IL

Start to Finish: 30 min.
Makes: 4 servings

- ⅓ cup apricot spreadable fruit
- 1 tablespoon white wine vinegar
- 1 tablespoon honey
- 1 garlic clove, minced
- ½ teaspoon grated lemon peel
- ⅛ teaspoon hot pepper sauce
- 2 turkey breast tenderloins (8 ounces each)
- ½ teaspoon salt
- ¼ teaspoon pepper

1. In a microwave, melt spreadable fruit; stir in vinegar, honey, garlic, lemon peel and pepper sauce. Reserve ¼ cup sauce for serving.
2. Sprinkle turkey with salt and pepper; place on an oiled grill rack over medium heat. Grill, covered, until a thermometer reads 165°, 7-10 minutes per side; brush with remaining sauce during the last minute of cooking. Let stand 5 minutes before slicing. Serve with reserved sauce.
Per 3 ounces cooked turkey with 1 tablespoon sauce: 200 cal., 2g fat (0 sat. fat), 65mg chol., 424mg sodium, 18g carb. (15g sugars, 0 fiber), 27g pro.
Diabetic Exchanges: 3 lean meat, 1 starch.

CHICKEN OLE FOIL SUPPER

EAT SMART FAST FIX ▸

CHICKEN OLE FOIL SUPPER

These Mexi-style packets can be assembled ahead and frozen if you like. Just thaw them overnight in the fridge, then grill as directed. I like to serve them with tortillas and fresh fruit on the side.
—Mary Peck, Salina, KS

Start to Finish: 30 min.
Makes: 4 servings

- 1 can (15 ounces) black beans, rinsed and drained
- 2 cups fresh or frozen corn (about 10 ounces), thawed
- 1 cup salsa
- 4 boneless skinless chicken breast halves (4 ounces each)
- ¼ teaspoon garlic powder
- ¼ teaspoon pepper
- ⅛ teaspoon salt
- 1 cup shredded cheddar cheese
- 2 green onions, chopped

1. Mix the beans, corn and salsa; divide among four 18x12-in. pieces of heavy-duty foil. Top with chicken. Mix seasonings; sprinkle over the chicken. Fold foil over chicken, sealing tightly.
2. Grill packets, covered, over medium heat until a thermometer inserted in chicken reads 165°, 15-20 minutes. Open foil carefully to allow steam to escape. Sprinkle with cheese and green onions.
Per serving: 405 cal., 13g fat (6g sat. fat), 91mg chol., 766mg sodium, 34g carb. (8g sugars, 6g fiber), 37g pro.
Diabetic Exchanges: 4 lean meat, 2 starch, 1 fat.

GREEK PORK CHOPS

My in-laws taught me a lot about cooking, so any time I come across a great new recipe, like these Greek-inspired pork chops, I enjoy making it for them. These grilled chops are bright, lemony and have become a quick new favorite.
—Geri Lipczynski, Oak Lawn, IL

Prep: 15 min. + marinating • **Grill:** 10 min.
Makes: 4 servings

- 2 tablespoons olive oil
- 4 teaspoons lemon juice
- 1 tablespoon Worcestershire sauce
- 2 teaspoons dried oregano
- 1 teaspoon salt
- 1 teaspoon onion powder
- 1 teaspoon garlic powder
- 1 teaspoon pepper
- ½ teaspoon ground mustard
- 4 boneless pork loin chops (¾ inch thick and 4 ounces each)

1. In a large resealable plastic bag, mix the first nine ingredients. Add pork chops; seal bag and turn to coat. Refrigerate 8 hours or overnight.
2. Drain pork, discarding marinade. Grill chops, covered, over medium heat or broil 4 in. from heat until a thermometer reads 145°, 4-5 minutes per side. Let stand for 5 minutes before serving.
Freeze option: Freeze chops with marinade in a resealable plastic freezer bag. To use, thaw in refrigerator overnight. Drain pork, discarding marinade. Grill as directed.
Per pork chop: 193 cal., 10g fat (3g sat. fat), 55mg chol., 349mg sodium, 2g carb. (0 sugars, 1g fiber), 22g pro.
Diabetic Exchanges: 3 lean meat, ½ fat
Greek Chicken Breasts: Substitute 4 boneless skinless chicken breasts (6 ounces each) for the pork. Proceed as directed. Grill or broil 5-7 minutes on each side or until a meat thermometer reads 170°.

GREEK PORK CHOPS

JALAPENO-SWISS TURKEY BURGERS

These easy turkey burgers are extra juicy and loaded with flavor. I think the spicy jalapenos give it just the right level of heat, but feel free to adjust the amount to amp it up or tone it down.
—Wanda Allende, Orlando, FL

Start to Finish: 25 min.
Makes: 4 servings

- 1 pound ground turkey
- 1 small onion, finely chopped
- ¾ teaspoon salt
- ¼ teaspoon pepper
- 8 slices Swiss cheese
- 1 jalapeno pepper, sliced
- 4 pretzel hamburger buns, split and toasted
  Optional toppings: sliced jalapeno, salsa and sour cream

1. Combine turkey, onion, salt and pepper; mix lightly but thoroughly. Shape into four ½-in.-thick patties.
2. Place burgers on an oiled grill rack or in a greased 15x10x1-in. pan. Grill, covered, over medium heat or broil 4 in. from heat until a thermometer reads 165°, about 4-6 minutes per side.
3. Top each burger with one slice cheese, jalapeno slices and a second slice of cheese. Grill or broil 1-2 minutes to melt cheese. Serve on buns; top as desired.
Per burger: 375 cal., 16g fat (6g sat. fat), 95mg chol., 767mg sodium, 25g carb. (4g sugars, 1g fiber), 33g pro.
HEALTH TIP You may be tempted to use ground turkey breast in this recipe. Don't! The patties are pretty simple, and they need the extra fat to keep them tender and juicy, and also to keep them from crumbling.

GRILLED PEACH, RICE & ARUGULA SALAD

¾ teaspoon salt
¾ teaspoon seasoned salt
¾ teaspoon poultry seasoning
¾ teaspoon onion powder
¾ teaspoon garlic powder
¾ teaspoon chili powder
⅛ teaspoon cayenne pepper
2 pork tenderloins (1 pound each)

Mix seasonings; sprinkle over tenderloins. Grill, covered, over medium heat until a thermometer reads 145°, 20-25 minutes, turning occasionally. Let stand 5 minutes before slicing.

Per 3 ounces cooked pork: 135 cal., 4g fat (1g sat. fat), 64mg chol., 416mg sodium, 1g carb. (0 sugars, 0 fiber), 23g pro.
Diabetic Exchanges: 3 lean meat.

EAT SMART FAST FIX ▸
HERBED BALSAMIC CHICKEN
PICTURED ON P. 207

Our kitchen is tiny and cramped, so we try to grill simple (but tasty) meals outside as often as possible during the summer months. Dried herbs work very well, but during the summer use fresh ones for the best taste.
—Kelly Evans, Denton, TX

Start to Finish: 30 min.
Makes: 6 servings

½ cup balsamic vinegar
3 tablespoons extra virgin olive oil
1 tablespoon minced fresh basil
1 tablespoon minced fresh chives
2 teaspoons grated lemon peel
1 garlic clove, minced
¾ teaspoon salt
¼ teaspoon pepper
6 boneless skinless chicken thighs (1½ pounds)

1. Whisk together all ingredients except chicken. In a bowl, toss chicken with ⅓ cup vinegar mixture; let stand 10 minutes.
2. Grill chicken, covered, over medium heat or broil 4 in. from heat until a thermometer reads 170°, for 6-8 minutes per side. Drizzle with remaining vinegar mixture before serving.

Per chicken thigh with 2 teaspoons sauce: 245 cal., 15g fat (3g sat. fat), 76mg chol., 358mg sodium, 6g carb. (5g sugars, 0 fiber), 21g pro.
Diabetic Exchanges: 3 lean meat, 1½ fat.

EAT SMART FAST FIX ▸
GRILLED PEACH, RICE & ARUGULA SALAD

This hearty salad was created when I needed to clear out some leftovers from the fridge—and it became an instant hit! The grilled peaches are the ultimate "tastes like summer" salad booster.
—Lauren Wyler, Dripping Springs, TX

Start to Finish: 30 min.
Makes: 6 servings

3 tablespoons cider vinegar
2 tablespoons Dijon mustard
2 tablespoons canola oil
2 tablespoons maple syrup
1 tablespoon finely chopped shallot
¼ teaspoon cayenne pepper
SALAD
1 package (8.8 ounces) ready-to-serve long grain and wild rice
2 medium peaches, quartered
6 cups fresh arugula (about 4 ounces)
6 bacon strips, cooked and crumbled
½ cup crumbled goat cheese

1. For dressing, whisk together the first six ingredients.

2. Prepare rice according to package directions; cool slightly. Place peaches on an oiled grill rack over medium heat. Grill, covered, until lightly browned, for 6-8 minutes, turning occasionally.
3. To serve, add bacon and ¼ cup dressing to rice. Line a platter with arugula; top with rice mixture and peaches. Drizzle with the remaining dressing; top with cheese.

Per serving: 218 cal., 11g fat (3g sat. fat), 20mg chol., 530mg sodium, 23g carb. (9g sugars, 2g fiber), 7g pro.
Diabetic Exchanges: 1 starch, 1 vegetable, 2 fat.

EAT SMART FAST FIX ▸
FLAVORFUL GRILLED PORK TENDERLOIN

Folks can find me grilling, no matter the weather. This pork tenderloin has a ton of flavor thanks to its special spice blend, and it doesn't get much easier to make. My wife especially likes the fact that she doesn't have to do the cooking!
—Steve Ehrhart, Villa Park, IL

Start to Finish: 30 min.
Makes: 8 servings

GRILLED BASIL CHICKEN & TOMATOES

Relax after work with a cold drink while this savory chicken marinates in an herby tomato blend for an hour, then toss it on the grill. It tastes just like summer.
—Laura Lunardi, West Chester, PA

Prep: 15 min. + marinating • **Grill:** 10 min.
Makes: 4 servings

- ¾ cup balsamic vinegar
- ¼ cup tightly packed fresh basil leaves
- 2 tablespoons olive oil
- 1 garlic clove, minced
- ½ teaspoon salt
- 8 plum tomatoes
- 4 boneless skinless chicken breast halves (4 ounces each)

1. For the marinade, place first five ingredients in a blender. Cut four tomatoes into quarters and add to blender; cover and process until blended. Halve remaining tomatoes for grilling.
2. In a bowl, combine chicken and ⅔ cup marinade; refrigerate, covered, 1 hour, turning occasionally. Reserve remaining marinade for serving.
3. Place chicken on an oiled grill rack over medium heat; discard marinade remaining in bowl. Grill chicken, covered, until a thermometer reads 165°, 4-6 minutes per side. Grill tomatoes, covered, over medium heat until lightly browned, 2-4 minutes per side. Serve chicken and tomatoes with reserved marinade.

Per serving: 177 cal., 5g fat (1g sat. fat), 63mg chol., 171mg sodium, 8g carb. (7g sugars, 1g fiber), 24g pro.
Diabetic Exchanges: 3 lean meat, 1 vegetable, ½ fat.

FREEZE IT

GRILLED MARINATED RIBEYES

These juicy steaks are a favorite meal of ours when we go camping. Let them sit in the tangy, barbecue-inspired marinade overnight and you've got a rich and hearty dinner ready to grill up the next day.
—Louise Graybiel, Toronto, ON

Prep: 10 min. + marinating • **Grill:** 10 min.
Makes: 4 servings

- ½ cup barbecue sauce
- 3 tablespoons Worcestershire sauce
- 3 tablespoons olive oil
- 2 tablespoons steak sauce
- 1 tablespoon red wine vinegar
- 1 tablespoon reduced-sodium soy sauce
- 2 teaspoons steak seasoning
- 1 teaspoon hot pepper sauce
- 1 garlic clove, minced
- 4 beef ribeye steaks (8 ounces each)

1. In a large resealable plastic bag, mix the first nine ingredients. Add steaks; seal bag and turn to coat. Refrigerate for 4 hours or overnight.
2. Drain steaks, discarding marinade. Grill, covered, over medium heat until meat reaches desired doneness (for medium-rare, a thermometer should read 135°; medium, 140°), 5-7 minutes per side.

Freeze option: Freeze steaks with marinade in a resealable plastic freezer bag. To use, thaw in refrigerator overnight. Drain the beef, discarding marinade. Grill as directed.
Note: This recipe was tested with McCormick's Montreal Steak Seasoning.
Per steak: 570 cal., 40g fat (15g sat. fat), 134mg chol., 592mg sodium, 8g carb. (6g sugars, 0 fiber), 40g pro.

GRILLED BASIL CHICKEN & TOMATOES

OKTOBERFEST BRATS WITH MUSTARD SAUCE

EAT SMART **FAST FIX** ▶

BRUSCHETTA STEAK

My husband and I love bruschetta, especially in the summertime with fresh tomatoes and herbs from our garden.
—Kristy Still, Broken Arrow, OK

Start to Finish: 25 min.
Makes: 4 servings

- 3 medium tomatoes, chopped
- 3 tablespoons minced fresh basil
- 3 tablespoons chopped fresh parsley
- 2 tablespoons olive oil
- 1 teaspoon minced fresh oregano or ½ teaspoon dried oregano
- 1 garlic clove, minced
- ¾ teaspoon salt, divided
- 1 beef flat iron or top sirloin steak (1 pound), cut into four portions
- ¼ teaspoon pepper
  Grated Parmesan cheese, optional

1. Combine first six ingredients; stir in ¼ teaspoon salt.
2. Sprinkle beef with pepper and remaining salt. Grill, covered, over

medium heat or broil 4 in. from heat until the meat reaches desired doneness (for medium-rare, a thermometer should read 135°; medium, 140°), 4-6 minutes per side. Top with tomato mixture. If desired, sprinkle with cheese.

Per steak with ½ cup tomato mixture: 280 cal., 19g fat (6g sat. fat), 73mg chol., 519mg sodium, 4g carb. (2g sugars, 1g fiber), 23g pro.
Diabetic Exchanges: 3 lean meat, 1½ fat, 1 vegetable.

FAST FIX ▶

OKTOBERFEST BRATS WITH MUSTARD SAUCE

I come from a town with a German heritage, and each year we have a huge Oktoberfest celebration. This recipe packs in all the traditional German flavors my whole family loves.
—Deborah Pennington, Decatur, AL

Start to Finish: 20 min.
Makes: 4 servings

- ⅓ cup half-and-half cream
- 2 tablespoons stone-ground mustard
- ½ teaspoon dried minced onion

- ¼ teaspoon pepper
  Dash paprika
- 4 fully cooked bratwurst links (about 12 ounces)
- 1 can (14 ounces) sauerkraut, rinsed and drained, warmed

1. For sauce, mix first five ingredients. Cut each bratwurst into thirds; thread the pieces onto four metal or soaked wooden skewers.
2. Grill brats, covered, over medium heat until golden brown and heated through, 7-10 minutes, turning occasionally. Serve with sauerkraut and sauce.

Per serving: 341 cal., 28g fat (10g sat. fat), 73mg chol., 1539mg sodium, 9g carb. (3g sugars, 3g fiber), 14g pro.

✳

TEST KITCHEN TIPS
Stone-ground mustard has more heat and a deeper flavor than yellow. You can substitute other mustards if you like.

Starting this recipe with cooked brats makes it speedy and convenient. If you decide to start with uncooked brats, grill them until fully cooked first, then cut into thirds and proceed with the recipe.

CALIFORNIA BURGER BOWLS

Burgers are a weekly staple at our house all year-round. Skip the fries, chips and bun—you won't need them with these loaded burger bowls. To spice up the mayo, add ½ teaspoon chipotle powder.
—Courtney Stultz, Weir, KS

Start to Finish: 25 min.
Makes: 4 servings

- 3 tablespoons fat-free milk
- 2 tablespoons quick-cooking oats
- ¾ teaspoon salt
- ½ teaspoon ground cumin
- ½ teaspoon chili powder
- ½ teaspoon pepper
- 1 pound lean ground turkey
- 4 cups baby kale salad blend
- 1½ cups cubed fresh pineapple (½ inch)
- 1 medium mango, peeled and thinly sliced
- 1 medium ripe avocado, peeled and thinly sliced
- 1 medium sweet red pepper, cut into strips
- 4 tomatillos, husks removed, thinly sliced
- ¼ cup reduced-fat chipotle mayonnaise

1. In a large bowl, mix milk, oats and seasonings. Add turkey; mix lightly but thoroughly. Shape mixture into four ½-in.-thick patties.
2. Place burgers on an oiled grill rack over medium heat. Grill, covered, until a thermometer reads 165°, 4-5 minutes per side. Serve over salad blend, along with remaining ingredients.

Per serving: 390 cal., 19g fat (4g sat. fat), 83mg chol., 666mg sodium, 33g carb. (22g sugars, 7g fiber), 26g pro.
Diabetic Exchanges: 3 lean meat, 2 vegetable, 1 fruit, 2½ fat.

HEALTH TIP Top these burger bowls with homemade guacamole instead of chipotle mayonnaise and they're gluten-free! Be sure to use certified gluten-free oats in the burger patties.

GRILLED GARDEN VEGGIE PIZZA

Pile the veggies onto this crisp, grilled crust! Here's a colorful, healthy pizza that looks as fresh as it tastes.
—Diane Halferty, Corpus Christi, TX

Start to Finish: 30 min.
Makes: 6 servings

- 1 medium red onion, cut crosswise into ½-inch slices
- 1 large sweet red pepper, halved, stemmed and seeded
- 1 each small zucchini and summer squash, cut lengthwise into ½-inch slices
- 2 tablespoons olive oil
- ½ teaspoon salt
- ¼ teaspoon pepper
- 1 prebaked 12-inch thin whole wheat pizza crust
- 3 tablespoons jarred roasted minced garlic
- 2 cups shredded part-skim mozzarella cheese, divided
- ⅓ cup torn fresh basil

1. Brush vegetables with oil; sprinkle with salt and pepper. Grill, covered, over medium heat until tender, 4-5 minutes per side for onion and pepper, 3-4 minutes per side for zucchini and squash.
2. Separate onion into rings; cut pepper into strips. Spread pizza crust with garlic; sprinkle with 1 cup cheese. Top with grilled vegetables, then remaining cheese.
3. Grill pizza, covered, over medium heat until bottom is golden brown and cheese is melted, 5-7 minutes. Top with basil.

Per slice: 324 cal., 15g fat (6g sat. fat), 24mg chol., 704mg sodium, 30g carb. (5g sugars, 5g fiber), 16g pro.
Diabetic Exchanges: 2 starch, 2 medium-fat meat, 1 fat.

CALIFORNIA BURGER BOWLS

GRILLED EGGPLANT
SANDWICHES

FAST FIX ▸

GRILLED EGGPLANT SANDWICHES

Grill this vegetarian eggplant, tomato and goat cheese sandwich to perfection for a tasty meatless meal.
—Jennifer Jaras, Corona, CA

Start to Finish: 25 min.
Makes: 2 servings

- 2 tablespoons olive oil
- 1 garlic clove, minced
- 2 ciabatta rolls, split
- 4 slices eggplant (½ inch thick)
- 1 medium heirloom tomato, cut into ½-inch slices
- ¼ teaspoon salt
- ⅛ teaspoon pepper
- 2 ounces fresh goat cheese, softened
- 6 fresh basil leaves

1. Mix oil and garlic; brush onto cut sides of rolls and both sides of vegetables. Sprinkle vegetables with salt and pepper.
2. Grill eggplant, covered, over medium heat, until tender, 4-5 minutes per side.

Grill the tomato, covered, until lightly browned, 1-2 minutes per side. Grill rolls, cut side down, until toasted, 1-2 minutes.
3. Spread roll bottoms with goat cheese. Top with basil, eggplant and tomato; close sandwiches.
Per sandwich: 538 cal., 21g fat (5g sat. fat), 19mg chol., 958mg sodium, 81g carb. (10g sugars, 7g fiber), 15g pro.
HEALTH TIP Make this hearty sandwich into a lower-calorie lunch or dinner by serving it open-face and using a knife and fork. You'll save more than 150 calories.

EAT SMART **FAST FIX** ▸

CILANTRO LIME SHRIMP

A quick garlicky-lime marinade works magic on these juicy shrimp. They come off the grill with huge flavors perfect for your next cookout.
—Melissa Rodriguez, Van Nuys, CA

Start to Finish: 30 min.
Makes: 4 servings

- ⅓ cup chopped fresh cilantro
- 1½ teaspoons grated lime peel
- ⅓ cup lime juice
- 1 jalapeno pepper, seeded and minced
- 2 tablespoons olive oil
- 3 garlic cloves, minced
- ¼ teaspoon salt
- ¼ teaspoon ground cumin
- ¼ teaspoon pepper
- 1 pound uncooked shrimp (16-20 per pound), peeled and deveined
   Lime slices

1. Mix first nine ingredients; toss with shrimp. Let stand 15 minutes.
2. Thread shrimp and lime slices onto four metal or soaked wooden skewers. Grill, covered, over medium heat until shrimp turn pink, 2-4 minutes per side.
Per kabob: 167 cal., 8g fat (1g sat. fat), 138mg chol., 284mg sodium, 4g carb. (1g sugars, 0 fiber), 19g pro.
Diabetic Exchanges: 3 lean meat, 1½ fat.

GINGER-GLAZED GRILLED SALMON

Our family loves salmon prepared this way, and it's a real treat to make on a warm summer evening. These fillets may be baked in the oven at 450 degrees for 18 minutes, basting occasionally.
—Wanda Toews, Cromer, MB

Start to Finish: 15 min.
Makes: 4 servings

- 2 tablespoons reduced-sodium soy sauce
- 2 tablespoons maple syrup
- 2 teaspoons minced fresh gingerroot
- 2 garlic cloves, minced
- 4 salmon fillets (6 ounces each)

1. For glaze, mix first four ingredients.
2. Place salmon on an oiled grill rack over medium heat, skin side up. Grill, covered, until fish just begins to flake easily with a fork, 4-5 minutes per side; brush top with half of the glaze after turning. Brush with remaining glaze before serving.

Per fillet: 299 cal., 16g fat (3g sat. fat), 85mg chol., 374mg sodium, 8g carb. (6g sugars, 0 fiber), 29g pro.
Diabetic Exchanges: 4 lean meat, ½ starch.

GRILLED CAPRESE QUESADILLAS
PICTURED ON P. 207

This is a quick and healthy summer recipe with ingredients right from the backyard garden. Feta or mozzarella cheese can be substituted for the goat cheese, or try it with grilled chicken.
—Amy Mongiovi, Lititz, PA

Start to Finish: 20 min.
Makes: 2 servings

- 4 whole wheat tortillas (8 inches)
- 6 ounces fresh mozzarella cheese, sliced
- 2 medium tomatoes, sliced and patted dry
- ⅓ cup julienned fresh basil
- ¼ cup pitted Greek olives, chopped
  Freshly ground pepper to taste

1. Layer one half of each tortilla with cheese and tomatoes; sprinkle with basil, olives and pepper to taste. Fold the tortillas to close.
2. Grill, covered, over medium-high heat until lightly browned and cheese is melted, 2-3 minutes per side.

Per serving: 535 cal., 25g fat (13g sat. fat), 67mg chol., 665mg sodium, 52g carb. (5g sugars, 8g fiber), 25g pro.

MUSHROOM BACON TURKEY BURGERS

If you ask me, a good burger needs mushrooms. But when you place them on top, they tend to slide around and fall out. So I decided to put mushrooms right into the patties—problem solved!
—Melissa Obernesser, Utica, NY

Start to Finish: 30 min.
Makes: 4 servings

- 1 cup finely chopped fresh mushrooms
- 3 tablespoons soft bread crumbs
- 3 tablespoons barbecue sauce
- ¾ teaspoon onion powder
- ½ teaspoon garlic powder
- ¼ teaspoon pepper
- 1 pound extra-lean ground turkey
- 4 turkey bacon strips, halved
- 4 thin slices cheddar cheese
- 4 whole wheat hamburger buns, split
  Additional barbecue sauce

1. Combine first six ingredients. Add turkey; mix lightly but thoroughly. Shape into four ½-in.-thick patties.
2. Place burgers on an oiled grill rack over medium heat; grill, covered, until a thermometer reads 165°, 4-5 minutes per side. Grill bacon strips, covered, until crisp, 2-3 minutes per side. Top burgers with cheese and bacon; grill, covered, until cheese is melted, 30 seconds.
3. Serve on buns. Top with additional barbecue sauce.

Per burger: 389 cal., 17g fat (4g sat. fat), 95mg chol., 727mg sodium, 30g carb. (9g sugars, 4g fiber), 32g pro.
Diabetic Exchanges: 4 lean meat, 2 starch, 2 fat.

GINGER-GLAZED GRILLED SALMON

Effortless Entertaining

Turn here for unique dishes that are surprisingly easy on the home cook. You'll find smart, uncomplicated recipes in this chapter for elegant lamb chops, tenderloin steak for two, salads for a summer barbecue, and irresistible game-day grub.

BARBECUE CHICKEN TOSTADAS

ROASTED SALMON WITH BROWN SUGAR GLAZE

Need a simple way to serve a whole salmon fillet to a group of friends? Here's the super easy recipe that finally made me a fan of the fish.

—Rachel Garcia, Colorado Springs, CO

Prep: 15 min. • **Bake:** 20 min.
Makes: 8 servings

- 1 tablespoon brown sugar
- 2 teaspoons butter
- 1 teaspoon honey
- 1 tablespoon olive oil
- 1 tablespoon Dijon mustard
- 1 tablespoon reduced-sodium soy sauce
- ½ to ¾ teaspoon salt
- ¼ teaspoon pepper
- 1 salmon fillet (2½ pounds)

1. In a small saucepan over medium heat, cook and stir the brown sugar, butter and honey until melted. Remove from the heat; whisk in the oil, mustard, soy sauce, salt and pepper. Cool for 5 minutes.

2. Place salmon in a large foil-lined baking pan; spoon brown sugar mixture over top. Bake at 350° for 20-25 minutes or until the fish flakes easily with a fork.
Per serving: 295 cal., 18g fat (3g sat. fat), 84mg chol., 403mg sodium, 3g carb. (2g sugars, 0 fiber), 28g pro.

BARBECUE CHICKEN TOSTADAS

Lots of my recipes start out as fun ways to use leftovers—like this one! My kids love tostadas, so this day-after-cookout dinner was a big hit.
—Lauren Wyler, Dripping Springs, TX

Start to Finish: 30 min.
Makes: 4 servings

- 2 tablespoons lemon juice
- 2 tablespoons mayonnaise
- 1 tablespoon light brown sugar
- ⅛ teaspoon pepper
- 2 cups coleslaw mix
- 2 green onions, thinly sliced

- 1 cup baked beans
- 2⅔ cups shredded cooked chicken
- ⅔ cup barbecue sauce
- 8 tostada shells
- 1 cup shredded smoked cheddar cheese

1. Preheat broiler. Mix the first four ingredients; toss with coleslaw mix and green onions. Refrigerate until serving.
2. Place beans in a small saucepan; mash with a potato masher until smooth. Cook over low heat until heated through, about 10 minutes, stirring frequently.
3. In another saucepan, mix chicken and barbecue sauce; cook over medium-low heat until hot, about 10 minutes, stirring mixture occasionally.
4. To assemble, place tostada shells on ungreased baking sheets. Spread with beans; top with chicken mixture and cheese. Broil 3-4 in. from heat until tostada shells are lightly browned and cheese is melted, 1-2 minutes. Top with slaw. Serve immediately.
Per 2 tostadas: 612 cal., 29g fat (10g sat. fat), 116mg chol., 1113mg sodium, 51g carb. (21g sugars, 6g fiber), 39g pro.

NUTTY CHICKEN STRIPS

I enjoy cooking things that are a little out of the ordinary. These crunchy chicken strips, seasoned with curry, are great for family game night.
—Betsy Baertlein, Mazeppa, MN

Prep: 20 min. • **Cook:** 20 min.
Makes: 6 servings

- 1 cup (8 ounces) plain yogurt
- 2 tablespoons minced fresh cilantro
- 1 tablespoon honey

CHICKEN
- 1 large egg
- ½ cup 2% milk
- 1 cup soft bread crumbs
- ½ cup chopped almonds
- 2 tablespoons minced fresh cilantro
- 1½ teaspoons curry powder
- 1½ pounds boneless skinless chicken breasts, cut into 1-inch-wide strips
- ¼ cup all-purpose flour
- ¼ cup canola oil

1. Mix yogurt, cilantro and honey. Refrigerate, covered, until serving.
2. In a shallow bowl, whisk together egg and milk. In another bowl, toss bread crumbs with almonds, cilantro and curry powder. Toss chicken strips with flour to coat lightly; shake off excess. Dip both sides of strips in egg mixture, then in crumb mixture.
3. In a large skillet, heat oil over medium heat. In batches, cook chicken until golden brown, 5-6 minutes per side. Drain on paper towels. Serve with sauce.
Note: To make soft bread crumbs, tear bread into pieces and place in a food processor or blender. Cover and pulse until crumbs form. One slice of bread yields ½ to ¾ cup crumbs.
Per 4 ounces cooked chicken with 1½ tablespoons sauce: 365 cal., 20g fat (3g sat. fat), 101mg chol., 132mg sodium, 16g carb. (7g sugars, 2g fiber), 30g pro.
Pecan Parmesan Chicken Strips: Omit almond, cilantro, curry powder, flour and yogurt dipping sauce. Reduce the bread crumbs to ½ cup. Combine with ⅓ cup each grated Parmesan cheese and ground pecans, 1 teaspoon dried oregano, ½ teaspoon each seasoned salt and dried basil, and ¼ teaspoon pepper. Proceed as directed. Serve with warmed spaghetti sauce if desired.

SLOPPY JOE DOGS

There are so many different ways to top a hot dog, but this tasty sloppy joe version beats them all!
—Kimberly Wallace, Dennison, OH

Prep: 20 min. • **Cook:** 15 min.
Makes: 16 servings

SLOPPY JOE TOPPING
- 2 pounds ground beef
- 2 celery ribs, chopped
- 1 small green pepper, finely chopped
- 1 small onion, chopped
- 1 can (10¾ ounces) condensed tomato soup, undiluted
- ¼ cup packed brown sugar
- ¼ cup ketchup
- 1 tablespoon cider vinegar
- 1 tablespoon prepared mustard
- 1½ teaspoons Worcestershire sauce
- 1 teaspoon pepper
- ½ teaspoon salt
- ¼ teaspoon garlic powder

DOGS
- 16 hot dogs
- 16 hot dog buns, split
  Warmed process cheese sauce and grilled onions, optional

1. In a Dutch oven, cook the beef, celery, green pepper and onion over medium heat until meat is no longer pink; drain. Stir in the soup, brown sugar, ketchup, vinegar, mustard, Worcestershire sauce, pepper, salt and garlic powder; heat through.
2. Grill hot dogs, covered, over medium heat for 6-10 minutes or until hot, turning occasionally. Serve on buns. Top each with ¼ cup beef mixture. Top with process cheese sauce and onions if desired.
Per serving: 422 cal., 23g fat (9g sat. fat), 68mg chol., 959mg sodium, 31g carb. (10g sugars, 1g fiber), 22g pro.

NUTTY CHICKEN STRIPS

Get Crackin'

Food stylist Lauren Knoelke does broiled lobster tail in just a few easy steps, with plenty of butter.

Cook Wow-Worthy Lobster Tails

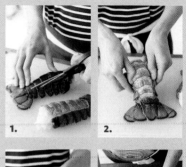

1. Snip
Using kitchen scissors, cut and remove a 2-inch-wide rectangle from the top shell of each lobster tail.

2. Loosen
Pull away the shell's edges to release the meat.

3. Separate
Gently pry the lobster meat loose from the bottom shell, keeping it attached at the tail end. Let the meat sit on top of the shell.

4. Broil
Line butter slices along the meat. Broil the lobster tails 5-6 in. from heat until the meat is opaque, 5-8 minutes. Season with salt and pepper; serve with lemon wedges. Clarified butter (next page) is optional but lovely.

---

(5) INGREDIENTS

BROILED LOBSTER TAIL

No matter where you live, these succulent, buttery lobster tails are just a few minutes away. Here in Wisconsin, we use frozen lobster with delicious results, but if you're near the ocean, by all means, use fresh!
—Lauren Knoelke, Milwaukee, WI

Prep: 30 min. • **Cook:** 5 min.
Makes:: 4 servings

4 lobster tails (5 to 6 ounces each), thawed
¼ cup cold butter, cut into thin slices
   Salt and pepper to taste
   Lemon wedges
   Clarified butter (see facing page), optional

Per lobster tail: 211 cal., 13g fat (8g sat. fat), 211mg chol., 691mg sodium, 0 carb. (0 sugars, 0 fiber), 24g pro.

FAST FIX
BREADED SEA SCALLOPS

I never liked seafood until my husband urged me to try scallops, and now I love them. He says my crispy breaded version is the best he's ever had.
—Martina Preston, Willow Grove, PA

Start to Finish: 15 min.
Makes: 2 servings

- 1 large egg
- ⅓ cup mashed potato flakes
- ⅓ cup seasoned bread crumbs
- ⅛ teaspoon salt
- ⅛ teaspoon pepper
- 6 sea scallops (about ¾ pound)
- 2 tablespoons all-purpose flour
- 2 tablespoons butter
- 1 tablespoon canola oil

1. In a shallow bowl, lightly beat egg. In another bowl, toss potato flakes and bread crumbs with salt and pepper. In a third bowl, toss scallops with flour to coat lightly. Dip in egg, then in potato mixture, patting to adhere.
2. In a large skillet, heat butter and oil over medium heat. Add scallops; cook until golden brown and scallops are firm and opaque, 2-3 minutes per side.
Per 3 scallops: 454 cal., 23g fat (9g sat. fat), 164mg chol., 1262mg sodium, 33g carb. (2g sugars, 2g fiber), 28g pro.
Almond-Crusted Sea Scallops: Substitute ⅓ cup ground almonds for the potato flakes. Add ½ teaspoon of grated lemon peel to the bread crumb mixture. Proceed as directed.

Butter Up!

Break out the bibs for some rich, velvety clarified butter. The ultimate lobster dunker is only a few minutes away.

⑤INGREDIENTS FAST FIX
CLARIFIED BUTTER

We make clarified butter to remove the milk solids, which are what burn when cooking with high heat. Keep a jar in the fridge to use for pan frying, or to drizzle over veggies, rice and, of course, seafood!
—*Taste of Home* Test Kitchen

Start to Finish: 20 min. • **Makes:** ¾ cup

- 1 cup unsalted butter, cubed

Per tablespoon: 130 cal., 14g fat (9g sat. fat), 40mg chol., 0 sodium, 0 carb. (0 sugars, 0 fiber), 0 pro.
Lemon-Chive Compound Butter: Add 2 tablespoons chopped fresh chives, 2 tablespoons chopped fresh parsley, 1 tablespoon minced shallot, 1 minced garlic clove, ½ teaspoon grated lemon peel and ¼ teaspoon salt to butter.
Chimichurri Compound Butter: Add 2 tablespoons chopped fresh cilantro, 2 tablespoons chopped fresh parsley, 1 tablespoon minced shallot, 1 teaspoon grated lemon peel, 1 teaspoon minced fresh oregano, 1 minced garlic clove, ¼ teaspoon salt and ⅛ teaspoon of crushed red pepper flakes to butter.

1. Simmer
Melt 1 cup of unsalted butter, cubed, in a heavy saucepan over low heat. Simmer until the solids and fat separate, about 10 minutes. Don't allow it to brown.

2. Skim
Remove from heat; skim and discard the surface foam. What's left should be clear yellow liquid.

3. Strain
Pour liquid into a bowl through fine-mesh or cheesecloth-lined strainer. Store in airtight container in the fridge for up to three months, or in the freezer for up to six months.

HOT SAUSAGE
& BEAN DIP

HOT SAUSAGE & BEAN DIP

This is a spin-off of a Mexican dip I once had. The original was wicked good, but since I was going through an I'm-so-over-Mexican-dip phase, I decided to switch it up. Take this to a party—I'll bet you no one else will bring anything like it!
—Mandy Rivers, Lexington, SC

Prep: 25 min. • **Bake:** 20 min.
Makes: 16 servings (¼ cup each)

- 1 pound bulk hot Italian sausage
- 1 medium onion, finely chopped
- 4 garlic cloves, minced
- ½ cup dry white wine or chicken broth
- ½ teaspoon dried oregano
- ¼ teaspoon salt
- ¼ teaspoon dried thyme
- 1 package (8 ounces) cream cheese, softened
- 1 package (6 ounces) fresh baby spinach, coarsely chopped
- 1 can (15 ounces) cannellini beans, rinsed and drained
- 1 cup chopped seeded tomatoes
- 1 cup shredded part-skim mozzarella cheese
- ½ cup shredded Parmesan cheese
  Assorted crackers or toasted French bread baguette slices

1. Preheat oven to 375°. In a large skillet, cook sausage, onion and garlic over medium heat until sausage is no longer pink, breaking up sausage into crumbles; drain. Stir in the wine, oregano, salt and thyme. Bring to a boil; cook until liquid is almost evaporated.
2. Add cream cheese; stir until melted. Stir in spinach, beans and tomatoes; cook and stir until spinach is wilted. Transfer to a greased 8-in. square pan or, if using an oven-proof skillet, leave in skillet. Sprinkle with cheeses.
3. Bake until bubbly, 20-25 minutes. Serve with crackers.
Per ¼ cup: 200 cal., 14g fat (7g sat. fat), 41mg chol., 434mg sodium, 7g carb. (2g sugars, 2g fiber), 10g pro.

⑤ INGREDIENTS
ROASTED CHICKEN
PICTURED ON P. 225
This beautiful, tender chicken is a real timesaver on busy weekends. A simple blend of pantry seasonings makes it a snap to prepare, and it smells heavenly as it roasts.
—Marian Platt, Sequim, WA

Prep: 10 min. • **Bake:** 1¼ hours + standing
Makes: 12 servings

- ¾ teaspoon onion salt
- ¾ teaspoon celery salt
- ¾ teaspoon seasoned salt
- ½ teaspoon pepper
- 2 broiler/fryer chickens (3 to 4 pounds each)

1. Preheat oven to 400°. Mix seasonings.
2. Place chickens on a rack in a roasting pan, breast side up. Rub seasonings over outside and inside of chickens. Tuck under wings; tie together drumsticks. Roast until a thermometer inserted in thickest part of thigh reads 170°-175°, 1¼-1½ hours. (Cover loosely with foil if chickens brown too quickly.)
3. Remove from oven; tent with foil. Let stand 15 minutes before carving.
Per serving: 293 cal., 17g fat (5g sat. fat), 104mg chol., 370mg sodium, 0 carb. (0 sugars, 0 fiber), 33g pro.

EAT SMART FAST FIX ▶
SUMMER SQUASH & WATERMELON SALAD
PICTURED ON P. 225

I always like to take this healthy option to parties and potlucks, and people seem to really appreciate it. No oil is necessary for this salad: the lemon juice combines with the feta to lightly coat the bright, fresh ingredients.
—Camille Parker, Chicago, IL

Start to Finish: 20 min.
Makes: 12 servings (¾ cup each)

- 6 cups cubed seedless watermelon
- 2 medium yellow summer squash, chopped
- 2 medium zucchini, chopped
- ½ cup lemon juice
- 12 fresh mint leaves, torn
- 1 teaspoon salt
- 8 cups fresh arugula or baby spinach
- 1 cup (4 ounces) crumbled feta cheese

In a large bowl, combine the first six ingredients. Just before serving, add arugula and cheese; toss ingredients gently to combine.
Per cup: 60 cal., 2g fat (1g sat. fat), 5mg chol., 297mg sodium, 11g carb. (8g sugars, 2g fiber), 3g pro.
Diabetic Exchanges: 1 vegetable, ½ fruit.

DIXIE LAMB CHOPS

These saucy lamb chops may seem fancy, but mine work for both special occasions and busy evenings. We love them with spinach salad and hearty bread.
—Barbara Burge, Los Gatos, CA

Start to Finish: 20 min.
Makes: 4 servings

- 4 lamb loin chops (5 to 6 ounces each)
- ½ teaspoon salt
- ¼ teaspoon pepper
- 1 tablespoon olive oil
- ¼ cup molasses
- 2 tablespoons steak sauce
- 1 tablespoon cider vinegar

1. Sprinkle chops with salt and pepper. In a large skillet, heat oil over medium heat; cook chops, covered, until bottoms are browned, 5-7 minutes.
2. Mix molasses, steak sauce and vinegar. Turn chops; pour molasses mixture over top. Cook, covered, over medium-low heat until lamb reaches desired doneness (for medium-rare, a thermometer should read 135°; medium, 140°), 5-7 minutes.

Per lamb chop with 1 tablespoon glaze: 225 cal., 9g fat (3g sat. fat), 57mg chol., 493mg sodium, 17g carb. (16g sugars, 0 fiber), 18g pro.
Diabetic Exchanges: 3 lean meat, 1 starch, ½ fat.

PORK CHOPS WITH NECTARINE SAUCE

As a dietitian, I'm always looking for ways to make meals healthy and delicious. These juicy chops are fast, too.
—Suellen Pineda, Victor, NY

Start to Finish: 30 min.
Makes: 4 servings

- 4 boneless pork loin chops (6 ounces each)
- ½ teaspoon salt
- ½ teaspoon dried thyme
- ¼ teaspoon pepper
- 3 tablespoons all-purpose flour
- 1 tablespoon canola oil
- 1 small onion, finely chopped
- 1 garlic clove, minced
- 3 medium nectarines or peeled peaches, cut into ½-inch slices
- ½ cup reduced-sodium chicken broth
- 1 tablespoon honey, optional

1. Sprinkle pork chops with seasonings. Dredge lightly with flour. In a large skillet, heat oil over medium heat; cook chops until a thermometer reads 145°, about 4-5 minutes per side. Remove from pan; keep warm.
2. Add onion to same pan; cook and stir over medium heat 2 minutes. Add garlic; cook and stir 1 minute. Add nectarines; cook until lightly browned on both sides. Stir in broth and, if desired, honey; bring to a boil. Reduce heat; simmer, uncovered, until nectarines are softened and sauce is slightly thickened, about 5 minutes. Serve with chops.

Per pork chop with ½ cup sauce: 330 cal., 14g fat (4g sat. fat), 82mg chol., 414mg sodium, 16g carb. (9g sugars, 2g fiber), 35g pro.
Diabetic Exchanges: 5 lean meat, 1 fruit, 1 fat.

DIXIE LAMB CHOPS

LEMON CREAM CHICKEN

⑤ INGREDIENTS FAST FIX ▶

TORTELLINI CARBONARA

Bacon, cream and Parmesan cheese make a classic pasta sauce that's absolutely heavenly. It's a great option for company!
—Cathy Croyle, Davidsville, PA

Start to Finish: 20 min.
Makes: 4 servings

- 1 package (9 ounces) refrigerated cheese tortellini
- 8 bacon strips, chopped
- 1 cup heavy whipping cream
- ½ cup grated Parmesan cheese
- ½ cup chopped fresh parsley

1. Cook tortellini according to package directions; drain.
2. Meanwhile, in a large skillet, cook bacon over medium heat until crisp, stirring occasionally. Remove with a slotted spoon; drain on paper towels. Pour off drippings.
3. In the same pan, combine cream, cheese, parsley and bacon; heat through over medium heat. Stir in the tortellini. Serve immediately.
Per cup: 527 cal., 36g fat (20g sat. fat), 121mg chol., 728mg sodium, 33g carb. (3g sugars, 2g fiber), 19g pro.

LEMON CREAM CHICKEN

If you want a dish that's quick, easy and elegant, you can't beat this one. The lemon cream sauce makes it irresistible, and it's a perfect complement to the chicken and mushrooms.
—Mary Anne McWhirter, Pearland, TX

Prep: 10 min. • **Cook:** 45 min.
Makes: 6 servings

- ½ cup plus 1 tablespoon all-purpose flour, divided
- ½ teaspoon salt
- ½ teaspoon pepper
- 6 boneless skinless chicken breast halves (4 ounces each)
- ¼ cup butter
- 1 cup chicken broth
- 1 cup heavy whipping cream, divided
- 3 tablespoons lemon juice
- ½ pound sliced fresh mushrooms

1. In a shallow bowl, mix ½ cup flour, salt and pepper. Dip chicken breasts in flour mixture to coat both sides; shake off excess flour.
2. In a large skillet, heat butter over medium heat. Cook the chicken in batches until a thermometer reads 165°, 5-7 minutes per side. Remove chicken, reserving drippings in pan.
3. Add broth to the skillet; bring to a boil. Simmer, uncovered, until liquid is reduced to ⅓ cup, about 10 minutes. Stir in ¾ cup cream, lemon juice and mushrooms; cook over medium-low heat 5 minutes.
4. In a small bowl, mix the remaining flour and cream until smooth; stir into sauce. Bring mixture to a boil; cook and stir until thickened, 1-2 minutes. Return chicken to the pan and heat through.
Per serving: 381 cal., 25g fat (15g sat. fat), 129mg chol., 488mg sodium, 12g carb. (2g sugars, 1g fiber), 27g pro.

RAMONA'S CHILAQUILES

A dear neighbor shared this recipe, which she used to make from scratch. My version takes a few snappy shortcuts.
—Marina Castle Kelley, Canyon Country, CA

Start to Finish: 30 min.
Makes: 4 servings

- ½ pound lean ground beef (90% lean)
- ½ pound fresh chorizo or bulk spicy pork sausage
- 1 medium onion, finely chopped
- 1 garlic clove, minced
- 1 can (14½ ounces) diced tomatoes with mild green chilies, undrained
- 1 can (10 ounces) diced tomatoes and green chilies, undrained
- 4 cups tortilla chips (about 6 ounces)
- 1 cup shredded Monterey Jack cheese Chopped fresh cilantro Optional toppings: sour cream, diced avocado and sliced red onion

1. Preheat oven to 350°. In a large skillet, cook and crumble beef and chorizo with onion and garlic over medium heat until beef is no longer pink, 5-7 minutes; drain. Stir in both tomatoes; bring to a boil. In a greased 1½-qt. or 8-in. square baking dish, layer 2 cups chips, half of the meat mixture and ½ cup cheese; repeat layers.
2. Bake, uncovered, until the cheese is melted, 12-15 minutes. Sprinkle with cilantro. If desired, serve with toppings.

Per serving: 573 cal., 35g fat (14g sat. fat), 110mg chol., 1509mg sodium, 28g carb. (5g sugars, 4g fiber), 33g pro.

HEALTH TIP Chilaquiles are indulgent any way you fix them, but they can be lightened up: Use chicken chorizo sausage and baked tortilla chips to lop off 15g fat per serving.

RAMONA'S CHILAQUILES

ITALIAN SAUSAGE WITH BOW TIES

PICTURED ON P. 225

When company comes for dinner, we often have our favorite sausage and pasta dish. I've shared this recipe several times. Now many of my friends make it for their families, too.
—Janelle Moore, Auburn, WA

Start to Finish: 25 min.
Makes: 6 servings

- 1 package (16 ounces) bow tie pasta
- 1 pound bulk Italian sausage
- ½ cup chopped onion
- ½ teaspoon crushed red pepper flakes
- 1½ teaspoons minced garlic
- 2 cans (14½ ounces each) Italian stewed tomatoes, drained and chopped
- 1½ cups heavy whipping cream
- ¼ teaspoon salt
- ¼ teaspoon dried basil Shredded Parmesan cheese

1. Cook pasta according to the package directions. Drain.
2. Meanwhile, in a 6-qt. stockpot, cook and crumble sausage with onion and pepper flakes over medium heat until no longer pink, 5-7 minutes. Add garlic; cook 1 minute. Drain.
3. Stir in tomatoes, cream, salt and basil; bring to a boil over medium heat. Reduce heat; simmer, uncovered, until thickened, 6-8 minutes, stirring occasionally. Stir in pasta; heat through. Serve with cheese.

Per 1¾ cups: 751 cal., 44g fat (21g sat. fat), 119mg chol., 989mg sodium, 67g carb. (9g sugars, 4g fiber), 23g pro.

★ ★ ★ ★ ★ **READER REVIEW**

"This was really good! I didn't have heavy cream so I used a half cup of whole milk and a half cup of Parmesan cheese. Tasted wonderful."

MRENDA TASTEOFHOME.COM

BEEF TENDERLOIN IN MUSHROOM SAUCE

FAST FIX ▶

BEEF TENDERLOIN IN MUSHROOM SAUCE

Just a skillet, a couple juicy steaks, some fresh mushrooms and a few simple ingredients prove it doesn't take much effort to fix a special meal for two.
—Denise McNab, Warminster, PA

Start to Finish: 25 min.
Makes: 2 servings

    4 tablespoons butter, divided
    1 teaspoon canola oil
    2 beef tenderloin steaks (1 inch thick
       and 4 ounces each)
    1 cup sliced fresh mushrooms
    1 tablespoon chopped green onion
    1 tablespoon all-purpose flour
    ⅛ teaspoon salt
       Dash pepper
    ⅔ cup chicken or beef broth
    ⅛ teaspoon browning sauce, optional

1. In a large skillet, heat 2 tablespoons butter and oil over medium-high heat; cook steaks to desired doneness (for medium-rare, a thermometer should read 135°; medium, 140°), 5-6 minutes per side. Remove from the pan, reserving drippings; keep warm.
2. In same pan, heat the drippings and remaining butter over medium-high heat; saute mushrooms and green onion until tender. Stir in flour, salt and pepper until blended; gradually stir in broth and, if desired, browning sauce. Bring to a boil, stirring constantly; cook and stir until thickened, 1-2 minutes. Serve with steaks.
Per serving: 417 cal., 32g fat (17g sat. fat), 112mg chol., 659mg sodium, 5g carb. (1g sugars, 1g fiber), 26g pro.

EAT SMART **FAST FIX** ▶

PISTACHIO SALMON

PICTURED ON P. 225

This simple salmon gets its crunch from a coating of crushed pistachios, panko bread crumbs and Parmesan cheese. Add colorful steamed veggies and some rice and it's dinnertime!
—Anthony Oraczewski, Port St. Lucie, FL

Start to Finish: 25 min.
Makes: 4 servings

    ⅓ cup pistachios, finely chopped
    ¼ cup panko (Japanese) bread crumbs
    ¼ cup grated Parmesan cheese
    1 salmon fillet (1 pound)
    ½ teaspoon salt
    ¼ teaspoon pepper

1. Preheat oven to 400°. In a shallow bowl, toss pistachios with bread crumbs and cheese.
2. Place salmon on a greased foil-lined 15x10x1-in. pan, skin side down; sprinkle with with salt and pepper. Top with the pistachio mixture, pressing to adhere. Bake, uncovered, until fish just begins to flake easily with a fork, 15-20 minutes.
Per 3 ounces cooked fish: 269 cal., 17g fat (3g sat. fat), 61mg chol., 497mg sodium, 6g carb. (1g sugars, 1g fiber), 23g pro.
Diabetic Exchanges: 3 lean meat, 1 fat, ½ starch.

HEALTH TIP Save leftover pistachios for snacking! One serving (about 50 nuts) has 6g protein, 3g fiber and more than 10 percent of the daily value for vitamin B6, thiamine, copper and phosphorous.

QUICK SESAME CHICKEN NOODLES

I love playing around with different ingredients and spices in my stir-fry recipes. As my children get older, I have more evenings when I need to whip up dinner quickly, and this dish with chicken strips and ramen noodles is perfect for our family.
—Heather Chambers, Largo, FL

Start to Finish: 25 min.
Makes: 4 servings

- 1 tablespoon sesame oil
- 1 package (22 ounces) frozen grilled chicken breast strips
- 1 medium yellow summer squash, thinly sliced
- 1 cup julienned carrots
- ⅓ cup halved fresh snow peas
- 3 garlic cloves, minced
- 2 packages (3 ounces each) chicken ramen noodles, broken into small pieces
- 1⅓ cups water
- ⅓ cup white wine or chicken broth
- 3 tablespoons reduced-sodium teriyaki sauce
- 4 green onions, sliced

1. In a large skillet, heat oil over medium-high heat; saute chicken, squash and carrots until chicken is heated through, 6-8 minutes. Add snow peas; cook until vegetables are crisp-tender, 3-4 minutes. Add garlic and contents of one ramen seasoning packet (discard or save second packet for another use); cook and stir for 1 minute.
2. Add noodles, water, wine and teriyaki sauce. Bring to a boil; cook, uncovered, until noodles are tender, 3-4 minutes, stirring occasionally.
3. Remove from heat; stir in green onions. Serve immediately.
Per 1½ cups: 460 cal., 15g fat (5g sat. fat), 93mg chol., 1626mg sodium, 37g carb. (6g sugars, 3g fiber), 45g pro.

QUICK SESAME CHICKEN NOODLES

RICOTTA, TOMATO & CORN PASTA

PICTURED ON P. 225

I love to make healthy meals with produce from my latest farmers market trip. This pasta takes only 30 minutes from pantry to dinner table. You can make it a meat entree by adding chicken, pork or shrimp.
—Jerilyn Korver, Bellflower, CA

Start to Finish: 30 min.
Makes: 8 servings

- 3 cups uncooked whole wheat elbow macaroni (about 12 ounces)
- 1 can (15 ounces) cannellini beans, rinsed and drained
- 2 cups cherry tomatoes, halved
- 1 cup fresh or frozen corn, thawed
- ½ cup finely chopped red onion
- ½ cup part-skim ricotta cheese
- ¼ cup grated Parmesan cheese
- 2 tablespoons minced fresh basil or 2 teaspoons dried basil
- 1 tablespoon olive oil
- 3 garlic cloves, minced
- 1 teaspoon salt
- 1 teaspoon minced fresh rosemary or ½ teaspoon dried rosemary, crushed
- ½ teaspoon pepper
- 3 cups arugula or baby spinach
  Chopped fresh parsley, optional

1. Cook pasta according to package directions. Drain and rinse with cold water; drain well.
2. In a large bowl, combine the beans, tomatoes, corn, onion, ricotta and Parmesan cheese, basil, oil, garlic, salt, rosemary and pepper. Stir in pasta. Add arugula; toss gently to combine. If desired, sprinkle with parsley. Serve immediately.
Per 1½ cups: 275 cal., 5g fat (1g sat. fat), 7mg chol., 429mg sodium, 46g carb. (4g sugars, 8g fiber), 13g pro.
Diabetic Exchanges: 3 starch, 1 lean meat.

✱

TEST KITCHEN TIP

For the ultimate flavor, use fresh produce when it's in season. In spring, that means asparagus, peas, artichokes and fennel. In the summer, eggplant, arugula, summer squash and tomatoes shine. Fall's finest? Butternut squash, Brussels sprouts and carrots, to name a few.

3

1

Baguette

Grab a loaf and raise a toast to these fresh ideas for crunchy crusts and genius toppings.

5

9

1 "My **Pomegranate Pistachio Crostini** are perfect for Christmas. Beat 4 oz. softened cream cheese, 2 Tbsp. OJ and 1 Tbsp. honey; spread over baguette toasts. Top toasts with 1 cup pomegranate seeds, ½ cup chopped pistachios and 2 oz. grated dark chocolate."
—Elisabeth Larsen, Pleasant Grove, UT

2 "French bread baguettes make awesome homemade pizzas."
—Lorraine Caland, Shuniah, ON

3 "**Mexican Sausage Crostini** make my brunch guests happy. Just scramble 6 eggs with 4 chopped green onions, ½ tsp. salt and ¼ tsp. pepper. Stir in a pound of cooked pork sausage. Top baguette toasts with ⅔ cup pico de gallo, egg mixture and ⅓ cup shredded Monterey Jack cheese. Bake crostini at 400° for 1-2 minutes. Top with cilantro and sour cream."
—Lisa Huff, Wilton, CT

4 "I mix mayo, Parm and artichokes and spread it on toasts, then top with sauted mushrooms, Italian seasoning and shredded Swiss. Then I bake them until they are bubbly."
—Nancy Mueller, Bloomington, MN

5 "I make **Sweet Potato Crostini**—they're like mini pies. Brush baguette slices with some melted butter and sprinkle with cinnamon sugar. Bake at 375° until lightly browned. Mix 2 cups mashed sweet potatoes, ¼ cup chopped pecans, 2 Tbsp. brown sugar and 2 Tbsp. melted butter; spread over the toasts. Place 1½ cups of mini marshmallows on top. Then broil until they're golden."
—Steve Westphal, Wind Lake, WI

6 "I top mine with Brie and bake till melty, then dollop on homemade cranberry compote. Such a good snack."
—Katherine Watson, Omaha, NE

7 "I make little open-faced sandwiches with potato salad, tomato, ham, pickle, red onion and hard-cooked eggs. So simple, but so fun!"
—Cara McDonald, Winter Park, CO

8 "I spread toasted baguette slices with avocado, then top with sliced steak and marinated red onions. They seem fancy, but they're super simple."
—Bonnie Hawkins, Elkhorn, WI

9 "My **Roasted Grape Crostini** are so elegant. Toss together 3 cups halved seedless red grapes, 2 Tbsp. each sherry vinegar and olive oil, ½ tsp. salt and ¼ tsp. pepper. Roast at 400° until lightly browned, about half an hour. Stir in 1 tsp. grated orange peel. Top baguette toasts with the grapes, shaved manchego cheese and sliced fresh basil."
—Janice Elder, Charlotte, NC

STEAK & BLUE CHEESE BRUSCHETTA WITH ONION & ROASTED TOMATO JAM

Some of my favorite steakhouse flavors—ribeye, tomato, sweet onion and blue cheese—inspired this bruschetta. It's hearty, delicious and shows up at all our parties and holiday gatherings.
—Debbie Reid, Clearwater, FL

Prep: 45 min. • **Grill:** 10 min.
Makes: 16 appetizers

- 5 tablespoons olive oil, divided
- 1 large sweet onion, halved and thinly sliced
- 1 cup grape tomatoes, halved
- ½ teaspoon kosher salt, divided
- ¼ teaspoon freshly ground pepper, divided
- 6 ounces cream cheese, softened
- 3 ounces crumbled blue cheese
- 3 garlic cloves, minced
- 16 slices French bread baguette (½ inch thick)
- 2 beef ribeye steaks (¾ inch thick and 8 ounces each)
- 1½ teaspoons Montreal steak seasoning
- 2 tablespoons balsamic vinegar

1. Preheat oven to 400°. In large skillet, heat 2 tablespoons oil over medium-high heat; saute onion until softened. Reduce heat to medium-low; cook until onions are golden brown, for 25-30 minutes, stirring occasionally.
2. Toss tomatoes with 1 tablespoon oil, ¼ teaspoon salt and ⅛ teaspoon pepper; spread in a 15x10x1-in. pan. Roast until softened, 10-15 minutes. Stir tomatoes into onion, mashing lightly. In small bowl, mix cream cheese, blue cheese, garlic and the remaining salt and pepper.
3. Brush bread slices with remaining oil; grill, covered, over medium heat until lightly toasted, 1-2 minutes per side. Sprinkle steaks with steak seasoning. Grill, covered, over medium heat until meat reaches desired doneness (for medium-rare, a thermometer should read 135°; medium, 140°; medium-well, 145°), for 3-5 minutes per side. Let stand 5 minutes before slicing.
4. To serve, spread toasts with cheese mixture; top with steak and onion mixture. Drizzle with vinegar.

Per appetizer: 185 cal., 14g fat (6g sat. fat), 32mg chol., 292mg sodium, 7g carb. (2g sugars, 0 fiber), 8g pro.

EAT SMART **FAST FIX**

WHITE WINE GARLIC CHICKEN

This garlic chicken is great with cooked brown rice or your favorite pasta. Add a sprinkle of Parmesan cheese, too.
—Heather Esposito, Rome, NY

Start to Finish: 30 min.
Makes: 4 servings

- 4 boneless skinless chicken breast halves (6 ounces each)
- ½ teaspoon salt
- ¼ teaspoon pepper
- 1 tablespoon olive oil
- 2 cups sliced baby portobello mushrooms (about 6 ounces)
- 1 medium onion, chopped
- 2 garlic cloves, minced
- ½ cup dry white wine or reduced-sodium chicken broth

1. Pound chicken breasts with a meat mallet to ½-in. thickness; sprinkle with salt and pepper. In a large skillet, heat oil over medium heat; cook chicken until no longer pink, 5-6 minutes per side. Remove from pan; keep warm.
2. Add mushrooms and onion to pan; cook and stir over medium-high heat until tender and lightly browned, 2-3 minutes. Add garlic; cook and stir 30 seconds. Add wine; bring to a boil, stirring to loosen browned bits from pan. Cook until liquid is slightly reduced, 1-2 minutes; serve over the chicken.

Per chicken breast half with ¼ cup mushroom mixture: 243 cal., 7g fat (2g sat. fat), 94mg chol., 381mg sodium, 5g carb. (2g sugars, 1g fiber), 36g pro.
Diabetic Exchanges: 5 lean meat, 1 fat.

BUCATINI WITH SAUSAGE & KALE

⑤ INGREDIENTS **FAST FIX**

BUCATINI WITH SAUSAGE & KALE

I was short on time, but I wanted to make an elegant dinner for my husband and me. That night, we enjoyed this simple pasta with spicy sausage and our homegrown kale. It was love at first bite.
—Angela Lemoine, Howell, NJ

Start to Finish: 30 min.
Makes: 6 servings

- 1 package (12 ounces) bucatini pasta or fettuccine
- 2 teaspoons plus 3 tablespoons olive oil, divided
- 1 pound regular or spicy bulk Italian sausage
- 5 garlic cloves, thinly sliced
- 8 cups chopped fresh kale (about 5 ounces)
- ¾ teaspoon salt
- ¼ teaspoon pepper
  Shredded Romano cheese

1. Cook pasta according to package directions, decreasing time by 3 minutes. Drain, reserving 2 cups pasta water. Toss pasta with 2 teaspoons oil.
2. In a 6-qt. stockpot, cook sausage over medium heat until no longer pink, about 5-7 minutes, breaking meat into large crumbles. Add garlic and remaining oil; cook and stir 2 minutes. Stir in kale, salt and pepper; cook, covered, over medium-low heat until kale is tender, about 10 minutes, stirring occasionally.
3. Add pasta and reserved pasta water; bring to a boil. Reduce heat; simmer, uncovered, until pasta is al dente and liquid is absorbed, about 3 minutes, tossing to combine. Sprinkle with cheese.

Per 1⅓ cups: 512 cal., 30g fat (8g sat. fat), 51mg chol., 898mg sodium, 43g carb. (2g sugars, 3g fiber), 19g pro.

BUTTERY WHISKEY-GLAZED PEARL ONIONS

I always have pearl onions on hand to add to stews and vegetable dishes—they're great pickled, too. Every Thanksgiving, I make this glazed onion dish. It can easily be made ahead of time and reheated.
—Ann Sheehy, Lawrence, MA

Start to Finish: 30 min.
Makes: 10 servings

- 2 packages (14.4 ounces each) pearl onions
- ⅓ cup cider vinegar
- ¼ cup butter, cubed
- ¼ cup whiskey or apple cider
- ¼ cup maple syrup
- ½ teaspoon dried thyme
- ½ teaspoon kosher salt
- ¼ teaspoon pepper
- 1⅓ cups water

1. Place all ingredients in a large nonstick skillet; bring to a boil. Reduce heat to medium-low; cook, covered, until onions are tender, 6-8 minutes.

2. Increase heat to medium-high; cook, uncovered, until the liquid is almost evaporated and onions are glazed, 10-12 minutes, stirring occasionally. Remove from heat.

Per ¼ cup: 100 cal., 5g fat (3g sat. fat), 12mg chol., 147mg sodium, 13g carb. (9g sugars, 1g fiber), 1g pro.

BLACKBERRY COBBLER

In summer, blackberries abound in fields and along country roads around here. It's fun to pick them, especially when we know this dessert will be the result.
—Tina Hankins, Laconia, NH

Prep: 10 min. • **Bake:** 45 min.
Makes: 8 servings

- ¼ cup butter, softened
- ½ cup sugar
- 1 cup all-purpose flour
- 2 teaspoons baking powder
- ½ cup milk
- 2 cups fresh or frozen blackberries
- ¾ cup unsweetened apple juice
  Ice cream or whipped cream, optional

1. In a small bowl, cream butter and sugar until light and fluffy. Combine flour and baking powder; add to creamed mixture alternately with milk just until moistened.

2. Pour into a greased 1½-qt. baking pan. Sprinkle with blackberries. Pour juice over all. Bake at 350° for 45-50 minutes or until golden brown. Serve warm; top with ice cream or cream if desired.

Per serving: 197 cal., 6g fat (4g sat. fat), 17mg chol., 169mg sodium, 33g carb. (19g sugars, 2g fiber), 2g pro.

BUTTERY WHISKEY-GLAZED PEARL ONIONS

Potlucks & Parties

Dazzle the hungry crowd at your next event with these simple party favorites. From snacks and sandwiches to sides and sweets, this chapter has all your potluck needs covered.

EAT SMART
SHRIMP GAZPACHO

Here's a refreshing take on the classic chilled tomato soup. Our twist features shrimp, lime and plenty of avocado.
—*Taste of Home* Test Kitchen

Prep: 15 min. + chilling
Makes: 12 servings (about 3 quarts)

- 6 cups spicy hot V8 juice
- 2 cups cold water
- ½ cup lime juice
- ½ cup minced fresh cilantro
- ½ teaspoon salt
- ¼ to ½ teaspoon hot pepper sauce
- 1 pound peeled and deveined cooked shrimp (31-40 per pound), tails removed
- 1 medium cucumber, seeded and diced
- 2 medium tomatoes, seeded and chopped
- 2 medium ripe avocados, peeled and chopped

In a large nonreactive bowl, mix first six ingredients. Gently stir in the remaining ingredients. Refrigerate, covered, 1 hour before serving.

Note: This recipe is best served the same day it's made.

Per cup: 112 cal., 4g fat (1g sat. fat), 57mg chol., 399mg sodium, 9g carb. (5g sugars, 3g fiber), 10g pro.
Diabetic Exchanges: 1 lean meat, 2 vegetable, 1 fat.

ROOT BEER BRATS

SLOW COOKER 🍲
ROOT BEER BRATS

Here's an easy recipe that's versatile, too. Serve the saucy brats over rice for one meal and have them on buns the next. For extra punch, add a splash of root beer concentrate to the sauce.
—Pamela Thompson, Girard, IL

Prep: 15 min. • **Cook:** 6 hours
Makes: 10 servings

- 1 can (12 ounces) root beer
- 3 tablespoons cornstarch
- 3 teaspoons ground mustard
- 3 teaspoons caraway seeds
- 10 uncooked bratwurst links
- 1 large onion, coarsely chopped
- 1 bottle (12 ounces) chili sauce
- 10 hoagie buns, toasted
  Thinly sliced red onion, optional
  Prepared mustard, optional

1. Whisk first four ingredients until blended. In a large nonstick skillet, brown the bratwursts over medium-high heat. Transfer to a 4- or 5-qt. slow cooker. Add onion, chili sauce and root beer mixture.
2. Cook, covered, on low 6-8 hours (a thermometer inserted in sausage should read at least 160°). Serve in buns. If desired, top with onion and mustard.
Per serving: 563 cal., 30g fat (10g sat. fat), 63mg chol., 1575mg sodium, 54g carb. (16g sugars, 2g fiber), 20g pro.

CAMPERS' COLESLAW

Crispy and crunchy, this no-fuss slaw makes a refreshing side dish for picnics and parties. It's an old family recipe.

—Kimberly Wallace, Dennison, OH

Prep: 15 min. + chilling
Cook: 5 min.
Makes: 12 servings (¾ cup each)

- 1½ cups sugar
- ¾ cup white vinegar
- ¾ cup olive oil
- 1 tablespoon salt
- 1 teaspoon celery seed
- 1 medium head cabbage, shredded (about 10 cups)
- 1 large onion, chopped
- 1 medium green pepper, chopped

1. In a small saucepan, combine first five ingredients. Bring to a boil; cook and stir until sugar is dissolved, 1-2 minutes. Remove from heat; cool completely.
2. In a large bowl, toss vegetables with dressing. Refrigerate, covered, until cold. Serve with a slotted spoon.

Per ¾ cup: 122 cal., 6g fat (1g sat. fat), 0 chol., 274mg sodium, 17g carb. (14g sugars, 2g fiber), 1g pro.

Crunchy Coleslaw: To the cabbage mixture, stir in 2 julienned medium Honeycrisp apples and 1 shredded large carrot. Sprinkle ½ cup coarsely chopped peanuts over the top.

CHOCOLATE MALT CRISPY BARS

This chunky, chewy square is a feast for your eyes. Malted milk flavor is loaded in the crispy bars from top to bottom.

—*Taste of Home* Test Kitchen

Start to Finish: 25 min.
Makes: 2 dozen

- 4 cups malted milk balls, divided
- 1 package (10 ounces) large marshmallows
- 3 tablespoons butter
- 5 cups crisp rice cereal
- 1 cup malted milk powder, divided
- 2 cups (12 ounces) semisweet chocolate chips

SLOW COOKER SRIRACHA CORN

1. Chop 1 cup malted milk balls; set aside. In a Dutch oven, combine marshmallows and butter. Cook and stir over medium-low heat until melted. Remove from the heat; stir in the cereal, ¾ cup malt powder and chopped candy. Press into a greased 13x9-in. pan.
2. In a microwave-safe bowl, melt the chocolate chips; stir until smooth. Stir in the remaining malt powder. Spread over cereal bars. Sprinkle with the remaining malted milk balls; press into chocolate. Let stand until set. Using a serrated knife, cut into squares.

Per bar: 256 cal., 10g fat (6g sat. fat), 7mg chol., 118mg sodium, 42g carb. (29g sugars, 1g fiber), 3g pro.

SLOW COOKER SRIRACHA CORN

A restaurant here had been advertising Sriracha corn on the cob, but I knew I could make my own. The golden ears turned out a little sweet, a little smoky and a little hot—perfect, if you ask my three teenage boys!

—Julie Peterson, Crofton, MD

Prep: 15 min. • **Cook:** 3 hours
Makes: 8 servings

- ½ cup butter, softened
- 2 tablespoons honey
- 1 tablespoon Sriracha Asian hot chili sauce
- 1 teaspoon smoked paprika
- ½ teaspoon kosher salt
- 8 small ears sweet corn, husks removed
- ¼ cup water
  Additional smoked paprika, optional

1. Mix first five ingredients. Place each ear of corn on a 12x12-in. piece of heavy-duty foil; spread with 1 tablespoon butter mixture. Wrap foil around corn, sealing tightly. Place in a 6-qt. slow cooker.
2. Add water; cook, covered, on low until corn is tender, for 3-4 hours. If desired, sprinkle the corn with additional paprika before serving.

Per ear of corn: 209 cal., 13g fat (8g sat. fat), 31mg chol., 287mg sodium, 24g carb. (11g sugars, 2g fiber), 4g pro.

✱

TEST KITCHEN TIP
Smoked paprika's rich, smoky and slightly sweet flavor adds complexity to dishes. The spice is especially good in lentil and bean soups and vegetable recipes, where it lends a robust, meaty flavor. You can also use it in recipes that call for ground chipotle pepper. Just add cayenne or chili powder to boost the heat if desired.

POPCORN

In a world where plain popcorn just isn't enough, we revamp movie night with tropical adventure, Italian drama and a love affair with peanut butter.

1

9

3

8

6

4

1 **Island Breeze:** Combine ⅓ cup softened butter, 2 teaspoons curry powder and 1 teaspoon sugar. Put it in the microwave to melt the butter. Drizzle over 3½ quarts of popcorn and toss. Sprinkle with toasted coconut, almonds, raisins and salt. Yum!
—Peggy Woodward, Food Editor

2 I like to mix up olive oil, Sriracha, maple syrup and a little kosher salt and toss it with popcorn. Spicy, sweet, salty!
—James Schend, Food Editor

3 **Peanut Butter Lovers:** Add 1 cup each sugar and honey to a saucepan. Stir while it comes to a boil over medium heat, and for 5 minutes while it boils. Off the heat, stir in 1 cup of peanut butter. Toss with 3½ quarts of popcorn. Spread it on waxed paper to cool. Top with M&M's and pretzels.
—Ellie Martin Cliffe, Senior Editor

4 **Party Time:** Mix ¼ cup grated Parmesan, 2 tablespoons ranch salad dressing mix, 1 teaspoon dried parsley and ¼ teaspoon onion powder. Melt ⅓ cup butter; drizzle over 3½ quarts popcorn. Toss with the Parmesan cheese blend. It's divine.
—Dana Meredith, Associate Editor

5 My favorite is Lawry's Seasoned Salt with some roasted peanuts.
—Sarah Farmer, Culinary Director

6 **Frosty Peppermint:** Combine 3½ quarts popcorn and ⅓ cup crushed peppermints. Melt ½ pound white candy coating; drizzle it over popcorn-candy mixture and toss. Cool on waxed paper, then break it up.
—Rachel Seis, Associate Editor

7 I'm happy with lots of real butter and salt.
—Susan Stetzel
Field Editor and Community Moderator

8 **Sesame-Ginger:** Melt ¼ cup butter; stir in ½ teaspoon sesame oil, a splash of soy sauce and a pinch of ginger. Drizzle over 3½ quarts popcorn and toss. Add wasabi pea-rice cracker mix and honey-roasted peanuts.
—Ellie Piper, Copy Editor

9 **Italian Cheese:** Mix 6 tablespoons grated Romano cheese, 2¼ teaspoons Italian seasoning and ¾ teaspoon garlic salt. Melt ⅓ cup butter; drizzle it over 3½ quarts popcorn and toss. Sprinkle on the Romano cheese mixture, toss and eat.
—Kristen Stecklein, Art Director

10 Being a Maryland native, I add a sprinkle of Old Bay seasoning. It gives popcorn a simple, savory kick. Sometimes I'm bold enough to bring a box of the stuff to the movie theater!
—Nicole Doster, Associate Digital Editor

11 My kids and I mix our popcorn with plain and peanut M&M's. Gotta say, this was a staple for us long before it was considered cool and started showing up on movie theater menus.
—Edwin Robles Jr.
Associate Creative Director

12 I love super savory popcorn loaded with grated Parmesan, garlicky butter and freshly ground black pepper.
—Bethany Van Jacobson, Lead Prep Cook

Beaches & Cream

Skip the glass; keep the umbrella. This pina colada dip is deliciously dunkable for the whole family.

Whisk 1¼ cups milk, ¾ cup pineapple yogurt and 1 package coconut pudding mix for about 2 minutes, then fold in a carton of whipped topping!

AUSSIE SAUSAGE ROLLS

EAT SMART FAST FIX ▶

SPRING ASPARAGUS

This fresh and colorful side dish is delicious served warm or cold. I get lots of compliments on the homemade dressing.
—Millie Vickery, Lena, IL

Start to Finish: 25 min.
Makes: 8 servings

- 1½ pounds fresh asparagus, trimmed and cut into 2-inch pieces
- 2 small tomatoes, cut into wedges
- 3 tablespoons cider vinegar
- ¾ teaspoon Worcestershire sauce
- ⅓ cup sugar
- 1 tablespoon grated onion
- ½ teaspoon salt
- ½ teaspoon paprika
- ⅓ cup canola oil
- ¼ cup sliced almonds, toasted
- ⅓ cup crumbled blue cheese, optional

1. In a large saucepan, bring 1 cup water to a boil. Add asparagus; cook, covered, until crisp-tender, 3-5 minutes. Drain; place in a large bowl. Add tomatoes; cover and keep warm.
2. Place vinegar, Worcestershire sauce, sugar, onion, salt and paprika in a blender; cover and process until smooth. While processing, gradually add oil in a steady stream. Toss with asparagus mixture. Top with almonds and, if desired, cheese.
Note: To toast nuts, bake in a shallow pan in a 350° oven for 5-10 minutes or cook in a skillet over low heat until nuts are lightly browned, stirring occasionally.
Per ¾ cup: 154 cal., 11g fat (1g sat. fat), 0 chol., 159mg sodium, 12g carb. (10g sugars, 1g fiber), 2g pro.
Diabetic Exchanges: 2 fat, 1 vegetable, ½ starch.

DID YOU KNOW?

Replacing saturated fats in the diet with unsaturated fats can have a positive impact on health, including improving your blood cholesterol levels. Canola oil and olive oil are both high in monounsaturated fat (and low in saturated fat). So you can use either oil in this recipe for great taste and good health!

AUSSIE SAUSAGE ROLLS

I was born and raised in Australia but moved to the U.S. when I married my husband. When I long for a taste of my homeland, I bake up a batch of these cute little sausage rolls and share them with my neighbors or co-workers.
—Melissa Landon, Port Charlotte, FL

Prep: 30 min. • **Bake:** 20 min.
MAKES: 3 dozen

- 1 medium onion, finely chopped
- 2 tablespoons minced fresh chives or 2 teaspoons dried chives
- 2 teaspoons minced fresh basil or ½ teaspoon dried basil
- 2 garlic cloves, minced
- ½ teaspoon salt
- ¼ teaspoon pepper
- 1 teaspoon paprika, divided
- 1¼ pounds bulk pork sausage
- 1 package (17.3 ounces) frozen puff pastry, thawed

1. Preheat oven to 350°. Combine first six ingredients and ¾ teaspoon paprika. Add sausage; mix lightly but thoroughly.
2. On a lightly floured surface, roll each pastry sheet into an 11x10½-in. rectangle. Cut lengthwise into three strips. Spread ½ cup sausage mixture lengthwise down the center of each strip. Fold over sides, pinching edges to seal. Cut each log into six pieces.
3. Place on a rack in a 15x10x1-in. pan, seam side down. Sprinkle with remaining paprika. Bake until golden brown and sausage is no longer pink, 20-25 minutes.
Per appetizer: 116 cal., 8g fat (2g sat. fat), 11mg chol., 198mg sodium, 8g carb. (0 sugars, 1g fiber), 3g pro.

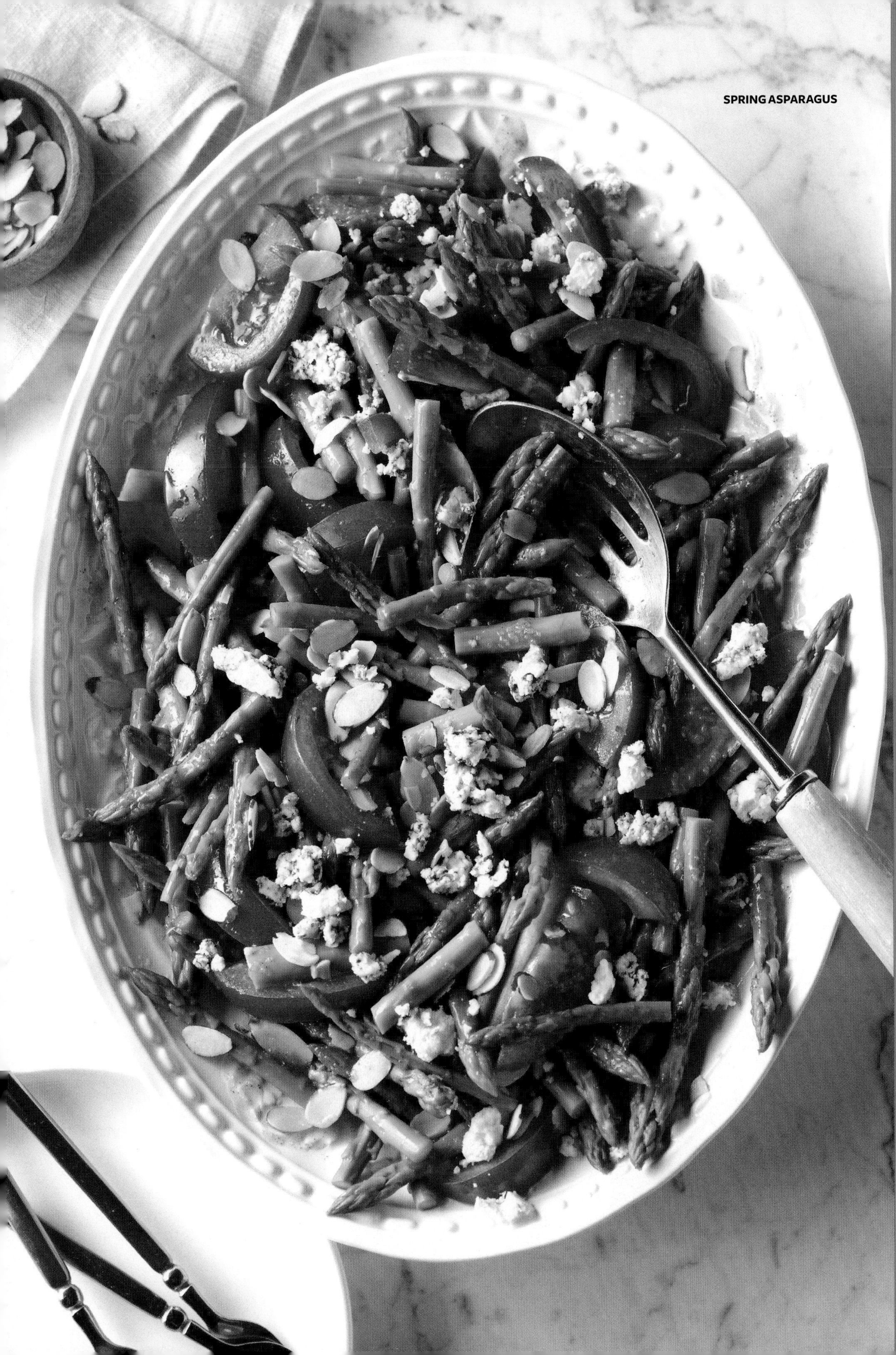

FAST FIX

PINA COLADA FRUIT SALAD

Give friends a taste of the tropics on warm summer days with this refreshing fruit blend. For a little extra punch, you might add a splash of coconut rum.
—Carol Farnsworth, Greenwood, IN

Start to Finish: 15 min.
Makes: 8 servings

- 1 can (10 ounces) frozen non-alcoholic pina colada mix, thawed
- ½ cup sugar
- ½ cup pineapple-orange juice
- ⅛ teaspoon almond extract
- ⅛ teaspoon coconut extract
- 1½ cups green grapes
- 1½ cups seedless red grapes
- 1½ cups fresh blueberries
- 1½ cups halved fresh strawberries
- 1 can (8 ounces) pineapple chunks, drained
- ½ cup fresh raspberries
  Thinly sliced fresh mint, optional

1. For dressing, mix first five ingredients until sugar is dissolved. Place fruit in a large bowl; toss gently with dressing.
2. Refrigerate, covered, until serving. If desired, top with mint.

Per ¾ cup: 225 cal., 2g fat (1g sat. fat), 0 chol., 17mg sodium, 53g carb. (49g sugars, 2g fiber), 1g pro.

SWEET & TART LEMON JELL-O

SWEET & TART LEMON JELL-O

With its sunny lemon color, this gelatin mold brightens up any table. I usually make two molds for parties because it disappears so quickly.
—Patricia Ryzow, Thousand Oaks, CA

Prep: 15 min. + chilling • **Cook:** 5 min.
Makes: 12 servings

- 1 envelope unflavored gelatin
- 1 cup cold water
- 2 cups boiling water
- 2 packages (3 ounces each) lemon gelatin
- 1 can (12 ounces) frozen limeade concentrate, thawed
- 2 cups heavy whipping cream
- 3 tablespoons confectioners' sugar
  Quartered fresh strawberries and fresh mint

1. In a small saucepan, sprinkle unflavored gelatin over cold water; let stand 1 minute. Heat and stir over low heat until gelatin is completely dissolved. Remove from heat.
2. In a large bowl, add boiling water to lemon gelatin; stir 2 minutes to completely dissolve. Stir in unflavored gelatin mixture and limeade concentrate. Refrigerate until slightly thickened.
3. In a bowl, beat cream until it begins to thicken. Add confectioners' sugar; beat until soft peaks form. Beat gelatin mixture until frothy; fold in whipped cream. Transfer to an 8-cup ring mold coated with cooking spray. Chill, covered, until set.
4. To serve, unmold onto a large plate. Serve with strawberries and mint.

Per slice: 252 cal., 15g fat (9g sat. fat), 45mg chol., 46mg sodium, 29g carb. (28g sugars, 0 fiber), 3g pro.

HEALTH TIP Sub 4 cups whipped topping for whipped cream to save 75 calories and 10g fat per serving.

SWEET GINGERED CHICKEN WINGS

When I prepare this recipe for a get-together, it's one of the first dishes to be snapped up. I first tasted the delicious chicken wings over a decade ago while attending a class on cooking with honey. Now I even serve the chicken as a main course.

—Debbie Dougal, Roseville, CA

Prep: 10 min. • **Bake:** 1 hour
Makes: 2 dozen

- 1 cup all-purpose flour
- 2 teaspoons salt
- 2 teaspoons paprika
- ¼ teaspoon pepper
- 24 chicken wings (about 5 pounds)

SAUCE
- ¼ cup honey
- ¼ cup thawed orange juice concentrate
- ½ teaspoon ground ginger
  Minced fresh parsley, optional

1. Preheat oven to 350°. Line two baking sheets with foil; coat with cooking spray.

2. In a large resealable plastic bag, combine flour, salt, paprika and pepper. Add chicken wings a few at a time; seal bag and toss to coat. Divide wings between prepared pans. Bake 30 minutes.

3. In a small bowl, combine honey, orange juice concentrate and ginger; brush over chicken wings. Bake 25-30 minutes or until juices run clear.

4. Preheat broiler. Broil wings 4 in. from heat 1-2 minutes or until lightly browned. If desired, sprinkle with parsley.

Per chicken wing: 134 cal., 7g fat (2g sat. fat), 29mg chol., 225mg sodium, 8g carb. (4g sugars, 0 fiber), 10g pro.

---

⑤INGREDIENTS FAST FIX
APRICOT-GLAZED BACON SPIRALS

PICTURED ON P. 241

Here's a real crowd-pleaser for an appetizer table or brunch buffet. Each spiral boasts a whole piece of crispy bacon, which contrasts with apricot preserves for a sweet-and-salty treat.

—Kellie Mulleavy, Lambertville, MI

Start to Finish: 25 min.
Makes: 15 servings

- 1 tablespoon butter
- ½ cup finely chopped onion
- 3 tablespoons apricot preserves
- 1 tube (8 ounces) refrigerated crescent rolls
- 1 package (2.1 ounces) ready-to-serve fully cooked bacon

1. Preheat oven to 375°. In a small skillet, heat butter over medium heat. Add onion; cook and stir 3-5 minutes or until tender. Reduce heat to low; add preserves. Cook and stir until melted.

2. Unroll crescent dough into one long rectangle. Roll into a 15x9-in. rectangle, sealing seams and perforations. Cut crosswise into fifteen 1-in. strips; top each with one piece of bacon. Roll up jelly-roll style, starting with a short side; pinch seam to seal. Place on an ungreased baking sheet, cut side down.

3. Spoon apricot mixture over each spiral. Bake 12-15 minutes or until golden brown. Let stand 5 minutes before serving. Refrigerate leftovers.

Per piece: 97 cal., 5g fat (2g sat. fat), 2mg chol., 185mg sodium, 9g carb. (3g sugars, 0 fiber), 3g pro.

SWEET GINGERED CHICKEN WINGS

SLOW COOKER 🍲
HOT PINEAPPLE HAM SANDWICHES
PICTURED ON P. 241

Your trusty slow cooker lets you make these gooey sandwiches without heating up your house on a hot day. The mustard and brown sugar give them a richness just about everybody loves.
—Nancy Foust, Stoneboro, PA

Prep: 25 min. • **Cook:** 3 hours
Makes: 10 servings

- 2 cans (20 ounces each) unsweetened crushed pineapple, undrained
- 1 medium onion, finely chopped
- ¾ cup packed light brown sugar
- ¼ cup Dijon mustard
- 2½ pounds thinly sliced deli ham
- 2 tablespoons cornstarch
- 2 tablespoons water
- 10 slices Swiss or cheddar cheese, optional
- 10 kaiser rolls, split

1. Mix first four ingredients. Place half of the mixture in a 5-qt. slow cooker; top with half of the ham. Repeat layers. Cook, covered, on low until heated through, 3-4 hours.

2. Using tongs, remove ham from slow cooker, leaving pineapple mixture behind; keep warm. In a large saucepan, mix cornstarch and water until smooth. Stir in pineapple mixture; bring to a boil. Reduce heat; simmer, uncovered, until mixture is slightly thickened, stirring occasionally. Serve the ham, pineapple mixture and, if desired, cheese on rolls.

Per sandwich: 468 cal., 8g fat (2g sat. fat), 60mg chol., 1540mg sodium, 69g carb. (36g sugars, 2g fiber), 29g pro.

✳
TEST KITCHEN TIP
Unless the recipe says you should stir or add ingredients, do not lift the lid while the slow cooker is operating. Every time you lift the lid, steam escapes, and you add to the cooking time.

KHMER PICKLED
VEGETABLE SALAD

KHMER PICKLED VEGETABLE SALAD

I grew up as a missionary kid in Cambodia, and most of my favorite foods have a Southeast Asian flair. Locals love eating this pickled salad for breakfast, but I like it for lunch or dinner as a side dish to satay chicken.
—Hannah Heavener, Belton, TX

Prep: 25 min. + chilling • **Cook:** 5 min.
Makes: 16 servings (¾ cup each)

- 2 medium daikon radishes (about 1¼ pounds each), peeled and thinly sliced
- 4 cups shredded cabbage (about ½ small)
- 1 large cucumber, thinly sliced
- 2 medium carrots, thinly sliced
- 1 cup cut fresh green beans (2 inch)
- ½ medium red onion, thinly sliced
- 1 piece fresh gingerroot (1 inch), thinly sliced
- 2 Thai chili or serrano peppers, halved lengthwise and seeded if desired
- 2 cups rice vinegar
- ¾ cup sugar
- 2 teaspoons salt
- 2 tablespoons chopped fresh cilantro

1. Place first eight ingredients in a large nonreactive bowl. Place vinegar, sugar and salt in a 2-cup or larger glass measure; microwave until warm, 2-3 minutes. Stir until sugar is dissolved. Stir dressing into vegetables. Refrigerate, covered, at least 1 hour before serving.

2. To serve, sprinkle with cilantro. Serve with a slotted spoon.

Per ¾ cup: 99 cal., 0 fat (0 sat. fat), 0 chol., 794mg sodium, 25g carb. (22g sugars, 2g fiber), 1g pro.

SHRIMP PASTA SALAD

PICTURED ON P. 241

I adore shrimp, so discovering it in this pasta salad recipe was a real treat for me. The lemon-dill sauce is light and bright.

—Traci Wynne, Denver, PA

Prep: 15 min. + chilling • **Cook:** 15 min.
Makes: 10 servings

- 8 ounces uncooked small pasta shells (about 2⅔ cups)
- 1 pound peeled and deveined cooked shrimp, chopped
- 1 cup frozen peas
- 4 green onions, chopped
- ¼ cup minced fresh parsley
- 1 cup mayonnaise
- 1 cup (8 ounces) plain yogurt
- ¼ cup lemon juice
- 2 tablespoons snipped fresh dill
- ½ teaspoon salt
- ¼ teaspoon white pepper

1. Cook pasta according to package directions. Drain, rinse with cold water; drain again.

2. In a large bowl, combine pasta, shrimp, peas, green onions and parsley. Mix remaining ingredients; stir into pasta mixture. Refrigerate, covered, at least 2 hours.

Per ¾ cup: 306 cal., 18g fat (3g sat. fat), 74mg chol., 326mg sodium, 21g carb. (3g sugars, 2g fiber), 14g pro.

FREEZE IT

THREE-BEAN BAKED BEANS

I got this recipe from an aunt and made a couple of changes to suit our tastes. With ground beef and bacon mixed in, these satisfying beans are a big hit at backyard barbecues and church picnics.

—Julie Currington, Gahanna, OH

Prep: 20 min. • **Bake:** 1 hour
Makes: 12 servings (¾ cup each)

- ½ pound ground beef
- 5 bacon strips, diced
- ½ cup chopped onion
- ⅓ cup packed brown sugar
- ¼ cup sugar
- ¼ cup ketchup
- ¼ cup barbecue sauce
- 2 tablespoons molasses
- 2 tablespoons prepared mustard
- ½ teaspoon chili powder
- ½ teaspoon salt
- 2 cans (16 ounces each) pork and beans, undrained
- 1 can (16 ounces) butter beans, rinsed and drained
- 1 can (16 ounces) kidney beans, rinsed and drained

1. Preheat oven to 350°. In a large skillet, cook and crumble beef with bacon and onion over medium heat until no longer pink; drain.

2. Stir in sugars, ketchup, barbecue sauce, molasses, mustard, chili powder and salt until blended. Stir in beans. Transfer to a greased 2½-qt. baking dish. Bake, covered, until beans reach desired thickness, about 1 hour.

Freeze option: Freeze cooled bean mixture in freezer containers. To use, partially thaw in refrigerator overnight. Heat through in a saucepan, stirring occasionally and adding a little water if necessary.

Per ¾ cup: 269 cal., 8g fat (2g sat. fat), 19mg chol., 708mg sodium, 42g carb. (21g sugars, 7g fiber), 13g pro.

THREE-BEAN BAKED BEANS

DILLY POTATO & EGG SALAD

Everyone has a favorite potato salad, and this is mine. As a young bride 36 years ago, I was eager to learn how to cook and make things that my husband would love. I combined my mom's and his mom's recipes, and this is the delicious result.
—Angela Leinenbach, Mechanicsville, VA

Prep: 20 min. + chilling
Cook: 20 min. + cooling
Makes: 12 servings (¾ cup each)

- 4 pounds medium red potatoes (about 14), peeled and halved
- 5 hard-boiled large eggs
- 1 cup chopped dill pickles
- 1 small onion, chopped
- 1½ cups mayonnaise
- 1 teaspoon celery seed
- ½ teaspoon salt
- ¼ teaspoon pepper
- Paprika

1. Place potatoes in a large saucepan; add water to cover. Bring to a boil. Reduce heat; cook, uncovered, until tender, about 15-20 minutes. Drain; cool completely.
2. Cut potatoes into ¾-in. cubes; place in a large bowl. Peel and chop four eggs; peel and slice remaining egg. Add chopped eggs, pickles and onion to potatoes. Mix mayonnaise, celery seed, salt and pepper; stir gently into potato mixture.

VEGGIE MACARONI & CHEESE

3. Sprinkle with paprika; top with sliced egg. Refrigerate, covered, at least 2 hours before serving.
Per ¾ cup: 326 cal., 22g fat (4g sat. fat), 80mg chol., 413mg sodium, 25g carb. (2g sugars, 3g fiber), 6g pro.

VEGGIE MACARONI & CHEESE

This creamy mac 'n' cheese definitely doesn't come from a box! Fresh veggies add crunch and color and will leave everyone saying, "More, please!"
—Marsha Morril, Harrisburg, OR

Prep: 30 min. • **Bake:** 15 min.
Makes: 12 servings

- 1½ cups uncooked elbow macaroni
- 3 cups fresh broccoli florets
- 2 cups fresh cauliflowerets
- 3 large carrots, halved and thinly sliced
- 2 celery ribs, sliced
- 1 tablespoon butter
- 1 medium onion, chopped
- ¼ cup all-purpose flour
- 1 cup 2% milk
- 1 cup chicken broth
- 3 cups shredded sharp cheddar cheese
- 1 tablespoon Dijon mustard
- ¼ teaspoon salt
- ⅛ teaspoon pepper
- ¼ teaspoon paprika

1. Preheat oven to 350°. In a 6-qt. stockpot, cook macaroni according to package directions, adding broccoli, cauliflower, carrots and celery during the last 6 minutes of cooking. Drain; transfer to a greased 13x9-in. baking dish.
2. Meanwhile, in a large saucepan, heat butter over medium-high heat; saute onion until tender. Stir in the flour until blended. Gradually stir in milk and broth; bring to a boil. Cook and stir sauce until thickened, about 2 minutes; stir in cheese, mustard, salt and pepper.
3. Add to macaroni mixture, stirring to coat; sprinkle with paprika. Bake macaroni, uncovered, until heated through, 15-20 minutes.
Per cup: 200 cal., 11g fat (6g sat. fat), 33mg chol., 391mg sodium, 15g carb. (3g sugars, 2g fiber), 10g pro.

⑤INGREDIENTS
FONTINA ASPARAGUS TART
PICTURED ON P. 241

This lemony tart is loaded with fontina cheese and fresh asparagus. It's a snap to make but looks really impressive. Be advised: your guests will be vying for the last tasty slice.
—Heidi Meek, Grand Rapids, MI

Prep: 15 min. • **Bake:** 20 min.
Makes: 16 servings

- 1 pound fresh asparagus, trimmed
- 1 sheet frozen puff pastry, thawed
- 2 cups shredded fontina cheese
- 1 teaspoon grated lemon peel
- 2 tablespoons lemon juice
- 1 tablespoon olive oil
- ¼ teaspoon salt
- ¼ teaspoon pepper

1. Preheat oven to 400°. In a large skillet, bring 1 in. of water to a boil; add the asparagus. Cook, covered, until crisp-tender, 3-5 minutes. Drain and pat dry.
2. On a lightly floured surface, roll pastry sheet into a 16x12-in. rectangle. Transfer to a parchment paper-lined large baking sheet. Bake until golden brown, about 10 minutes.
3. Sprinkle 1½ cups cheese over pastry to within ½-in. of edges. Place asparagus over top; sprinkle with the remaining cheese. Mix remaining ingredients; drizzle over top. Bake tart until the cheese is melted, 10-15 minutes. Serve warm.
Per piece: 142 cal., 9g fat (4g sat. fat), 16mg chol., 202mg sodium, 10g carb. (1g sugars, 1g fiber), 5g pro.

12-HOUR SALAD
PICTURED ON P. 241

This recipe was Mom's scrumptious scheme to get her kids to eat vegetables. She never had any trouble when she served this colorful, crunchy salad.
—Dorothy Bowen, Thomasville, NC

Prep: 20 min. + chilling
Makes: 12 servings

- 8 cups torn mixed salad greens
- 1½ cups chopped celery
- 2 medium green peppers, chopped
- 1 medium red onion, chopped

SWEET ITALIAN HOLIDAY BREAD

- 2½ cups frozen peas (about 10 ounces), thawed
- 1 cup mayonnaise
- 1 cup (8 ounces) sour cream
- 3 tablespoons sugar
- 1 cup shredded cheddar cheese
- ½ pound bacon strips, cooked and crumbled

1. Place greens in a 3-qt. bowl or 13x9-in. dish. Layer with the celery, peppers, onion and peas.
2. Mix mayonnaise, sour cream and sugar; spread over top. Sprinkle with cheese and bacon. Refrigerate the salad, covered, for 12 hours or overnight.
Per cup: 280 cal., 23g fat (7g sat. fat), 22mg chol., 347mg sodium, 11g carb. (6g sugars, 3g fiber), 8g pro.

SWEET ITALIAN HOLIDAY BREAD

This is authentic ciambellotto, *a sweet loaf my great-grandmother used to bake in Italy. I still use her traditional recipe—the only update I made was for modern appliances.*
—Denise Perrin, Vancouver, WA

Prep: 15 min. • **Bake:** 45 min.
Makes: 1 loaf (20 slices)

- 4 cups all-purpose flour
- 1 cup sugar
- 2 tablespoons grated orange peel
- 3 teaspoons baking powder
- 3 large eggs
- ½ cup 2% milk
- ½ cup olive oil
- 1 large egg yolk
- 1 tablespoon coarse sugar

1. Preheat oven to 350°. In a large bowl, whisk flour, sugar, orange peel and baking powder. In another bowl, whisk eggs, milk and oil until blended. Add to flour mixture; stir just until moistened.
2. Shape into a 6-in. round loaf on a greased baking sheet. Brush top with egg yolk; sprinkle with coarse sugar. Bake for 45-50 minutes or until a toothpick inserted in the center comes out clean. Cover top loosely with foil during the last 10 minutes if needed to prevent bread from overbrowning. Remove from pan to a wire rack; serve warm.
Per slice: 197 cal., 7g fat (1g sat. fat), 38mg chol., 87mg sodium, 30g carb. (11g sugars, 1g fiber), 4g pro.

Holiday & Seasonal Pleasers

Find dozens of mouthwatering ways to celebrate in this big chapter. From St. Patrick's Day to your holiday-season open house, and from frosty Fourth of July treats to warm Christmas cookie-tray sweets, these dishes bring delight the whole year through.

St. Patrick's Day Traditional Dinner

Celebrate the wearing o' the green with old-time boiled corned beef & cabbage dinner, colcannon, soda bread and a spritely drink. Party punch not your style? Then treat your clan to homemade Irish cream (p. 272).

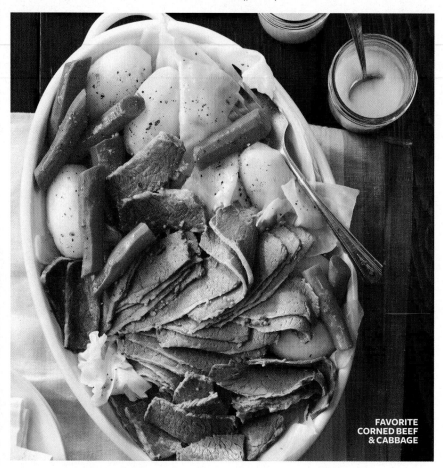

FAVORITE CORNED BEEF & CABBAGE

FAVORITE CORNED BEEF & CABBAGE

This Irish dish is classic comfort food, and it's simpler to make at home than you might think. We love it as an early springtime dinner.
—Evelyn Kenney, Trenton, NJ

Prep: 10 min. • **Cook:** 2¾ hours
Makes: 10 servings

- 1 corned beef brisket (about 4 pounds) with spice packet
- 2 tablespoons brown sugar
- 2 bay leaves
- 3½ pounds small potatoes (10-15), peeled
- 8 medium carrots, halved crosswise
- 1 medium head cabbage, cut into wedges

HORSERADISH SAUCE
- 3 tablespoons butter
- 2 tablespoons all-purpose flour
- 1 to 1½ cups reserved cooking juices from corned beef
- 1 tablespoon sugar
- 1 tablespoon cider vinegar
- ¼ cup horseradish

MUSTARD SAUCE (OPTIONAL)
- 1 cup (8 ounces) sour cream
- 2 tablespoons Dijon mustard
- ¼ teaspoon sugar

1. Place brisket, contents of seasoning packet, brown sugar and bay leaves in a large Dutch oven or stockpot; cover with water. Bring to a boil. Reduce heat; simmer, covered, 2 hours.

2. Add potatoes and carrots; return to a boil. Reduce heat; simmer, covered, just until beef and vegetables are tender, for 30-40 minutes. (If the pot is full, remove potatoes and carrots before adding the cabbage; reheat before serving.)

3. Add cabbage to pot; return to a boil. Reduce heat; simmer, covered, until cabbage is tender, about 15 minutes. Remove vegetables and corned beef; keep warm.

4. Strain and reserve 1½ cups cooking juices for horseradish sauce; skim fat from reserved juices. Discard remaining juices. Prepare sauces as desired.

5. Cut beef across the grain into slices. Serve with vegetables, horseradish sauce and, if desired, mustard sauce.

Horseradish Sauce: In a small saucepan, melt butter over medium heat; stir in flour until smooth. Gradually whisk in 1 cup reserved juices. Stir in sugar, vinegar and horseradish; bring to a boil, stirring constantly. Cook and stir until thickened. If desired, thin with additional juices. Season to taste with additional sugar, vinegar or horseradish.

Mustard Sauce: Mix all ingredients.

Per serving with horseradish sauce: 564 cal., 28g fat (10g sat. fat), 134mg chol., 1616mg sodium, 50g carb. (11g sugars, 8g fiber), 29g pro.

Sip Me, I'm Irish

Ladle St. Patrick's Day punch into glasses dressed in full leprechaun regalia. For belts, grab black ribbon and double-sided tape, plus rhinestone stickers for a wee bit o' bling.

✳ Beat 1 qt. softened lime sherbet, 1/2 cup thawed limeade concentrate and 2 Tbsp. sugar. Stir in 2 cans (12 oz. each) chilled lemon-lime soda and 1-2 cups crushed ice. Serves 6.

EAT SMART **FAST FIX ▸**

COLCANNON IRISH POTATOES

My mother came from Ireland as a teen and brought this traditional, homey recipe with her. If your family is reluctant to even try eating cooked cabbage like mine is, just serve it hidden in Grandma's irresistible mashed potatoes!
—Marie Pagel, Lena, WI

Start to Finish: 30 min.
Makes: 10 servings

- 2½ **pounds potatoes (about 6 medium), peeled and cut into 1-inch pieces**
- 2 **cups chopped cabbage**
- 1 **large onion, chopped**
- 1 **teaspoon salt**
- ¼ **teaspoon pepper**
- ¼ **cup butter, softened**
- 1 **cup 2% milk**

1. Place potatoes in a 6-qt. stockpot; add water to cover. Bring to a boil. Reduce heat to medium; cook, covered, until almost tender, 8-10 minutes.

2. Add the cabbage and onion; cook, covered, until cabbage is tender, 5-7 minutes. Drain; return to pot. Add salt and pepper; mash to desired consistency, gradually adding butter and milk.
Per ¾ cup: 129 cal., 5g fat (3g sat. fat), 14mg chol., 290mg sodium, 19g carb. (4g sugars, 2g fiber), 3g pro.
Diabetic Exchanges: 1 starch, 1 fat.

SLOW COOKER 🍲

GARLIC-DILL SODA BREAD
PICTURED ON P. 255

It's amazing how bread can be made in a slow cooker, which is why this recipe is so awesome— who knew it could be so simple! Let the inviting aroma of dill and cheese fill your kitchen.
—Melissa Hansen, Milwaukee, WI

Prep: 15 min. • **Cook:** 1½ hours
Makes: 1 loaf (12 wedges)

- 4 **cups all-purpose flour**
- 2 **tablespoons dried parsley flakes**
- 1 **tablespoon dried minced onion**
- 2 **teaspoons garlic powder**
- 1½ **teaspoons dill weed**
- 1 **teaspoon salt**
- 1 **teaspoon baking soda**
- 1 **teaspoon ground mustard**
- 1¾ **cups buttermilk**
- 1 **cup shredded sharp cheddar cheese**

1. In a large bowl, whisk the first eight ingredients. Add buttermilk and cheese; stir just until moistened. Turn onto a lightly floured surface; knead gently 6-8 times or just until dough comes together. Shape dough into a 6-in. round loaf. Using a sharp knife, score surface with 1-in. deep cuts in a crisscross pattern. Place in a greased 5-qt. slow cooker.

2. Cook, covered, on high 1½ to 2 hours or until a thermometer reads 190°-200°.

3. Preheat broiler. Remove bread; place on a baking sheet. Broil 6-8 in. from heat 2-3 minutes or until golden brown. Remove to a wire rack to cool completely.
Per wedge: 209 cal., 4g fat (2g sat. fat), 11mg chol., 434mg sodium, 35g carb. (2g sugars, 1g fiber), 8g pro.

Red, White & Cool!

Up the chill factor at your Fourth of July party with these festive and frosty treats straight from your icebox.

PATRIOTIC ICE CREAM CUPCAKES

PATRIOTIC ICE CREAM CUPCAKES

These frosty cupcakes are practically a fireworks display on their own. The little treats feature red velvet cake, blue moon ice cream, a creamy white topping and star-spangled sprinkles.
—*Taste of Home* Test Kitchen

Prep: 30 min. + freezing
Bake: 15 min. + cooling
MAKES: 3 dozen

    1 package red velvet cake mix (regular
       size)
    1½ quarts blue moon ice cream,
       softened if necessary
    1 jar (7 ounces) marshmallow creme
    3 cups heavy whipping cream
       Red, white and blue sprinkles

1. Preheat oven to 350°. Line 36 muffin cups with paper liners.

2. Prepare cake batter according to package directions. Fill prepared cups about one-third full. Bake until a toothpick inserted in the center comes out clean, 11-14 minutes. Cool cupcakes 10 minutes before removing from pans to wire racks; cool completely.

3. Working quickly, spread ice cream onto cupcakes. Freeze until firm, at least 1 hour.

4. Place marshmallow creme in a large bowl. Add whipping cream; beat until blended and stiff peaks form. Pipe or spread over cupcakes. Decorate with sprinkles. Serve immediately or freeze until firm.

Note: Blue moon ice cream may be substituted with vanilla ice cream tinted with blue food coloring.

Per cupcake: 220 cal., 13g fat (6g sat. fat), 46mg chol., 139mg sodium, 21g carb. (16g sugars, 0 fiber), 4g pro.

FAST FIX

EASY BERRY CHEESECAKE PARFAITS

These sweet little parfaits take everything that's good about cheesecake and make it way easier. You get the rich creaminess, graham cracker crunch and bright berry flavor all in a fun individual portion.
—*Taste of Home* Test Kitchen

Start to Finish: 15 min.
MAKES: 2 servings

    2 ounces cream cheese, softened
    ⅔ cup marshmallow creme
    ½ cup frozen whipped topping
    4 tablespoons graham cracker crumbs
    1 cup fresh raspberries
    1 cup fresh blueberries

1. Beat cream cheese and marshmallow creme until blended; fold in whipped topping.

2. Sprinkle 2 tablespoons cracker crumbs into each of two glasses or dessert dishes. Layer each with ½ cup cream cheese mixture, ¼ cup raspberries and ¼ cup blueberries; repeat layers. Refrigerate, covered, until serving.

Per parfait: 396 cal., 15g fat (9g sat. fat), 29mg chol., 174mg sodium, 54g carb. (39g sugars, 6g fiber), 4g pro.

STRAWBERRY WATERMELON SLUSH

We like to relax on the back porch after a long day in the sun with glasses of my slush. What could be more refreshing on a hot summer day?
—Patty Howse, Great Falls, MT

Start to Finish: 10 min.
Makes: 4 servings

- ⅓ cup lemon juice
- ⅓ cup sugar
- 2 cups cubed seedless watermelon
- 2 cups fresh strawberries, halved
- 2 cups ice cubes

Place first four ingredients in a blender; cover and process until smooth. Add ice; process, covered, until slushy. Serve immediately.

Per 1¼ cups: 112 cal., 0 fat (0 sat. fat), 0 chol., 4mg sodium, 30g carb. (27g sugars, 2g fiber), 1g pro.

PRETZEL JELL-O DESSERT

This is one of my mother's absolute favorite desserts. The salty pretzel crust is the perfect complement to the sweet cream cheese filling.
—Erin Frakes, Moline, IL

Prep: 30 min. + chilling
Makes: 12 servings

- 2 cups crushed pretzels
- ¾ cup butter, melted
- 2 tablespoons sugar

FILLING
- 1 package (8 ounces) cream cheese, softened
- 1 cup sugar
- 1 carton (8 ounces) frozen whipped topping, thawed

TOPPING
- 2 packages (3 ounces each) strawberry gelatin
- 2 cups boiling water
- ½ cup cold water
  Fresh strawberries and additional whipped topping, optional

1. Preheat oven to 350°. Mix crushed pretzels, melted butter and sugar; press onto bottom of an ungreased 13x9-in. baking dish. Bake 10 minutes. Cool crust completely.
2. For filling, beat cream cheese and sugar until smooth. Stir in whipped topping; spread over crust. Refrigerate, covered, until cold.
3. In a small bowl, dissolve gelatin in boiling water. Stir in cold water; refrigerate until partially set. Pour carefully over filling. Refrigerate, covered, until firm, 4-6 hours.
4. Cut into squares. If desired, serve dessert with strawberries and additional whipped topping.

Per piece: 401 cal., 22g fat (14g sat. fat), 50mg chol., 401mg sodium, 48g carb. (37g sugars, 1g fiber), 4g pro.

★ ★ ★ ★ ★ **READER REVIEW**

"Very easy to lighten up. I used fat-free cream cheese and sugar-free Jell-O. I didn't cut the butter in half this time, but next time I will. Very tasty and good for those with diabetes."

AVONLADY54555 TASTEOFHOME.COM

STRAWBERRY WATERMELON SLUSH

PATRIOTIC POPS

EAT SMART 🄯 **INGREDIENTS**

PATRIOTIC POPS

My kids love homemade ice pops, and I love knowing that the ones we make are good for them. We whip up a big batch with multiple flavors so they have many choices, but these patriotic red, white and blueberry ones are a favorite!
—Shannon Carino, Frisco, TX

Prep: 15 min. + freezing
Makes: 1 dozen

1¾ cups (about 14 ounces) vanilla yogurt, divided

2 tablespoons honey, divided
1¼ cups sliced fresh strawberries, divided
1¼ cups fresh or frozen blueberries, thawed, divided
12 freezer pop molds or 12 paper cups (3 ounces each) and wooden pop sticks

1. Place 2 tablespoons of yogurt, 1 tablespoon of honey and 1 cup strawberries in a blender; cover and process until blended. Remove to a small bowl. Chop remaining strawberries; stir into strawberry mixture.

2. In blender, process 2 tablespoons yogurt, remaining honey and 1 cup blueberries until blended; remove to another bowl. Stir in the remaining blueberries.

3. In each mold, layer 1 tablespoon strawberry mixture, 2 tablespoons yogurt and 1 tablespoon blueberry mixture. Top with holders. (If using paper cups, top with foil and insert sticks through the foil.) Freeze until firm.

Per pop: 55 cal., 1g fat (0 sat. fat), 2mg chol., 24mg sodium, 11g carb. (10g sugars, 1g fiber), 2g pro.
Diabetic Exchanges: 1 starch.

RED, WHITE & BLUEBERRY PIE

This is a wonderful light dessert for any summer get-together, festive and tasty.
—Kimberly Mason, Broken Arrow, OK

Prep: 20 min. + chilling
Makes: 8 servings

- 2 ounces white baking chocolate, melted
  One 9-inch graham cracker crust (about 6 ounces)
- ¾ cup sliced fresh strawberries
- 1 package (8 ounces) cream cheese, softened
- ¾ cup confectioners' sugar
- ¾ cup 2% milk
- 1 package (3.3 ounces) instant white chocolate pudding mix
- 1 cup whipped topping
- 8 fresh strawberries, halved lengthwise
- 1 cup fresh blueberries

1. Spread melted chocolate onto the bottom and sides of crust. Arrange sliced strawberries over chocolate.
2. In a bowl, beat cream cheese and confectioners' sugar until smooth; gradually beat in milk. Add pudding mix; beat on low speed until thickened, about 2 minutes. Spread the mixture over the strawberries.
3. Decorate pie with whipped topping, blueberries and halved strawberries. Refrigerate until serving.

Per piece: 383 cal., 19g fat (10g sat. fat), 30mg chol., 395mg sodium, 50g carb. (44g sugars, 1g fiber), 4g pro.

RED, WHITE
& BLUEBERRY PIE

---

(5) INGREDIENTS

FOURTH OF JULY ICE CREAM CAKE

This pretty layered dessert is actually super easy to prepare and keeps well in the freezer for days.
—Anne Scholovich, Waukesha, WI

Prep: 20 min. + freezing
Makes: 16 servings

- 1 prepared angel food cake (8 to 10 ounces)
- 2 quarts strawberry ice cream, softened if necessary
- 1 quart vanilla ice cream, softened if necessary
- 2½ cups heavy whipping cream
- 2 tablespoons confectioners' sugar

1. Cut cake horizontally into four equal layers. Place bottom layer on a serving plate; spread with half of the strawberry ice cream. Place in freezer.
2. Spread second cake layer with vanilla ice cream; place over strawberry layer in freezer. Spread third cake layer with remaining strawberry ice cream; place over vanilla layer in freezer. Top with remaining cake layer. Freeze until ice cream is firm.
3. Beat cream until it begins to thicken. Add confectioners' sugar; beat until stiff peaks form. Spread over top and sides of cake. Freeze until serving.

Per slice: 363 cal., 23g fat (14g sat. fat), 76mg chol., 182mg sodium, 36g carb. (9g sugars, 1g fiber), 5g pro.

Halloween Bites

Give 'em something good to eat, like spooky tomato soup, stuffed spider biscuits and pumpkin-head pizzas.

EYEBALL TACO SALAD

EYEBALL TACO SALAD

Topped with creepy peepers, this tasty taco salad is packed with ground beef, cheese, tomato and satisfying southwest flavor to make everyone in your freaky family happy.
—Jolene Young, Union, IL

Prep: 45 min. • **Bake:** 25 min.
Makes: 10 servings

- 2½ pounds lean ground beef (90% lean)
- 1 envelope taco seasoning
- 1 can (8 ounces) tomato sauce
- ¾ cup water
- 1 package (15½ ounces) nacho-flavored tortilla chips, crushed
- 2 cups shredded Monterey Jack cheese
- 2 cups shredded cheddar cheese
- 4 cups torn iceberg lettuce
- 1 medium red onion, finely chopped
- 10 slices tomato, halved
- 1 cup (8 ounces) sour cream
- 10 pitted ripe olives, halved

1. Preheat oven to 325°. In a 6-qt. stockpot, cook and crumble beef over medium-high heat until no longer pink, 7-9 minutes. Stir in seasoning, tomato sauce and water; bring to a boil. Reduce heat; simmer, uncovered, 15 minutes, stirring occasionally.
2. Spread chips evenly in a greased 15x10x1-in. baking pan; sprinkle with Jack cheese. Top with beef mixture; sprinkle with cheddar cheese. Bake until bubbly, 25-30 minutes.
3. Cut into ten 5x3-in. portions. Top each with lettuce and onion. Add tomatoes, sour cream and olives to make eyeballs.
Per serving: 569 cal., 35g fat (13g sat. fat), 99mg chol., 962mg sodium, 35g carb. (4g sugars, 3g fiber), 32g pro.

JACK-O'-LANTERN PIZZAS

Set out a variety of toppings and let the kids decorate their pumpkin-head pizzas. It will be so much fun they won't realize that they're eating their veggies!
—Rachel DeVault, Grove City, OH

Start to Finish: 30 min.
Makes: 1 dozen

- 1 pound ground beef
- ½ teaspoon salt
- ¼ teaspoon pepper
- 1 package (12 ounces) English muffins, split and toasted
- 1 jar (14 ounces) pizza sauce
- 2 cups shredded part-skim mozzarella cheese
  Sliced ripe olives
  Chopped and slivered sweet red, yellow and green peppers

1. Preheat oven to 425°. In a large skillet, cook and crumble beef over medium heat until no longer pink, 5-7 minutes; drain. Stir in salt and pepper.
2. Place muffins in 15x10x1-in. pans. Spread tops with pizza sauce; top with beef. Sprinkle with cheese.
3. Bake until cheese is melted, about 5 minutes. Add olives and peppers to make Jack-o'-lantern faces.
Per mini pizza: 216 cal., 9g fat (4g sat. fat), 35mg chol., 511mg sodium, 19g carb. (3g sugars, 1g fiber), 15g pro.

BAT WING SOUP

Start to Finish: 30 min.
Makes: 6 servings

- 2 tablespoons canola oil
- 4 garlic cloves, peeled
- 4 cans (14½ ounces each) stewed tomatoes, undrained
- ½ cup heavy whipping cream
- 6 slices bread
- 2 tablespoons butter, melted
- 2 teaspoons Italian seasoning
  Freshly ground pepper, optional

1. In a large saucepan, heat oil over medium heat; saute garlic until tender, but not browned. Stir in tomatoes. Puree soup using an immersion blender. Or puree in batches in a blender and return to pan.
2. Bring soup to a boil. Stir in cream; heat through over low heat. Keep warm.
3. Preheat oven to 400°. For the wings, flatten bread on a work surface using a rolling pin. Cut each slice diagonally in half; remove crusts. Using kitchen scissors, cut long sides to resemble bat wings. Place on an ungreased baking sheet.
4. Brush tops with butter; sprinkle with Italian seasoning. Bake until lightly toasted, 5-8 minutes, flipping once.
5. Serve soup with wings. If desired, sprinkle with pepper.

Per cup soup with 2 bat wings: 257 cal., 16g fat (7g sat. fat), 33mg chol., 589mg sodium, 27g carb. (15g sugars, 3g fiber), 4g pro.

> "This spooky tomato soup gets extra richness from a splash of cream. It's laced with garlic (to keep those vampires away!) and garnished with toasty bat wings."
>
> —RACHEL DEVAULT, GROVE CITY, OH

CREEPY-CRAWLY PASTA SALAD

A sweet-and-sour dressing tops off this easy pasta salad that's ghoulishly good for you!
—*Taste of Home* Test Kitchen

Prep: 15 min. + chilling • **Cook:** 15 min.
Makes: 12 servings (¾ cup each)

- 8 ounces uncooked fusilli or other spiral pasta
- 1 medium zucchini, julienned
- 1 cup fresh cauliflower florets
- 1 cup cherry tomatoes, halved
- 1 small green pepper, chopped
- ½ cup chopped red onion
- 1 cup colossal ripe olives, halved
- ¾ cup pimiento-stuffed olives

DRESSING
- ¼ cup ketchup
- 2 tablespoons sugar
- 2 tablespoons white vinegar
- 1 garlic clove, peeled
- 1 teaspoon paprika
- ¼ teaspoon salt
- ½ small onion, cut into wedges
- ¼ cup canola oil

1. Cook pasta according to the package directions. Drain; rinse with cold water and drain well. Transfer to a large bowl. Add vegetables and olives.

2. Place first seven dressing ingredients in a blender; cover and process until blended. While processing, gradually add oil in a steady stream; process until thickened. Add to salad; toss to coat. Refrigerate, covered, at least 2 hours before serving.

Per ¾ cup: 162 cal., 7g fat (1g sat. fat), 0 chol., 380mg sodium, 22g carb. (6g sugars, 2g fiber), 3g pro.
Diabetic Exchanges: 1½ starch, 1 fat.

(5) INGREDIENTS

CANDY CORN COOKIES

Get a head start on these buttery cookies by shaping and chilling the homemade dough ahead of time. When you're ready, just slice and bake the tricolor treats.
—*Taste of Home* Test Kitchen

Prep: 35 min. + chilling
Bake: 10 min./batch
Makes: about 5 dozen

- 1½ cups butter, softened
- 1½ cups sugar
- ½ teaspoon vanilla extract
- 3 cups all-purpose flour
- 1 teaspoon baking soda
- ½ teaspoon salt
  Yellow and orange paste food coloring

1. Cream butter and sugar until light and fluffy. Beat in vanilla. In another bowl, whisk together flour, baking soda and salt; gradually beat into creamed mixture.

2. Divide dough in half. Tint one portion yellow. Divide remaining dough into two-thirds and one-third portions. Color the larger portion orange; leave smaller portion plain.

3. Shape each portion of dough into two 8-in. logs. Flatten top and push sides in at a slight angle. Place orange logs on yellow logs; push sides in at a slight angle. Top with plain logs, forming a slightly rounded top. Wrap each in plastic; refrigerate until firm, about 4 hours.

4. Preheat oven to 350°. Unwrap and cut dough into ¼-in. slices. Place 2 in. apart on ungreased baking sheets.

5. Bake until set, 10-12 minutes. Remove from pans to wire racks to cool.

Per cookie: 83 cal., 5g fat (3g sat. fat), 12mg chol., 77mg sodium, 10g carb. (5g sugars, 0 fiber), 1g pro.

CANDY CORN COOKIES

GHOULISH CITRUS PUNCH

On Halloween, I give classic citrus punch an eye-catching twist with strategically splashed grenadine.
—Dianne Conway, London, ON

Prep: 10 min. + chilling
Makes: 8 servings (1 cup each)

- 2 cups pineapple juice
- 2 cups orange juice
- 1 cup white grapefruit juice
- 1 cup lemonade
- 2 cups chilled ginger ale
  Grenadine syrup

1. In a pitcher, mix first four ingredients; refrigerate, covered, until cold.
2. To serve, stir in ginger ale; pour into glasses. Slowly add grenadine.

Per cup: 107 cal., 0 fat (0 sat. fat), 0 chol., 8mg sodium, 26g carb. (23g sugars, 0 fiber), 1g pro.

HAM & CHEESE SPIDERS

Kids really enjoy eating these creepy spider-shaped sandwiches. It's worth the effort to put them together.
—Kendra Barclay, De Kalb, IL

Prep: 30 min. • **Bake:** 15 min.
Makes: 5 sandwiches

- 1 cup chopped fully cooked ham
- 2 tablespoons finely chopped onion
- 2 tablespoons butter, softened
- 1½ teaspoons prepared mustard
- 2 tubes (6 ounces each) small refrigerated flaky biscuits (5 count), divided
- 1 tube (11 ounces) refrigerated breadsticks
- 5 slices American cheese
- 1 large egg yolk
- 1 teaspoon water
- 10 ripe olive slices (about 2 tablespoons)
- 1 tablespoon diced pimientos
- 1 teaspoon poppy seeds

1. Preheat oven to 375°. Using small pieces of foil, make forty ½-in. foil balls for shaping spider legs; coat lightly with cooking spray.
2. For filling, mix first four ingredients. On greased baking sheets, pat five biscuits into 3½-in. circles. For legs, cut each of 10 breadsticks crosswise in half; cut each piece lengthwise in half. (Reserve the remaining breadsticks for another use.) Attach eight legs to each biscuit, twisting and pressing onto pan to adhere. Tuck a foil ball under the center of each leg.
3. Spoon filling over biscuits. Fold cheese slices into quarters; place over top. Pat remaining biscuits into 4-in. circles; place over cheese, pressing edges to seal.
4. Whisk together egg yolk and water; brush over tops. Attach olives for eyes; fill centers with pimientos. Sprinkle with poppy seeds.
5. Bake until golden brown, for about 15-20 minutes. Serve warm.

Per ½ sandwich: 264 cal., 12g fat (5g sat. fat), 35mg chol., 827mg sodium, 28g carb. (5g sugars, 1g fiber), 10g pro.

✱

TEST KITCHEN TIP

American cheese is a perennial kid favorite, but feel free to substitute cheddar, Swiss or mozzarella cheese in these spooky spiders.

GHOULISH CITRUS PUNCH

Fast & Fabulous Thanksgiving Feast

Get ahead of the game with make-ahead potatoes, shortcut cranberries, slow-cooked dressing and a gorgeous glazed turkey that's oven-ready in minutes.

FRUIT-GLAZED ROAST TURKEY

FRUIT-GLAZED ROAST TURKEY

To give roast turkey an update, we use apple, cranberry and raspberry flavors and fresh herbs in the glaze. This tangy bird is amazing.
—Aysha Schurman, Ammon, ID

Prep: 20 min. • **Bake:** 2½ hours + standing
Makes: 14 servings

- ¼ cup unsweetened applesauce
- ¼ cup whole-berry cranberry sauce
- ¼ cup fresh raspberries
- 2 tablespoons orange juice
- 2 tablespoons olive oil
- 1 tablespoon molasses
- 1 tablespoon fresh parsley leaves
- 1 tablespoon fresh cilantro leaves
- 1 teaspoon pepper
- ½ teaspoon salt
- 1 turkey (14 to 16 pounds)

1. Preheat oven to 400°. Place the first 10 ingredients in a blender; cover and process until blended. Place turkey on a rack in a shallow roasting pan, breast side up. Tuck wings under turkey; tie drumsticks together. Roast, uncovered, 1 hour.

2. Reduce oven setting to 325°. Brush turkey with half of the glaze. Roast 1½ - 2 hours longer or until a thermometer inserted in thickest part of thigh reads 170°-175°, brushing turkey with the remaining glaze during the last 45 minutes. (Cover loosely with foil if turkey browns too quickly.)

3. Remove turkey from oven; tent with foil. Let stand 20 minutes before carving.

Per 8 ounces cooked turkey: 563 cal., 26g fat (7g sat. fat), 246mg chol., 261mg sodium, 4g carb. (3g sugars, 0 fiber), 72g pro.

---

⑤ INGREDIENTS

RED WINE CRANBERRY SAUCE

We were feeling festive when we started our holiday cooking, but a bottle of wine was a bit more than we wanted to drink. I added half a cup to the cranberry sauce, in place of juice, and a new recipe was born!
—Helen Nelander, Boulder Creek, CA

Prep: 5 min. • **Cook:** 20 min. + chilling
Makes: about 2⅓ cups

- 1 package (12 ounces) fresh or frozen cranberries
- 1 cup sugar
- 1 cup water
- ½ cup dry red wine or grape juice

1. In a large saucepan, combine all ingredients, bring to a boil, stirring to dissolve sugar. Reduce heat to medium; cook, uncovered, until most of the berries pop, about 15 minutes, stirring occasionally.

2. Transfer to a bowl; cool slightly. Refrigerate, covered, until cold (sauce will thicken upon cooling).

Per ¼ cup: 122 cal., 0 fat (0 sat. fat), 0 chol., 1mg sodium, 30g carb. (27g sugars, 2g fiber), 0 pro.

✱

TEST KITCHEN TIPS
Wine makes this a little more tart and less sweet than some cranberry sauces. We tested this recipe with cabernet sauvignon, but you could use merlot, pinot noir or sangiovese.

Cranberries are high in pectin. When heated with sugar, the pectin gives cranberry sauce its jam-like consistency.

CHEDDAR & CHIVE MASHED POTATOES

My husband swears that my cheddar mashed potatoes are the world's best. We always have some in the freezer. Sometimes I dollop individual servings into muffin cups and reheat them that way instead.

—Cynthia Gerken, Naples, FL

Prep: 45 min. + chilling • **Bake:** 1 hour
Makes: 16 servings (¾ cup each)

- 5 pounds Yukon Gold potatoes, peeled and cut into 1-inch pieces (about 10 cups)
- 1 cup butter, cubed
- 1 cup sour cream
- 2 teaspoons salt
- ¾ teaspoon pepper
- ½ cup heavy whipping cream
- 1½ cups shredded cheddar cheese
- 1½ cups shredded Monterey Jack cheese
- ¼ cup grated Parmesan cheese
- 2 tablespoons minced fresh chives

TOPPINGS
- 1 cup shredded cheddar cheese
- 1 can (6 ounces) french-fried onions

1. Place potatoes in a 6-qt. stockpot; add water to cover. Bring to a boil. Reduce heat to medium; cook, uncovered, until tender, 10-15 minutes. Drain potatoes; transfer to a large bowl.
2. Add butter, sour cream, salt and pepper; beat until blended. Beat in whipping cream. Stir in the cheeses and chives. Transfer to a 13x9-in. baking dish. Refrigerate, covered, overnight.
3. To serve, preheat the oven to 350°. Remove potatoes from refrigerator while oven heats.
4. Bake, covered, 45 minutes, stirring after 30 minutes. Sprinkle with toppings; bake, uncovered, until heated through, about 15 minutes.
Per ¾ cup: 474 cal., 32g fat (18g sat. fat), 70mg chol., 693mg sodium, 37g carb. (3g sugars, 2g fiber), 11g pro.

SOUTHERN GREEN BEANS WITH APRICOTS

Green beans and apricots have become a family tradition. Enhanced with balsamic vinegar, the flavors will make your taste buds pop.

—Ashley Davis, Easley, SC

Prep: 15 min. • **Cook:** 20 min.
Makes: 8 servings

- 2 pounds fresh green beans, trimmed
- 1 can (14½ ounces) chicken broth
- ½ pound bacon strips, chopped
- 1 cup dried apricots, chopped
- ¼ cup balsamic vinegar
- ¾ teaspoon salt
- ¾ teaspoon garlic powder
- ¾ teaspoon pepper

1. Place beans and broth in a large saucepan. Bring to a boil. Cook, covered, 4-7 minutes or until beans are crisp-tender; drain.
2. In a large skillet, cook bacon over medium heat until crisp; stir occasionally. Remove with a slotted spoon; drain on paper towels. Discard drippings, reserving 1 tablespoon drippings in pan.
3. Add apricots to drippings; cook and stir over medium heat until softened. Stir in vinegar, salt, garlic powder, pepper and beans; cook and stir 2-3 minutes longer or until beans are coated. Sprinkle with bacon.
Per ¾ cup: 149 cal., 6g fat (2g sat. fat), 12mg chol., 464mg sodium, 21g carb. (14g sugars, 5g fiber), 6g pro.

CHEDDAR & CHIVE MASHED POTATOES

**BLOOD ORANGE
AVOCADO SALAD**

BLOOD ORANGE AVOCADO SALAD

My refreshing side salad is such a nice addition to our calorie-loaded Thanksgiving dinner. Use regular oranges if you can't find blood oranges. Finely chopped walnuts work well in place of the pomegranate seeds, too.
—Nancy Heishman, Las Vegas, NV

Prep: 30 min. + chilling
Makes: 10 servings

⅓ cup orange juice
⅓ cup extra virgin olive oil
3 tablespoons lime juice
2 tablespoons honey
1 tablespoon minced Italian parsley
¼ teaspoon ground cardamom
¼ teaspoon kosher salt
¼ teaspoon coarsely ground pepper
4 medium ripe avocados, peeled and sliced
4 large red grapefruit, sectioned
2 medium blood oranges, peeled and sliced
½ cup finely chopped red onion
⅓ cup pomegranate seeds
⅓ cup crumbled feta cheese

1. For dressing, whisk together the first eight ingredients.
2. In a serving dish, combine avocados, grapefruit and oranges; sprinkle with onion and pomegranate seeds. Drizzle with dressing. Top with cheese. Refrigerate, covered, 1 hour before serving.

Per serving: 241 cal., 16g fat (3g sat. fat), 2mg chol., 89mg sodium, 24g carb. (17g sugars, 6g fiber), 3g pro.
Diabetic Exchanges: 3 fat, 1 fruit, ½ starch.

✳

TEST KITCHEN TIPS

The acid from the citrus keeps the avocados from browning while the salad chills.

This recipe is versatile: Regular olive oil also works well; skip the cardamom (although we loved it!) if you don't have it on hand; and use dried cranberries in place of pomegranate seeds.

CHEDDAR CORN BISCUITS

Everyone asks for my biscuits with cheddar and corn, especially when I serve soup. If you're lucky and have leftovers, rewarm and pass the butter and jam.
—Susan Braun, Swift Current, SK

Prep: 20 min. • **Bake:** 20 min.
Makes: 16 biscuits

4¼ cups all-purpose flour
2 tablespoons baking powder
1 teaspoon ground mustard
¾ teaspoon salt
¾ cup cold butter, cubed
1 can (14¾ ounces) cream-style corn
1½ cups shredded cheddar cheese
2 large eggs, lightly beaten
2 tablespoons 2% milk

1. Preheat oven to 425°. In a large bowl, whisk flour, baking powder, mustard and salt. Cut in butter until mixture resembles coarse crumbs. Add corn, cheese and eggs; stir just until moistened.
2. Turn onto a lightly floured surface; knead gently 8-10 times. Pat or roll dough to 1-in. thickness; cut with a floured 2½-in. biscuit cutter. Place biscuits 2 in. apart on ungreased baking sheets; brush with milk. Bake 18-22 minutes or until golden brown. Serve warm.
Per biscuit: 270 cal., 13g fat (8g sat. fat), 57mg chol., 476mg sodium, 30g carb. (1g sugars, 1g fiber), 7g pro.

SAUSAGE-HERB DRESSING

SLOW COOKER
SAUSAGE-HERB DRESSING

To make time for last-minute Thanksgiving essentials, I prep the sausage part of this recipe a day or two ahead of time, then finish the dressing in my slow cooker on the big day. It has stood the holiday test two years running!
—Judy Batson, Tampa, FL

Prep: 20 min. • **Cook:** 2 hours
Makes: 10 servings

1 pound bulk sage pork sausage
1 medium sweet onion, chopped (about 2 cups)
2 celery ribs, chopped
¼ cup brewed coffee
½ teaspoon poultry seasoning
½ teaspoon dried oregano
½ teaspoon rubbed sage
½ teaspoon dried thyme
½ teaspoon pepper
1½ cups chicken or turkey broth
1 package (12 ounces) seasoned stuffing cubes (8 cups)
Chopped fresh parsley

1. In a 6-qt. stockpot, cook and crumble sausage with onion and celery over medium heat until no longer pink, about 5-7 minutes; drain. Stir in coffee and seasonings; cook 3 minutes, stirring occasionally.
2. Add broth; bring to a boil. Remove from heat; stir in stuffing cubes. Transfer to a greased 4- or 5-qt. slow cooker.
3. Cook, covered, on low until heated through and edges are lightly browned, about 2-2½ hours, stirring once. Sprinkle with parsley.
Note: Don't be tempted to add more broth. The dressing will moisten as it cooks.
Per ¾ cup: 254 cal., 11g fat (3g sat. fat), 25mg chol., 919mg sodium, 29g carb. (4g sugars, 2g fiber), 9g pro.

Very Merry Party Starters

Savor quick-prep party foods and beverages this holiday season. Entertain with ease when you keep these smart recipes on hand.

HOLIDAY MIMOSA

(5)INGREDIENTS FAST FIX
HOLIDAY MIMOSA
Add a splash of color to your brunch table with this lovely rosy mimosa. It has a fantastic sweet-tart taste.
—Jessie Sarrazin, Livingston, MT

Start to Finish: 5 min
Makes: 1 serving

- 1 tablespoon red coarse sugar
- ½ ounce raspberry liqueur
- 2 ounces ruby red grapefruit juice
- 2 ounces champagne
  Grapefruit twist

1. Sprinkle sugar on a plate. Moisten the rim of a champagne flute with water; hold glass upside down and dip rim into sugar.
2. Pour the raspberry liqueur and the grapefruit juice into the glass; top with champagne. Garnish with a grapefruit twist.

Note: To make a batch of mimosas (12 servings), slowly pour one bottle (750 ml) chilled champagne into a pitcher. Stir in 3 cups cranberry juice and ¾ cup raspberry liqueur.

Per serving: 121 cal., 0 fat (0 sat. fat), 0 chol., 0 sodium, 13g carb. (6g sugars, 0 fiber), 0 pro.

FAST FIX
CHILI CON QUESO
Years ago, my husband invented this gooey cheese dip. I may be biased, but I have to say it's excellent. If you like heat, rev it up with finely chopped jalapenos.
—Patricia Leinheiser, Albuquerque, NM

Start to Finish: 20 min.
Makes: 24 servings (2 tablespoons each)

- 2 tablespoons butter
- 1 medium onion, chopped
- 1 to 2 garlic cloves, minced
- 1 can (4 ounces) chopped green chilies
- 2 tablespoons cornstarch
- 1 cup whole milk
- 2½ cups shredded cheddar cheese
- 2 cups shredded Monterey Jack cheese
  Tortilla chips
  Chopped tomato and sliced jalapeno pepper, optional

1. In a saucepan, heat butter over medium-high heat; saute onion and garlic until tender. Add chilies; cook and stir 5 minutes. In a small bowl, mix cornstarch and milk until smooth; stir into onion mixture. Bring to a boil; cook and stir until thickened, 1-2 minutes.
2. Reduce heat to low; gradually stir in cheeses, adding in small amounts and allowing cheese to melt between additions. Serve warm with chips. If desired, top with tomato and jalapeno.

Per 2 tablespoons: 95 cal., 7g fat (5g sat. fat), 25mg chol., 155mg sodium, 2g carb. (1g sugars, 0 fiber), 5g pro.

MULLED WINE

This mulled wine is soothing and satisfying with a delightful blend of spices warmed to perfection. Refrigerating the wine mixture overnight allows the flavors to blend, so don't omit this essential step.
—*Taste of Home* Test Kitchen

Prep: 15 min. • **Cook:** 30 min. + chilling
Makes: 5 servings

- 1 bottle (750 milliliters) fruity red wine
- 1 cup brandy
- 1 cup sugar
- 1 medium orange, sliced
- 1 medium lemon, sliced
- ⅛ teaspoon ground nutmeg
- 2 cinnamon sticks (3 inches)
- ½ teaspoon whole allspice
- ½ teaspoon aniseed
- ½ teaspoon whole peppercorns
- 3 whole cloves
  Optional garnishes: orange slices, star anise and additional cinnamon sticks

1. In a large saucepan, combine first six ingredients. Place remaining spices on a double thickness of cheesecloth. Gather corners of cloth to enclose spices; tie securely with string. Place in pan.
2. Bring to a boil, stirring occasionally. Reduce heat; simmer gently, covered, 20 minutes. Transfer to a covered container cool slightly. Refrigerate, covered, overnight.
3. Strain wine mixture into a large saucepan, discarding fruit and spice bag; reheat. Serve warm. Garnish as desired.
Note: This recipe was tested with Rioja wine. Merlot would also work well.
Per ¾ cup: 379 cal., 0 fat (0 sat. fat), 0 chol., 10mg sodium, 46g carb. (41g sugars, 0 fiber), 0 pro.

FREEZE IT **5** INGREDIENTS

MAKE-AHEAD SAUSAGE PINWHEELS

Filled with sausage, sweet pepper and cream cheese, these roll-ups are excellent for unexpected visitors, a cocktail party or for a halftime snack. Besides being easy to make, they can be done way ahead and kept in the freezer. All you have to do is pop them into a hot oven!
—Cindy Nerat, Menominee, MI

Prep: 1 hour + freezing • **Bake:** 15 min.
Makes: about 6½ dozen

- 1 pound bulk regular or spicy pork sausage
- ½ cup diced sweet red pepper
- 1 green onion, chopped

- 1 package (8 ounces) cream cheese, cubed
- 2 tubes (8 ounces each) refrigerated crescent rolls

1. Preheat oven to 350°. In a large skillet, cook and crumble sausage over medium-high heat until no longer pink, 5-7 minutes; drain. Add pepper and green onion; cook and stir 2 minutes. Transfer to a bowl; cool 10 minutes. Stir in the cream cheese until blended; cool completely.
2. Unroll one can of crescent dough and separate into four rectangles; pinch perforations to seal. Press each rectangle to 6x4½ in.; spread each with ⅓ cup filling to within ¼ in. of edges. Roll up jelly-roll style, starting with a short side; pinch seam to seal. Roll gently to make logs smooth. Place on a waxed paper-lined baking sheet, seam side down. Repeat with remaining crescent dough. Freeze logs, covered, until firm, about 1 hour.
3. Cut each log into 10 slices. Bake on parchment paper-lined baking sheets until golden brown, about 15-18 minutes. Serve warm.
Freeze option: Freeze pinwheels in freezer containers, separating layers with waxed paper. To use, bake the frozen pinwheels as directed, increasing time by 3-5 minutes.
Per appetizer: 46 cal., 3g fat (1g sat. fat), 6mg chol., 89mg sodium, 2g carb. (1g sugars, 0 fiber), 1g pro.

MULLED WINE

SESAME CHICKEN DIP

A co-worker made this dip for one of our many parties, and it went over so well that I adopted the recipe as my own. It's a smart choice for potlucks because you can make it ahead, it serves a crowd, and folks can't get enough of it.
—Dawn Schutte, Sheboygan, WI

Prep: 30 min. + chilling
Makes: 36 servings (¼ cup each)

- 2 tablespoons reduced-sodium soy sauce
- 4 teaspoons sesame oil
- 2 garlic cloves, minced
- 4 cups shredded cooked chicken breast
- 3 packages (8 ounces each) reduced-fat cream cheese
- 1 jar (10 ounces) sweet-and-sour sauce
- 2 cups chopped fresh baby spinach
- 1 cup thinly sliced green onions (about 8)
- ½ cup chopped salted peanuts
   Sesame rice crackers

1. Mix soy sauce, sesame oil and garlic; toss with chicken. Refrigerate, covered, at least 1 hour.
2. Spread cream cheese onto a large serving plate; top with sweet-and-sour-sauce, spinach and chicken. Sprinkle with green onions and peanuts. Refrigerate, covered, at least 2 hours. Serve with crackers.

Per ¼ cup dip: 97 cal., 6g fat (3g sat. fat), 25mg chol., 176mg sodium, 4g carb. (2g sugars, 0 fiber), 7g pro.

EASY IRISH CREAM

FAST FIX

EASY IRISH CREAM

Stir up this fast and easy recipe for a potluck brunch. There's plenty of coffee flavor in every cozy cup.
—Anna Hansen, Park City, UT

Start to Finish: 15 min.
Makes: 5 cups

- 2 cups half-and-half cream
- 1 can (13.4 ounces) dulce de leche or sweetened condensed milk
- 1¼ cups Irish whiskey
- ¼ cup chocolate syrup
- 2 tablespoons instant coffee granules
- 2 teaspoons vanilla extract
   Hot brewed coffee or ice cubes

Pulse all ingredients in a blender until smooth. Stir 1-2 tablespoons into a mug of hot coffee, or pour over ice.

Per ½ cup: 415 cal., 21g fat (13g sat. fat), 79mg chol., 116mg sodium, 35g carb. (34g sugars, 0 fiber), 4g pro.

Toasted Hazelnut: Pulse 2 cups heavy whipping cream, 1 can dulce de leche or sweetened condensed milk, 1¼ cups hazelnut liqueur and 2 tablespoons instant coffee granules in a blender until smooth.

Butter Mint: Pulse 2 cups heavy whipping cream, 1 can dulce de leche or sweetened condensed milk, 1¼ cups peppermint schnapps and 2 tablespoons butter extract in a blender until smooth.

Salted Caramel: Pulse 2 cups heavy whipping cream, 1 can dulce de leche or sweetened condensed milk, 1¼ cups butterscotch schnapps and ¼ teaspoon salt in a blender until smooth.

Chocolate Covered Cherry: Pulse 2 cups heavy whipping cream, 1 can dulce de leche or sweetened condensed milk, 1¼ cups amaretto and ½ cup chocolate syrup in a blender until smooth.

MEDITERRANEAN TOMATO BITES

My friend Mary served these lovely appetizers at a summer gathering several years ago, and I adapted it a bit to my taste. It's a great August recipe when tomatoes and herbs are at their freshest.
—Susan Wilson, Milwaukee, WI

Prep: 20 min. • **Bake:** 15 min.
Makes: 32 appetizers

- 1 package (17.3 ounces) frozen puff pastry, thawed
- 1½ cups shredded Gouda cheese
- 6 plum tomatoes, thinly sliced
- ¼ cup pitted ripe olives, coarsely chopped
- 1 cup (4 ounces) crumbled feta cheese
  Minced fresh basil
  Minced fresh oregano

1. Preheat oven to 400°. Unfold puff pastry. Cut each sheet into 16 squares; place on parchment paper-lined baking sheets.
2. Sprinkle with Gouda cheese; top with tomatoes, olives and feta cheese. Bake until golden brown, 14-18 minutes. Sprinkle with herbs.

Freeze option: Cover and freeze unbaked pastries on waxed paper-lined baking sheets until firm. Transfer to freezer containers, separating layers with waxed paper; return to freezer. To use, bake pastries as directed, increasing time as necessary to heat through. Top as directed.

Per appetizer: 106 cal., 6g fat (2g sat. fat), 8mg chol., 136mg sodium, 9g carb. (0 sugars, 1g fiber), 3g pro.

✴

TEST KITCHEN TIP

Puff pastry is convenient, but it's very rich. Lighten up this appetizer a bit by serving on toasted French bread slices. Decrease bake time slightly and skip the freeze option.

MEDITERRANEAN TOMATO BITES

CRANBERRY MEATBALLS

Lots of people have asked me to share these family-favorite meatballs, but I knew I had a real winner when my grandmother asked me for the recipe!
—Tammy Neubauer, Ida Grove, IA

Prep: 20 min. • **Bake:** 20 min.
Makes: 6 dozen

- 2 large eggs, lightly beaten
- 1 cup cornflake crumbs
- ⅓ cup ketchup
- 2 tablespoons dried minced onion
- 2 tablespoons soy sauce
- 1 tablespoon dried parsley flakes
- ½ teaspoon salt
- ¼ teaspoon pepper
- 2 pounds ground pork

SAUCE
- 1 can (14 ounces) jellied cranberry sauce
- 1 cup ketchup
- 3 tablespoons brown sugar
- 1 tablespoon lemon juice

1. Preheat oven to 350°. Mix first eight ingredients. Add pork; mix lightly but thoroughly. Shape into 1-in. meatballs. Place on a greased rack in a 15x10x1-in. pan. Bake until a thermometer reads 160°, 20-25 minutes. Drain the meatballs on paper towels.
2. In a large skillet, cook and stir sauce ingredients over medium heat until blended. Stir in meatballs; heat through.
Per meatball: 58 cal., 2g fat (1g sat. fat), 16mg chol., 142mg sodium, 6g carb. (4g sugars, 0 fiber), 3g pro.

★ ★ ★ ★ ★ **READER REVIEW**
"I cheated and used 2 pounds frozen Italian meatballs. Cooked in the crock for 4½ hours on low. The sauce is terrific. I'll definitely make them again. Leftovers reheat well in the microwave and are very, very tasty!"
PARKSVILLE TASTEOFHOME.COM

BAKED SPINACH DIP LOAF

Any round loaf works as a serving bowl for this cream-cheesy dip, with spinach, cheddar, water chestnuts and, yes, bacon. Scoop the dip with the extra bread and veggies—then eat the bowl!
—Frieda Meding, Trochu, AB

Prep: 25 min. • **Bake:** 1 hour 25 min.
Makes: 16 servings (¼ cup each)

- 6 bacon strips, cooked and crumbled, divided
- 2 packages (8 ounces each) cream cheese, softened
- 1 cup mayonnaise
- 1 package (10 ounces) frozen chopped spinach, thawed and squeezed dry
- 1 can (8 ounces) sliced water chestnuts, drained and chopped
- 1¼ cups shredded cheddar cheese, divided
- 2 green onions, chopped, divided
- 1 garlic clove, minced
- 2 teaspoons dill weed
- ½ teaspoon seasoned salt
- ⅛ teaspoon pepper
- 1 unsliced round loaf (1 pound) sourdough bread
  Cucumber slices

1. Preheat the oven to 375°. Reserve 1 tablespoon crumbled bacon for topping. Beat cream cheese and mayonnaise until smooth. Stir in spinach, water chestnuts, 1 cup cheese, half of the green onions, garlic, seasonings and remaining bacon.
2. Cut a 1½-in. slice off top of bread. Hollow out the bottom, leaving a ½-in.-thick shell. Cut all removed bread into cubes for serving. Fill shell with dip. Wrap in heavy-duty foil, tenting foil over dip. Bake on a baking sheet 1¼ hours.
3. Open foil carefully, allowing steam to escape. Sprinkle dip with remaining cheese and green onion and the reserved bacon. Bake until the cheese is melted, 10-15 minutes. Serve the dip warm with cucumber slices and cubed bread.
Per ¼ cup dip: 254 cal., 24g fat (9g sat. fat), 41mg chol., 334mg sodium, 5g carb. (2g sugars, 1g fiber), 6g pro.

FESTIVE GUACAMOLE APPETIZERS

For ages, my brother's family and I have gotten together on Christmas Eve, and we always eat snacks while we open our presents. This Tex-Mex spin on classic appetizer pizza is one we have again and again.
—Laurie Pester, Colstrip, MT

Prep: 1 hour • **Bake:** 10 min. + cooling
Makes: 40 appetizers

- 2 tubes (8 ounces each) refrigerated seamless crescent dough sheet
- 1½ teaspoons taco seasoning, divided
- 20 pretzel sticks, broken in half
- 4 ounces cream cheese, softened
- 1 cup guacamole
- 2 medium sweet yellow peppers
- 1 medium sweet red pepper
- 1 medium green pepper
  Chopped fresh cilantro, optional

1. Preheat the oven to 375°. On an ungreased baking sheet, unroll one tube of crescent dough and press into a 13x8-in. rectangle. Prick with a fork; sprinkle with ¾ teaspoon taco seasoning. Repeat with remaining dough and seasoning.
2. Bake dough until golden brown, for 10-12 minutes. Transfer to wire racks to cool completely.
3. Cut each rectangle crosswise to make four strips (about 8x4-in.). For trees, cut each strip into five triangles, reserving scraps at each end for another use. For trunks, insert a pretzel piece into the base of each triangle.
4. Beat cream cheese and guacamole until smooth; spread over trees. Halve and seed peppers. Cut 40 stars from yellow peppers using a ¾-in. star-shaped cookie cutter. Dice and julienne the remaining peppers for tree decorations. Decorate trees with pepper pieces and, if desired, cilantro. Refrigerate until serving.
Per appetizer: 57 cal., 3g fat (1g sat. fat), 3mg chol., 133mg sodium, 6g carb. (1g sugars, 1g fiber), 1g pro.

CRANBERRY
MEATBALLS

BAKED SPINACH
DIP LOAF

FESTIVE GUACAMOLE
APPETIZERS

Christmas Cookies Made Easy

The holidays just got sweeter, thanks to no-bake treats, quick-prep cookies and foolproof fudge. You're sure to find a new Christmas tradition among these festive reader favorites.

CHOCOLATE RUM BALLS

CHOCOLATE RUM BALLS

Roll these truffle-like rum balls in crushed Oreos to get just the right amount of crunch. I've been known to freeze them for emergencies.
—Dauna Harwood, Elkhart, IN

Prep: 30 min. + chilling
Makes: about 3 dozen

  1 teaspoon instant coffee granules
  ¼ cup dark rum, warmed
  4 ounces cream cheese, softened
  1 cup confectioners' sugar
  1 cup ground almonds
  3 ounces unsweetened chocolate, melted
  8 Oreo cookies, finely crushed

1. Dissolve coffee granules in warm rum. Beat cream cheese, confectioners' sugar, almonds and rum mixture until blended. Stir in melted chocolate. Refrigerate until firm enough to roll, about 1 hour.
2. Shape mixture into 1-in. balls; roll in crushed cookies. Store in an airtight container in the refrigerator, separating layers with waxed paper.
Per rum ball: 70 cal., 4g fat (2g sat. fat), 3mg chol., 21mg sodium, 7g carb. (5g sugars, 1g fiber), 1g pro.

SNICKERDOODLES

The history of these whimsically named treats is widely disputed, but their popularity is undeniable! Help yourself to one of our soft cinnamon-sugared cookies and see for yourself.
—*Taste of Home* Test Kitchen

Prep: 20 min. • **Bake:** 10 min./batch
Makes: 2½ dozen

  ½ cup butter, softened
  1 cup plus 2 tablespoons sugar, divided
  1 large egg
  ½ teaspoon vanilla extract
  1½ cups all-purpose flour
  ¼ teaspoon baking soda
  ¼ teaspoon cream of tartar
  1 teaspoon ground cinnamon

1. Preheat oven to 375°. Cream butter and 1 cup sugar until light and fluffy; beat in egg and vanilla. In another bowl, whisk together flour, baking soda and cream of tartar; gradually beat into the creamed mixture.
2. In a small bowl, mix cinnamon and remaining sugar. Shape dough into 1-in. balls; roll in cinnamon sugar. Place 2 in. apart on ungreased baking sheets.
3. Bake until light brown, 10-12 minutes. Remove from pans to wire racks to cool.
Per cookie: 81 cal., 3g fat (2g sat. fat), 15mg chol., 44mg sodium, 12g carb. (7g sugars, 0 fiber), 1g pro.

NICE & SOFT SUGAR COOKIES

My family's all-time favorite Christmas cookie has had a million shapes over the years. Little ones have fun choosing their own designs.

—Cathy Hall, Lyndhurst, VA

Prep: 45 min. + chilling
Bake: 5 min./batch + cooling
Makes: about 3 dozen

- 1 cup butter, softened
- 1½ cups confectioners' sugar
- 1 large egg
- 1½ teaspoons vanilla extract
- 2½ cups self-rising flour

ICING
- 2½ cups confectioners' sugar
- ¼ cup water
- 4 teaspoons meringue powder
- ¼ cup light corn syrup
  Food coloring of choice
  Colored sugar and sprinkles, optional

1. Cream butter and confectioners' sugar until light and fluffy; beat in egg and vanilla. Gradually beat in flour. Divide the dough in half. Wrap each in plastic; refrigerate 2 hours or until firm enough to roll.

2. Preheat oven to 375°. On a floured surface, roll each portion of dough to ³⁄₁₆-in. thickness. Cut with floured 3-in. cookie cutters. Place 2 in. apart on ungreased baking sheets. Bake until set, 5-7 minutes. Cool on pans 2 minutes; remove to wire racks to cool completely.

3. Beat confectioners' sugar, water and meringue powder on low speed until blended; beat on high until soft peaks form, about 4 minutes. Add corn syrup; beat 1 minute.

4. Tint with food coloring as desired. (Always keep unused icing covered with a damp cloth; if necessary, beat again on high speed to restore texture.) Pipe or spread icing on cookies; decorate as desired. Let dry.

Note: As a substitute for 2½ cups of self-rising flour, place 3¾ teaspoons baking powder and 1¼ teaspoons salt in a 1-cup measuring cup. Add all-purpose flour to measure 1 cup; combine with an additional 1½ cups all-purpose flour. Meringue powder is available from Wilton Industries. Visit _wilton.com_.

Per cookie: 138 cal., 5g fat (3g sat. fat), 19mg chol., 150mg sodium, 22g carb. (15g sugars, 0 fiber), 1g pro.

NICE & SOFT SUGAR COOKIES

---

⑤ INGREDIENTS

EASY CINNAMON THINS

When a co-worker's husband came home from Iraq, we had a potluck for him. These cookies with coarse red sugar matched our patriotic theme.
—Janet Whittington, Heath, OH

Prep: 20 min. + standing
Makes: 2½ dozen

- 12 ounces white candy coating, chopped
- 1 teaspoon cinnamon extract
- 30 Ritz crackers
- 12 finely crushed cinnamon hard candies
  Red colored sugar

1. In a microwave, melt candy coating; stir until smooth. Stir in extract.
2. Dip crackers in candy coating mixture; allow excess to drip off. Place on waxed paper. Decorate with candies and colored sugar as desired. Let stand until set.
Per cookie: 75 cal., 4g fat (3g sat. fat), 0 chol., 36mg sodium, 10g carb. (8g sugars, 0 fiber), 0 pro.

COCONUT CLOUDS

FREEZE IT

WHITE ALMOND NO-BAKE COOKIES

My daughter and I like to try new recipes. We were out of chocolate chips one day, so we came up with this cookie using white baking chips.
—Debbie Johnson, Winona Lake, IN

Prep: 25 min. • **Cook:** 5 min. + chilling
Makes: about 3½ dozen

    2   cups sugar
    ½   cup butter, cubed
    ½   cup 2% milk
    1   cup white baking chips
    ½   teaspoon almond extract
    3   cups old-fashioned oats
    1   cup dried cherries or dried
        cranberries, optional

1. In a large saucepan, combine sugar, butter and milk. Cook and stir over medium heat until butter is melted and sugar is dissolved. Remove from heat. Stir in baking chips and extract until smooth. Add the oats and, if desired, cherries; stir until coated.
2. Drop by rounded tablespoonfuls onto waxed paper-lined baking sheets. Refrigerate until set, about 30 minutes. Store cookies in an airtight container in the refrigerator.
Per cookie: 101 cal., 4g fat (2g sat. fat), 7mg chol., 23mg sodium, 16g carb. (12g sugars, 1g fiber), 1g pro.

COCONUT CLOUDS

The big dollop of buttercream and a sprinkle of roasty-toasty coconut make these soft cookies the first to disappear from Christmas cookie trays. Take care to toast the coconut for absolutely heavenly flavor.
—Donna Scofield, Yakima, WA

Prep: 45 min.
Bake: 10 min./batch + cooling
Makes: about 5½ dozen

    ¼   cup butter, softened
    ¼   cup shortening
    1   cup sugar
    ½   cup packed brown sugar
    2   large eggs
    1   teaspoon coconut extract
    1   teaspoon vanilla extract
    1   cup (8 ounces) sour cream
    2¾ cups all-purpose flour
    1   teaspoon salt
    ½   teaspoon baking soda
    1   cup sweetened shredded coconut,
        toasted

BROWNED BUTTER FROSTING
    ⅓   cup butter, cubed
    3   cups confectioners' sugar
    3   tablespoons evaporated milk
    1   teaspoon coconut extract

    1   teaspoon vanilla extract
    2   cups sweetened shredded coconut,
        toasted

1. Preheat oven to 375°. Cream the butter, shortening and sugars until light and fluffy; beat in eggs and extracts. Stir in sour cream. In another bowl, whisk together flour, salt and baking soda; gradually beat into creamed mixture. Stir in coconut.
2. Drop dough by tablespoonfuls 2 in. apart onto lightly greased baking sheets. Bake until set, 8-10 minutes. Remove to wire racks to cool completely.
3. In a small heavy saucepan, heat butter over medium heat until golden brown, about 5-7 minutes, stirring constantly. Transfer to a bowl; gradually beat in confectioners' sugar, milk and extracts. Spread over cookies. Dip in coconut; let stand until set. Store the cookies in an airtight container.
Note: To toast coconut, bake in a shallow pan in a 350° oven for 5-10 minutes or cook in a skillet over low heat until golden brown, stirring occasionally.
Per cookie: 110 cal., 5g fat (3g sat. fat), 13mg chol., 72mg sodium, 16g carb. (11g sugars, 0 fiber), 1g pro.

CHOCOLATE MINT DREAMS

My favorite flavor combo is chocolate-mint, so these frosted cookies are hard to resist. Luckily, I always manage to save some for my cookie trays so friends and family can enjoy some, too.
—Anne Revers, Omaha, NE

Prep: 30 min. • **Bake:** 5 min./batch + cooling
Makes: about 3 dozen

- ¾ cup butter, softened
- ½ cup confectioners' sugar
- 2 ounces unsweetened chocolate, melted and cooled
- ¼ teaspoon peppermint extract
- 1½ cups all-purpose flour
- 1 cup miniature semisweet chocolate chips

ICING
- 2 tablespoons butter, softened
- 1 cup confectioners' sugar
- ¼ teaspoon peppermint extract
- 1 to 2 tablespoons 2% milk
- 1 to 2 drops green food coloring, optional

DRIZZLE
- ½ cup semisweet chocolate chips
- ½ teaspoon shortening

1. Preheat oven to 375°. Cream butter and confectioners' sugar until light and fluffy. Beat in the cooled chocolate and extract. Gradually beat in flour. Stir in chocolate chips. (Dough will be soft.)
2. Drop dough by tablespoonfuls 2 in. apart onto ungreased baking sheets. Bake until firm, 5-7 minutes. Cool on pans 2 minutes. Remove to wire racks to cool completely.
3. For icing, mix butter, confectioners' sugar, extract and enough milk to achieve desired consistency. If desired, tint green with food coloring. Spoon over cookies.
4. In a microwave, melt chocolate chips and shortening; stir until smooth. Drizzle over tops.
Per cookie: 123 cal., 8g fat (5g sat. fat), 12mg chol., 37mg sodium, 14g carb. (9g sugars, 1g fiber), 1g pro.

CHOCOLATE MINT DREAMS

(5) INGREDIENTS FAST FIX

HOLIDAY CORNFLAKE COOKIES

I can't seem to make enough of these cornflake wreaths around the holidays. The cookies firm up quickly, so you'll need to place the Red Hots right away.
—Kathleen Hedger, Godfrey, IL

Start to Finish: 15 min.
Makes: 16 cookies

- ½ cup butter, cubed
- 40 large marshmallows
- 4 cups frosted cornflakes
  Red Hots
  Assorted sprinkles

1. In a 6-qt. stockpot, melt butter over medium heat. Add marshmallows; cook and stir until melted. Remove from heat.
2. Fold in cornflakes. Working quickly, fill 16 greased muffin cups two-thirds full. Using the end of a wooden spoon, make holes in centers to resemble wreaths. Decorate immediately with Red Hots and sprinkles.
Per cookie: 147 cal., 6g fat (4g sat. fat), 15mg chol., 109mg sodium, 24g carb. (14g sugars, 0 fiber), 1g pro.

⑤ INGREDIENTS
MEXICAN WEDDING CAKES

As part of a Mexican tradition, I tucked these sugar-dusted cookies into small gift boxes for the guests at my sister's wedding. Most folks said the cookies never made it home! We bake them around the holidays, too.
—Sarita Johnston, San Antonio, TX

Prep: 30 min. • **Bake:** 15 min.
Makes: about 6 dozen

- 2 **cups butter, softened**
- 1 **cup confectioners' sugar**
- 1 **teaspoon vanilla extract**
- 4 **cups all-purpose flour**
- 1 **cup finely chopped pecans**
  Additional confectioners' sugar

1. Preheat oven to 350°. Cream butter and 1 cup confectioners' sugar until light and fluffy; beat in vanilla. Gradually beat in flour. Stir in pecans.
2. Shape tablespoons of dough into 2-in. crescents. Place 2 in. apart on ungreased baking sheets.
3. Bake until light brown, 12-15 minutes. Roll cookies in additional confectioners' sugar while warm; cool on wire racks.
Per cookie: 88 cal., 6g fat (3g sat. fat), 14mg chol., 41mg sodium, 7g carb. (2g sugars, 0 fiber), 1g pro.

"These buttery cookies are so simple to prepare, with only a few ingredients."
—PATTIE PRESCOTT, MANCHESTER, NH

EASY 3-INGREDIENT SHORTBREAD COOKIES

⑤ INGREDIENTS
EASY 3-INGREDIENT SHORTBREAD COOKIES

Prep: 10 min. • **Bake:** 30 min. + cooling
Makes: 16 cookies

- 1 **cup unsalted butter, softened**
- ½ **cup sugar**
- 2 **cups all-purpose flour**
  Confectioners' sugar, optional

1. Preheat oven to 325°. Cream butter and sugar until light and fluffy. Gradually beat in flour. Press dough into an ungreased 9-in. square baking pan. Prick with a fork.
2. Bake until light brown, 30-35 minutes. Cut into squares while warm. Cool completely on a wire rack. If desired, dust with confectioners' sugar.
Per cookie: 183 cal., 12g fat (7g sat. fat), 31mg chol., 2mg sodium, 18g carb. (6g sugars, 0 fiber), 2g pro.

HOLIDAY SPRITZ

I swapped rum extract for vanilla in a classic spritz recipe, and my cookies ended up tasting like eggnog! Measure the flour carefully so you can easily press the dough into those shapes we all love.
—Lisa Varner, El Paso, TX

Prep: 30 min. • **Bake:** 10 min./batch
Makes: about 7 dozen

- 1 cup butter, softened
- 1 cup confectioners' sugar
- ¼ teaspoon salt
- 1 large egg
- 1½ teaspoons rum extract
- 2½ cups all-purpose flour

OPTIONAL DECORATIONS
- 1 cup confectioners' sugar
- 2 to 3 tablespoons water
  Colored sugar

1. Preheat oven to 375°. Cream butter, confectioners' sugar and salt until light and fluffy; beat in egg and extract. Gradually beat in flour.
2. Using a cookie press fitted with a disk of your choice, press dough 1 in. apart onto ungreased baking sheets.
3. Bake until bottoms are light brown, 6-9 minutes. Cool on pans 2 minutes; remove to wire racks to cool completely.

For optional decorations: Place confectioners' sugar in a small bowl; stir in enough water to reach desired consistency. Dip tops of cookies in glaze; sprinkle with sugar. Let stand until set.

Per serving: 1 cookie: 39 cal., 2g fat (1g sat. fat), 8mg chol., 23mg sodium, 4g carb. (1g sugars, 0 fiber), 0 pro.

HOLIDAY SPRITZ

THUMBPRINT BUTTER COOKIES

The buttery little rounds add beautiful color to a platter of Christmas treats. Fill the thumbprint in the center with any fruit preserves you like.
—*Taste of Home* Test Kitchen

Prep: 25 min. • **Bake:** 10 min./batch
Makes: 2½ dozen

- 6 tablespoons butter, softened
- ½ cup sugar
- 1 large egg
- 2 tablespoons canola oil
- 1 teaspoon vanilla extract
- ¼ teaspoon butter flavoring
- 1½ cups all-purpose flour
- ¼ cup cornstarch
- 1 teaspoon baking powder
- ¼ teaspoon salt
- 3 tablespoons apricot or other fruit preserves

1. Preheat oven to 350°. Cream butter and sugar until light and fluffy; beat in egg, oil, vanilla and butter flavoring. In another bowl, whisk together flour, cornstarch, baking powder and salt; gradually beat into creamed mixture.
2. Shape dough into 1-in. balls; place 2 in. apart on greased baking sheets. Press a deep indentation in center of each with the end of a wooden spoon handle. Bake until edges are light brown, 8-10 minutes.
3. Remove from pans to wire racks to cool. Fill with preserves.

Per cookie: 75 cal., 3g fat (2g sat. fat), 13mg chol., 52mg sodium, 10g carb. (4g sugars, 0 fiber), 1g pro.

CATHEDRAL COOKIES

Children love the colorful marshmallows in these no-bake slices, which mimic the look of stained-glass windows. They really light up the cookie tray at our holiday parties.

—Carol Shaffer, Cape Girardeau, MO

....

Prep: 10 min. + freezing
Cook: 10 min. + chilling
Makes: about 5 dozen

- 1 cup (6 ounces) semisweet chocolate chips
- 2 tablespoons butter
- 1 large egg, lightly beaten
- 3 cups pastel miniature marshmallows
- ½ cup chopped pecans or walnuts
- 1 cup sweetened shredded coconut

1. In a heavy saucepan, melt chocolate chips and butter over low heat, stirring occasionally. Stir a small amount into the egg, then return all to pan. Cook and stir over low heat for 2 minutes. Pour into a bowl; let cool for 15 minutes. Gently stir in the marshmallows and nuts. Chill for 30 minutes.

2. On a sheet of waxed paper, shape mixture into a 1½-in.-diameter log. Place coconut on another sheet of waxed paper. Gently roll log over coconut to coat sides. Wrap up tightly, twisting ends to seal.

3. Freeze for 4 hours or overnight. Remove waxed paper. Cut into ¼-in. slices. Store in an airtight container in the refrigerator.

Per 2 cookies: 81 cal., 5g fat (3g sat. fat), 9mg chol., 21mg sodium, 9g carb. (7g sugars, 1g fiber), 1g pro.

(5)INGREDIENTS
EASY PEANUT BUTTER FUDGE

My sister shared the recipe for this unbelievably easy candy. I prefer using creamy peanut butter, but the chunky style works just as well.

—Mary Jane Rummel, Linglestown, PA

....

Prep: 15 min. + chilling
Makes : 2 pounds (64 pieces)

- 2 teaspoons butter, softened
- 2 cups sugar
- ½ cup whole milk
- 1⅓ cups peanut butter
- 1 jar (7 ounces) marshmallow creme

1. Line an 8-in. square pan with foil; grease with butter.

2. In a heavy saucepan, combine sugar and milk; bring to a boil over medium heat, stirring constantly. Boil 3 minutes, stirring constantly. Remove from heat.

3. Stir in peanut butter and marshmallow creme until blended. Immediately spread into prepared pan; cool slightly.

4. Refrigerate until firm. Using foil, lift fudge out of pan. Remove foil; cut into squares. Store between layers of waxed paper in an airtight container.

Per piece: 67 cal., 3g fat (1g sat. fat), 0 chol., 28mg sodium, 10g carb. (9g sugars, 0 fiber), 1g pro.

CATHEDRAL COOKIES

CHOCOLATE-DIPPED
ORANGE COOKIES

⑤ INGREDIENTS
BUTTERY LEMON
SANDWICH COOKIES

*My grandson approves of these lemony
sandwich cookie made with crackers and
prepared frosting. Decorate them with
whatever sprinkles you like.*
—Nancy Foust, Stoneboro, PA

Prep: 20 min. + standing
Makes: 2½ dozen

  ¾ **cup lemon frosting**
  60 **Ritz crackers**
  24 **ounces white candy coating, melted**
      **Nonpareils, jimmies or sprinkles,
      optional**

Spread frosting on bottoms of half of the
crackers; cover with remaining crackers.
Dip sandwiches in melted candy coating;
allow excess to drip off. Place on waxed
paper; decorate as desired. Let stand until
set. Store in an airtight container in the
refrigerator.
Per sandwich cookie: 171 cal., 9g fat
(6g sat. fat), 0 chol., 70mg sodium,
23g carb. (19g sugars, 0 fiber), 0 pro.

CHOCOLATE-DIPPED
ORANGE COOKIES

*With dark chocolate,
orange and almond,
these melt-in-your-
mouth cookies have
the perfect amount of
sweetness. And we can't resist dunking
them, they're so cute!*
—Linda Call, Falun, KS

Prep: 40 min.
Bake: 20 min./batch + cooling
Makes: about 6 dozen

  1 **cup butter, softened**
  1 **package (8 ounces) cream cheese,
    softened**
  1 **cup sugar**
  ½ **teaspoon salt**
  2 **tablespoons grated orange peel**
  ½ **teaspoon vanilla extract**
2½ **cups all-purpose flour**
  1 **cup finely chopped blanched
    almonds**

GLAZE
  5 **ounces semisweet chocolate,
    chopped**
  3 **tablespoons butter**
  ¼ **cup finely chopped blanched
    almonds**

1. Preheat oven to 325°. In a large bowl,
beat butter, cream cheese, sugar and
salt until blended. Beat in orange peel
and vanilla. Gradually beat in flour. Stir
in almonds.
2. Shape dough into 1-in. balls; place 2 in.
apart on ungreased baking sheets. Flatten
with bottom of a glass dipped in sugar.
3. Bake until firm, 20-25 minutes. Remove
from pans to wire racks to cool completely.
4. For the glaze, in a microwave, melt
chocolate and butter; stir until smooth.
Dip each cookie halfway in chocolate; allow
excess to drip off. Sprinkle with almonds.
Place on waxed paper; let stand until set.
Per cookie: 81 cal., 6g fat (3g sat. fat),
12mg chol., 57mg sodium, 7g carb. (3g
sugars, 0 fiber), 1g pro.

Delectable Desserts

Irresistible sweets turn an ordinary day into a celebration! Here, find our favorite cookie-jar temptations, dessert-table stars, no-bake treats and even homemade ice cream—made with no special equipment whatsoever.

CINNAMON APPLE TART

CINNAMON APPLE TART

I got the idea for this delicious fall dessert from a lovely Italian woman who's also a fabulous cook. It's so simple to make—and cleanup is just as easy! I often make two and freeze one.
—Stacie Blemings, Heath, TX

Prep: 20 min. • **Bake:** 20 min.
Makes: 6 servings

- 1 large apple, peeled and chopped
- 1 teaspoon lemon juice
- 1 sheet refrigerated pie pastry
- 2 tablespoons apple jelly
- 2 tablespoons sugar
- ¼ cup cinnamon baking chips
- ⅓ cup sliced almonds
- 1 teaspoon 2% milk

ICING
- 1 cup confectioners' sugar
- ¼ teaspoon almond extract
- 1 to 2 tablespoons 2% milk

1. Preheat oven to 400°. Toss apple with lemon juice.
2. On a large sheet of parchment paper, roll pastry into a 14-in. circle; transfer to a baking sheet. Spread jelly onto pastry to within 2 in. of edges. Sprinkle with apple, sugar, baking chips and almonds. Fold up edges of pastry over filling, leaving opening in center. Brush folded pastry with milk.
3. Bake the tart until golden brown, 20-25 minutes. Transfer to a wire rack to cool.
4. Mix icing ingredients, using enough milk to reach desired consistency. Drizzle over tart.

Per piece: 370 cal., 15g fat (6g sat. fat), 7mg chol., 159mg sodium, 57g carb. (39g sugars, 1g fiber), 3g pro.

TEXAS TUMBLEWEEDS

⑤ INGREDIENTS
TEXAS TUMBLEWEEDS

Tumbleweeds blow across the roads in some parts of Texas, and I think these cute little stacks resemble them quite well. I've been make these sweets with my sister for years.
—Karen LeMay, Seabrook, TX

Prep: 20 min. + chilling
Makes: about 4 dozen

- 1 cup butterscotch chips
- 1 cup creamy peanut butter
- 1 can (9 ounces) potato sticks (about 6 cups)

1. In a microwave or large metal bowl over simmering water, melt butterscotch chips and peanut butter; stir until smooth. Gently stir in potato sticks.
2. Drop the mixture by rounded tablespoonfuls onto waxed paper-lined baking sheets. Refrigerate 10-15 minutes or until set.

Per piece: 76 cal., 5g fat (2g sat. fat), 0 chol., 57mg sodium, 6g carb. (3g sugars, 0 fiber), 2g pro.

✱
TEST KITCHEN TIPS
Swap any kind of chocolate chips for the butterscotch and Nutella for the peanut butter. Heavenly!

If you can't find potato sticks, try using crushed potato chips.

LEMON BERRY
DUMP CAKE

LEMON BERRY DUMP CAKE

This sweet-tart cake recipe is so much fun to make with my grandkids. They love just dumping it all in and watching it magically become a pretty, delicious dessert.
—Nancy Heishman, Las Vegas, NV

Prep: 10 min. • **Bake:** 45 min. + cooling
Makes: 15 servings
(3 cups lemon topping)

- 6 **cups fresh or frozen blueberries**
- 1 **teaspoon ground cinnamon**
- ¾ **cup butter, melted, divided**
- 1 **package lemon cake mix (regular size)**

TOPPING

- 2 **containers (6 ounces each) lemon yogurt**
- 1 **container (8 ounces) frozen whipped topping, thawed**
- ½ **cup marshmallow creme**
- ⅓ **cup lemon curd**
    Additional blueberries, optional

1. Preheat oven to 350°. Toss blueberries with cinnamon; spread into a greased 13x9-in. baking dish. Drizzle with half of the melted butter. Sprinkle with cake mix; drizzle with remaining butter.
2. Bake cake until golden brown and fruit is bubbly, about 45-55 minutes. Cool on a wire rack.
3. Beat together the yogurt, whipped topping, marshmallow creme and lemon curd. Serve dump cake with the yogurt mixture and, if desired, additional blueberries.
Per serving: 340 cal., 15g fat (9g sat. fat), 31mg chol., 297mg sodium, 48g carb. (33g sugars, 1g fiber), 3g pro.

JAM-TOPPED MINI CHEESECAKES

PICTURED ON P. 285
Presto! We turned cheesecake into irresistible finger food with these cute little treats.
—*Taste of Home* Test Kitchen

Prep: 20 min. • **Bake:** 15 min. + chilling
Makes: 1 dozen

- 1 **cup graham cracker crumbs**
- 3 **tablespoons butter, melted**
- 1 **package (8 ounces) cream cheese, softened**
- ⅓ **cup sugar**
- 1 **teaspoon vanilla extract**
- 1 **large egg, lightly beaten**
    Assorted jams, warmed

1. In a small bowl, combine graham cracker crumbs and butter. Press gently onto the bottom of 12 paper-lined muffin cups. In another small bowl, beat the cream cheese, sugar and vanilla until smooth. Add egg; beat on low speed just until combined. Spoon over crusts.
2. Bake at 350° for 15-16 minutes or until centers are set. Cool for 10 minutes before removing from pan to a wire rack to cool completely. Refrigerate for at least 1 hour.
3. Remove paper liners; top each cheesecake with 1 teaspoon jam.
Per serving: 149 cal., 11g fat (6g sat. fat), 46mg chol., 124mg sodium, 11g carb. (8g sugars, 0 fiber), 2g pro.

RASPBERRY CHOCOLATE PUFFS

This chocolaty, flaky dessert is one of my favorite show-off recipes because it makes a spectacular presentation. Although it looks like you toiled, it's actually really easy and quick to make!
—Anneliese Deising, Plymouth, MI

Prep: 25 min. • **Bake:** 20 min. + cooling
Makes: 8 servings

- 1 cup milk chocolate chips
- 1 cup white baking chips
- 1 cup chopped pecans
- 1 package (17.3 ounces) frozen puff pastry, thawed
- 1 package (12 ounces) frozen unsweetened raspberries, thawed
- 1 cup confectioners' sugar
  Additional confectioners' sugar
  Optional ingredients: fresh raspberries and additional chocolate and white baking chips

1. Preheat oven to 425°. Toss together chocolate chips, baking chips and pecans. On a lightly floured surface, roll each pastry sheet into a 12-in. square; cut each sheet into quarters, making four 6-in. pastry squares.

2. Place squares on ungreased baking sheets; top each with about ⅓ cup chocolate mixture. Lightly brush edges of pastry with water; bring together all corners, pinching seams to seal.

3. Bake until golden brown, 18-20 minutes. Remove to a wire rack to cool slightly. Puree frozen raspberries with 1 cup confectioners' sugar in a food processor. Strain to remove seeds.

4. Dust the pastries with confectioners' sugar. Serve with raspberry sauce and, if desired, fresh berries and additional chips.
Per serving: 699 cal., 39g fat (13g sat. fat), 9mg chol., 238mg sodium, 81g carb. (40g sugars, 7g fiber), 9g pro.

PEAR-BLACKBERRY CRISP

I love to make this in the fall when I have an abundance of fresh pears from a nearby orchard. The unique combination of pears and blackberries makes it special.
—Beth Fleming, Downers Grove, IL

Prep: 25 min.
Bake: 45 min.
Makes: 12 servings

- 10 medium pears (about 4 pounds), peeled and sliced
- 2 cups fresh or frozen blackberries
- ⅓ cup sugar
- ¼ cup all-purpose flour
  TOPPING
- 1⅓ cups all-purpose flour
- 1⅓ cups quick-cooking oats
- 1 cup packed brown sugar
- 1 teaspoon ground cinnamon
- ½ teaspoon salt
- 1 cup cold butter, cubed

1. Preheat oven to 375°. Place pears and blackberries in a large bowl. Mix sugar and flour; toss with fruit. Transfer to a greased 13x9-in. baking dish.

2. In a bowl, mix the first five topping ingredients; cut in butter until crumbly. Sprinkle over filling. Bake until filling is bubbly and topping is golden brown, 45-50 minutes.
Per serving: 415 cal., 16g fat (10g sat. fat), 41mg chol., 228mg sodium, 67g carb. (39g sugars, 7g fiber), 4g pro.

COCONUT RUM BALLS

My mom has made rum balls for as long as I can remember. They look beautiful in a dessert buffet and can be easily given as gifts. When I switched the traditional rum to coconut rum and added shredded coconut, I think I made these tasty treats even better!
—Jana Walker, Macomb, MI

Prep: 25 min. + standing
Makes: about 4½ dozen

- 1 package (12 ounces) vanilla wafers, finely crushed
- 1 cup confectioners' sugar
- 2 tablespoons baking cocoa
- 1 cup sweetened shredded coconut
- 1 cup chopped pecans
- ½ cup light corn syrup
- ¼ cup coconut rum
  Additional confectioners' sugar

1. Whisk crushed wafers, confectioners' sugar and cocoa. Stir in coconut and pecans. In a separate bowl, whisk corn syrup and rum; stir into wafer mixture. Shape into 1-in. balls; let stand 1 hour.

2. Roll in additional confectioners' sugar. Store in an airtight container.
Per rum ball: 73 cal., 3g fat (1g sat. fat), 1mg chol., 31mg sodium, 10g carb. (8g sugars, 1g fiber), 0 pro.

RASPBERRY
CHOCOLATE PUFFS

EAT SMART ⑤ INGREDIENTS
LIGHT & CREAMY CHOCOLATE PUDDING

This pudding is exactly what its name promises: light and creamy. Since it uses soy milk, it's a great choice if you're lactose intolerant or are having a guest who doesn't drink milk.

—Deborah Williams, Peoria, AZ

Prep: 10 min. • **Cook:** 15 min. + chilling
Makes: 4 servings

- 3 tablespoons cornstarch
- 2 tablespoons sugar
- 2 tablespoons baking cocoa
- ⅛ teaspoon salt
- 2 cups chocolate soy milk
- 1 teaspoon vanilla extract

1. In a small heavy saucepan, mix the cornstarch, sugar, cocoa and salt. Whisk in milk. Cook and stir over medium heat until thickened and bubbly. Reduce heat to low; cook and stir 2 minutes longer.
2. Remove from heat. Stir in vanilla. Cool 15 minutes, stirring occasionally.
3. Transfer to dessert dishes. Refrigerate, covered, 30 minutes or until cold.

Per ½ cup: 127 cal., 2g fat (0 sat. fat), 0 chol., 112mg sodium, 25g carb. (16g sugars, 1g fiber), 3g pro.
Diabetic Exchanges: 1½ starch.

APPLE DUMPLING BAKE

APPLE DUMPLING BAKE

I received this recipe from a friend of mine, then tweaked it to suit my family's tastes. Mountain Dew is the secret ingredient in this rich apple dessert that's a snap to make.

—Chris Shields, Monrovia, IN

Prep: 15 min. • **Bake:** 35 min.
Makes: 8 servings

- 2 medium Granny Smith apples
- 2 tubes (8 ounces each) refrigerated crescent rolls
- 1 cup sugar
- ⅓ cup butter, softened
- ½ teaspoon ground cinnamon
- ¾ cup Mountain Dew soda
  Vanilla ice cream

1. Preheat oven to 350°. Peel, core and cut each apple into eight wedges. Unroll both tubes of crescent dough; separate each into eight triangles. Wrap a triangle around each wedge. Place in a greased 13x9-in. baking dish.
2. In a bowl, mix sugar, butter and cinnamon until blended; sprinkle over dumplings. Slowly pour soda around the rolls (do not stir).
3. Bake, uncovered, until golden brown and apples are tender, 35-40 minutes. Serve warm with ice cream.

Per 2 dumplings: 414 cal., 20g fat (9g sat. fat), 20mg chol., 510mg sodium, 55g carb. (35g sugars, 1g fiber), 4g pro.

PEACH COBBLER DUMP CAKE

This recipe gives you tender cake with a beautifully crisp cobbler topping over sweet peaches. You can make it any time of year. Add a scoop of vanilla ice cream on the side, and dessert's golden.
—Keri Sparks, Little Elm, TX

Prep: 10 min.
Bake: 35 min.
Makes: 15 servings

2 cans (15 ounces each) sliced peaches in extra-light syrup
2 tablespoons brown sugar
1 teaspoon ground cinnamon
1 package yellow cake mix (regular size)
¾ cup sliced almonds
½ cup cold butter

1. Preheat oven to 350°. Place one can of peaches in a greased 13x9-in. baking dish. Drain remaining can of peaches and add to baking dish; sprinkle with brown sugar and cinnamon. Sprinkle with cake mix and almonds.
2. Cut butter into very thin slices; arrange over top, spacing evenly. Bake until golden brown and fruit is bubbly, 35-40 minutes. Serve warm.

Per serving: 234 cal., 11g fat (5g sat. fat), 16mg chol., 242mg sodium, 34g carb. (22g sugars, 1g fiber), 2g pro.

CRANBERRY CHOCOLATE CHIP PECAN PIE

I've been using this rich pecan pie recipe for 30 years, changing it up when the mood strikes. We love it any way I make it! It's awesome baked a day ahead, too.
—Joan Hallford, North Richland Hills, TX

Prep: 20 min. • **Bake:** 40 min.
Makes: 8 servings

1 sheet refrigerated pie pastry
4 large eggs
1 cup dark corn syrup
⅔ cup sugar
¼ cup butter, melted
¾ teaspoon ground cinnamon
¼ teaspoon ground nutmeg
1½ cups fresh or frozen cranberries, thawed, chopped
1 cup miniature semisweet chocolate chips
1 cup pecan halves

1. Preheat oven to 375°. Unroll pastry sheet into a 9-in. pie plate; flute edge. Refrigerate while preparing filling.
2. Whisk together eggs, corn syrup, sugar, melted butter and spices. Sprinkle cranberries and chocolate chips onto bottom of crust; top with egg mixture. Arrange pecans over filling.
3. Bake on a lower oven rack until the crust is golden brown and filling is puffed, 40-50 minutes. Cool pie on a wire rack. Refrigerate leftovers.

Per piece: 576 cal., 30g fat (12g sat. fat), 113mg chol., 239mg sodium, 78g carb. (62g sugars, 3g fiber), 6g pro.

✱
TEST KITCHEN TIPS
Dark corn syrup gives this pie a robust flavor, but you can use light corn syrup if you prefer.

For a perfectly browned crust, be sure to preheat your oven and bake the pie on a lower oven rack.

Not sure if it's done? Bake until a thermometer inserted in the center reads 200°.

CRANBERRY CHOCOLATE CHIP PECAN PIE

Vanilla Dream

Almost as fun as eating ice cream: making it at home with just four ingredients, a freezer and a friend. So sweet, so simple.

1. Make the Base
Stir whipping cream, half-and-half, sugar and vanilla until sugar is dissolved.

2. Grab a Dish
Place a 13x9-in. dish in freezer until cold. Pour cream mixture into prepared dish and freeze until the edges of the mixture begin to set, 20-30 minutes.

3. Mix It Up
Remove dish from freezer. Using a hand mixer, beat the mixture until it's nice and smooth. Cover the dish and place it back in the freezer.

4. Make It Creamy
Continue to beat the mixture again every 30 minutes, covering and freezing it in the meantime. You'll have ice cream in about 3 hours.

⑤ INGREDIENTS
HOMEMADE VANILLA ICE CREAM

We don't want to brag, but this vanilla ice cream recipe really is the best ever. And with only four ingredients, it just might be the easiest, too. No ice cream maker? No problem. Just follow the directions below.
—Taste of Home Test Kitchen

2 **cups heavy whipping cream**
2 **cups half-and-half cream**
1 **cup sugar**
2 **teaspoons vanilla extract**

Per ½ cup: 308 cal., 22g fat (14g sat. fat), 78mg chol., 37mg sodium, 23g carb. (23g sugars, 0 fiber), 3g pro.

Prep: 20 min. + freezing
Makes: 1¼ quarts

IRISH WHISKEY FLOAT

Here's a tasty adult spin on a favorite childhood ice cream treat. Every sip is cool, creamy and fun!

—Nick Iverson, Denver, CO

Start to Finish: 5 min.
Makes: 1 serving

- 1 scoop vanilla ice cream
- 1 cup cola
- 1 ounce Irish whiskey

Place ice cream in a tall glass; top with cola and whiskey. Serve immediately.

Per serving: 299 cal., 7g fat (4g sat. fat), 29mg chol., 63mg sodium, 41g carb. (37g sugars, 0 fiber), 2g pro.

CARROT DUMP CAKE

Our family loves carrot cake so much that I experimented to find an easier way to make it so we could enjoy it all the time. This supermoist version makes my family smile when it suddenly appears on the table.

—Bonnie Hawkins, Elkhorn, WI

Prep: 10 min. • **Bake:** 25 min. + cooling
Makes: 12 servings

- 1 can (8 ounces) crushed pineapple
- 1 cup shredded carrots (2 medium carrots)
- 1 cup finely chopped walnuts
- 1 package spice cake mix (regular size)
- ¾ cup unsalted butter, melted
  Whipped cream, optional

1. Preheat oven to 350°. Mix pineapple, carrots and walnuts; spread into a greased 11x7-in. baking dish. Sprinkle with cake mix; drizzle with butter.
2. Bake until golden brown, 25-30 minutes. Cool on a wire rack. If desired, serve with whipped cream.

Per piece: 339 cal., 21g fat (9g sat. fat), 31mg chol., 263mg sodium, 37g carb. (20g sugars, 1g fiber), 4g pro.

COOKIE CRUST DEEP-DISH APPLE PIE

COOKIE CRUST DEEP-DISH APPLE PIE

One of my favorite make-and-take desserts, this deep-dish pie is based on an old Hungarian recipe that's popular in this part of Ohio. The easy cookie crust is the best part.

—Diane Shipley, Mentor, OH

Prep: 45 min. + chilling • **Bake:** 40 min.
Makes: 15 servings

- 1 cup butter, softened
- ½ cup sugar
- ½ teaspoon salt
- 3 large egg yolks
- 1 teaspoon vanilla extract
- 3 tablespoons sour cream
- 3 cups all-purpose flour

FILLING

- 1 cup sugar
- 2 tablespoons all-purpose flour
- 1 teaspoon ground cinnamon
- 8 cups sliced peeled Granny Smith apples
- 2 tablespoons butter, cubed

TOPPING

- 1 large egg white
- ¼ cup finely chopped pecans

1. Beat the butter, sugar and salt until blended; beat in egg yolks and vanilla. Beat in sour cream. Gradually beat in flour. Divide dough in half. Shape each into a rectangle; wrap in plastic. Refrigerate until firm, about 1 hour.
2. Preheat oven to 375°. On waxed paper, roll one half of dough into a 14x10-in. rectangle. Transfer to a greased 13x9-in. pan; press onto bottom and ½ in. up sides of pan. (Dough may crack; pinch together to patch.)
3. Mix sugar, flour and cinnamon; toss with apples. Place in crust; dot with butter. On waxed paper, roll remaining dough into a 14x10-in. rectangle; place over filling. Pinch edges to seal.
4. Whisk egg white until frothy; brush over top. Sprinkle with pecans. Cut slits in top crust. Bake on a lower oven rack until golden brown, 40-45 minutes. Cool on a wire rack.

Per piece: 357 cal., 17g fat (10g sat. fat), 74mg chol., 196mg sodium, 49g carb. (26g sugars, 2g fiber), 4g pro.

✳

TEST KITCHEN TIP
Use a gentle touch when brushing the egg white over the top crust; the dough is delicate. Some juices from the filling might ooze out during baking, and that's OK. Consider it a caramelly bonus.

EAT SMART
CHOCOLATE CHIP CREAM CHEESE BARS

Lower in fat and calories than you might ever guess, these bars couldn't be easier to whip up. They make a fun, quick dessert to bring to parties or serve to company!
—Jennifer Rafferty, Milford, OH

Prep: 15 min. • **Bake:** 20 min. + cooling
Makes: 2 dozen

- 1 package German chocolate cake mix (regular size)
- ⅓ cup canola oil
- 1 large egg

FILLING
- 1 package (8 ounces) reduced-fat cream cheese
- ⅓ cup sugar
- 1 large egg, lightly beaten
- 1 cup miniature semisweet chocolate chips

1. Preheat oven to 350°. Combine cake mix, oil and egg; mix until blended. Reserve 1 cup mixture for topping. Press remaining mixture into a 13x9-in. baking pan coated with cooking spray. Bake until set, 10-12 minutes.

2. For filling, beat cream cheese and sugar until smooth. Beat in egg. Spread over crust. Sprinkle with chocolate chips and reserved topping.

3. Bake until set, 18-20 minutes. Cool on a wire rack. Cut into bars. Store cream cheese bars in refrigerator.

Per bar: 187 cal., 9g fat (3g sat. fat), 24mg chol., 207mg sodium, 25g carb. (18g sugars, 0 fiber), 3g pro.
Diabetic Exchanges: 1½ starch, 1½ fat.

RHUBARB MALLOW COBBLER

RHUBARB MALLOW COBBLER

My mom used to make this when I was growing up. Now, we take fresh rhubarb to my son in Texas so he can share this treat with his family.
—Judy Kay Warwick, Webster City, IA

Prep: 15 min.
Bake: 40 min.
Makes: 12 servings

- 4 cups diced fresh or frozen rhubarb
- 2½ cups sugar, divided
- 1 cup miniature marshmallows
- ½ cup butter, softened
- 1 teaspoon vanilla extract
- 1¾ cups all-purpose flour
- 3 teaspoons baking powder
- ½ teaspoon salt
- ½ cup whole milk

1. In a large bowl, combine rhubarb and 1½ cups sugar. Transfer to a greased 11x7-in. baking dish. Sprinkle with the marshmallows.

2. In a small bowl, cream the butter, vanilla and remaining sugar until light and fluffy. Combine the flour, baking powder and salt; add to creamed mixture alternately with milk. Beat just until moistened; spoon over rhubarb.

3. Bake at 350° for 40-45 minutes or until topping is golden brown. Serve warm.

Note: If using frozen rhubarb, measure rhubarb while still frozen, then thaw completely. Drain in a colander, but do not press liquid out.

Per serving: 323 cal., 8g fat (5g sat. fat), 22mg chol., 285mg sodium, 61g carb. (45g sugars, 1g fiber), 3g pro.

ALMOND PEAR TART

I had never seen a pie without a pan until my daughter brought back this wonderful recipe from a Rotary Club exchange program in Belgium. Now it's a favorite.
—Sherry LaMay, Capitan, NM

Prep: 15 min. • **Bake:** 20 min. + cooling
Makes: 8 servings

    Pastry for single-crust pie (9 inches)
¾ cup plus 2 teaspoons sugar, divided
3 tablespoons all-purpose flour
4 cups sliced peeled fresh pears (about
    4 medium)
3 tablespoons sliced almonds

1. On a lightly floured surface, roll pastry into a 10-in. circle. Transfer crust to a parchment paper-lined baking sheet.
2. In a large bowl, combine ¾ cup sugar and flour; add pears and toss to coat. Spoon over the pastry to within 2 in. of edges. Fold up edges of pastry over filling, leaving center uncovered. Sprinkle with remaining sugar.

3. Bake at 450° for 15 minutes or until crust is golden and filling is bubbly. Sprinkle with almonds; bake 5 minutes longer. Using the parchment paper, slide tart onto a wire rack to cool.
Per slice: 269 cal., 8g fat (3g sat. fat), 5mg chol., 100mg sodium, 48g carb. (29g sugars, 2g fiber), 2g pro.

CARAMEL APPLE CUPCAKES

 Bring these extra-special cupcakes to your next event and watch how quickly they disappear! With a caramel topping and spice cake base, they're the perfect mix of two fall favorite treats.
—Diane Halferty, Corpus Christi, TX

Prep: 25 min. • **Bake:** 20 min. + cooling
Makes: 1 dozen

1 package spice or carrot cake mix
    (regular size)
2 cups chopped peeled tart apples
    (about 2 medium)
20 caramels

3 tablespoons 2% milk
1 cup finely chopped pecans, toasted
12 wooden skewers (4½ inch)

1. Preheat oven to 350°. Line 12 jumbo muffin cups with paper liners.
2. Prepare cake mix batter according to package directions; fold in apples. Fill prepared cups three-fourths full. Bake until a toothpick inserted in center comes out clean, about 20 minutes. Cool for 10 minutes before removing from pans; cool completely on a wire rack.
3. In a small saucepan, cook caramels and milk over low heat until smooth, stirring constantly. Spread over cupcakes. Sprinkle with pecans. Insert a wooden skewer in each cupcake.
Note: To toast nuts, bake in a shallow pan in a 350° oven for 5-10 minutes or cook in a skillet over low heat until lightly browned, stirring occasionally.
Per cupcake: 365 cal., 19g fat (3g sat. fat), 48mg chol., 315mg sodium, 48g carb. (30g sugars, 1g fiber), 5g pro.

CARAMEL APPLE CUPCAKES

FAVORITE DUTCH APPLE PIE

Everything about this dessert makes it the top request for family gatherings. Its oat crust reminds me of a cookie, and the tart apple filling just can't be beat.
—Brenda DuFresne, Midland, MI

Prep: 20 min. • **Bake:** 40 min. + cooling
Makes: 8 servings

- 2 cups all-purpose flour
- 1 cup packed brown sugar
- ½ cup quick-cooking oats
- ¾ cup butter, melted

FILLING
- ⅔ cup sugar
- 3 tablespoons cornstarch
- 1¼ cups cold water
- 4 cups chopped peeled tart apples (about 2 large)
- 1 teaspoon vanilla extract

1. Preheat oven to 350°. Mix flour, brown sugar, oats and butter; reserve 1½ cups mixture for topping. Press remaining mixture onto bottom and up sides of an ungreased 9-in. pie plate.
2. In a large saucepan, mix the sugar, cornstarch and water until smooth; bring to a boil. Cook and stir until thickened, about 2 minutes. Remove from heat; stir in apples and vanilla. Pour mixture into crust. Crumble topping over filling.
3. Bake until crust is golden brown and filling is bubbly, 40-45 minutes. Cool on a wire rack.

Per piece: 494 cal., 18g fat (11g sat. fat), 46mg chol., 146mg sodium, 81g carb. (49g sugars, 2g fiber), 4g pro.

SPICED CAPPUCCINO KISS COOKIES

SPICED CAPPUCCINO KISS COOKIES

This recipe combines two of my favorite flavors: coffee and cinnamon. You can always find these cookies on my holiday treat trays.
—Cynthia Messenger, Mount Pleasant, SC

Prep: 30 min. + chilling
Bake: 10 min./batch • **Makes:** 2 dozen

- ½ cup unsalted butter, softened
- ¼ cup packed brown sugar
- ¾ cup sugar, divided
- 1 large egg
- 1½ teaspoons instant espresso powder
- 1 teaspoon vanilla extract
- 1¼ cups all-purpose flour
- ¼ teaspoon baking soda
- ¼ teaspoon salt
- 2 teaspoons ground cinnamon
- 24 striped chocolate kisses

1. Beat butter, brown sugar and ¼ cup sugar until light and fluffy. Beat in egg, espresso powder and vanilla. In another bowl, whisk together flour, baking soda and salt; gradually beat into creamed mixture. Refrigerate, covered, until firm enough to shape, about 1 hour.
2. Preheat oven to 350°. Mix cinnamon and remaining sugar. Shape dough into twenty-four 1-in. balls; roll in cinnamon sugar. Place 2 in. apart on ungreased baking sheets.
3. Bake until lightly browned, about 10-12 minutes. Immediately top with chocolate kisses, pressing lightly. Cool slightly on pans before removing to wire racks to cool.

Per cookie: 117 cal., 5g fat (3g sat. fat), 19mg chol., 46mg sodium, 17g carb. (11g sugars, 0 fiber), 1g pro.

✱

TEST KITCHEN TIPS
Add the espresso powder with the eggs and vanilla instead of the flour mixture to ensure that it dissolves.

This dough is a little sticky, but it can be rolled into balls after chilling for an hour.

These cookies taste like a snickerdoodle with a hint of espresso.

COCONUT-LAYERED POUND CAKE

If you love chocolate, almonds and coconut, this cake is for you. It comes together in a flash and tastes just like an Almond Joy candy bar!
—Linda Nichols, Steubenville, OH

Start to Finish: 10 min.
Makes: 8 servings

- 1 package (7 ounces) sweetened shredded coconut
- 1 can (14 ounces) sweetened condensed milk
- ½ cup chopped almonds, toasted
- 1 loaf (16 ounces) frozen pound cake, thawed
- 1 cup chocolate fudge frosting

Mix coconut, milk and almonds. Cut cake horizontally into four layers. Place bottom layer on a serving plate; top with half of the coconut mixture, one cake layer and ½ cup frosting. Repeat layers. Refrigerate, covered, until serving.

Note: To toast nuts, bake in a shallow pan in a 350° oven for 5-10 minutes or cook in a skillet over low heat until lightly browned, stirring occasionally.

Per slice: 715 cal., 35g fat (19g sat. fat), 98mg chol., 426mg sodium, 93g carb. (72g sugars, 3g fiber), 10g pro.
Cannoli Torte: Combine 2 cups ricotta cheese with ⅓ cup each sugar and miniature chocolate chips. Assemble cake, using cheese mixture instead of coconut mixture.

PUMPKIN TORTE

This beautiful layered cake has a creamy, pumpkin spice filling. It's quick and always turns out so well. The nuts and caramel topping add a nice finishing touch.
—Trixie Fisher, Piqua, OH

Prep: 30 min. • **Bake:** 25 min. + cooling
Makes: 12 servings

- 1 package yellow cake mix (regular size)
- 1 can (15 ounces) solid-pack pumpkin, divided
- 4 large eggs
- ½ cup 2% milk
- ⅓ cup canola oil
- 1½ teaspoons pumpkin pie spice, divided
- 1 package (8 ounces) cream cheese, softened
- 1 cup confectioners' sugar
- 1 carton (16 ounces) frozen whipped topping, thawed
- ¼ cup caramel ice cream topping
  Pecan halves, toasted

1. Preheat oven to 350°. Line bottom of two greased 9-in. round baking pans with parchment paper; grease paper.
2. Combine cake mix, 1 cup pumpkin, eggs, milk, oil and 1 teaspoon pie spice; beat on low speed 30 seconds. Beat on medium 2 minutes. Transfer batter to prepared pans.
3. Bake until a toothpick inserted in center comes out clean, 25-30 minutes. Cool 10 minutes before removing from pans to wire racks; cool completely.
4. Beat cream cheese until light and fluffy. Beat in confectioners' sugar and the remaining pumpkin and pie spice until smooth. Fold in whipped topping.
5. Using a long serrated knife, cut each cake horizontally in half. Place one cake layer on a serving plate; spread with a fourth of the filling. Repeat three times. Drizzle with caramel topping; sprinkle with pecans. Store in refrigerator.

Per slice: 476 cal., 24g fat (12g sat. fat), 82mg chol., 367mg sodium, 58g carb. (41g sugars, 1g fiber), 6g pro.

PUMPKIN TORTE

CRANBERRY CAKE WITH ALMOND-BUTTER SAUCE

Make room for this recipe in your collection. Tart cranberries and sweet almond glaze turn this simple cake into something truly special.
—Betsy King, Duluth, MN

Prep: 20 min. Bake 35 min. + cooling
Makes: 9 servings (1¼ cups sauce)

- 3 **tablespoons butter, softened**
- 1 **cup sugar**
- 1 **cup 2% milk**
- 2 **cups all-purpose flour**
- 2 **teaspoons baking powder**
- 1 **teaspoon salt**
- 2 **cups fresh or frozen cranberries**

SAUCE
- ½ **cup butter, cubed**
- 1 **cup sugar**
- ½ **cup half-and-half cream**
- 1 **teaspoon almond extract**

1. Preheat oven to 350°. Grease an 8-in. square baking pan. Beat butter and sugar until crumbly. Beat in milk. Whisk together flour, baking powder and salt; stir into the butter mixture. Stir in the cranberries. Transfer to prepared pan.
2. Bake until a toothpick inserted in center comes out clean, 35-40 minutes. Cool in pan on a wire rack.
3. For sauce, in a saucepan, melt butter over medium heat. Add sugar and cream; cook and stir until sugar is dissolved, about 5 minutes. Remove sauce from heat; stir in extract. Serve warm with cake.
Per piece with about 2 tablespoons sauce: 442 cal., 16g fat (10g sat. fat), 46mg chol., 501mg sodium, 70g carb. (47g sugars, 2g fiber), 4g pro.

FREEZE IT · ⑤ INGREDIENTS

NO-BAKE CHOCOLATE MINT TREATS
PICTURED ON P. 285

At our house, everyone lends a hand to make these simple chocolate-covered cookies. Decorate them with sprinkles to match any occasion.
—Lily Julow, Lawrenceville, GA

Prep: 15 min. + freezing
Makes: about 3 dozen

- 3 **cups crushed chocolate wafers (about 65 wafers)**
- 6 **ounces cream cheese, softened**
  Sugar
- 1 **pound chocolate mint candy coating disks, chopped**
- 2 **tablespoons shortening**
  Green and white sprinkles, optional

1. In a large bowl, combine chocolate wafer crumbs and cream cheese. Shape into 1-in. balls. Coat bottom of a glass with cooking spray, then dip in sugar; flatten balls to ¼-in. thickness. (Re-dip glass in sugar as needed.) Freeze 30 minutes or until firm.
2. In a microwave, melt candy coating disks and shortening; stir until smooth. Dip cookies in coating mixture; allow excess to drip off. Place on waxed paper; if desired, decorate immediately with sprinkles. Store between layers of waxed paper in an airtight container in the refrigerator.
Note: Chocolate candy coating disks are sometimes called chocolate melts. Look for them in the baking aisle at the supermarket.
Per cookie: 113 cal., 6g fat (4g sat. fat), 5mg chol., 78mg sodium, 14g carb. (10g sugars, 1g fiber), 1g pro.

---

⑤ INGREDIENTS · FAST FIX

TOASTED COCONUT MILK SHAKES

I created this recipe as a reminder of my oldest brother, Brad, a picky eater but one who loved any dessert with coconut. It has a short list of ingredients, but it's certainly tall on coconut flavor!
—Laurie Hudson, Westville, FL

Start to Finish: 15 min.
Makes: 4 servings

- ½ **cup flaked coconut**
- ⅔ **cup coconut milk, stirred before measuring then chilled**
- ½ **cup cream of coconut, stirred before measuring then chilled**
- 4 **cups vanilla ice cream**
  Sweetened whipped cream

1. In a small skillet, cook and stir coconut over medium-low heat until toasted, about 6-8 minutes. Cool completely.
2. Place coconut milk, cream of coconut, ¼ cup toasted coconut and ice cream in a blender; cover and process until blended.
3. Pour into four glasses. Top with whipped cream; sprinkle with remaining coconut. Serve immediately.
Per cup: 502 cal., 30g fat (23g sat. fat), 58mg chol., 161mg sodium, 54g carb. (51g sugars, 1g fiber), 6g pro.

---

⑤ INGREDIENTS

CHOCOLATE TOFFEE CRUNCHIES

Prep: 20 min. • **Bake:** 20 min. + cooling
Makes: 4 dozen

- 2 **cups vanilla wafer crumbs (about 60 wafers)**
- ¼ **cup packed brown sugar**
- ½ **cup butter, melted**

TOPPING
- ½ **cup butter, cubed**
- ½ **cup packed brown sugar**
- 1 **cup (6 ounces) semisweet chocolate chips**
- ½ **cup finely chopped pecans**

1. Preheat oven to 350°. Toss wafer crumbs with brown sugar and butter; press into an ungreased 13x9-in. pan. Bake until lightly browned, 8-10 minutes.
2. For topping, place butter and brown sugar in a small saucepan. Bring to a boil over medium heat; cook and stir 1 minute. Pour evenly over crust.
3. Bake 10 minutes. Remove from the oven; let stand 2 minutes. Sprinkle with the chocolate chips; let stand until chips have softened. Spread evenly over top; sprinkle with pecans. Cool completely before cutting.
Per bar: 93 cal., 6g fat (3g sat. fat), 11mg chol., 55mg sodium, 9g carb. (7g sugars, 0 fiber), 0 pro.

CHOCOLATE TOFFEE CRUNCHIES

**BLACK FOREST
ICEBOX COOKIES**

CHOCOLATE-COVERED-
CHERRY DUMP CAKE

PICTURED ON P. 285

*My mother-in-law loves chocolate-
covered cherries, and I used to make this
cake every year for her birthday. Now
we've moved away, but I make this for my
kids on her birthday so they still feel close
to her.*
—Angela Lively, Conroe, TX

Prep: 10 min. • **Bake:** 35 min.
Makes: 15 servings

- 1 **can (21 ounces) cherry pie filling**
- ½ **cup semisweet chocolate chips**
- 2 **teaspoons almond extract**
- 1 **package chocolate cake mix (regular
   size)**
- ¾ **cup pecan halves**
- 1 **cup unsalted butter, melted**

1. Preheat oven to 350°. Mix pie filling,
chocolate chips and extract; spread into a
greased 13x9-in. baking dish. Sprinkle with
the cake mix and pecans; drizzle with
melted butter.
2. Bake until top is set and filling is bubbly,
35-40 minutes. Serve warm.
Per serving: 331 cal., 20g fat (10g sat.
fat), 33mg chol., 197mg sodium, 38g
carb. (15g sugars, 2g fiber), 2g pro.

BLACK FOREST
ICEBOX COOKIES

*You'll want to keep extra batches of these
tasty cookies on hand for when company
drops by. The chocolate wafers and
sweet-tart filling go perfectly together.*
—*Taste of Home* Test Kitchen

Prep: 15 min. + chilling
Cook: 5 min. + cooling
Makes: 20 cookies

- 3 **tablespoons granulated sugar**
- 4 **teaspoons cornstarch**
   Dash salt
- ¾ **cup fresh or frozen pitted tart
   cherries (thawed), coarsely chopped**
- ¾ **cup cherry juice blend**
- 1½ **teaspoons lemon juice**
- 1 **to 2 drops red food coloring, optional**
- ½ **cup mascarpone cheese**
- 1 **tablespoon confectioners' sugar**
- 1 **teaspoon cherry brandy**
- 1 **package (9 ounces) chocolate
   wafers**
- ½ **cup semisweet chocolate chips**
- ¼ **cup heavy whipping cream**

1. In a small saucepan, combine the
granulated sugar, cornstarch and salt. Add
the cherries, juice blend and lemon juice.
Bring to a boil; cook and stir for 2 minutes

or until thickened. Remove from the heat
and stir in food coloring if desired. Cool to
room temperature.
2. In a small bowl, combine mascarpone
cheese, confectioners' sugar and brandy.
Spread about 1 teaspoon cheese mixture
onto 20 wafers; top with 2 teaspoons
cherry mixture and remaining wafers.
Place on a waxed paper-lined baking pan.
Place chocolate chips in a small bowl. In a
small saucepan, bring cream just to a boil.
Pour over chips; whisk until smooth.
Drizzle over cookies. Refrigerate, covered,
for up to 4 hours before serving.
Per sandwich cookie: 139 cal., 9g fat (4g
sat. fat), 17mg chol., 81mg sodium, 15g
carb. (9g sugars, 1g fiber), 2g pro.

DID YOU KNOW?

Dark sweet cherries are larger and
firmer than sour cherries. While sweet
cherries are popular and delicious for
eating out of hand, they're often too
sweet for baked goods and confections.
Sour cherries are generally considered
better for making sweets. However,
sweet cherries in a dessert recipe can
mean using less sugar.

CINNAMON PECAN BARS

I'm a special ed teacher, and we bake these bars in my life-skills class. It's an easy recipe that my special-needs students have fun preparing.
—Jennifer Peters, Adams Center, NY

Prep: 10 min. • **Bake:** 25 min.
Makes: 2 dozen

- 1 package butter pecan cake mix (regular size)
- ½ cup packed dark brown sugar
- 2 large eggs
- ½ cup butter, melted
- ½ cup chopped pecans
- ½ cup cinnamon baking chips

1. Preheat oven to 350°. In a large bowl, combine cake mix and brown sugar. Add eggs and melted butter; mix well. Stir in pecans and baking chips. Spread into a greased 13x9-in. baking pan.
2. Bake until golden brown, 25-30 minutes. Cool in pan on a wire rack. Cut into bars.
Per bar: 185 cal., 9g fat (4g sat. fat), 26mg chol., 190mg sodium, 25g carb. (17g sugars, 0 fiber), 2g pro.

⑤ INGREDIENTS CHOCOLATE BUTTERSCOTCH HAYSTACKS
PICTURED ON P. 285

My grandmother made haystacks like these and gave them to my cousin Vonnie and me when our parents didn't want us to have any more sweets.
—Christine Schwester, Divide, CO

Prep: 25 min. + chilling • **Makes:** 3 dozen

- 2 cups (12 ounces) semisweet chocolate chips
- 1 package (10 to 11 ounces) butterscotch chips
- 4 cups crispy chow mein noodles

1. In a microwave or large metal bowl over simmering water, melt chocolate chips and butterscotch chips; stir until smooth. Gently stir in noodles.
2. Drop by rounded tablespoonfuls onto waxed paper-lined baking sheets. Refrigerate 10-15 minutes or until set.
Per cookie: 160 cal., 9g fat (5g sat. fat), 0 chol., 84mg sodium, 22g carb. (15g sugars, 1g fiber), 1g pro.

APPLE SNICKERDOODLE DUMP CAKE
PICTURED ON P. 285

With an apple farm just down the road, I'm always looking for creative ways to use up those bushels. We love this cozy cake with caramel drizzle and a scoop of vanilla or cinnamon ice cream.
—Rachel Garcia, Colorado Springs, CO

Prep: 15 min. • **Bake:** 35 min.
Makes: 10 servings

- 6 cups sliced, peeled tart apple (about 8 medium)
- ⅓ cup packed brown sugar
- ¼ cup sugar
- ¼ cup orange juice
- 1 tablespoon lemon juice
- 1 package (17.9 ounces) snickerdoodle cookie mix
- ½ cup butter, melted
- 1 cup coarsely chopped pecans or walnuts

1. Preheat oven to 350°. Toss the apples with sugars and fruit juices; spread into a greased 11x7-in. baking dish.
2. Place cookie mix in a bowl; stir in contents of cinnamon-sugar packet. Sprinkle over apples. Drizzle with butter. Top with pecans.
3. Bake until golden brown and apples are tender, 35-40 minutes. Serve warm.
Per serving: 475 cal., 23g fat (7g sat. fat), 24mg chol., 193mg sodium, 67g carb. (48g sugars, 3g fiber), 3g pro.

★ ★ ★ ★ ★ **READER REVIEW**

"While I wouldn't call this a cake, I will call it delicious! I didn't peel the apples—I never peel apples for a dessert. It may not look as pretty, but none of the nutrients are lost."

MS11145 TASTEOFHOME.COM

CINNAMON PECAN BARS

WHITE CHOCOLATE CRANBERRY BLONDIES

EAT SMART

BLUEBERRY WALNUT BARS

With power-packing oats, walnuts and blueberries, this sweet treat will be a favorite of both the kids and adults.
—Dawn Onuffer, Crestview, FL

Prep: 20 min. • **Bake:** 10 min. + cooling
Makes: 12 servings

- ⅔ cup ground walnuts
- ½ cup graham cracker crumbs
- 2 tablespoons plus ⅓ cup sugar, divided
- ⅓ cup old-fashioned oats
- 3 tablespoons reduced-fat butter, melted
- 1 package (8 ounces) reduced-fat cream cheese
- 1 tablespoon orange juice
- ½ teaspoon vanilla extract
- ½ cup reduced-fat whipped topping
- 2 tablespoons blueberry preserves
- 1½ cups fresh blueberries

1. In a small bowl, combine the walnuts, cracker crumbs, 2 tablespoons sugar, oats and butter. Press onto the bottom of an 8-in. square baking dish coated with cooking spray.
2. Bake at 350° for 9-11 minutes or until set and edges are lightly browned. Cool on a wire rack.
3. In a large bowl, beat cream cheese and remaining sugar until smooth. Beat in orange juice and vanilla. Fold in whipped topping. Spread over crust.
4. In a microwave-safe bowl, heat preserves on high for 15-20 seconds or until warmed; gently stir in blueberries. Spoon over filling. Refrigerate until serving.
Note: This recipe was tested with Land O'Lakes light stick butter.
Per piece: 167 cal., 9g fat (4g sat. fat), 17mg chol., 125mg sodium, 19g carb. (14g sugars, 1g fiber), 3g pro.
Diabetic Exchanges: 2 fat, 1 starch.

WHITE CHOCOLATE CRANBERRY BLONDIES

The family often requests these bars. If you want a fancier presentation, cut them into triangles and drizzle white chocolate over each one individually.
—Erika Busz, Kent, WA

Prep: 35 min. • **Bake:** 20 min. + cooling
Makes: 3 dozen

- ¾ cup butter, cubed
- 1½ cups packed light brown sugar
- 2 large eggs
- ¾ teaspoon vanilla extract
- 2¼ cups all-purpose flour
- 1½ teaspoons baking powder
- ¼ teaspoon salt
- ⅛ teaspoon ground cinnamon
- ½ cup dried cranberries
- 6 ounces white baking chocolate, coarsely chopped

FROSTING
- 1 package (8 ounces) cream cheese, softened
- 1 cup confectioners' sugar
- 1 tablespoon grated orange peel, optional
- 6 ounces white baking chocolate, melted
- ½ cup dried cranberries, chopped

1. Preheat oven to 350°. In a large microwave-safe bowl, microwave butter until melted; stir in brown sugar. Cool slightly.
2. Beat in eggs, one at a time, and vanilla. In another bowl, whisk together flour, baking powder, salt and cinnamon; stir into butter mixture. Stir in cranberries and chopped chocolate (batter will be thick). Spread into a greased 13x9-in. pan.
3. Bake until golden brown and a toothpick inserted in center comes out clean (do not overbake), 18-21 minutes. Cool completely on a wire rack.
4. For frosting, beat cream cheese, confectioners' sugar and, if desired, orange peel until smooth. Gradually beat in half of the melted white chocolate; spread over blondies. Sprinkle with cranberries; drizzle top with remaining melted chocolate.
5. Cut into triangles. Store in an airtight container in the refrigerator.
Per blondie: 198 cal., 9g fat (6g sat. fat), 27mg chol., 100mg sodium, 28g carb. (22g sugars, 0 fiber), 2g pro.

ORANGE-DRIZZLED GRAPE TARTLETS

Sugar cookie dough and cream cheese make it easy to build these cute little fruit tartlets.
—Julie Sterchi, Campbellsvlle, KY

Start to Finish: 20 min.
Makes: 1 dozen

- 1 tube (16½ ounces) refrigerated sugar cookie dough
- 1 package (8 ounces) cream cheese, softened
- ½ cup confectioners' sugar
- ½ teaspoon vanilla extract
- ¾ cup seedless red grapes, halved
- ¾ cup green grapes, halved
- ¼ cup orange marmalade

1. Preheat oven to 350°. Cut cookie dough into twelve slices, about ¾ in. thick. On ungreased baking sheets, pat each slice to form ½-in.-thick circles. Bake 10-12 minutes or until golden brown. Remove to wire racks to cool completely.

2. Meanwhile, in a small bowl, beat cream cheese, confectioners' sugar and vanilla until blended. Spread over cookie crusts. Top with grapes.

3. In a microwave-safe dish, microwave marmalade, covered, on high 15-20 seconds or until warmed. Drizzle over grapes.

Per serving: 286 cal., 15g fat (6g sat. fat), 32mg chol., 225mg sodium, 36g carb. (20g sugars, 1g fiber), 3g pro.

NO-BAKE OREO CHEESECAKE

With Oreo cookies and cheesecake — how can you go wrong? I made 20 of these crowd-pleasing desserts in all different sizes for my wedding, and they were a hit.
—Leanne Stinson, Carnduff, SK

Prep: 40 min. + chilling
Makes: 8 servings

- 24 Oreo cookies, crushed
- 6 tablespoons butter, melted

FILLING
- 1 envelope unflavored gelatin
- ¼ cup cold water
- 1 package (8 ounces) cream cheese, softened
- ½ cup sugar
- ¾ cup 2% milk
- 1 cup whipped topping
- 10 Oreo cookies, coarsely chopped

1. In a small bowl, mix crushed cookies and butter. Press onto bottom of a greased 9-in. springform pan. Refrigerate until ready to use.

2. In a small saucepan, sprinkle gelatin over cold water; let stand 1 minute. Heat and stir over low heat until gelatin is completely dissolved. Let stand 5 minutes.

3. In a large bowl, beat cream cheese and sugar until smooth; gradually add milk. Beat in gelatin mixture. Fold in whipped topping and chopped cookies. Spoon over the crust.

4. Refrigerate, covered, overnight. Loosen sides of cheesecake with a knife; remove rim from pan.

Per slice: 499 cal., 30g fat (16g sat. fat), 53mg chol., 374mg sodium, 53g carb. (37g sugars, 1g fiber), 7g pro.

NO-BAKE OREO CHEESECAKE

Easy Odds & Ends

Who doesn't want big restaurant flavor they can easily make at home? We've got you covered with favorite restaurant copycats in this chapter. Plus, you'll find 15 creative ideas for pasta salads and homemade gifts.

The Best Restaurant Copycats

Dinner's at the coziest spot in town. These DIY restaurant knockoffs were inspired by readers' famous favorites.

Crunchy Asian Chicken Salad

TASTES LIKE APPLEBEE'S

FAST FIX ▶

CRUNCHY ASIAN CHICKEN SALAD

I love this crunchy, citrusy salad. Once I even made my husband drive an hour to the nearest Applebee's restaurant just so I could eat it! That's when I decided to come up with my own version that's a great stand-in for the original. I'm happy and my husband is, too!
—Mandy Bird, Holbrook, ID

Start to Finish: 25 min.
Makes: 4 servings

- 4 frozen breaded chicken tenders (about 8 ounces)
- ⅓ cup mayonnaise
- 3 tablespoons honey
- 2 tablespoons rice vinegar
- 1½ teaspoons Dijon mustard
- ¼ teaspoon sesame oil
- 1 package (10 ounces) hearts of romaine salad mix
- 1 package (14 ounces) coleslaw mix
- ¼ cup crispy chow mein noodles
- ⅓ cup sliced almonds, toasted

1. Cook chicken tenders according to package directions. Meanwhile, whisk together mayonnaise, honey, vinegar, mustard and sesame oil.

2. To serve, place romaine and coleslaw mixes in a large bowl; toss with dressing. Divide among four plates. Cut chicken into bite-sized pieces; place over salads. Sprinkle with noodles and almonds.

Note: To toast nuts, bake in a shallow pan in a 350° oven for 5-10 minutes or cook in a skillet over low heat until lightly browned, stirring occasionally.

Per serving: 419 cal., 25g fat (3g sat. fat), 11mg chol., 602mg sodium, 42g carb. (20g sugars, 7g fiber), 12g pro.

DID YOU KNOW?

Chicken tenderloins, also commonly called chicken tenders, come from the breast meat closest to the breastbone. Tenderloins are white meat and taste just like chicken breast. Chicken tenders is a looser term. It may indicate ground or chopped meat that's been shaped into a strip, breaded and fried.

LOADED DELI SUB SANDWICH

When I can't decide between a turkey or roast beef sandwich, I go for both, then pile on fresh, crunchy veggies and two kinds of cheese. For those who like a little bit of everything, this sub more than satisfies.

—Jamie Fanning, Creighton, NE

Start to Finish: 15 min.
Makes: 4 servings

  4 hoagie buns, split
  ½ cup mayonnaise
TOPPINGS
  3 cups fresh baby spinach
  ½ cup thinly sliced red onion
  ½ cup chopped green or red pepper
  ¼ cup sliced ripe olives
  ¼ cup dill pickle slices
  ⅓ pound sliced deli roast beef
  ⅓ pound sliced deli turkey
  8 thin slices cheddar cheese
  8 thin slices provolone cheese
     Optional seasonings: dried oregano, grated Parmesan cheese and pepper

Spread buns with mayonnaise. Layer with toppings. Sprinkle with seasonings as desired; close sandwiches.

Per sandwich: 709 cal., 44g fat (14g sat. fat), 86mg chol., 1661mg sodium, 42g carb. (7g sugars, 3g fiber), 38g pro.

HEALTH TIP Most of the sodium here comes from the big piece of bread, plus the deli meat and cheeses. Use a mini bun or kaiser roll, cut back the meat and load on veggies for a healthier version.

Loaded Deli
Sub Sandwich
*TASTES LIKE
SUBWAY*

Slow Cooker
Carnitas
*TASTES LIKE
CHIPOTLE*

SLOW COOKER CARNITAS

We shared these flavor-packed tacos with friends from church who came over to help us move. The slow cooker makes this recipe extra easy, and I love that whenever I make it, I'm reminded of the wonderful people back in Michigan.

—Abigail Raines, Hamden, CT

Prep: 25 min. • **Cook:** 8 hours
Makes: 12 servings

  ½ cup salsa
  3 bay leaves
  1 tablespoon salt
  2 teaspoons ground cumin
  2 teaspoons dried oregano
  2 teaspoons pepper
 1½ teaspoons garlic powder
  4 whole cloves
 1¼ cups water
  2 medium onions, chopped
  1 bone-in pork shoulder roast (6 to 7 pounds)
 24 corn tortillas (6 inches) or taco shells, warmed
     Optional toppings: shredded cheese, sour cream and chopped tomato, onion and cilantro

1. In a small bowl, mix the first nine ingredients. Place onions in a 6-qt. oval slow cooker. Place roast over onions; pour salsa mixture over roast. Cook, covered, on low until pork is tender, 8-10 hours.

2. Remove roast; remove and discard bone. Shred pork with two forks. Serve in tortillas with toppings as desired.

Freeze option: Freeze cooled pork mixture in freezer containers. To use, partially thaw in refrigerator overnight. Microwave, covered, on high in a microwave-safe dish until heated through, stirring occasionally and adding a little water or broth if necessary.

Per 2 tacos: 393 cal., 18g fat (6g sat. fat), 100mg chol., 757mg sodium, 25g carb. (2g sugars, 4g fiber), 32g pro.

Cajun Chicken
& Pasta
TASTES LIKE
CHILI'S

Cheesy Broccoli Soup
in a Bread Bowl
TASTES LIKE
PANERA

CAJUN CHICKEN & PASTA

This kicked-up pasta dish is a family favorite and my most requested recipe. It's easy to adapt, too. Swap in shrimp for the chicken, add your favorite veggies, adjust the spice level to your family's taste—you can't go wrong!
—Dolly Kragel, Smithland, IA

Prep: 10 min. + standing
Cook: 35 min.
Makes: 6 servings

- 1 pound boneless skinless chicken breasts, cut into 2x½-in. strips
- 3 teaspoons Cajun seasoning
- 8 ounces uncooked penne pasta (about 2⅓ cups)
- 2 tablespoons butter, divided
- 1 small sweet red pepper, diced
- 1 small green pepper, diced
- ½ cup sliced fresh mushrooms
- 4 green onions, chopped
- 1 cup heavy whipping cream
- ½ teaspoon salt
- ¼ teaspoon dried basil
- ¼ teaspoon lemon-pepper seasoning
- ¼ teaspoon garlic powder
  Pepper to taste
  Chopped plum tomatoes
  Minced fresh basil
  Shredded Parmesan cheese

1. Toss chicken with Cajun seasoning; let stand 15 minutes. Cook pasta according to package directions; drain.
2. In a large skillet, heat 1 tablespoon butter over medium-high heat; saute chicken until no longer pink, 5-6 minutes. Remove from pan.
3. In same pan, heat remaining butter over medium-high heat; saute peppers, mushrooms and green onions until peppers are crisp-tender, 6-8 minutes. Stir in cream and seasonings; bring to a boil. Cook and stir until slightly thickened, 4-6 minutes. Stir in pasta and chicken; heat through. Top with tomatoes and basil. Sprinkle with cheese.
Per serving: 398 cal., 21g fat (12g sat. fat), 97mg chol., 357mg sodium, 31g carb. (4g sugars, 2g fiber), 22g pro.

CHEESY BROCCOLI SOUP IN A BREAD BOWL

This creamy, cheesy broccoli soup tastes just like Panera's! My family requests it all the time. You can even make your own homemade bread bowls.
—Rachel Preus, Marshall, MI

Prep: 5 min. • **Cook:** 30 min.
Makes: 6 servings

- ¼ cup butter, cubed
- ½ cup chopped onion
- 2 garlic cloves, minced
- 4 cups fresh broccoli florets (about 8 ounces)
- 1 large carrot, finely chopped
- 3 cups chicken stock
- 2 cups half-and-half cream
- 2 bay leaves
- ½ teaspoon salt
- ¼ teaspoon ground nutmeg
- ¼ teaspoon pepper
- ¼ cup cornstarch
- ¼ cup water or additional chicken stock
- 2½ cups shredded cheddar cheese
- 6 small round bread loaves (about 8 ounces each), optional

1. In a 6-qt. stockpot, heat butter over medium heat; saute onion and garlic until tender, 6-8 minutes. Stir in the broccoli, carrot, stock, cream and seasonings; bring to a boil. Simmer, uncovered, until the vegetables are tender, 10-12 minutes.
2. Mix cornstarch and water until smooth; stir into soup. Bring to a boil, stirring occasionally; cook and stir until thickened, 1-2 minutes. Remove bay leaves. Stir in cheese until melted.
3. If using bread bowls, cut a slice off the top of each bread loaf; hollow out the bottoms, leaving ¼-in.-thick shells (save removed bread for another use). Fill with soup just before serving.
Per cup soup: 422 cal., 32g fat (19g sat. fat), 107mg chol., 904mg sodium, 15g carb. (5g sugars, 2g fiber), 17g pro.

✳
TEST KITCHEN TIP
These make for a hearty meal on their own, but are also delicious as appetizers. Smaller, sturdy breads such as hard rolls are a good choice.

Get Creative with Pasta Salad

Warm weather calls for a cool and crispy garden-fresh salad. Here's how to create your ultimate picnic side dish, summertime dinner or lunch box winner. Just start with a pound of pasta, choose your mix-ins and add a simple dressing. Presto!

CUCUMBER SHELL SALAD

Ranch dressing is the mild coating for this pleasant pasta salad chock-full of crunchy cucumber, onion and green peas. Wherever I take it, I'm always asked for the recipe.

—Paula Ishii, Ralston, NE

Prep: 20 min. + chilling
Makes: 16 servings

- 1 package (16 ounces) medium pasta shells
- 1 package (16 ounces) frozen peas, thawed
- 1 medium cucumber, halved and sliced
- 1 small red onion, chopped
- 1 cup ranch salad dressing

Per ¾ cup: 165 cal., 1g fat (0 sat. fat), 0 chol., 210mg sodium, 33g carb. (0 sugars, 3g fiber), 6g pro.
Diabetic Exchanges: 2 starch.

HOW-TO
Create Any Pasta Salad

1. Cook Pasta
Boil a pound of pasta in salted water according to package directions for al dente; drain.

2. Rinse and Drain
Rinse pasta well in cold water to stop the cooking. Drain well.

3. Pick Your Mix-Ins
Add your favorite mix-ins. Go for a variety of flavors, colors and textures.

4. Dress and Accent
Add a cup or more of dressing and stir well to combine. (Pasta salad tends to absorb dressing as it sits.) Add some bold flavor accents such as crisp bacon, spicy curry powder, crunchy nuts or tangy lemon. Refrigerate until serving.

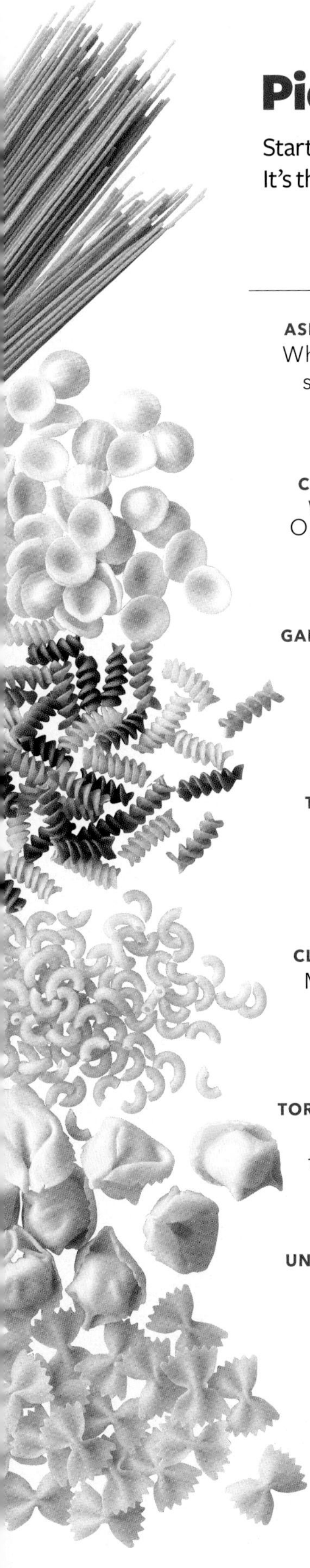

Pick a Pasta Salad

Start with a shape. Toss with mix-ins. Add dressing and flavorful accents.
It's the simplest, most delicious equation that adds up to potluck perfection.

PASTA	MIX-INS	DRESSING	ACCENTS
ASIAN NOODLE Whole-wheat spaghetti	Cubed chicken, coleslaw mix, mandarin oranges	Sesame-ginger vinaigrette	Chow mein noodles
CALIFORNIA WALDORF Orecchiette	Smoked turkey, apples, celery, strawberries	2-1 mix of plain yogurt and mayo	Walnuts, Dijon mustard
GARDEN RANCH Tricolor rotini	Broccoli, cucumbers, tomatoes	Ranch dressing	Crumbled bacon
TACO BEEF Rotini	Taco meat, cheddar, tomatoes, peppers	Catalina dressing	Tortilla chips, black olives
CLASSIC MAC Macaroni	Ham, cheddar, peas, green onions	Mayo thinned with vinegar	Pickle relish
TORTELLINI TIME Cheese tortellini	Broccoli, red peppers	Red wine vinaigrette	Prosciutto, green olives
UNDER THE SEA Shells	Imitation crab, peas	Mayonnaise	Dill
SPINACH BOW TIES Farfalle	Baby spinach, yellow pepper, dried apricots	Balsamic vinaigrette	Sliced almonds

Jolly in a Jar

Readers share their secret for easy holiday gift-giving. Just put a lid on it!

RICH HOT
FUDGE SAUCE

SLOW COOKER PEAR BUTTER

This is a tasty spread for toast, muffins, biscuits or any of your favorite breads. It is easy to make and has a rich pear flavor with hints of cinnamon, star anise and lemon.
—Geraldine Saucier, Albuquerque, NM

Prep: 25 min. • **Cook:** 6 hours
Makes: 6 cups

- 1 cinnamon stick (3 inches)
- 4-5 star anise points (about ½ whole)
- 5 pounds pears, peeled and chopped (about 12 cups)
- 1 cup packed light brown sugar
- 1 teaspoon grated lemon peel

1. Place spices on a double thickness of cheesecloth. Gather corners of cloth to enclose spices; tie securely with string. In a 5- or 6-qt. slow cooker, toss remaining ingredients. Add spice bag, covering with pears.
2. Cook, covered, on low until pears are tender, 5-6 hours. Remove spice bag.
3. Puree pear mixture using an immersion blender. Or, cool slightly and puree pear mixture in a blender in batches; return to slow cooker.
4. Cook, uncovered, on high until mixture is thickened to the desired consistency, 1-2 hours, stirring occasionally. Store the cooled pear butter in an airtight container in the refrigerator up to 1 week.
Freeze option: Freeze cooled pear butter in freezer containers up to 3 months. To use, thaw in refrigerator.
Per 2 tablespoons: 41 cal., 0 fat (0 sat. fat), 0 chol., 2mg sodium, 11g carb. (9g sugars, 1g fiber), 0 pro.

❋
TEST KITCHEN TIPS

For an intense licorice flavor, use whole star anise.

Liquids expand as they freeze, so leave extra room at the top of the freezer container.

To turn this into a pear sauce, which is thinner than spreadable pear butter, cook for a shorter time after pureeing.

RICH HOT FUDGE SAUCE

I've been making this scrumptious topping since the early 1980s. It always turns out smooth and yummy, and it satisfies any chocoholic's cravings.
—Carol Hunihan, Ann Arbor, MI

Start to Finish: 30 min.
Makes: 3½ cups

- ¾ cup butter, cubed
- 1 cup heavy whipping cream
- 1⅓ cups packed brown sugar
- ¼ cup sugar
- 1 cup baking cocoa
- ½ cup plus 2 tablespoons light corn syrup
-    Pinch salt
- 2 ounces unsweetened chocolate
- 1 tablespoon vanilla extract
- 1 to 2 teaspoons rum extract

1. Place butter and cream in a heavy saucepan; cook and stir over medium-low heat until butter is melted. Add sugars; cook and stir until dissolved, 3-4 minutes.
2. Add cocoa, corn syrup and salt; cook and stir until blended, about 3 minutes. Stir in chocolate until melted. Reduce heat to low; cook and stir until mixture reaches desired thickness, 10-15 minutes.
3. Remove from heat; stir in extracts. Serve warm. Refrigerate leftovers.
Per 2 tablespoons: 166 cal., 9g fat (6g sat. fat), 25mg chol., 103mg sodium, 21g carb. (18g sugars, 1g fiber), 1g pro.

SLOW COOKER PEAR BUTTER

CRANBERRY DARK
CHOCOLATE TRAIL MIX

HOMEMADE RANCH
DRESSING & DIP MIX

HOT BUTTERED CIDER MIX

ESPRESSO STEAK RUB

HOMEMADE RANCH DRESSING & DIP MIX

Keep this versatile blend on hand to whip up a delicious veggie dip or salad dressing on a moment's notice. The jar of mix also makes a great holiday gift—just attach a copy of the recipe.

—Joan Hallford, North Richland Hills, TX

Prep: 10 min. + chilling
Makes: 1 cup dressing or 2 cups dip per batch

- 2 tablespoons dried parsley flakes
- 1 tablespoon garlic powder
- 1 tablespoon dried minced chives
- 2 teaspoons lemon-pepper seasoning
- 1½ teaspoons dried oregano
- 1½ teaspoons dried tarragon
- 1 teaspoon salt

ADDITIONAL INGREDIENTS FOR SALAD DRESSING (FOR EACH BATCH)
- ½ cup mayonnaise
- ½ cup buttermilk

ADDITIONAL INGREDIENTS FOR DIP (FOR EACH BATCH)
- 1 cup mayonnaise
- 1 cup (8 ounces) sour cream

Mix seasonings until well blended. Transfer to an airtight container. Store in a cool, dry place for up to 1 year. Shake to redistribute seasonings before using.
Note: 4 batches dressing or 2 batches dip (about 4 tablespoons mix).
To prepare salad dressing: Whisk together mayonnaise, buttermilk and 1 tablespoon mix. Refrigerate, covered, at least 1 hour before serving.

Per 2 tablespoons dressing: 108 cal., 11g fat (2g sat. fat), 6mg chol., 198mg sodium, 1g carb. (1g sugars, 0 fiber), 1g pro.
To prepare dip: Mix mayonnaise, sour cream and 2 tablespoons mix until blended. Refrigerate, covered, at least 2 hours before serving.
Per ¼ cup dip: 262 cal., 27g fat (7g sat. fat), 30mg chol., 297mg sodium, 1g carb. (1g sugars, 0 fiber), 1g pro.

FAST FIX ▶
CRANBERRY DARK CHOCOLATE TRAIL MIX

A close friend once gave me a jar of trail mix that was absolutely delicious. My re-creation comes close and is a favorite!

—Nancy A Johnson, Laverne, OK

Start to Finish: 5 min.
Makes: 24 servings

- 1 package (10 ounces) dark chocolate chips
- 1½ cups dried cranberries
- 1½ cups sliced almonds
- 1 cup raisins
- 1 cup coarsely chopped walnuts
- ½ cup pistachios

Toss together all ingredients. Store in airtight containers.
Per ¼ cup: 176 cal., 11g fat (3g sat. fat), 0 chol., 16mg sodium, 21g carb. (15g sugars, 3g fiber), 3g pro.

FAST FIX ▶
HOT BUTTERED CIDER MIX

Put the butter base for this beverage in a decorative jar and attach a copy of the recipe for a great gift from your kitchen.
—*Taste of Home* Test Kitchen

Start to Finish: 10 min.
Makes: 64 servings
(2 cups buttered cider mix)

- 1 cup butter, softened
- 1 cup packed brown sugar
- ½ cup honey
- 1 teaspoon ground cinnamon
- ½ teaspoon ground cardamom
- ¼ teaspoon ground cloves

EACH SERVING
- ¾ cup hot apple cider or juice
- 1 ounce apple brandy, optional

Beat the butter and brown sugar until blended; beat in the honey and spices. Transfer to an airtight container. Store in refrigerator up to 2 weeks.
To prepare hot cider: Place 1½ teaspoons buttered cider mix in mug. Stir in hot cider and, if desired, brandy.
Per ¾ cup prepared cider: 136 cal., 3g fat (2g sat. fat), 8mg chol., 40mg sodium, 28g carb. (25g sugars, 0 fiber), 0 pro.

FAST FIX ▶
ESPRESSO STEAK RUB

I'm always entering cooking contests and experimenting with big, bold flavor combinations. This espresso-laced spice rub is equal parts sweet, hot and exotic and is awesome for grilled ribeye.
—Sandi Sheppard, Norman, OK

Start to Finish: 5 min.
Makes: about 1 cup

- ⅓ cup instant espresso powder
- ¼ cup packed brown sugar
- 3 teaspoons kosher salt
- 3 teaspoons lemon-pepper seasoning
- 1 teaspoon cayenne pepper
- ¼ teaspoon Chinese five-spice powder
- ¼ teaspoon garlic powder

Mix all ingredients until well blended. Transfer to an airtight container. Store in a cool, dry place for up to 6 months.
Per 1½ teaspoons: 9 cal., 0 fat (0 sat. fat), 0 chol., 211mg sodium, 2g carb. (2g sugars, 0 fiber), 0 pro.

CRANBERRY DARK CHOCOLATE TRAIL MIX

General Recipe Index

This handy index lists every recipe by food category, major ingredient and cooking method, so you can easily locate the recipes that suit your needs.

||||||||||||||||||||||||||||||||||||||||||||||||||||||||||||||||||

BUTTERNUT THYME TARTLETS, P. 8

WEEKNIGHT
PASTA SKILLET,
P. 82

MINI SHEPHERD'S
PIES, P.150

ONE-BOWL
CHOCOLATE CHIP
BREAD, P. 174

APPLE CHICKEN
STEW, P.187

Lemony Turkey Rice Soup, 50
Slow Cooker Stuffed Pepper Soup, 200

SALADS
Dressing
Cilantro Salad Dressing, 26
Main Dishes
Asian Noodle & Beef Salad, 210
Asian Slaw with Steak, 215
Chicken Quinoa Salad, 24
Crunchy Asian Chicken Salad, 306
Egg-Topped Wilted Salad, 159
Eyeball Taco Salad, 262
Garlic Shrimp & Rice Salad, 20
Grilled Chicken Salad with Blueberry
    Vinaigrette, 215
Pesto Corn Salad with Shrimp, 28
Salmon & Feta Wilted Spinach Salad, 21
Shrimp Scampi Spinach Salad, 123
Skinny Cobb Salad, 139
Spicy Mongolian Beef Salad, 138
Spinach Salad with Tortellini & Roasted
    Onions, 36
Thai Chicken Coleslaw, 37
Turkey & Pasta Ranch Salad, 38
Side Dishes
Almond Strawberry Salad, 40
Bacon Avocado Salad, 20
Berry Nectarine Salad, 23
Blood Orange Avocado Salad, 268
Broccoli Slaw, 41
Campers' Coleslaw, 243
Cucumbers with Dressing, 24
Creepy-Crawly Pasta Salad, 264
Cucumber Shell Salad, 310
Curried Quinoa Salad, 41
Delicious Apple Salad, 152
Dutch Waffle Cookies, 151
Dilly Potato & Egg Salad, 252
Grandma's Spinach Salad, 32
Green Bean Salad with Creamy
    Dressing, 28
Grilled Apple Tossed Salad, 208
Grilled Peach, Rice & Arugula
    Salad, 218
Khmer Pickled Vegetable Salad, 250
Mango & Jicama Salad, 39
Minty Pineapple Fruit Salad, 36
Nectarine & Beet Salad, 29
Pina Colada Fruit Salad, 248
Sesame-Ginger Cucumber Salad, 22
Sesame Ramen Salad, 40
Shrimp Pasta Salad, 251
Spinach Blueberry Salad, 26
Spinach Salad with Warm Bacon
    Dressing, 29
Strawberry Kale Salad, 38

GINGER-GLAZED
GRILLED SALMON, P. 223

Strawberry Salad with Poppy Seed
    Dressing, 22
Summer Squash & Watermelon
    Salad, 230
Tarragon Asparagus Salad, 41
12-Hour Salad, 253
Yummy Corn Chip Salad, 30

SANDWICHES & WRAPS
(*also see Burgers*)
Cold
Blue Cheese Chicken Salad
    Sandwiches, 54
Curried Egg Salad, 56
Loaded Avocado BLT, 49
Loaded Deli Sub Sandwich, 307
Sesame Chicken Veggie Wraps, 57
Hot
Apple Chicken Quesadillas, 51
Bacon & Egg Sandwiches, 160
Bistro Turkey Sandwich, 46
Broccoli-Cheddar Beef Rolls, 67
Cheesy Chicken Wafflewiches, 66
Grilled Bean Burgers, 209
Grilled Brats with Sriracha Mayo, 212

Grilled Caprese Quesadillas, 223
Grilled Cheese & Pepper
    Sandwiches, 55
Grilled Eggplant Sandwiches, 222
Grilled Hummus Turkey Sandwich, 50
Ham & Cheese Spiders, 265
Honey Buffalo Meatball Sliders, 12
Hot Antipasto Subs, 64
Hot Pineapple Ham Sandwiches, 250
Indian Spiced Chickpea Wraps, 53
Italian Joes on Texas Toast, 45
Jalapeno-Swiss Turkey Burgers, 217
Mozzarella Beef Roll-Ups, 48
Mushroom Bacon Turkey Burgers, 223
Oktoberfest Brats with Mustard
    Sauce, 220
Parmesan Chicken Sandwiches, 51
Portobello Melts, 46
Pulled Pork Grilled Cheese, 56
Root Beer Brats, 242
Sloppy Cheesesteaks, 63
Sloppy Joe Dogs, 227
Southern Fried BLT, 61
Thai Chicken Wraps, 59
Turkey Dijon Melts, 63

PINA COLADA DIP, P. 245

BLOOD ORANGE
AVOCADO SALAD, P. 268

Alphabetical Recipe Index

This index lists every recipe in alphabetical order so you can easily find all of your favorites.

||||||||||||||||||||||||||||||||||||||||||||||||||||||||||||||||||||||||||||||||||||||||||||||||

APPLE PEAR SALSA
WITH CINNAMON CHIPS, P. 11

CHEESY CHEDDAR BROCCOLI CASSEROLE, P. 31